D1506232

DISCOVER
WINDOWS 95

BY DAN GOOKIN AND
SANDRA HARDIN GOOKIN

IDG
BOOKS
WORLDWIDE

IDG BOOKS WORLDWIDE, INC.

AN INTERNATIONAL
DATA GROUP COMPANY

FOSTER CITY, CA • CHICAGO, IL •
INDIANAPOLIS, IN • SOUTHLAKE, TX

Discover Windows 95

Published by
IDG Books Worldwide, Inc.
An International Data Group Company
919 E. Hillsdale Blvd., Suite 400
Foster City, CA 94404

www.idgbooks.com (IDG Books WorldWide Web site)

Library of Congress Catalog Card No.: 96-80456

ISBN: 0-7645-3078-X

Printed in the United States of America

10 9 8 7 6 5 4 3 2

1E/SX/RQ/ZX/IN

Distributed in the United States by IDG Books Worldwide, Inc.

Distributed by Macmillan Canada for Canada; by Contemporanea de Ediciones for Venezuela; by Distribuidora Cuspide for Argentina; by CITEC for Brazil; by Ediciones ZETA S.C.R. Ltda. for Peru; by Editorial Limusa SA for Mexico; by Transworld Publishers Limited in the United Kingdom and Europe; by Academic Bookshop for Egypt; by Levant Distributors S.A.R.L. for Lebanon; by Al Jassim for Saudi Arabia; by Simron Pty. Ltd. for South Africa; by Pustak Mahal for India; by The Computer Bookshop for India; by Toppan Company Ltd. for Japan; by Addison Wesley Publishing Company for Korea; by Longman Singapore Publishers Ltd. for Singapore, Malaysia, Thailand, and Indonesia; by Unalis Corporation for Taiwan; by WS Computer Publishing Company, Inc. for the Philippines; by WoodsLane Pty. Ltd. for Australia; by WoodsLane Enterprises Ltd. for New Zealand. Authorized Sales Agent: Anthony Rudkin Associates for the Middle East and North Africa.

For general information on IDG Books Worldwide's books in the U.S., please call our Consumer Customer Service department at 800-762-2974. For reseller information, including discounts and premium sales, please call our Reseller Customer Service department at 800-434-3422.

For information on where to purchase IDG Books Worldwide's books outside the U.S., please contact our International Sales department at 415-655-3172 or fax 415-655-3295.

For information on foreign language translations, please contact our Foreign & Subsidiary Rights department at 415-655-3021 or fax 415-655-3281.

For sales inquiries and special prices for bulk quantities, please contact our Sales department at 415-655-3200 or write to the address above.

For information on using IDG Books Worldwide's books in the classroom or for ordering examination copies, please contact our Educational Sales department at 800-434-2086 or fax 817-251-8174.

For press review copies, author interviews, or other publicity information, please contact our Public Relations department at 415-655-3000 or fax 415-655-3299.

For authorization to photocopy items for corporate, personal, or educational use, please contact Copyright Clearance Center, 222 Rosewood Drive, Danvers, MA 01923, or fax 508-750-4470.

 is a trademark under exclusive license to IDG Books Worldwide, Inc., from International Data Group, Inc.

DISCOVER
WINDOWS 95

ABOUT IDG BOOKS WORLDWIDE

Welcome to the world of IDG Books Worldwide.

IDG Books Worldwide, Inc., is a subsidiary of International Data Group, the world's largest publisher of computer-related information and the leading global provider of information services on information technology. IDG was founded more than 25 years ago and now employs more than 8,500 people worldwide. IDG publishes more than 275 computer publications in over 75 countries (see listing below). More than 60 million people read one or more IDG publications each month.

Launched in 1990, IDG Books Worldwide is today the #1 publisher of best-selling computer books in the United States. We are proud to have received eight awards from the Computer Press Association in recognition of editorial excellence and three from *Computer Currents'* First Annual Readers' Choice Awards. Our best-selling ...*For Dummies*® series has more than 30 million copies in print with translations in 30 languages. IDG Books Worldwide, through a joint venture with IDG's Hi-Tech Beijing, became the first U.S. publisher to publish a computer book in the People's Republic of China. In record time, IDG Books Worldwide has become the first choice for millions of readers around the world who want to learn how to better manage their businesses.

Our mission is simple: Every one of our books is designed to bring extra value and skill-building instructions to the reader. Our books are written by experts who understand and care about our readers. The knowledge base of our editorial staff comes from years of experience in publishing, education, and journalism — experience we use to produce books for the '90s. In short, we care about books, so we attract the best people. We devote special attention to details such as audience, interior design, use of icons, and illustrations. And because we use an efficient process of authoring, editing, and desktop publishing our books electronically, we can spend more time ensuring superior content and spend less time on the technicalities of making books.

You can count on our commitment to deliver high-quality books at competitive prices on topics you want to read about. At IDG Books Worldwide, we continue in the IDG tradition of delivering quality for more than 25 years. You'll find no better book on a subject than one from IDG Books Worldwide.

John J. Kilcullen
John Kilcullen
CEO
IDG Books Worldwide, Inc.

Steven Berkowitz
Steven Berkowitz
President and Publisher
IDG Books Worldwide, Inc.

Eighth Annual Computer Press Awards ≥1992

Ninth Annual Computer Press Awards ≥1993

Tenth Annual Computer Press Awards ≥1994

Eleventh Annual Computer Press Awards ≥1995

IDG Books Worldwide, Inc., is a subsidiary of International Data Group, the world's largest publisher of computer-related information and the leading global provider of information services on information technology. International Data Group publishes over 275 computer publications in over 75 countries. Sixty million people read one or more International Data Group publications each month. International Data Group's publications include: **ARGENTINA:** Buyer's Guide, Computerworld Argentina, PC World Argentina; **AUSTRALIA:** Australian Macworld, Australian PC World, Australian Reseller News, Computerworld, IT Casebook, Network World, Publish, Webmaster; **AUSTRIA:** Computerwelt Osterreich, Networks Austria, PC Tip Austria; **BANGLADESH:** PC World Bangladesh; **BELARUS:** PC World Belarus; **BELGIUM:** Data News; **BRAZIL:** Annuário de Informática, Computerworld, Connections, Macworld, PC Player, PC World, Publish, Reseller News, Supergamepower; **BULGARIA:** Computerworld Bulgaria, Network World Bulgaria, PC & MacWorld Bulgaria; **CANADA:** CIO Canada, Client/Server World, ComputerWorld Canada, InfoWorld Canada, NetworkWorld Canada, WebWorld; **CHILE:** Computerworld Chile, PC World Chile; **COLOMBIA:** Computerworld Colombia, PC World Colombia; **COSTA RICA:** PC World Centro America; **THE CZECH AND SLOVAK REPUBLICS:** Computerworld Czechoslovakia, Macworld Czech Republic, PC World Czechoslovakia; **DENMARK:** Communications World Danmark, Computerworld Danmark, Macworld Danmark, PC World Danmark, Techworld Denmark; **DOMINICAN REPUBLIC:** PC World Republica Dominicana; **ECUADOR:** PC World Ecuador; **EGYPT:** Computerworld Middle East, PC World Middle East; **EL SALVADOR:** PC World Centro America; **FINLAND:** MikroPC, Tietoverkko, Tietoviikko; **FRANCE:** Distributique, Hebdo, Info PC, Le Monde Informatique, Macworld, Reseaux & Telecoms, WebMaster France; **GERMANY:** Computer Partner, Computerwoche, Computerwoche Extra, Computerwoche FOCUS, Global Online, Macwelt, PC Welt; **GREECE:** Amiga Computing, GamePro Greece, Multimedia World; **GUATEMALA:** PC World Centro America; **HONDURAS:** PC World Centro America; **HONG KONG:** Computerworld Hong Kong, PC World Hong Kong, Publish in Asia; **HUNGARY:** ABCD CD-ROM, Computerworld Szamitastechnika, Internetto online Magazine, PC World Hungary, PC-X Magazin Hungary; **ICELAND:** Tolvuheimur PC World Island; **INDIA:** Information Communications World, Information Systems Computerworld, PC World India, Publish in Asia; **INDONESIA:** InfoKomputer PC World, Komputek Computerworld, Publish in Asia; **IRELAND:** ComputerScope, PC Live!; **ISRAEL:** Macworld Israel, People & Computers/Computerworld; **ITALY:** Computerworld Italia, Macworld Italia, Networking Italia, PC World Italia; **JAPAN:** DTP World, Macworld Japan, Nikkei Personal Computing, OS/2 World Japan, SunWorld Japan, Windows NT World, Windows World Japan; **KENYA:** PC World East African; **KOREA:** Hi-Tech Information, Macworld Korea, PC World Korea; **MACEDONIA:** PC World Macedonia; **MALAYSIA:** Computerworld Malaysia, PC World Malaysia, Publish in Asia; **MALTA:** PC World Malta; **MEXICO:** Computerworld Mexico, PC World Mexico; **MYANMAR:** PC World Myanmar; **NETHERLANDS:** Computer! Totaal, LAN Internetworking Magazine, LAN World Buyers Guide, Macworld Netherlands, Net, WebWereld; **NEW ZEALAND:** Absolute Beginners Guide and Plain & Simple Series, Computer Buyer, Computer Industry Directory, Computerworld New Zealand, MTB, Network World, PC World New Zealand; **NICARAGUA:** PC World Centro America; **NORWAY:** Computerworld Norge, CW Rapport, Datamagasinet, Financial Rapport, Kursguide Norge, Macworld Norge, Multimediaworld Norge, PC World Ekspress Norge, PC World Nettverk, PC World Norge, PC World ProduktGuide Norge; **PAKISTAN:** Computerworld Pakistan; **PANAMA:** PC World Panama; **PEOPLE'S REPUBLIC OF CHINA:** China Computer Users, China Computerworld, China InfoWorld, China Telecom World Weekly, Computer & Communication, Electronic Design China, Electronics Today, Electronics Weekly, Game Software, PC World China, Popular Computer Week, Software Weekly, Software World, Telecom World; **PERU:** Computerworld Peru, PC World Profesional Peru, PC World SoHo Peru; **PHILIPPINES:** Click!, Computerworld Philippines, PC World Philippines, Publish in Asia; **POLAND:** Computerworld Poland, Computerworld Special Report Poland, Cyber, Macworld Poland, Networld Poland, PC World Komputer; **PORTUGAL:** Cerebro/PC World, Computerworld/Correio Informático, Dealer World Portugal, Mac*In/PC*In Portugal, Multimedia World; **PUERTO RICO:** PC World Puerto Rico; **ROMANIA:** Computerworld Romania, PC World Romania, Telecom Romania; **RUSSIA:** Computerworld Russia, Mir PK, Publish, Seti; **SINGAPORE:** Computerworld Singapore, PC World Singapore, Publish in Asia; **SLOVENIA:** Monitor; **SOUTH AFRICA:** Computing SA, Network World SA, Software World SA; **SPAIN:** Communicaciones World España, Computerworld España, Dealer World España, Macworld España, PC World España; **SRI LANKA:** Infolink PC World; **SWEDEN:** CAP&Design, Computer Sweden, Corporate Computing Sweden, Internetworld Sweden, it.branschen, Macworld Sweden, MaxiData Sweden, MikroDatorn, Natverk & Kommunikation, PC World Sweden, PCaktiv, Windows World Sweden; **SWITZERLAND:** Computerworld Schweiz, Macworld Schweiz, PCtip; **TAIWAN:** Computerworld Taiwan, Macworld Taiwan, NEW ViSiON/Publish, PC World Taiwan, Windows World Taiwan; **THAILAND:** Publish in Asia, Thai Computerworld; **TURKEY:** Computerworld Turkiye, Macworld Turkiye, Network World Turkiye, PC World Turkiye; **UKRAINE:** Computerworld Kiev, Multimedia World Ukraine, PC World Ukraine; **UNITED KINGDOM:** Acorn User UK, Amiga Action UK, Amiga Computing UK, Apple Talk UK, Computing, Macworld, Parents and Computers UK, PC Advisor, PC Home, PSX Pro, The WEB; **UNITED STATES:** Cable in the Classroom, CIO Magazine, Computerworld, DOS World, Federal Computer Week, GamePro Magazine, InfoWorld, I-Way, Macworld, Network World, PC Games, PC World, Publish, Video Event, THE WEB Magazine, and WebMaster; online webzines: JavaWorld, NetscapeWorld, and SunWorld Online; **URUGUAY:** InfoWorld Uruguay; **VENEZUELA:** Computerworld Venezuela, PC World Venezuela; and **VIETNAM:** PC World Vietnam. 3/24/97

Welcome to the Discover Series

Do you want to discover the best and most efficient ways to use your computer and learn about technology? Books in the Discover series teach you the essentials of technology with a friendly, confident approach. You'll find a Discover book on almost any subject — from the Internet to intranets, from Web design and programming to the business programs that make your life easier.

We've provided valuable, real-world examples that help you relate to topics faster. Discover books begin by introducing you to the main features of programs, so you start by doing something *immediately*. The focus is to teach you how to perform tasks that are useful and meaningful in your day-to-day work. You might create a document or graphic, explore your computer, surf the Web, or write a program. Whatever the task, you learn the most commonly used features, and focus on the best tips and techniques for doing your work. You'll get results quickly, and discover the best ways to use software and technology in your everyday life.

This book contains the following elements:

Screen Shots. Just to give you an idea of what you should be seeing on your screen.

Bonus. As if this book isn't enough of a bonus, the end of each chapter has additional information about Windows 95.

Side Trip. The Side Trips found in this books supply, "Oh, by the way" information.

Discovery Center. What you'll discover is that most of the important steps on how to do things in Windows are found in this part of the book. The steps in the Discovery Center have very little explanations (you'll have to read the book for that), but contain bone-downed steps. Just the facts, ma'am.

Visual Index. People in general don't all learn the same way. Some learn from hearing, some from doing, and some from seeing. The Visual Index is for those people that like to *see* how Windows 95 looks when it's up and running.

Tear-out Cheat Sheet. You know how there are some things you just *can't* remember, like your mother-in-law's birthday? I understand. I can never remember that `ctrl+v` is the command for paste. Just doesn't make sense. Keep the cheat sheet on your desk and save those brain cells for something else.

Icons. You'll see that certain paragraphs in Discover are highlighted by icons. These icons denote text of special interest. The following is a guide to the icons used in this book:

 Scattered throughout the chapters, you'll find Tips that give you quick, simple information on the topic at hand.

 You can't cover everything all at once. The cross reference is to help guide you so you know where to go for more information.

 Just some cool stuff on the World Wide Web.

Credits

ACQUISITIONS EDITOR
Gregory Croy

DEVELOPMENT EDITOR
Michael Koch

COPY EDITORS
Tracy Brown
Marcia Baker

TECHNICAL EDITOR
Yael Li-Ron

PROJECT COORDINATOR
Katy German

GRAPHICS AND PRODUCTION SPECIALISTS
Mario F. Amador
Laura Carpenter
Elizabeth Cârdenas-Nelson
Kurt Krames
Jude Levinson
Ed Penslien
Dina F Quan
Mark Schumann
Deirdre Smith

QUALITY CONTROL SPECIALIST
Mick Arellano

PROOFREADERS
Desne Border
Kelli Botta
Michelle Croninger
Andrew Davis
Stacey Lynn
Candace Ward
Anne Weinberger

INDEXER
Sherry Massey

BOOK DESIGN
Seventeenth Street Studios
Phyllis Beaty

About the Authors

Dan Gookin considers himself a writer and computer guru whose job is to remind everyone computers are not to be taken *too* seriously. His approach to computers is light and humorous, yet very informative. He knows the complex beasts are important and can do a great deal to help people become productive and successful.

Dan's most recent titles include the best-selling *Word 97 for Windows For Dummies; PCs For Dummies, 5th Edition;* and *Web Wambooli.* He is the author of the original Dummies book, *DOS For Dummies.* All told, Dan has written over 60 books on computers. Dan holds a degree in Communications-Visual Arts (okay, let's be honest: Art!) from the University of California-San Diego, and lives with his wife and four sons in the Pacific Northwest. You can e-mail Dan at: dang@idgbooks.com

Sandra Hardin Gookin has an amazing ability to make difficult tasks easy to understand. This comes, in part, from her Speech Communications degree from Oklahoma State University, but mainly from having to communicate with her five boys (four children + one husband, Dan).

Sandra works with Dan to make Windows 95 easy for you to understand. If she can understand it, you will too. Sandra's other book is *Parenting For Dummies.* You can e-mail Sandra at: sandyg@iea.com

PREFACE

Welcome to *Discover Windows 95*, a book written just for you. This is the unofficial manual — the human being guidebook — a new approach to explaining only what's useful and not rambling on about the rest. I promise to tell you exactly what's important in Windows and exactly what can be cheerfully ignored.

Honestly, Windows 95 is a *massive* program. Even the *complete* reference books — the hefty 1,000+ pagers — only scratch the surface of what the Windows 95 operating system can do. But do *you* really want to know all that stuff?

Of course not! You want to know what's important. You want to know it now. The other stuff? Forget it. Just getting the job done in the quickest possible way is the philosophy of this book. The other stuff, the details and boring technical matter, are all omitted — not even glanced at here. And don't be surprised if, on the way to getting the most from Windows 95, you have a little fun as well. This book educates *and* entertains. Such a deal!

Brazen Assumptions

I'm assuming you have a computer and that computer has the Windows 95 operating system installed. That's about all you really need to get started here. This book takes care of the rest.

While this book does detail the operation of Windows 95, it does not discuss older versions of Windows. In fact, you should forget everything about Windows 3.11 or Windows for Workgroups and concentrate instead on getting your work done in Windows 95 — which is what this book does best.

How This Book Is Organized

Like discovering anything, you need to know your way around first. After all, finding the lost city of Nubi-Nubi is pointless if you can't get back out of the forest. To make it easier for you to find your way around Windows 95, we've broken this book down into six major parts:

Part I, "Breaking into Windows," is about getting your bearings in Windows 95. You'll learn how to maneuver through the dense forest of icons, open and close treasured files, navigate the help system, and be able to find your way back again without getting lost and while feeling you've actually accomplished something.

Part II, "Getting Work Done," covers working with programs in depth, including specifics on the freebie programs that come with Windows 95.

Part III, "Disks, Folders, Files, and Whatnot," imparts invaluable advice on how to deal with your disk drives, files, and folders in order to give the impression that you're organized, even if you know you're not.

Part IV, "Dinking," tells you how to change the way Windows works, also known as dinking. Common dinking tasks covered include messing with fonts, adjusting your printer, and networking.

Part V: "Having Fun," introduces you to some strange and wonderful stuff that can be found in Windows 95. Believe it or not, in addition to being aggravating, Windows does offer a choice selection of diversions, including the ever-popular Solitaire game. Not that you ever would ….

Part VI: "Windows is as Windows Does," tells you all about the gizmos and graphical gadgets that come with Windows to (supposedly) help you get your work done. Intuitive? Maybe. Frustrating? Just about all the time. Hence we included a chapter on troubleshooting Windows, "Problems and Solutions."

Let's Get Started

Now that you've got the basic road map, you're ready to get started. Be prepared to discover what Windows 95 can do for you — at home or at work — and rest assured that once you've finished this book, you'll get your job done easier and faster.

Acknowledgments

To Jordan, Simon, Jonah, and Jeremiah for sitting on our desks and helping us type, in addition to your patience when we weren't always so good at playing *Star Wars* with you. (Dan, it's your turn to be Darth Vader!)

To Shirley and Virgil for the countless hours of extra help and all that great Seattle's Best coffee.

To Michael Koch for being a great editor (even though he made us use words such as *enable*, egads!)

To Tracy Brown and Marcia Baker for copyediting this book virtually overnight.

To Yael Li-Ron for her technical tips and insights.

To the many people in the production department who worked hard to get this book out on time.

To Silicon Valley for creating the mess that makes a book like this one necessary.

CONTENTS AT A GLANCE

Preface, ix
Acknowledgments, xi

PART ONE—BREAKING INTO WINDOWS

1 THE BIG PICTURE   3

2 A QUICK TOUR OF MY COMPUTER   17

3 STARTING YOUR WORK   31

4 FROM HELL TO HELP: USE ONE PROGRAM,
  YOU'VE USED THEM ALL   41

PART TWO—GETTING WORK DONE

5 ALL ABOUT THE START THING   61

6 GETTING TO KNOW THE TASKBAR   75

7 INTRODUCING THE APPLETS   87

8 MULTITASKING — SHARING AND LOVING   103

9 VISITING PLANET INTERNET AND OTHER ONLINE STUFF   113

10 DEALING WITH ANCIENT DOS APPLICATIONS   133

11 INSTALLING NEW SOFTWARE   143

PART THREE—DISKS, FOLDERS, FILES, AND WHATNOT

12 WHAT DRIVES YOUR DISK DRIVES   155

13 ORGANIZING FOLDERS AND FILES   167

14 MANIPULATE THEM FILES   177

15 THE POLITICALLY CORRECT RECYCLE BIN   189

PART FOUR—DINKING

16   KEEPING MR. DISK DRIVE HEALTHY AND HAPPY   201

17   MESSING WITH YOUR PRINTER   215

18   DINKING FRENZY AT THE CONTROL PANEL   227

19   FUN WITH FONTS   241

20   WINDOWS AND EVERYONE ELSE'S PC (THE JOYS OF NETWORKING)   249

21   INSTALLING NEW HARDWARE   269

PART FIVE—HAVING FUN

22   CHANGING THE LOOK OF WINDOWS   281

23   INTERESTING, WEIRD, AND NEAT STUFF   295

24   FUN, GAMES, AND FRIVOLITY   307

PART SIX—WINDOWS IS AS WINDOWS DOES

25   YOUR BASIC WINDOWS' WINDOWS CONCEPTS   321

26   TRAPPED IN A DIALOG BOX   333

27   MOUSY CONCEPTS   345

28   WORKING WITH TEXT AND GRAPHICS   355

29   PROBLEMS AND SOLUTIONS   363

Appendix A Error Messages (and How to Deal with Them), 375

Appendix B Freebies, 383

Discovery Center, 385

Visual Index, 427

Index, 431

CONTENTS

Preface, ix

Acknowledgments, xi

PART ONE—BREAKING INTO WINDOWS, 1

---

1 THE BIG PICTURE, 3

Start Your Computer!, 3

Welcome to Windows, but You Still Can't Work Yet , 5
Log In, Mystery Guest — but Only if You're on a Network, 5
"But I Don't Wanna Type a Name and Password!", 7
Uh-oh! Windows Doesn't Know Who You Are, 7
Windows Says Hello for the *n*th Time, 8

The First Stop Is the Desktop, 9

The Start Thing, the Heart of Windows, 10

What to Do in Windows, 12
Working in Windows, 12
Playing in Windows, 12
Dinking with Windows, 13

Quitting Windows and Turning Off Your PC, 13

Suspending Your Computer, 15

Summary, 15

2 A QUICK TOUR OF MY COMPUTER, 17

My Computer, Your Computer, 17
Opening My Computer and Looking Inside, 18
Opening Stuff Inside My Computer, 19
Closing Stuff, 19

The Things That Lurk Inside My Computer, 20
Disk Drives Are the Big Spinning Storage Thingamabobs, 20
Just Because They're Called Folders Doesn't Mean Anything Is Folded in Them, 21
"Oh, Lordy, I Have Too Many Windows Open!", 22
File Away the Hours, 23

Different Ways to Look at the Stuff in My Computer, 24
Whip Out the Toolbar, 24
The Big Icon View (Most Popular), 25
The Details View (Nerds Love This), 26
Sorting It All Out, 26

What About the Explorer?, 26

The Single Window Approach to Using My Computer, 27

Summary, 29

3 STARTING YOUR WORK, 31

Starting Programs, from the Obvious to the Obtuse, 31
    Marching Through the Start Button March, 32
    Starting an Icon Clinging to the Desktop, 33
    Starting a Program in My Computer, 34
    Running to the Run Command to Start a Program, 34

Starting a Document Instead of a Program, 35
    Finding Your Document Lurking in the Documents Menu, 36
    Finding a Document Nestled in My Computer, 36

Quitting Any Program, 37
    The Common, Polite, Almost Civilized Way to Quit, 37
    Quitting by Closing a Window, 38
    The Drastic Way to Quit, 38

Clearing the Documents Menu, 39

Sticking Popular Documents on Your Desktop, 40

Summary, 40

4 FROM HELL TO HELP: USE ONE PROGRAM, YOU'VE USED THEM ALL, 41

Scent of a Windows Application, 41
    What's on the Menu?, 42
    Hanging Out at the Toolbar, 43
    Status Bars: Your Application's Cheat Sheet, 44

Going About Your Business, 44
    Making Stuff, 45
    Printing Your Stuff, 45
    Saving Your Stuff, 46
    Opening Stuff, 48
    Starting New Stuff, 49
    Closing Stuff, 50

The Windows Way of Offering Help, 50
    The Quick and Desperate Jab at the F1 Key, 50
    Using the Help System, 51
    Finding a Specific Topic Using the Index, 53
    Finding a Specific Topic Using the Find Panel, 53
    Quitting the Help System, 54

Done for the Day? To Quit or Put Away?, 56

The Meaning of Menus, 56
    Hot, Hot, Hot Keys, 57
    Quick Key Shortcuts, 57

Summary, 58

PART TWO—GETTING WORK DONE, 59

5 ALL ABOUT THE START THING, 61

Onto the Start Menu, 61
　Stuff That Lives on the Main Start Thing Menu, 62
　Sticking Something on the Main Start Thing Menu, 63
　Adding a Program to a Start Thing Submenu, 64
　Zapping a Program from a Start Thing Submenu, 66

Applications That Start Automatically (Amazing!), 68
　Adding and Moving Programs to the StartUp Submenu, 68
　Running a Program Minimized When It Starts, 70

Some Cool Programs to Add to the StartUp Submenu, 72

A Really Nerdy Way to Add a Program, 73

Summary, 74

6 GETTING TO KNOW THE TASKBAR, 75

Buttons and Windows Galore, 75

Too Many Buttons on the Taskbar!, 76

"My Taskbar Is Gone!", 78

Having Fun with the Loud Time, 79
　Setting the PC's Speaker Volume, 80
　Hanging Out with Printer Dude, 81
　Messing with the Modem Guy, 81
　Fooling with the Time (Setting the Time on Your PC), 83

Other Taskbar Stuff , 85

The Envelope, Please, 85

Summary, 86

7 INTRODUCING THE APPLETS, 87

Secret Background Information on the Applets, 87

Making Purty Pictures with Paint, 88

Let WordPad Bring Out the Shakespeare in You, 94

Notepad, Windows' Feeble Text Editor, 99

Figure It Out Yourself (the Calculator), 99

Is This the Party to Whom I'm Speaking? (the Phone Dialer), 100
　Making the Call, 101
　Keeping Track of Who You Call, 101
　Hold on for Speed Dialing, 101

Summary, 102

8 MULTITASKING — SHARING AND LOVING, 103

An Episode in Multitasking, 104
Switching Applications with the Taskbar, 104
A Multitasking Tutorial Involving Paint and WordPad, 104
Using the Cool Switch to Switch Applications, 106

Sharing Information — the Three Amigos, 107
Sharing Between Paint and WordPad, 108
Ending the Tutorial, 110

Everything Goes to the Clipboard, 112

Summary, 112

9 VISITING PLANET INTERNET AND OTHER ONLINE STUFF, 113

Internet Folderol, 114
Modem Mayhem, 115
Internet Software, 116
Get Yourself an Internet Service Provider, 117
Get Important Information from Your Provider, 117
Gotta Have the Cash, 117

Installing Your Internet Software, 118

Connecting to the Internet, 119
Running Your Internet Programs, 122
Disconnecting from the Internet, 123

A Shortcut to the Internet on the Desktop, 124

The Joys of HyperTerminal, 124
Grazing Through the HyperTerminal Window, 125
Creating a New Session in HyperTerminal, 125
Dialing a Something You Already Created, 127

Doing the Online Thing, 128

Hanging Up, 129

Other Modem Programs You May Have, 129

What About the Speed, Data Word Format, and All That?, 131
Uploading and Downloading, 131

Summary, 132

10 DEALING WITH ANCIENT DOS APPLICATIONS, 133

Starting Your Old, Favorite DOS Program, 134
Messing with a DOS Window, 135
Copying and Pasting Between DOS Programs, 137
Quitting a DOS Program, 138
Installing DOS Software (Is a Pain), 139

Messing with a DOS Program's Properties, 139

Troubleshooting MS-DOS Program Problems, 141

Summary, 142

11 INSTALLING NEW SOFTWARE, 143

And Now for Something New, 143

Adding the Rest of Windows, 146

The Subtle Art of Uninstalling, 149
Officially Uninstalling Stuff, 149
Uninstalling Bits and Pieces of Windows, 150
Unofficially Uninstalling Stuff, 150

Updating Windows, 151

Summary, 151

PART THREE—DISKS, FOLDERS, FILES, AND WHATNOT, 153

12 WHAT DRIVES YOUR DISK DRIVES, 155

The Big Spinnin' Deal with Disk Drives, 155
Disk Drive (A:), (B:), (C:), 156
Giving Your Disk a Proper Name, 158
Checking on Disk Usage, or "Fills up Fast, Doesn't It?", 159

The Thrill of Formatting a Floppy Disk, 160

Creating a Disk to Start Your Computer: The Fun Yet Useful Emergency
Boot Disk, 163

Playing a Musical CD, 163

RAM Drives Belong in the Past, 164

Summary, 165

13 ORGANIZING FOLDERS AND FILES, 167

How Folders Helped Tame the Wild West, 167
What's up with the Root Folder?, 168
Crazy Folder Terminology, 169
Conjuring Up a New Folder, 169
Creating a New Folder as You Save Something to Disk, 170

Climbing the Folder Tree, 171
Let's Go Exploring, 172
Working with Folder Trees in the Save As, Open, and Browse Dialog Boxes, 173

Setting Up Folders Just So, 174
The Useful Work Folder Organizational Strategy, 174
Random Folders for Random Stuff, 175

Beating a Pathname to a File's Door, 176

Summary, 176

14 MANIPULATE THEM FILES, 177

Blessing a File with a New Name, 177

Copying Files, 180

Taking a Shortcut Instead of Copying Files, 180
  Making a New Shortcut, 181
  Don't Make a Shortcut This Way, 181

Deeply Moving Files, 182

Some Files Just Hafta Go, or Deleting Files, 182

Undo Thy File Manipulation Sins!, 183

Crowd Control, or Working with Groups of Files, 184
  The Best Way to Select a Rag-Tag Rogue Group of Files, 184
  Calf Ropin' Files, 185
  Selecting Scads of Files with SHIFT + Click, 185
  Selecting the Whole Dang Doodle, 187

More Stuff on File Manipulation, 187
  File Renaming Tips, 188
  Creating a File Copy in the Same Folder, 188
  The Old Drag-and-Drop, 188

Summary, 188

15 THE POLITICALLY CORRECT RECYCLE BIN, 189

How to Find a Recycle Bin Near You, 189

"But the File Whatever Is a Program!", 190

Using the Recycle Bin Just Once to See How It Works, 191

A Quick, Odorless Peek into the Recycle Bin to Restore Something, 192

Flushing the Recycle Bin Empty, 194

Tweaking the Recycle Bin, 195

Reducing Disk Space the Recycle Bin Hogs Up, 196

Summary, 197

PART FOUR—DINKING, 199

16 KEEPING MR. DISK DRIVE HEALTHY AND HAPPY, 201

Some Mild Ranting, 201

Finding the Disk Tool', Tool Shed, 202

Backup Drudgery, 203
  What to Back Up and When to Do It, 204
  How It's Done, 204
  Restoring Something You Backed Up, 208

Weaseling Out Errors with ScanDisk, 209

Removing Those Nasty Fragments from Your Disks, 211

Doing It All Automatically, 213

All About Disk Compression, 213

Summary, 214

17 MESSING WITH YOUR PRINTER, 215

Where the Printer Lurks, 215

Peeping at the Printers Folder, 217
 Yo, My Main Printer, 217
 Printer Setup and Properties Nonsense, 217

Playing with the Queue, 219
 The Theoretical Hockey Puck of a Printing Queue, 219
 Looking at the Printing Queue, 220
 Pausing Your Printing, 220
 Moving Documents in the Queue, 221
 Killing Documents in the Queue, 221

Basic Fax, 222

Summary, 225

18 DINKING FRENZY AT THE CONTROL PANEL, 227

The Great Control Panel Hunt, 227

Items Not Covered Elsewhere in This Book, 229
 Accessibility Options, or Making Windows Friendly to Everyone, 229
 Happy, Happy, Joystick, 230
 Spicing Up a Keyboard, 231
 Merry Modems, 233
 Other Strange and Wonderful Goodies, 234

Items Covered Elsewhere in This Book, 235

Items You Just Don't Need, 238

Summary, 239

19 FUN WITH FONTS, 241

Where the Fonts Folder Lurks, 241

Playing with the Fonts Folder, 243
 Here a Font, There a Font, Everywhere a Font Font, 243
 My Font's Uglier than Your Font!, 244
 Adding Fonts to Your Collection, 245
 Removing an Old Cruddy Font, 246

Weeding Out Cool Characters with the Character Map Program, 246

Summary, 248

20 WINDOWS AND EVERYONE ELSE'S PC
(THE JOYS OF NETWORKING), 249

Networking Nonsense, 250

It's a Beautiful Day in the Network Neighborhood, 250
Prowling Around the Network Neighborhood, 250
Browsing Other Computers à la My Computer, 251
Spanning the Globe, 252
Using the Explorer/Network Neighborhood Connection, 253

Messing with Someone Else's Computer, 253
Saving Files Elsewhere, 254
Opening Files Elsewhere, 255
Using an Alien Printer, 257

Surrendering Your Hardware to the Network, 258
Sharing Hard Drives and Folders, 259
Sharing Your Printer, 260

Stop! Oh, Yes, Wait a Minute, Mr. Postman!, 262
Fussing with the Exchange (i.e., Mail) Program, 262
Checking Your Mail, 263
Sending Mail, 264
The Joys of WinPopup, 266

Strange Filenames on Older Windows Computers, 268

Summary , 268

21 INSTALLING NEW HARDWARE, 269

Adding a New Something to Your Computer, 269

Installing a Brand New Printer, 273

"There's a Stupid Printer Installed Here and I Want to Get Rid of It", 277

It's a Drag to Drag-and-Drop to a Printer, 277

Summary, 277

PART FIVE—HAVING FUN, 279

22 CHANGING THE LOOK OF WINDOWS, 281

Background Information, 281
The First Step to Change the Look of Windows, 283
Choosing One of Them Fancy Desktop Patterns, 284
Wallpaper Without the Glue, 285

The Screen Resolution Revolution, 286

Making Windows' Color Scheme Match Your Office, 288

Messing with the Taskbar, 290
  Whipping About the Taskbar, 290
  Stretching the Taskbar, 291
  Tweaking the Way the Taskbar Works, 291

Make Up Your Own Color Scheme, 293

Create Your Own Desktop Pattern and Wallpaper, 293

Summary, 294

23 INTERESTING, WEIRD, AND NEAT STUFF, 295

Saving the Screen from Boredom, 295
  Has Your Screen Been Saved?, 296
  Shhh! Using the Password Option, 297

A More Lively Mouse Pointer, 298

A More Euphonious PC, 299
  Making Windows Noisy, 300
  Scheming Sound Schemes, 301
  Making Music mit MIDI, 302
  Recording Your Own Sounds for Fun and Profit, 303

Behold Computer Video!, 305

Summary, 306

24 FUN, GAMES, AND FRIVOLITY, 307

Finding the Games, 307

Solitaire: The Art of Playing by Yourself, 308

Minesweeper, or How Not to Blow Up Bob, 309

FreeCell (Another Annoying Solitaire-like Game), 311

Hearts Attack, 312

Other Games Abounding, 313

Wrestling with DOS Games, 314
  DOS Games? Forget Windows!, 314
  Properly Configuring a DOS Game Session in Windows, 315

How to Cheat the Games, 317
  3D Space Cadet Pinball, 317

Summary, 318

PART SIX—WINDOWS IS AS WINDOWS DOES, 319

25 YOUR BASIC WINDOWS' WINDOWS CONCEPTS, 321

Windows' Windows (or "Pains of Glass") , 321
  I've Been Framed!, 322
  Inside Information, 323

Adjusting a Window's Position and Size, 324
The Joy of Stretch, 324
The Wonder of Maximize and Restore, 326
Moving Windows, 326
Cleaning Stray Windows, 327

To Deal with Scrollbars, 327
Scrolling for Dollars, 328
Working a Scrollbar (Scrollin', Scrollin', Scrollin'), 328

Chasing Menus, 329
Working the Menus, 329
Beware the Instant Menu!, 328
Working Menus With Your Keyboard, 330

The Old Multidocument Interface Gag, 331

Summary, 332

26   TRAPPED IN A DIALOG BOX, 333

Anatomy of a Dialog Box, 334
Basic Pieces' Parts, 335
Panels, Pages, and Tabs, 336
Areas, Regions, and Asylums, 336

Working the Dialog Box, 336
The Mousy Way of Using a Dialog Box, 336
The Keyboardy Way of Using a Dialog Box, 336
Time to Commit to Something, 337

All Them Gizmos, 337
Buttons, 338
Check Boxes, 338
The Collapsible Tree Structure Thing, 339
Drop-Down Lists, 340
Drop-Down Palettes, 340
Input Boxes, 341
List Boxes, 341
On/Off Buttons, 342
Option Buttons, 342
Sliders, 343

Spinners, 343

Summary, 344

27   MOUSY CONCEPTS, 345

"Here I Come to Save the Day!" (Using Mr. Mouse), 345

Know These Mouse Terms, 347

Behavior Patterns Common to the Computer Mouse, 347
Getting to the Point, 347

Some Things Just Click, 348
Doing the Right-Click, 349
Moving Can Be Such a Drag, 350
Selective Service, 351

The Ever-Changing Mouse Pointer, 351

The Double-Quick Double-Click, 352

Summary, 353

28 WORKING WITH TEXT AND GRAPHICS, 355

Basic Messing with Text Stuff, 355
All Hail the Flashing Toothpick Cursor, 356
Basic Text Editing Stuff, 356
Making Text Feel Special by Selecting It, 357

Changing the Way Text Looks, 358
A Font of Typefaces, 358
Text Sizes from Petite to Full-Figured, 359

Basic Messing with Graphics Stuff (Stretching), 360

Funky Things to Do with Text (Attributes), 361

Summary, 361

29 PROBLEMS AND SOLUTIONS, 363

The All-Purpose Amazing Windows Troubleshooter, 364

Dealing with Annoying Hardware Conflicts, 367

Special Ways to Start Your Computer, 368
Windows' Special Startup Key Commands, 368
Mayday! Mayday! Stick in That Emergency
Boot Disk!, 369

File? File? Here File! C'mon, Boy! Where'd You Go?, 371

Finding Files — The Relaxed Explanation, 372

Other Options You May Want to Try in the Find Dialog Box, 374

Summary, 374

Appendix A Error Messages (and How to Deal with Them), 375

Appendix B Freebies, 383

Discovery Center, 385

Visual Index, 427

Index, 431

BREAKING INTO WINDOWS

THIS PART CONTAINS THE FOLLOWING CHAPTERS

CHAPTER **1** THE BIG PICTURE

CHAPTER **2** A QUICK TOUR OF MY COMPUTER

CHAPTER **3** STARTING YOUR WORK

CHAPTER **4** FROM HELL TO HELP: USE ONE
PROGRAM, YOU'VE USED THEM ALL

"I'm back," Heracles announced. He dropped the hulking carcass of the hellhound in the middle of the temple floor. A muffled thud echoed through the pillared building. A final whumph of air escaped from the rotting dog's three heads.

Eurystheus turned from his sacrifice, astonished to see Heracles, standing strong and alive after his twelve labours. Heracles was caked with a mixture of dried blood and soot from the underworld. A sour stink filled the temple, though Eurystheus couldn't tell whether it came from the dead hellhound or from Heracles.

"I, uh, see you found Cerberus," Eurystheus began. He had not expected Heracles to do so, let alone return intact from Hell. But if anyone could, it would be Heracles. And in his heart, Eurystheus knew how Heracles had dreamed of the moment he would dump Cerberus' body on the temple floor. He had probably thought of it the whole time he dragged, carried, and rolled the beast up from the depths of the earth.

"Eurystheus, I completed the ten tasks you set for me," Heracles said.

"Twelve," Eurystheus said.

"Whatever. Now, will you grant me my sanity?" Heracles asked.

Eurystheus couldn't respond. Ancient Greek tradition prescribed that you not annoy one who'd been to Hell, killed the guard dog, and dragged its 800-pound corpse up to civilization. Something about that said, "Here's a guy you don't want to tick off." Eurystheus had to try reason.

"Hercules," he began.

"It's Heracles," Heracles corrected. "Hera! Hera! Hera!"

Eurystheus said, "Shhh! You don't want to wake her! That vexing goddess is the last thing you need. What you do need is . . ."

"Another task?" Heracles asked, sheepishly. How amazing such a brute of a man could humble himself before such a spindly little king.

Eurystheus nodded. "Yes, I've been dabbling with something. You see, just last week I decided to get into this Internet thing."

The two men walked to the palace, Heracles still covered in blood and soot and smelling like a ripe goat. They entered a small room to one side of the throne room. There, sitting atop an acacia wood box, was a Pentium PC. It was running Windows 500 B.C.

"Heracles, you are a man among men," Eurystheus began. "If anyone can tame this nasty computer, it's you. Here's a book, a stool, and a jug of wine. Good luck."

Heracles opened the book, preparing for what he hoped would be his last — the thirteenth — labour. His only wish was that Eurystheus had offered him a bath first. But soon Heracles' eyes opened wide and his spirit lifted as the computer began to sing to him the Windows theme song. . . .

THE BIG PICTURE

IN THIS CHAPTER YOU LEARN THESE KEY SKILLS

HOW TO START YOUR COMPUTER   PAGE   3

LOGGING IN TO WINDOWS 95   PAGE   5

USING THE START THING   PAGE   10

WORKING, PLAYING, AND DINKING WITH
   WINDOWS   PAGE   12

QUITTING WINDOWS AT THE END OF
   THE DAY   PAGE   13

Two things exist to help you and your computer get something done: an operating system and application programs. And two things are there to get in your way: an operating system and application programs. Welcome to the world of computer software!

Software is the stuff that controls your computer hardware. It tells the hardware what to do, how to start in the morning, and how to get your work done. The whole idea is to put *you* in the driver's seat when it comes to using the computer. And the main program in charge of all that is your computer's operating system, Windows 95.

Start Your Computer!

You can't get anything done until you turn on your computer. This is not as basic as it sounds. You'll find the big box thing has a switch, the monitor has a switch, and the printer and the modem have switches. And yes, they all have to be turned on.

To start your computer, flip on the switch on the computer box, and then turn on the switch on the computer's monitor. If you're going to print, turn on the printer. If you're going to use some other external device — a modem, scanner, external disk drive, whatever — turn on that switch as well.

Your computer comes to life. This will take a while, depending on how much stuff you have crammed into your computer's innards or hanging onto your computer through that ganglia of cables 'round back. Your computer may beep. It may snort. It may even make beautiful "I'm having a great dream" kind of music! Eventually you'll see the message *Starting Windows 95* displayed, and then Windows explodes on the screen. Yeah, yeah, yeah. Windows 95. Hurrah for Microsoft. Let's have another stock split. Whoopty-doo.

TIP You can save a lot of time and hassle by plugging all your computer gadgets into a power strip, which you can buy at any hardware or computer store. Be sure to look for power strips that offer surge protection, as well as spike protection.

X-REF If you've just started your computer after adding a new piece of equipment, say a modem, printer, or some other hardware, refer to Chapter 21 for information on the software side of that hardware setup.

SIDE TRIP

EVEN MORE WAYS TO SAY "START YOUR COMPUTER"

Starting a computer is easy. (Getting it to do what you want is the problem.) But to make starting a computer more difficult, the computer whiz kids have come up with a battalion of terms, each of which means "start the computer." Here's a sampling:

Power-up	Geekish for turning on the computer, very nuclear-reactor sounding.
Power-on	Same as power-up, though it doesn't have any weight-lifter attachments.
Boot	Classic computer term for starting a computer, though it refers specifically to starting your computer's main piece of software, the operating system.
Reset	This interrupts the computer from whatever it's doing and forces it to start all over. (A warm boot.) Only reset as a last, drastic measure to get control. You'll find a reset button on the big boxy part of your computer next to your power button.

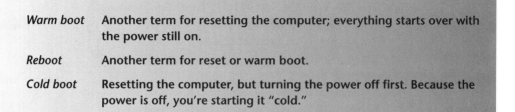

Warm boot	Another term for resetting the computer; everything starts over with the power still on.
Reboot	Another term for reset or warm boot.
Cold boot	Resetting the computer, but turning the power off first. Because the power is off, you're starting it "cold."

SIDE TRIP

Welcome to Windows, but You Still Can't Work Yet

One problem with Windows is that it prevents you from getting to your work right away. You have to sit there and watch its rah-rah and then wade through one, possibly two, dialog boxes before you get anything done.

 X-REF You have to use a mouse to use Windows. See Chapter 27 for information on using a mouse if the concept is alien to you or if you just fear rodents.

For more details on dialog boxes check out Chapter 26.

Log In, Mystery Guest — but Only if You're on a Network

The first dialog box you may encounter urges you to log in, either to your office computer network or just to Windows (see Figure 1-1). If you're not on a network, you probably won't see this message. You can safely skip down to the section titled "Windows Says Hello for the *n*th Time."

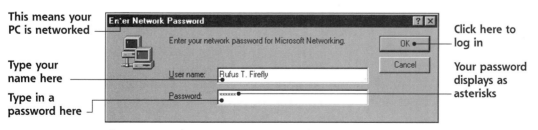

Figure 1-1a Here the prisoners identify themselves to the warden.

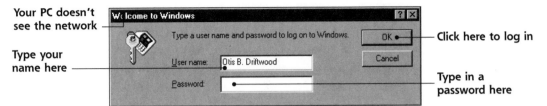

Your PC doesn't see the network

Type your name here

Click here to log in

Type in a password here

Figure 1-1b These are special prisoners — they have their own computers.

TIP Notice the question mark in the upper-right corner of these dialog boxes. If you click this question mark and then point and click any other part of the box, you'll see the pop-up Help.

Follow these steps to log in:

1. Type your first and last name or login ID (given to you by your network administrator to identify you on a network) in the box labeled *User name*, and then press the TAB key. For example, this is what the Pope types to log in to the Vatican computer: **John Paul II**; and this is what Bill Gates types in to log on to the network at Microsoft: **billg**.

TIP As with DOS, you're limited to the number of characters and spaces you can use for your log-in name. If your user name (or login ID) is already displayed in the box, then you don't need to retype it; just skip ahead to Step 2.

2. In the box labeled *Password*, type your secret password. For example, type **None,** which is the password I use at my office. Windows displays asterisks as you type. This is part of its security, but it means you'll have to erase the whole thing when you make a mistake. Use the BACKSPACE key. By the way, passwords can be from one to several characters long. Keeping them short and memorable is always a good idea. (If you've never typed in your name and password before, you'll see another dialog box appear. See the section "Uh-oh! Windows Doesn't Know Who You Are" below for how to deal with it.)

3. Click the OK button. The dialog box goes away, but Windows remembers who you are.

X-REF If you're using a network, it's a good idea to log in every time. Chapter 20 discusses networking aspects of Windows.

"But I Don't Wanna Type a Name and Password!"

If you don't want to log in to Windows, just click the Cancel button in the "who are you?" dialog box. Click. The box goes away.

If more than one person uses your computer, then logging in is a way to identify yourself as someone special. That way Doris can use the computer with her special settings and Oscar can do the same, each without bothering the other. Or if you're on a network, others can recognize that so-and-so is using a particular computer.

Also, if you're on a network and you choose not to log in, then your computer won't be able to access other computers on the network. It's your choice.

Uh-oh! Windows Doesn't Know Who You Are

Windows isn't rude to you if you've never typed in your name and a password before. It merely wants to confirm the password you're using. You'll see a dialog box similar to the one shown in Figure 1-2.

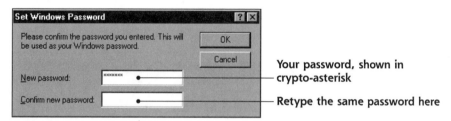

Figure 1-2   Windows wants you to remember your password.

The *New password* box contains the password you just entered, shown in crypto-asterisk.

1. Type that same password again in the *Confirm new password* box. (This is an argument for making brief, memorable passwords.)

2. Click OK and Windows will remember you. But it's now up to you to remember your password. Windows will demand it each time it starts (unless you followed my original advice and clicked Cancel when the box first appeared).

"HELP! I FORGOT MY PASSWORD"

If you forget your old password, click the Cancel button in the log-in dialog box. So much for security.

Windows will warn you when you forget your password or type in something goofy. A "naughty-naughty" dialog box is displayed, but you can still click the Cancel button to use Windows.

The only true way around this pickle is to create a new user name for yourself. Refer to the previous sections for what to do next.

Windows Says Hello for the *n*th Time

Finally (and this may or may not be finally, depending on Windows' mood), you'll see the Welcome to Windows 95 dialog box, shown in Figure 1-3. You can dawdle here, or just click the Close button to start your work.

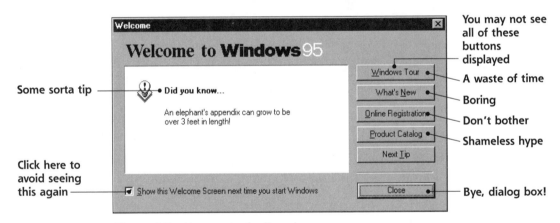

Figure 1-3 Now you're finally welcome.

If you click the Close button, you're ready to use the desktop. Refer to the next section.

Other windows may be open on the screen, which will cover all or part of the Welcome to Windows box. To see the Welcome box up front, click the Welcome button on the taskbar at the bottom of the screen.

X-REF For more information on using a dialog box, especially filling in various fields, refer to Chapter 26.

TURNING OFF THE "WELCOME TO WINDOWS 95" THING FOREVER

If you really don't want to be bothered with the Welcome to Windows 95 box, you can turn it off forever. Just click in the *Show this Welcome Screen next time you start Windows* box. (You can also press the ALT+S key combination to uncheck this item. Press and hold the ALT key, and then tap the S key. Release both keys.) The ✔ check mark in the box disappears. You're done.

The First Stop Is the Desktop

When you operate a car, you sit in the driver's seat. In a plane, the captain and copilot control things from the cockpit. In Windows, your center of control is the desktop (see Figure 1-4). That's Windows' front door to everything in your computer, the place where you work, the end result of all the hoopla it took to get the thing started. Table 1-1 tells you what the desktop icons are.

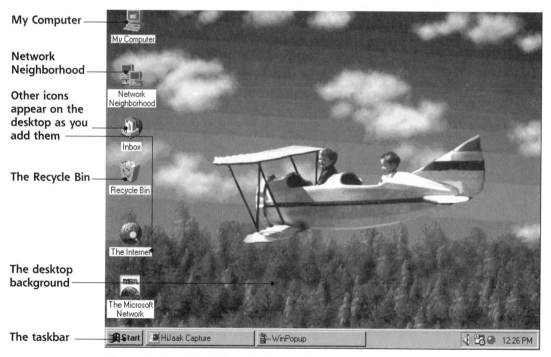

My Computer

Network Neighborhood

Other icons appear on the desktop as you add them

The Recycle Bin

The desktop background

The taskbar

Figure 1-4   The Windows desktop

TABLE 1-1 The Desktop Icons

Screen Item	Description
TASKBAR	The taskbar is located at the bottom of your screen. You use the taskbar to switch quickly between the windows of programs or documents you have open. The taskbar is covered in Chapter 6.
MY COMPUTER	My Computer is used to see everything on your computer. It's covered in Chapter 2.
RECYCLE BIN	The Recycle Bin is a temporary holding bin for the stuff you want to delete. You can go back and take things out of the Recycle Bin should you have a change of heart about deleting something. For more details look at Chapter 15.
NETWORK NEIGHBORHOOD	The Network Neighborhood is an icon on your desktop that, when clicked, enables you to peek at the other computers in your network. It's like a Peeping Tom icon. There's more about the Network Neighborhood in Chapter 20.
INBOX	The Inbox works with Microsoft Exchange. You can get mail and faxes from the Inbox. See Chapter 20 for more details.
THE INTERNET	The Internet is not a program in Windows. Instead, it's a collection of computers that all exchange information. You'll need Internet software and a modem to use the Internet. You'll see how in Chapter 9.

As a cockpit, the Windows desktop is disappointing. They do this on purpose. Microsoft figures too many knobs, dials, and buttons get in your way. However, the minimalist approach tends to be cryptic, so it's an unusual trade-off.

 X-REF Note, too, Figure 1-4 shows what the desktop may look like on your screen. If what you see is different and you want to change it, refer to Chapter 22, the section "Background Information." (You can change everything about the desktop. It's completely customizable.)

The Start Thing, the Heart of Windows

To one side of the taskbar is the Start button, or *Start Thing* as I like to call it. It's a *thing* because when you click on the Start button, up pops a menu full of selections that lead to even more selections, that lead to even more selections. It can be pretty unwieldy if you're not careful. If you don't see the taskbar on your screen (say, something else is covering it), you can press CTRL+ESC — press the CTRL (control) key, and then tap the ESC (escape) key — to pop up the Start Thing menu.

Follow these steps to activate the Start Thing, and then close it again:

1. Click your mouse on the Start button and the Start menu pops up. If you're using one of the new Windows 95 keyboards, you can press the Windows button (between the CTRL and ALT buttons on the lower-left side of the keyboard) to pop up the Start Thing menu.

2. There are several items on the Start Thing menu, as seen in Figure 1-5. Each plays some role in working Windows. Hover your mouse over Programs and you'll see even more items.

TIP If you're using a laptop or energy-efficient PC, you'll also see a second item at the bottom of the Start Thing menu, just above the **Shut Down** item. It's the Suspend button, which is covered near the end of this chapter.

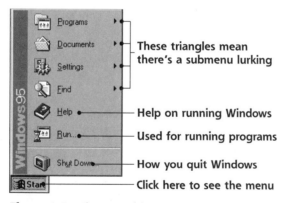

Figure 1-5 The Start Thing menu

3. Click the Start Thing button again and the pop-up menu disappears. You can also just click your mouse anywhere on the desktop or press the ESC key. Poof! It's gone.

What to Do in Windows

Windows doesn't exist for itself. Yes, it does look impressive on the screen. But if you want to impress people that way, turn the TV to PBS and have *Masterpiece Theatre* running on your desk, not a computer. To get the most from a computer, you need to do something. In Windows, you can do the following things:

* You can work
* You can play
* You can dink

Working is what you'll be doing most of the time. Playing is what you'll be doing when you should be working. And dinking is what you'll be doing when you'd rather be doing anything else.

Working in Windows

You get your work done in Windows using various applications, such as Microsoft Word, Netscape, Lotus 1-2-3, WordPerfect, or whatever software you have. After all the hoopla of Windows starting, you'll get down to work by running one or more of these programs.

 See Chapter 3 for more information on the various ways you can get work done in Windows.

Playing in Windows

Playing is just like working in Windows. The only difference is you start a fun program instead of something that has to do with "productivity."

Windows comes with many fun programs for playing and generally wasting time. There's the ever-popular Solitaire game (which is something many companies were thinking of banning as an antiproductivity tool!). And there are other numerous ways to pass the hours in a fun and graphical way.

Follow these steps to start a game:

1. Click the Start Thing to pop up the menu.

2. Select `Programs` → `Accessories` → `Games`. That's where you'll find most of the Windows games. Notice how you needn't actually *click* Programs, Accessories, and Games. You just hover your mouse pointer over it and then more stuff magically appears. You do have to click your final

choice, though. For example, hover your arrow over Programs, and then hover over Accessories, and then hover over Games. Now you actually get to *click* the game you want.

X-REF Believe it or not, all of Part V covers having fun in Windows. And the subject of Solitaire is covered specifically in Chapter 24.

Dinking with Windows

Dinking is the art of adjusting the way something works on a computer. If you're a dinker, then Windows 95 is paradise. If you hate messing with things, then Windows 95 is hell.

Before bubbling with elation or drowning in despair, you should know that there are two kinds of dinking. First there's dinking to get something to work. That's a pain. Then there's dinking just because. You can change the way Windows looks and works all over the place. This can be fun and also an incredible time-waster.

X-REF Part IV of this book covers dinking in-depth. Most dinking, however, is done in Windows' Control Panel. For more details see Chapter 18.

Quitting Windows and Turning Off Your PC

When you're done for the day, you should shut down Windows and turn off your computer.

Follow these steps to shut down Windows and wrap things up:

1. Activate the Start Thing pop-up menu. You do this most quickly by pressing CTRL+ESC. You can also click the Start Thing button if you see the taskbar, or press the Windows key (if your keyboard has one). Up pops the menu.

2. Select the bottom item, Shut Down . Don't think a movie is about to start because the screen dims. Instead a dialog box appears, giving you various options for putting away Windows (see Figure 1-6).

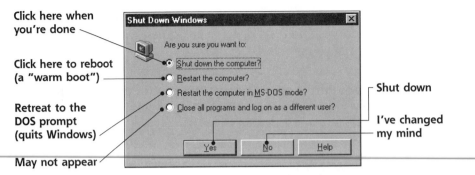

Click here when you're done

Click here to reboot (a "warm boot")

Retreat to the DOS prompt (quits Windows)

May not appear

Shut down

I've changed my mind

Figure 1-6 Windows is ready for bed.

3. Make sure the option *Shut down the computer?* is selected. Click the option button if there isn't a black dot by it.

4. Click on the Yes button. Yes, you want to quit and shut down. If you change your mind, click No and Windows will return to normal.

5. Windows will hum. It will stir. It will wrap things up for you. If you haven't yet saved any documents to disk, you'll be informed of that now and given a chance to save. Otherwise, Windows hums and stirs some more. If someone else on the network is using your computer, you'll see a warning dialog box displayed. Click on No so you don't shut down your computer and accidentally peeve them.

6. All done. The final screen displays the Windows 95 logo and tells you it's okay (*safe,* actually) to turn off your computer.

Never turn off your computer unless Windows tells you it's okay to do so. This is the best way to ensure your computer lives a safe and happy life and that you never lose anything accidentally.

7. Turn off the computer. Flip off the power switch on the computer box and monitor, plus anything else attached to your PC.

8. Get out and get some fresh air.

See the section "Saving Your Stuff" in Chapter 4 for information on saving your stuff.

See Chapter 20 for more information on networking.

Suspending Your Computer

All Windows 95 laptops and some of the newer energy-efficient desktop models have a Suspend command sitting right on top of the Shut Down command on the Start Thing menu. If you plan on being away from your computer for an hour or so, choose the Suspend item instead of Shut Down.

When you choose Suspend your monitor goes blank and you might even hear the PC's hard drive wind down. That's the energy-saving mode where your computer merely sips power, saving the planet for our children (who probably won't be as mindful) and their future.

To restart the computer while it's suspended, just jiggle the mouse back and forth a few times or press the ENTER key on the keyboard. Your PC or laptop springs instantly back to life.

If you really want to save time, choose the Suspend command all the time instead of Shut Down. That's a real time-saver, because reactivating the computer is as easy as jiggling the mouse.

Summary

This chapter covered starting your computer and getting your feet wet with Windows 95. Twasn't too bad, now was it? Before you head on out to Chapter 2, make sure you learned the following:

- ☑ How to turn on your computer.
- ☐ How to log in if you're on a network.
- ☑ What the different items on your desktop are.
- ☑ How to activate the Start Thing.
- ☑ How to start a game.
- ☑ How to shut down Windows and your computer.

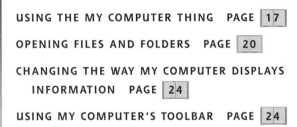

CHAPTER TWO

A QUICK TOUR OF MY COMPUTER

2

IN THIS CHAPTER YOU LEARN THESE KEY SKILLS

USING THE MY COMPUTER THING   PAGE   17

OPENING FILES AND FOLDERS   PAGE   20

CHANGING THE WAY MY COMPUTER DISPLAYS
   INFORMATION   PAGE   24

USING MY COMPUTER'S TOOLBAR   PAGE   24

My Computer is really Your Computer, the one sitting on your desk right now. The one running Windows 95. What the My Computer icon on the desktop represents is all the stuff on your computer. Everything. It's kind of an anchor point for the things you do with your stuff, a way to get at your stuff. Of course, Windows has many programs that do the same thing, from the nerdy Explorer to the disgusting DOS prompt. But of all of them, My Computer (aka Your Computer) is the best way to see your stuff.

My Computer, Your Computer

My Computer represents all the things inside your computer, the stuff you have stored there. It contains a visual representation of your computer's hard drives, folders, and files, showing you how and where information is stored. This is perhaps the best way to deal with that sort of stuff, though Windows has other ways to display or get at that information as well — which you can cheerfully ignore if you're just starting.

My Computer

The My Computer icon is stuck on the desktop. You can move it around or rename it, but you cannot remove or delete it. Just about everything else on the desktop, however, can be rearranged.

X-REF See Chapter 14, the section "Blessing a File with a New Name," for information on renaming icons (and files).

Opening My Computer and Looking Inside

Open the My Computer icon by double-clicking on it. Go ahead, double-click and see what happens. This displays a window on the screen that shows certain goodies lurking inside your computer, similar to what you see in Figure 2-1.

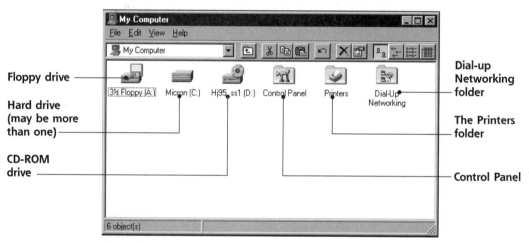

Floppy drive

Hard drive (may be more than one)

CD-ROM drive

Dial-up Networking folder

The Printers folder

Control Panel

Figure 2-1 My Computer's first window

At this stage, you'll see two types of items: disk drives and special folders. The disk drives represent your computer's disk drives and the special folders hold other things.

The shape and appearance of the disk drives in My Computer depend on what types of disk drives live inside or nearby. Disk drives, no matter what type, are given letters and names. The letters have a colon after them and appear in parentheses. The names are optional.

The Control Panel and Printers folders are included in My Computer because they are important parts of your computer, just like the disk drives. Sections covering each of these items appear later in this chapter.

The "serving hand" thing you may see under a disk drive means the drive is up for grabs on the network, a *shared* drive. Likewise, a drive that looks like it's connected to the sewer system is a drive on someone else's computer on the network, one your computer is currently "borrowing."

Behemoth (C:)

C on 'Koby' (F:)

X-REF You can find out more about this networking stuff in Chapter 20.

Opening Stuff Inside My Computer

My Computer displays the goodies inside your computer as icons. To see what's inside an icon — a disk drive or folder or whatever — you double-click on the icon, just as you double-clicked on My Computer to open it.

Opening an icon displays a window on the screen, detailing what the icon represents. When you open a disk drive icon in My Computer, a window appears displaying folders and files on that disk drive.

(C:)

When you double-click to open a folder, a window appears displaying files and folders inside that folder.

X-REF You can open file icons as well, but I wouldn't recommend doing so on a random basis; opening the file typically starts the application that created the file. See Chapter 3, the section "Starting a Document Instead of a Program" for more information.

Closing Stuff

To close a window in Windows, click on its Close button (the X button in the upper-right corner).

This closes that window, removing it from the screen. In case you're wondering, closing a window *does not* delete it or its contents. It simply closes the window.

You can close any window you like in any order, it doesn't matter which ones you opened first.

X-REF Chapter 25 has more information on working with windows if you need to brush up.

The Things That Lurk Inside My Computer

The main My Computer window contains three different things: disk drives, folders, and files. The bottom line here is the file. That's the basic storage container for information on a computer. All computer programs are files; you put your stuff in files and other files exist "just because." Everything is organized and represented by an appropriate icon inside My Computer.

Disk Drives Are the Big Spinning Storage Thingamabobs

Files and folders are stored on various disk drives inside your computer. Those disk drives appear as icons inside the main My Computer window.

To see what files or folders lurk on your disk drives, double-click a disk drive icon to open its window. The window details the contents of the disk drive, which will be a bunch of folders and files. Figure 2-2 shows the contents of drive (C:), *Too loud* on my test computer.

SIDE TRIP

FINDING A LOST WINDOW

To find a lost window, use the taskbar. All open windows have their names plastered on the taskbar as a button. To go to a specific window, just click that window's button on the taskbar. For example, to return to the *My Computer* folder, locate the *My Computer* button on the taskbar and click it once. This brings that window front and center.

If you forget what a toolbar icon represents, hover the mouse pointer over it for a few seconds (but don't click!). This displays a tiny bubble with the name of the toolbar button's command on it. The bubble is called a *tooltip*.

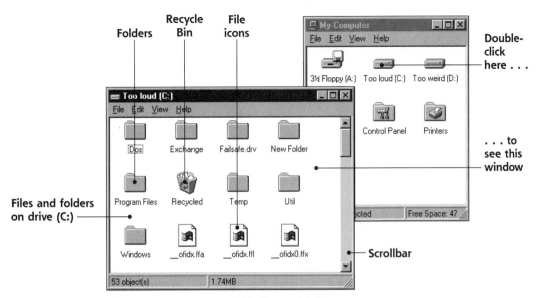

Figure 2-2 Drive (C:) yields files and folders.

All the file and folder icons have names, located directly beneath the icon. The file icons may also have pictures on them, which clues you in to what the file does or which program created it.

 X-REF Why isn't drive (C:) called *Betty* or something? See Chapter 12, the section "Giving Your Disk a Proper Name."

Just Because They're Called Folders Doesn't Mean Anything Is Folded in Them

Folders are used in your computer to store files and to help you stay organized. A disk drive may have tens of thousands of files. If all of them were in one place it would be a mess. Imagine having to look through some massive window in My Computer for one teensy file. Instead, things are put into folders.

Fold Me

Folders contain files, usually files of a related type. For example, all the documents used to create this book live in a folder. This keeps them separate from other files and whatnot floating around my disk drive.

Follow these steps to open a folder:

1. Double-click a disk drive icon, such as your drive (C:) icon. This opens drive (C:) and enables you to see what files and folders live there.

2. Look around. Double-click a folder. This opens a folder and you see another window full of files and maybe even more folders.

3. To open another folder, double-click its icon. As an example, double-click the Windows folder to open it. This displays another window, with even more files and folders inside.

4. Close the folder when you're done snooping by clicking the folder window's Close button.

TIP To keep you from getting lost (and because a lot of windows on the desktop can drive one insane), the name of the current folder you're looking at appears at the top of the window, in the line called the title bar. See Figure 2-3 for an example of the "Windows" folder, where Windows and its hoard of files and folders live.

"Oh, Lordy, I Have Too Many Windows Open!"

It isn't a problem to have several windows open on the desktop at a time. In fact, the only sin committed is one of clutter.

Follow these steps to organize your windows:

1. Find the taskbar that should be the line on the bottom of the desktop, like the annoying scroll of stock quotes during the day on *CNN Headline News*. If you don't see the taskbar, move the mouse pointer down to the bottom of the screen and the taskbar should pop up.

2. Point the mouse at a "blank" part of the taskbar, where there aren't any buttons. Click the right mouse button once and the taskbar shortcut menu pops up.

3. Choose Cascade from the menu. This arranges all the windows on the screen in a nice, overlapping fashion. Click Tile Horizontally or Tile Vertically to arrange the windows in a tiled (not overlapping) fashion.

X-REF See Chapter 6 for more information on using the taskbar.

File Away the Hours

The most basic element you'll find in any My Computer window is a file. A *file* appears as an icon on the screen with a name floating beneath it. Hopefully, one or the other will clue you in to what the file is and does.

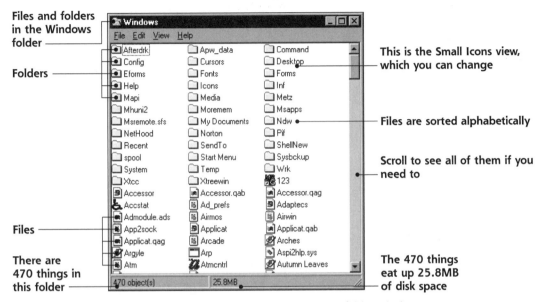

Files and folders in the Windows folder

Folders

Files

There are 470 things in this folder

This is the Small Icons view, which you can change

Files are sorted alphabetically

Scroll to see all of them if you need to

The 470 things eat up 25.8MB of disk space

Figure 2-3 Files lurking inside the Windows folder window

You can actually "open" some files to start a program or document (covered in Chapter 3). Other files cannot be opened or, if you try, you'll be greeted with an Open With dialog box. Press the ESC key when this happens.

A QUICK TOUR OF MY COMPUTER

If the name or the icon's picture doesn't help you identify the file's usefulness, then you can peer into it and examine its contents. This is covered in Chapter 13.

Mostly you'll be working with the files in My Computer by copying, renaming, moving, or deleting them. All this fun stuff is covered in Chapter 14.

Different Ways to Look at the Stuff in My Computer

You can change the way My Computer shows you files and folders on your disk drives. There are big icons, little icons, filename lists, and other boring stuff. Although I personally favor the big icon approach, you may find yourself delighted with one of the other options, each of which is detailed in the following sections.

 As you discover new ways to look at information inside a window, you'll want to change the window's size on the screen. You can zoom it up big if you like, or you can grab the window's edges with the mouse and drag the thing to the perfect size. See Chapter 25, the section "Adjusting a Window's Position and Size," for more information.

Whip Out the Toolbar

All the windows in My Computer can have a toolbar — which is a row of buttons — attached to them. If you don't see it now, choose | View | → | Toolbar | from the menu. The toolbar appears, as shown in Figure 2-4.

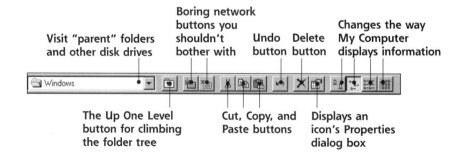

Visit "parent" folders and other disk drives

Boring network buttons you shouldn't bother with

Undo button

Delete button

Changes the way My Computer displays information

The Up One Level button for climbing the folder tree

Cut, Copy, and Paste buttons

Displays an icon's Properties dialog box

Figure 2-4 My Computer's toolbar

BAR HOPPING: THE STATUS BAR

In addition to the toolbar, windows in My Computer also boast a status bar. This is a strip of information along the bottom of the window, used by most programs to display extra information or options (see Chapter 4, "Status Bars: Your Application's Cheat Sheet").

The status bar in My Computer tells you how many files or folders are selected and their total size. If no files or folders are selected, then the status bar tells you how many files and folders are in the current window and their total size. If you select one file or folder, then that number and the total size is displayed on the status bar.

In My Computer, you can take a look at the status bar by choosing View → Status bar. Or you can choose this command again to remove the status bar, enabling you to see more of your stuff in the window.

Many of the buttons have similar menu commands that you can use when you can't see the toolbar: The File menu has the Delete and Properties commands; the Edit menu has the Undo, Cut, Copy, and Paste commands; the View menu has commands equivalent to the last four toolbar buttons, Large Icons, Small Icons, List, and Details.

The Big Icon View (Most Popular)

The most popular way to view information in My Computer is the big icon view, called Large Icons in the View menu. This is the way My Computer initially shows you information (see Figures 2-1 and 2-2), and it can be quite handy because you can really see the icons.

To switch to big icon view, choose View → Large Icons. Or you can click the Large Icon button from the toolbar.

The only time you may want to try the Small Icons view is when a folder contains too many files (such as the Windows folder in Figure 2-3) and you want to see more of them in a window at a time. If so, choose View → Small Icons or select the Small Icons button from the toolbar.

In either view, Large or Small Icons, you can move the icons around in the window, arranging them as you please. Just drag an icon to a new spot in the window and it stays there. (This isn't possible with the List view, which always shows smaller icons in neat columns.)

The Details View (Nerds Love This)

Fans of DOS will appreciate the Details view of stuff in My Computer windows. Choose View → Details or click the Details button on the toolbar. This displays the files by icon, name, size in bytes, the type of file, and, finally, the date it was created or last modified, each in a neat little column (see Figure 2-5).

Sorting It All Out

You can sort the items in a window in a number of ways, using the View menu. Choose View → Arrange Icons . A submenu appears from which you can choose how to sort the icons in the window:

> By Name
> By Type
> By Size
> By Date (the time the file was created or last modified)

If you like constant order, you can choose the View → Arrange Icons → Auto Arrange command. This automatically "snaps" all the icons to a grid all the time.

TIP **When you use the Large Icon or Small Icon view, the icons can become disorderly in the window — especially if you're dragging them around, copying, or pasting. To align things, choose the View → Line Up Icons command. This instantly makes any sloppy window neat and tidy.**

What About the Explorer?

The Microsoft Explorer is another way to work with and manipulate files in Windows. It's more of an advanced program, designed for use by folks who *really* know their disk drives and what's stored on them. Part III of this book deals with using the Explorer. If you're just starting with Windows 95, use My Computer for now.

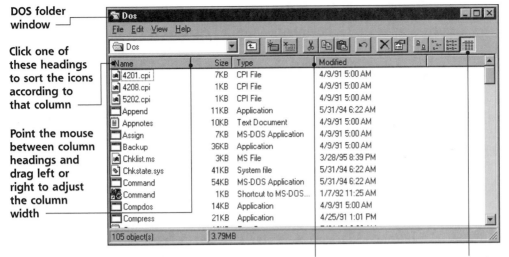

DOS folder window ——

Click one of these headings to sort the icons according to that column ——

Point the mouse between column headings and drag left or right to adjust the column width ——

Or double-click between column headings to set the width equal to the widest item in that column

Details view is active

Figure 2-5 The DOS folder, à la Details view with the toolbar hanging out

BONUS

The *Single Window* Approach to Using My Computer

You don't have to see everything in My Computer using a different window for each disk drive or folder. It's possible to use only one window for everything. That way, when you go to a new folder, its contents appear in the window rather than a new window appearing. You may find this a neater approach to working with files and folders in My Computer.

Follow these steps to use the single-window approach in My Computer:

1. Choose ⟨View⟩ → ⟨Options⟩. This displays the Options dialog box for My Computer.

2. Make sure the Folder panel is up front by clicking the Folder tab if it's not in front.

3. Click the text *Browse folders by using a single window that changes as you open each folder.* A dot will appear in the option button by this text after you click it.

4. Click on the OK button.

Now the essence of how My Computer works has changed. When you open a disk drive or folder, no new window appears. Instead, the contents of that disk drive or folder appear in the current window. Obviously, this means some changes should take place to the way you use My Computer.

The best way to work things is to switch on the toolbar, as covered in the section "Whip Out the Toolbar" earlier in this chapter. Because you'll only see one folder in the window at a time, you need a way to view other folders.

To view the contents of any folder in the current window, just double-click it. This opens that folder and you see its goodies — but in the current window.

To see the contents of the previous folder (the folder containing the current folder), click the Up One Level button on the toolbar.

Clicking the Up One Level button closes the current folder. Then you see the next folder up. Keep clicking this button and, eventually, you'll be back at My Computer's main level, with all the disk drives, Control Panel, and Printers folders.

If your fingers are resting comfortably on the keyboard, you can go up one level without having to click the Up One Level button. Instead, whack the BACK-SPACE key. This displays the previous window just like the button, which is handy when you're typing or too lazy to use the mouse. (By the way, this works if you're using the one-window approach to My Computer.)

To go to any disk drive or folder quickly, use the Go-to-a-different-folder button on the toolbar. It enables you to zoom to a folder you've previously opened or to another disk drive on the computer.

 See "Climbing the Folder Tree" in Chapter 13 for more information on this goodie.

To change My Computer back to where one folder equals one window, go through the steps in this section again, but choose *Browse folders using a separate window for each folder* in Step 3.

Summary

The My Computer thing is a tool you'll be using a lot in addition to the toolbar. If you didn't grasp these concepts very well, go back and glance over the chapter.

- ☑ How to open My Computer.
- ☑ How to open and close stuff in My Computer.
- ☐ How to organize your windows.
- ☐ How to change the size of icons.

2

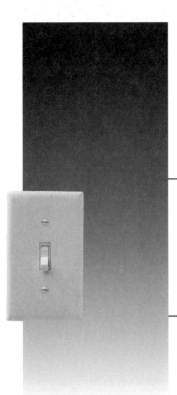

CHAPTER THREE

STARTING YOUR WORK

IN THIS CHAPTER YOU LEARN THESE KEY SKILLS

THE EASY WAYS TO START A PROGRAM   PAGE 31

STARTING A DOCUMENT IN MY COMPUTER   PAGE 35

QUITTING A PROGRAM (THE EASY WAY)   PAGE 37

CLEARING THE DOCUMENTS MENU   PAGE 39

Windows tries its best to make you happy all by itself. Alas, it just doesn't cut it. While you can dink with Windows all day — you can even make a lifetime hobby of it and, because it's so involving, no one else would think you're doing anything other than work — you eventually do need to settle down and get something done. To make that happen, you need to start an application, run a program, or just get something going so that you and your computer can be happy and productive together.

Starting Programs, from the Obvious to the Obtuse

In its vain effort to make everything in Windows 95 simple and organized, Microsoft has created a veritable beef stew of contraptions you can use to start your programs. Prepare to be overwhelmed with options. Microsoft can't make up its mind! Just because the button on the screen reads Start doesn't necessarily mean that's the place where everything begins. However, for the most part, it is true.

X-REF Before you can start any program, it must be installed on your computer. Refer to Chapter 11 for information on installing programs. If you would like your Windows programs to start up automatically each time you start Windows, refer to Chapter 5, the section "Applications That Start Automatically (Amazing!)."

Marching Through the Start Button March

The obvious way to run a program is to use the Start Thing button, located on one side of the taskbar. It says Start, which means "to start a program" because your computer is already on and running at this point.

Follow these steps to start a new program:

1. Click the Start Thing button. You can also pop up the Start menu by pressing CTRL+ESC or the Windows button on your keyboard, if available.

2. Select Programs . The Programs submenu appears (see Figure 3-1). It contains programs and folders. Folders live near the top of the menu, and they lead to even more submenus (hence the little arrows pointing off to the right). If one of your programs appears at the top of the Start Thing menu, you're ready to start it now. Move on to Step 4.

3. If you don't see the program you want, click on a submenu folder to look for more programs. This is "marching through the Start menu march." There are lots of folders with lots of programs in them. Once you get used to Windows, you'll know right where everything is.

4. When you find your program, click on it. You only need to click once, using the left (main) mouse button. This starts the program, running it on the screen.

Items in a submenu should pertain somewhat to the name of the menu: *Accessories* contains miscellaneous Windows programs; *Microsoft Works* contains its own programs; *Multimedia* contains those types of files; and so on.

Programs on the menu have their own icon next to the name. The icon is just a cute little picture, often not representing what it is the program does at all. The name is more descriptive.

If the submenu in which you're looking does not contain the file you want, press the ESC key. This pops down the most recent menu and saves your sanity.

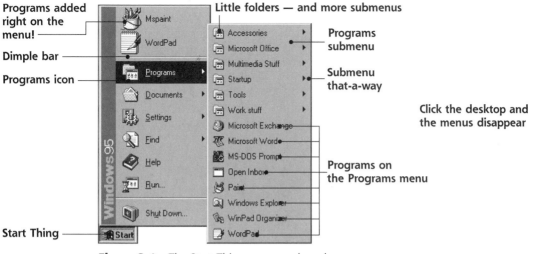

Programs added right on the menu!

Little folders — and more submenus

Dimple bar

Programs icon

Programs submenu

Submenu that-a-way

Click the desktop and the menus disappear

Programs on the Programs menu

Start Thing

Figure 3-1 The Start Thing menu and a submenu

Starting an Icon Clinging to the Desktop

Some programs live on the desktop, pictured as little icons. For example, you may see programs named Inbox, The Internet, or Outlook already on your desktop.

To start an icon on the desktop, double-click on it just as you would the My Computer icon. The program starts and its window soon appears on the desktop.

X-REF Anyone can place an icon on the desktop. It's an incredible shortcut and makes running popular programs a cinch. Refer to Chapter 14 to see how it's done.

SIDE TRIP

THOSE SUBMENUS ARE SLIPPERY!

The Start Thing menus are very sensitive about where you hover your mouse. If you move the mouse off a menu just slightly, it may disappear. And if the mouse is hovering over another submenu item (the ones with the triangles by them), another menu pops right up. Annoying.

Alas, there is no way around this predicament. The only advice I can offer is to be careful. Or you can choose one of the alternate methods of starting a program covered in this chapter.

Starting a Program in My Computer

My Computer shows you a graphical representation of the stuff in your computer. There are disk drives, folders, and files. And of course, some of those files are really programs that you can double-click on to start.

To get things rolling, pretend you want to use the calculator to add some numbers. You want this calculator because you're rebelling against your parents who always said you had to add things up in your head or you'd lose your math ability. Yeah, right.

Follow these steps to start a new program in My Computer:

1. Double-click on the My Computer icon. It'll open right up.

2. Double-click on the drive (C:) icon. This enables you to open that disk drive and see what lives there — mostly a collection of folders and files. Your goal is to find the folder that contains the files in which you're interested.

3. Double-click on the Windows folder and you see more files. The one you want is Calc, which is the Windows calculator program. (You may need to scroll down until you see it. To scroll down, click on the down-pointing arrow on the right side of the window.)

4. Double-click on the Calc icon file. There's your calculator. Add. Subtract. Divide. Do the SQRT thing (which is *square root* and not *squirt*). Click the Calculator's Close button when you're done.

 See Chapter 7 for more Calculator program information.

Running to the Run Command to Start a Program

No one in his or her right mind will run to the **Run** command to start a program. Most sane people will run *from* it. Although it works, there are just easier, more graphical methods for starting a program. The **Run** command exists only for those situations when you'll be asked to start a program that way, typically from some crusty old user manual. You will also be asked to use the **Run** command if you ever install an old DOS program or game.

Follow these steps to use the Run command:

1. Activate the Start Thing menu. Press CTRL+ESC to pop that sucker up, or click on the Start Thing button if a mouse is handy.

2. Click **Run** (or press the R key if you're mouse-lazy). The Run dialog box appears, similar to the one shown in Figure 3-2.

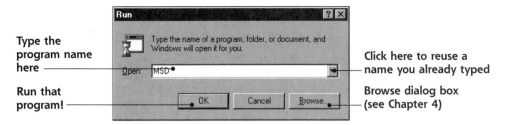

Type the program name here ———

Run that program! ———

Click here to reuse a name you already typed

Browse dialog box (see Chapter 4)

Figure 3-2 The Run command's dialog box

3. Type the name of the program you want to run in the *Open* box. For example, if you were told to run the MSD program you would type **MSD** in the box.

TIP If you're using the [Run] command to rerun a program, you can click the mouse on the arrow next to the *Open* box. This displays a drop-down list of all the previous programs typed into the box. Click on one to run it again. If Windows 95 is new on your PC, you won't have anything listed in this drop-down list.

4. Click on the OK button. Windows will go out, hunt down the program you typed, and hopefully, run it. If the program can't be found, an insulting dialog is displayed. Check what you typed and then try the command again.

5. If you've opened the Run box (because, well, I told you to) but you really don't have anything to run, just click the Cancel button (or press ESC) and the whole Run box will disappear.

X-REF If you've done everything right and the program still hasn't been found, refer to Chapter 29, "File? File? Here File! C'mon, Boy! Where'd You Go?" for help tracking it down.

Starting a Document Instead of a Program

Y
ou use programs to create *documents*. In fact, documents are the whole reason for having a computer. They're the stuff you do. Your effort. Your work. Your soul.

Here's a Windows secret: You can start your work easily and quickly by opening the document on which you want to work instead of opening an application and then opening the document. You save one step by starting a document instead of a program. Of course, this works only *after* you've created the document. But because most folks work on the same documents day after day, it's a handy shortcut.

Finding Your Document Lurking in the Documents Menu

Lurking in the Start Thing menu is a submenu called *Documents*. It doesn't contain a list of all the documents on your PC, just the most recent ones you've opened. Whatever. You can choose one of those documents from the menu to instantly start working on it again.

Follow these steps to start working on a document in the Documents menu:

1. Click on the Start Thing, or press CTRL+ESC or the Windows key (if your keyboard sports one).

2. Choose . You can hover over the word *Documents* with your mouse pointer or press the D key. This slides out the Documents submenu, which contains a list of documents you've messed with recently (Figure 3-3). If you see the hollow word Empty in the menu, there are no documents to open there. Oh well.

[Empty]

3. Pluck out a recent document. For example, if you see your *Household Inventory* report looming there, click on it.

4. The document is opened. Opening the document runs the program that created it, which gets you off and running (and working) as quickly as possible.

Finding a Document Nestled in My Computer

Just as you can use My Computer to open a program, you can use it to open documents. Basically, follow the same steps as you would for opening a program, but choose a document you created instead. See the section "Starting a Program in My Computer" earlier in this chapter for the details.

 TIP Don't randomly open icons in My Computer! Only double-click those icons representing documents *you* created. If you didn't create the document, or you don't know what it is, don't mess with it!

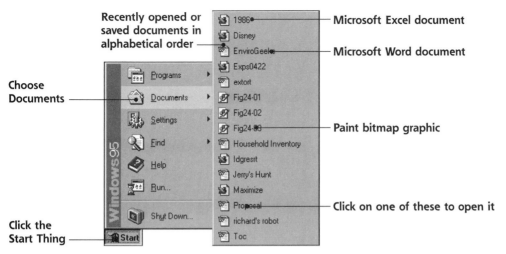

Recently opened or saved documents in alphabetical order

Microsoft Excel document

Microsoft Word document

Choose Documents

Paint bitmap graphic

Click on one of these to open it

Click the Start Thing

Figure 3-3 The Documents menu shows recently opened files.

Quitting Any Program

After you start a program, you'll use it for a while, and then you'll want to quit. (Sometimes you may want to quit sooner.) Not to be shy about it, Windows has lots of ways to quit a program. The most popular is the most polite, though there are other strange and often esoteric ways to wave bye-bye to your programs.

The Common, Polite, Almost Civilized Way to Quit

Quit any program by selecting the Exit command at the bottom of the File menu. Choose `File` → `Exit` and you're out. The command may be called Close, and in some rare instances you may even see the word Quit used. They're all the same.

Using the `Exit` command is the best, but not the only, way to quit. The following sections illustrate other ways to quit, which you can try if you ever have the time.

X-REF If you haven't yet saved before quitting, Windows will alert you and give you a chance to save. See Chapter 4 for more information on saving your stuff.

Quitting by Closing a Window

In Windows, closing a window is often the same as quitting. (This is why some Quit commands are called Close.) You can close a window by clicking the X in the window's upper-right corner.

The Drastic Way to Quit

Windows has a really scary way to kill off any program: Press CTRL+ALT+DELETE. This is the old DOS reset command, which used to restart the entire computer. You can do that in Windows to shut down any program or *dead* programs. I recommend this only as a last resort.

When you first press CTRL+ALT+DELETE, you'll see the Close Program window (see Figure 3-4).

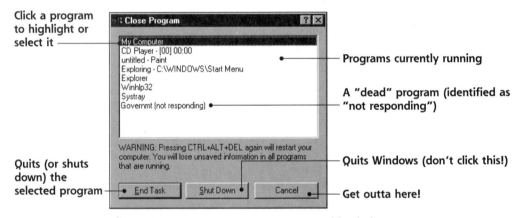

Figure 3-4 Press CTRL + ALT + DELETE to see this window.

The Close Program window lists all the programs currently humming away in Windows. To close any program, highlight its name in the window and then click the End Task button. The program closes — just as if you selected its Exit command — and you can continue working.

If the program doesn't close, a dialog box appears announcing that the program is *busy*. It's best to wait and try to shut down the program in a more traditional way, as described in the previous two sections.

When a program dies, it will say *not responding* by its name. You can click on that program, and then click on the End Task button to kill it off. After doing this, I would quit Windows and start everything all over again just to be safe. (Dead programs may cause other programs to come tumbling down as well.)

SOME THINGS YOU JUST DON'T WANT TO DO

There are a few things in Windows you just don't want to do. Trust me on this. If you press CTRL+ALT+DELETE twice, you'll reset your computer for sure. This is a desperate thing. Don't do it unless you absolutely have to.

Another thing you won't want to do, but probably will anyway from time to time: Don't click on the Shut Down button. Sometimes, without thinking, you may click on the Shut Down button when you really want to click the End Task button. If you do, Windows will quit and shut down your computer without warning. This is probably *not* what you intended.

Clearing the Documents Menu

The Documents menu continues to fill with the names of documents, up to the last 15 items you've opened or saved. (Not all Windows applications stick documents there.) Eventually this can get really junky. To clean up the Documents menu, follow these steps:

1. Choose Settings → Taskbar from the Start Thing menu. The Taskbar Properties dialog box appears.

2. Click on the Start Menu Programs panel. This brings the panel forward if it's not already in front.

3. Click on the Clear button in the bottom Documents Menu area. Clicking on the button instantly clears the Documents menu; there is no warning here!

4. Close the Taskbar Properties dialog box. Click on its Close button in the upper-right corner.

BONUS

Sticking Popular Documents on Your Desktop

Most folks use the same documents over and over: Travel Reports, P&L spreadsheets, endless projects you'll probably never finish, and so on. To make getting at these documents a lot easier, you can slap them right down on your desktop. Or if you like, you can put them all in a folder and put that on your desktop. Either way you get easy access to your most commonly used documents.

Follow these steps to stick a document on your desktop:

1. Click on the folder or document once to highlight the folder.

2. Copy the folder/file by typing CTRL+C on the keyboard. This is the copy command, which you can also get by choosing **Edit** → **Copy** from the menu if you're in love with your mouse.

3. Point anywhere on the desktop and click once on the mouse's main button.

4. Press CTRL+V to paste the folder/file. This puts a copy of your folder or file on the desktop for easy access.

Summary

This whole chapter was about *Starting*. You can now start the Start Thing menu, start icons on the desktop, start a document in My Computer, and start a new document. Now if we could only start a diet this easily.

Did you learn these things? If you didn't, go back and read again.

- ☐ How to start a new program.
- ☐ How to start an icon on the desktop.
- ☐ How to use the Run command.
- ☐ How to start a document in the Documents menu.
- ☐ The different ways to quit a program.
- ☐ How to clear the Documents menu.

FROM HELL TO HELP: USE ONE PROGRAM, YOU'VE USED THEM ALL

IN THIS CHAPTER YOU LEARN THESE KEY SKILLS

USING MENUS AND TOOLBARS   PAGE 41

CREATING, PRINTING, AND SAVING STUFF   PAGE 44

OPENING AND CLOSING STUFF   PAGE 48

USING THE HELP SYSTEM   PAGE 50

KNOWING WHEN TO QUIT VERSUS PUT ASIDE   PAGE 56

There's something charming about consistency. Mankind just loves it when things can be expected: the car starts, the check comes in the mail, it rains when you plan a picnic; you get the idea. These things assure us that everything's okay and allow the concept of *normal* to exist. Windows draws upon this need, serving up its applications in a similar, predictable and easy-to-get-used-to manner; almost all Windows programs work alike or have features so similar you will feel at home with any application.

Scent of a Windows Application

All Windows applications share a common approach. The look of each will be similar and you can count on several items working the same way. The bonus here is you'll find few surprises, even when you work with something new. This helps you get your work done quickly.

Figure 4-1 shows a typical Windows program, WordPad. Everything common to most Windows applications is pointed out in the figure. In the following example, you'll use WordPad. This is a good program to start with because it's typical of Windows' applications.

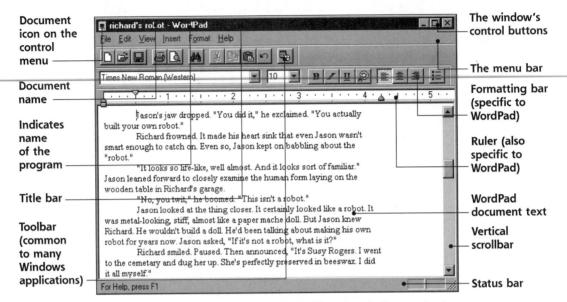

Figure 4-1 The WordPad program looks like a lot of other applications.

Follow these steps to start WordPad:

1. Start the Start Thing by pressing CTRL+ESC to pop up the menu or click on Start .

2. Choose Programs → Accessories . WordPad should be listed in the Accessories submenu, probably toward the bottom.

3. Click WordPad . WordPad starts in its own window on the desktop. Keep WordPad on the screen for the rest of the chapter. You'll be using it for a tutorial — fun!

 Chapter 7, the section "Let WordPad Bring Out the Shakespeare in You," has more information on WordPad, should you be interested.

What's on the Menu?

Computer programs work only when you give them commands. The commands are clustered in two places: the menu bar or a toolbar. Generally speaking, all the commands are attached to the menu bar. The toolbar contains only handy commands (covered in the next section).

The menu bar appears near the top of the program's window. It contains several key words, each of which supposedly describes a category of command: File, Edit, View, and so on. Each of these words is the name of a menu. Figure 4-2 shows the File menu.

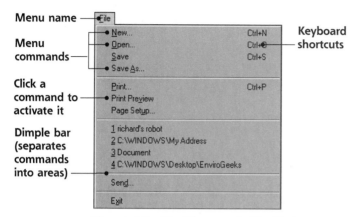

Figure 4-2 The File menu in WordPad

To activate a menu, click on its name using the mouse. For example, to see what commands are in the File menu, click File. To activate a command, click it or use its quick-key shortcut if one is available.

Hanging Out at the Toolbar

Some programs offer quick shortcuts to common commands. These appear on a toolbar or strip o' buttons somewhere below the menu or occasionally on *floating palettes* (tiny windows that hover over your work). The idea here is simple: Click on a button with the mouse to get at some command quickly.

The only drawback to toolbars is the wee li'l pictures on the buttons don't often fully explain what the button does. So to make things easier, point the mouse pointer at the button briefly and a bubble or balloon (like a cartoon balloon) appears over the icon. The bubble is called a *tooltip*, as in "Tiptoe through the tooltips," and it tells what the button does. Figure 4-3 shows how the disk button in WordPad is really a shortcut to the Save command.

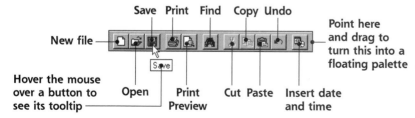

Figure 4-3 The bubble says this button is really the Save command.

TOOLBARS AND FLOATING TOOL PALETTES

By day, WordPad's toolbar sits under the menu. By night, it's a wild floating palette you can drag anywhere in WordPad's window. How? Just point the mouse to a blank part of the toolbar and drag it elsewhere. Depending on where you drag it, you'll have a toolbar (like Figure 4-3) or a floating palette. Personally, I prefer the toolbar because a floating palette tends to get in the way of my text.

By the way, this trick can be applied to just about any toolbar in Windows.

 X-REF Some buttons you press once to activate some command. Other buttons are more like on/off switches. See Chapter 26, the section "On/Off Buttons," for more information on which is which. Also see "Drop-Down Lists" in that chapter for information on drop-down lists, which often appear on toolbars.

Status Bars: Your Application's Cheat Sheet

A status bar is nothing more than a strip of information across a window. In WordPad, the status bar may say "For Help, Press F1" or it may tell you more about a command. Other applications use the status bar to tell you about the document you're working on or other information regarding the program. In a way, it's a cheat sheet.

Going About Your Business

You use a Windows application to create something, what I call *stuff*. For example, you use a word processor to write a nasty letter to your bank; you use a spreadsheet to figure out how you can afford a sports car to help you survive a midlife crisis; your kids use a Paint program for hours to create and then print a solid black sheet of paper; and so on. No matter what it is you do or whatever stuff you create, there are common approaches taken to work with it in Windows. Basically you can do six things with stuff:

* Make new stuff
* Print stuff

* Save stuff to disk
* Open and modify stuff already created
* Close stuff you're working on
* Start over again to make more stuff

These items are common to *all* Windows applications. The only programs that don't do these things are utilities, which are used for dinking and games.

Making Stuff

What you create with your application depends on the application. In all cases, you'll use the keyboard, mouse, and the various menu commands and tools in the application to get your work done. The end result? You've made stuff.

Follow these steps to make stuff in WordPad:

1. Start WordPad. (See the instructions at the start of the section "Scent of a Windows Application" if you haven't already started WordPad.)

2. Type your name and address. Just use the keyboard like you would a typewriter. Press ENTER at the end of each line and after typing the last line. Here's what I'd type:

   Dan Gookin
   919 E. Hillsdale Blvd., Suite 400
   Foster City, CA 94404

And there you go. You have a wonderful little document that you're going to print in a moment.

Printing Your Stuff

Having your creation inside the computer just isn't enough. In most cases you'll want a *hard copy*, or a printout, of your stuff. The application will take your work and hopefully make something beautiful of it, something that will come churning out of the printer in a matter of seconds.

Your printer should be on and ready to print before you use the print command. If it is and everything is set up correctly, then the file should print right away. If not, you have a problem!

X-REF See Chapter 29 for information on troubleshooting printer problems. See the section "The All-Purpose Amazing Windows Troubleshooter."

Follow these steps to print your name and address:

1. Click **File** on the menu. You can also press ALT+F if your fingers are glued to the keyboard.

2. Click **Print**, or press the P key. This brings up the Print dialog box with further instructions, as in Figure 4-4.

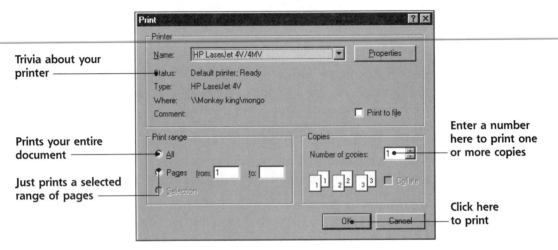

Trivia about your printer

Prints your entire document

Just prints a selected range of pages

Enter a number here to print one or more copies

Click here to print

Figure 4-4 The standard Print dialog box

3. Click OK to start printing.

You really don't need to mess with the rest of the dialog box, just click on OK and your stuff prints. You may see a tiny "I'm printing now" dialog box displayed. Whatever.

 TIP **Another quick way to print is to click on the print button on the toolbar — provided one is available. This button prints your document instantly without displaying the standard Print dialog box, it just prints.**

Saving Your Stuff

Sometimes you'll use an application to make something really quickly, print it, and then be done with it. Most of the time, however, you'll want to save what you make. You save it for two reasons. First, it's nice to save things so you don't have to do that work all over again. Second, by saving your stuff to disk, you allow yourself the freedom to look at it later, edit, modify, and otherwise change it.

Follow these steps to save your name and address:

1. Click **File** on the menu bar.

2. Click **Save**. You can also press ALT+F and then the S key, or you can press all three keys one at a time: ALT, F, and S. Eventually the Save As dialog box appears, similar to the one shown in Figure 4-5. You will be saving your stuff in three steps, so keep Figure 4-5 close at hand to help you find things.

Save As dialog box —

Start here —

Type a file name in here —

Save a file as a specific type —

Optionally choose a folder here as well

Click here to save

Figure 4-5 The Save As dialog box

3. Choose a disk drive for your document. Click the arrow by the drop-down list at the top of the Save As dialog box. From the list that appears, choose drive (C:). (You may have to scroll up to see the (C:) label.)

4. Choose a folder for your document. If you have a *My Documents* folder, choose it from the list. Otherwise you're done. (Later chapters will show you how to create special folders and save your documents there.)

5. Click once in the *File name* box and type in a document name. You may already see the text *Document* in there. Go ahead and type in something else, something descriptive, short, and to the point. For this example, type **My Address,** as shown in Figure 4-5. Use the BACKSPACE key to backup and erase if you make a typing boo-boo.

6. Choose a document type. Word for Windows 6.0 may already be showing, which is fine.

7. Press ENTER, or click the Save button; either way your stuff is now saved to disk.

Your clue to whether a document has been saved is right on the main title bar of the application's window. Many applications change the window name after a document has been saved. If WordPad's window name is now *My Address—WordPad*, you can rest assured your document was saved on disk.

TIP   **The quickest way to save is to press the CTRL+S shortcut key.**

Opening Stuff

Because you never can finish all your work in a day, all Windows programs enable you to open files you've previously saved to disk. Once you open them, they sit right there on the screen ready for you to play with them, edit them, print them, and then save them again when you're happy.

Follow these steps to open a file:

1. Choose File → Open from the menu to summon the Open dialog box, or press the handy CTRL+O shortcut. You can even use an open button on the toolbar. The Open dialog box (see Figure 4-6) is a common part of almost every Windows program. You use it to scour your hard drive and folders, hunting down a file on the disk with which you want to work.

2. Locate the folder or disk drive where the file is located. In this example, the file you want to open is right there in the dialog box. Look for the *My Address* file. (You may have to use the scrollbar.)

3. Double-click on the file, and there's the address you typed in earlier.

Look for your
document's
folder here

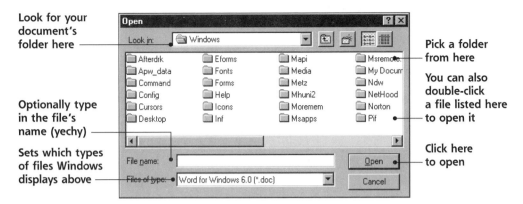

Pick a folder
from here

You can also
double-click
a file listed here
to open it

Optionally type
in the file's
name (yechy)

Sets which types
of files Windows
displays above

Click here
to open

Figure 4-6   The Open dialog box

 X-REF   If you don't see your file lurking in the Open dialog box and it's ticking you off, then you'll need to hunt for it. See Chapter 29, "Finding Files — The Relaxed Explanation."

Starting New Stuff

If you're done with one document and want to start working on another, choose the New command from the File menu. This is a lot quicker than quitting the program and starting over.

Most Windows programs use the CTRL+N shortcut key to start a new document. They may also sport a New button on the toolbar, which looks like a blank sheet of paper.

Some applications may ask you to save your current work when you select the New command. Select the Yes button when asked, and then see "Saving Your Stuff" earlier in this chapter for information on how to use the Save dialog box.

How to Open Your Most Recent Stuff Quickly

Some Windows applications keep track of the last few things you've been working on. These are kept in a list located in the File menu, usually numbered 1 through 4 (see Figure 4-2). You can quickly open recently used files by selecting them from the file menu.

SIDE TRIP

Closing Stuff

When you're done with your toys, you should put them away. The Close command closes a window (or document), but does not close the program. Close commands typically appear in programs that have a "Window" menu, which enables you to use several windows to work on several things at once. (WordPad lacks a Close command because you can work on only one document at a time.)

To close your document, choose `File` → `Close` from the menu. The window closes, the document is gone, but you haven't quit your program.

No universal shortcut key exists for the Close command, though many programs may use CTRL+W (where the W means what? Window? Walk away? Whatever?). And you can almost always use CTRL+F4 to close a window, and ALT+F4 will close both the window and the program.

Close is not the same as Save. You save when you think what you have is good. You close when you're done messing with it. As a side effect, closing something that hasn't been saved will prompt Windows to ask you whether you want it saved.

The idea behind the Close command is you don't have to quit your programs when you're done working on something. You can simply close your document and then work on something else.

The Windows Way of Offering Help

A common feature of nearly every Windows program is its extensive, online help. Of course, how you define help and what the program gives you are usually two different things. In a Windows program, Help usually refers to an electronic version of the manual. In fact, Microsoft has made it a point to shift their manual text to a Help program and only print scant information in the traditional, bound manuals. (While this may save a lot of trees, it's not going to do you any good when the computer won't start.)

The Quick and Desperate Jab at the F1 Key

The F1 key is the Help key. All Windows programs obey this law. Anywhere you are, at any time, you can stab the F1 key to get help. And not only that, the help you see will be related to whatever you're doing; press the F1 key in a Save dialog box and you'll see helpful information on saving files — that kind of thing.

When you're done reviewing the helpful information, press the ESC key to return to your document.

When you first press F1, you may see a little window with a book and a magic pen. The magic pen writes something in the book — something about Microsoft stock being overinflated in value — and then you'll see the Help system on your screen. (If you're lucky, you'll actually see the magic pen fill several pages.)

Using the Help System

The Windows Help system is designed like a book. There are chapters, sections, and a table of contents. Figure 4-7 shows you the main contents panel in the Help system. This is where you see an organized overview of information in the Help system, like chapters in a manual. In fact, that's what it is — an online version of the manual. If you don't see the Contents panel, click on the Contents tab in the upper part of the Help system window.

 X-REF See Chapter 26, the section "Panels, Pages, and Tabs," for more information on these tabs and panels if you need help.

More panels
with different
ways to display
the information

Major "chapters"

An open chapter

Contents inside
the chapter

Double-click this
to read its
information

Click here to
print the
topic's text

All done!

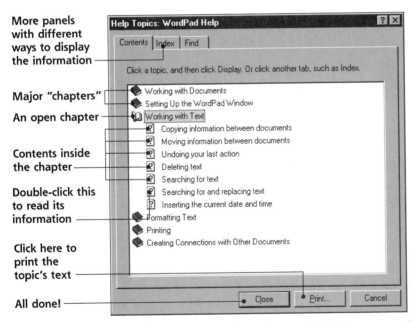

Figure 4-7 The Help system for WordPad, Contents panel

To open a chapter, double-click on its name. This changes the icon by the chapter name from a closed book to an open book and you'll see a list of topics in that chapter (see Figure 4-7).

To close a chapter, and make the screen a little more readable, double-click its name again.

To open a topic, double-click on its name. This opens a separate window that details information about the topic, often including step-by-step instructions (see Figure 4-8).

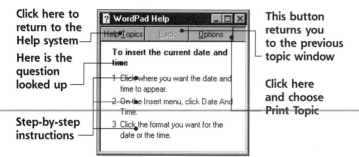

Figure 4-8 A sample topic window

Some text in the Help window may appear with a dotted underline in the helpful description. Usually these are terms or jargon that may baffle you. To see a definition of the text, hover the mouse pointer over it. The mouse pointer changes into a little hand with a pointy finger. Click the mouse once to see a pop-up definition. Click the mouse again to make the definition go away.

A square by some text indicates a *link* to that particular topic. If you move the mouse pointer over the square, it changes to a pointy finger hand. Click the mouse once and you'll be instantly zoomed to that topic for more information.

TIP To return to the main Help system screen at any time, click on the Contents button.

THE WEIRD "?" BUTTON ON SOME WINDOWS

See the little question-mark button in the upper-right corner of a dialog box? This activates a feature where you can point and click anything in the window to get help on it. After clicking the "?" button, the mouse pointer changes to an arrow with a question mark by it. At this point you can click several items in the window to see a pop-up bubble explaining what the item is or how it works. Click the mouse again (or press ESC) to make the bubble go away.

SIDE TRIP

Finding a Specific Topic Using the Index

All information about a specific program or topic is organized into the Help system's index. You can use the index to find a topic if you know exactly what it is.

Follow these steps to find a specific topic:

1. In your application (WordPad), press the F1 key to activate the Help system. You don't need to do this if the Help screen is already visible.

2. Click the Index tab. This brings that panel to the front if it isn't already. You'll see a list of topics and subtopics displayed just as you would find in any good index (see Figure 4-9).

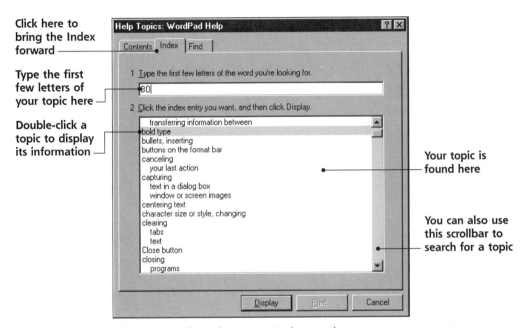

Figure 4-9 The Help system's Index panel

3. Search for your topic by typing the first few letters of the word in the box at the top of the panel. For example, type **BO** for *bold type* and — behold! — the topic is displayed in the lower window.

4. Double-click the index entry you're looking for and read up on the topic you've chosen. Or, you can click the Display button at the bottom-right corner of the window to get to your information.

Finding a Specific Topic Using the Find Panel

Another way to hunt down information is to use the Find panel in the Help system. It lists helpful information based on an alphabetically sorted list of words, commands, and meaningless jargon.

Follow these steps to use the Find panel:

1. In the Help system, click the Find panel using the mouse. The Find panel comes up, looking something like Figure 4-10.

First type what you're looking for ————

Second, choose a topic ————

Finally, double-click the subjects that interest you ————

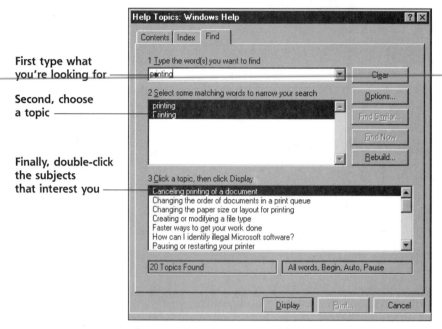

Figure 4-10 The Find panel for WordPad's help

2. Type the subject you want to find in the box at the top. For example, type the word **printing** to look up information on printing. Normally, you need to type only the first few letters of your subject. This produces a short list of topics in box number 2.

3. Select the topic from box number 2. For example, if *printing* is listed there, click the word *printing* (actually, in this case, there are two different *printing* topics). This narrows the list of subjects in box number 3 to only a few, one of which is probably what you need.

4. Select the help you need from box number 3. Highlight the help topic with the mouse and click the Display button at the bottom of the dialog box. Hopefully, this displays the information you need.

Quitting the Help System

When you're done with the Help system, you must quit it — just like any other program. Click the Cancel button in the bottom-right corner of the Help system's window. You can also quit by closing the Help system's window. The easiest way to quit the Help system and close its window is to press the ESC key.

MAJOR HELP FOR WINDOWS

One of the main items stuck to the Start Thing menu is Help. When you select this item you'll be tossed into the Help system with all the chapters, topics, and subjects related to everything Windows does — a substantial amount of substance!

Everything in Windows Help works as described in this chapter. You have a Contents, Index, and Find panel for looking up individual topics. The Contents panel even has subchapters and sub-sub-subtopics, which can be very tiresome to wade through. For that reason, I recommend using either the Index or Find panels to look up something that interests you.

As with the Help system for any program, you should quit before you return to Windows to get your work done. Just press the ESC key and the Help system disappears.

TIP There may be times when you don't want to quit the Help system. For example, you may want to switch back and forth between your program and Help. To do so, press the ALT+TAB keys. Press it once to switch back to your application. Press it again to switch back to the Help system.

KEEPING THE HELP TABS ORGANIZED

Get familiar with the three tabs in the Help menu: Contents, Index, and Find. They will be close friends to you the more you get acquainted with Windows. Look at the Contents, Index, and Find section of Help like this:

Contents   Contents is for general, overall ideas and directions.

Index   The Index is good if you're not quite sure what particular word you're looking for. For example, you know you've seen a word, starts with a T, maybe, and it makes the cursor move to the right in intervals. Now, what's it called? Oh yeah, a Tab! (Wait, I thought a Tab was a nasty-tasting cola beverage.)

Find   Find is when you know the exact word you want to find. That makes sense.

Done for the Day? To Quit or Put Away?

Quitting your program isn't always necessary when you're done working. In fact, you'll probably have two or three programs you use all the time. Instead of quitting them when you're done working on your stuff, I recommend you put them aside.

Putting aside an application makes it easier for you to use it again later quickly. This is part of *multitasking*, which is covered in detail later in this book. For now, to put aside your document click the *minimize* button in the window's upper-right corner.

Thwoop! This zooms the window down to a small button on the taskbar. The program isn't dead, it's just put away so you can easily use it later.

To get the application back, just click its button on the taskbar. This zooms the application back up to its previous size and location, ready for you to continue working.

 If you think this putting away stuff sounds cool, check out Chapter 8 which goes into fine, yet perky, detail.

BONUS

The Meaning of Menus

You can activate a menu using the keyboard. The underlined letter in a menu title or command name is called a *hot key*. If you press the ALT key on your keyboard and then that hot key, it's the same as choosing a particular menu item with the mouse.

Some menus have submenus attached to them.

Menus appear left to right, the most commonly used menu supposedly appearing on the left. Likewise, the most common menu commands appear on the top of a drop-down menu. The only exception here is the Exit command, which usually appears at the bottom of the first menu.

The first menu, typically the File menu, is the most important. It contains the saving, printing, opening, and other important commands.

The Help menu usually appears last in the menu bar (whether or not it's most important to you). At the bottom of most Help menus is the About command. This command displays a tiny box that tells you something about the program, its name or version, or other information. Unfortunately it doesn't tell you what the program actually does. Hopefully, you'll know that *before* you install the software.

X-REF And, yes, there is *still* more to be learned in Chapter 25, "Chasing Menus."

Hot, Hot, Hot Keys

It's not always necessary to use that little mouse creature. You can get just as much work done by keeping your hands on the keyboard. The following list of hot keys should help you with this.

Hot Key	Function
ALT+F	File Menu
ALT+E	Edit Menu
ALT+V	View Menu
ALT+I	Insert Menu
ALT+O	Format Menu
ALT+H	Help Menu

Quick Key Shortcuts

The following shortcuts will help you regardless of which program you're using in Windows. Nifty, eh?

Key Combo	Command
CTRL+A	Select All
CTRL+C	Copy

(continued)

Key Combo	Command
CTRL+F	Find
CTRL+N	New
CTRL+O	Open
CTRL+P	Print
CTRL+S	Save
CTRL+V	Paste
CTRL+X	Cut
CTRL+Z	Undo
F1	Help
ALT+F4	Quit/Exit

Summary

By now, you should understand a little more about how Windows programs work. In fact, you should understand the following:

☐ How to start WordPad.

☐ How to read a menu (not meaning those in a restaurant).

☐ What the icons mean in the toolbar.

☐ How to make, print, and save something in WordPad.

☐ How to open and close a file.

☐ How to use the Help System.

PART TWO

GETTING WORK DONE

THIS PART CONTAINS THE FOLLOWING CHAPTERS

CHAPTER 5 ALL ABOUT THE START THING

CHAPTER 6 GETTING TO KNOW THE TASKBAR

CHAPTER 7 INTRODUCING THE APPLETS

CHAPTER 8 MULTITASKING — SHARING, AND LOVING

CHAPTER 9 VISITING PLANET INTERNET AND OTHER ONLINE STUFF

CHAPTER 10 DEALING WITH ANCIENT DOS APPLICATIONS

CHAPTER 11 INSTALLING NEW SOFTWARE

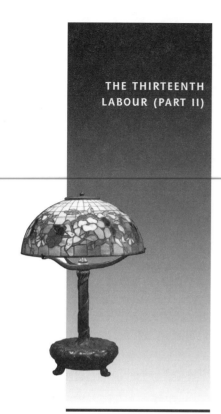

"**G**ood morning," Eurystheus announced, entering the small room where Heracles laboured for the thirteenth time. He pulled the cloak around him tighter to ward off the morning chill. These marbled palaces were pretty but they certainly lacked proper heating.

Heracles grunted. He took a loud sip from a Jolt cola, sucking the last of the sweetened caffeinated juice from the container. He crushed the empty can against his skull.

Eurystheus couldn't read Heracles' mood. He tried to step in a little closer, to look at the screen. "Um, how's it been going? Have you figured it out yet?"

"It's like a Hydra."

Eurystheus jumped back. He didn't want anything to do with the slimy multiheaded beast. "That bad?"

"No," Heracles said. "But killing this thing is nonintuitive. There're too many ways to do it and if you think too long, one of the heads comes up and bites you in the . . ."

"What are you doing now?" Eurystheus asked.

Heracles, in all his bulging strength, gently rolled the mouse over to the Start Thing button and clicked to start a program.

"That's amazing," Eurystheus exclaimed. "What is that?"

"It's WordPad," Heracles said, his voice unenthusiastic. "It's like a little word processor, but it lacks the beefier functions such as a spelling checker and the capability to save in the HTML format."

Heracles turned and looked Eurystheus in the eye. He told the timid king, "Eventually you'll have to get some *real* software for this thing."

Eurystheus nodded silently.

"Now I'm doing Copy and Paste," Heracles said. "Then I'm going to try some multitasking. That would have saved time over the past few years." Heracles burst out laughing, slapping his thigh for telling such a clever joke.

Eurystheus nervously laughed. Then he said, "What do you mean multitasking would save you time?"

"Well," said Heracles, starting a Paint document and sketching a stick figure fighting a Hydra, "I could have doubled-up on some of those annoying tasks you assigned me. Imagine cleaning out the stables while I'm killing the Nemean lion *and* getting that Amazon lady's girdle. Think of the time I would have saved doing all those tasks simultaneously. By Zeus! I'd be done now, fully sane, and back in my own country with my wife and kin."

"Then," Eurystheus began, realizing his plan may backfire, "you'll eventually show *me* how all this works, right?"

Heracles was silent.

"Maybe you can multitask right now and tell me what's going on," Eurystheus tried again.

Silence.

Then Heracles said, "A-ha! Here is where I learn about the Internet."

ALL ABOUT THE START THING

IN THIS CHAPTER YOU LEARN THESE KEY SKILLS

UTTERLY MESSING WITH THE START
THING MENU   PAGE 61

ADDING PROGRAMS TO THE MENU   PAGE 64

REMOVING PROGRAMS FROM THE MENUS   PAGE 66

MAKING SOME PROGRAMS START
AUTOMATICALLY   PAGE 68

RUNNING APPLICATIONS MINIMIZED OR
MAXIMIZED   PAGE 70

5

The Start Thing is where everything starts. Almost. Actually, the Start Thing looks like one of Microsoft's attempts to make things that turned out wrong look easier. And then when they found out it was bad, they tried to fix it instead of to kill it, which just made it worse — like some massive, but well-intentioned, government project gone awry. But I digress.

The Start Thing isn't really that ugly to use. It's unwieldy, but the true point you should remember is the Start Thing can help you fire up your favorite programs, if you know how to tame it. That's the subject of this chapter, beating the Start Thing into shape.

Onto the Start Menu

There are so many ways to start an application in Windows, it's just best to forget all of them and concentrate instead on using the Start Thing menu. It may not be perfect, but it's handy.

To pop up the Start menu, click the Start button, press CTRL+ESC, or press the Windows key if your keyboard has one.

Stuff That Lives on the Main Start Thing Menu

Seven definite items are on the Start Thing menu, divided into two groups. A thin dimple line separates the two groups. Table 5-1 lists everything.

TABLE 5-1   The Start Menu

Icon	Text	What It Does
	PROGRAM	Lists a submenu of programs (see Chapter 3)
	DOCUMENTS	Lists a submenu of recent documents
	SETTINGS	Lists a submenu for quick access to Windows' dinking tools
	FIND	A special command that helps you find files, folders, and programs on disk
	HELP	Activates Windows' main Help system
	RUN	Brings up a dialog box where you can type the name of a command to run
	SHUTDOWN	Forces Windows into bankruptcy; seriously, offers several options for quitting Windows or shutting down for the day
	SUSPEND	This works like Shutdown, but forces energy-efficient and laptop computers into a "sleep" mode, saving energy

In addition to the basics, you may also see a second dimple line and even more items on the top of the Start Thing menu totem pole (such as in Figure 5-1). These are quick-access programs and stuff you can stick on the menu yourself. It's a snap to do, and it's covered in the next section.

Sticking Something on the Main Start Thing Menu

You can easily avoid marching through the Start Thing menu march by sticking your favorite and most popular programs right there on the Start Thing main menu. That way you need only pop up the menu and you're just one mouse click away from your favorite program. Figure 5-1 shows an example with two popular programs used throughout this book, Paint and WordPad.

Click here to start Paint

Click here to start WordPad

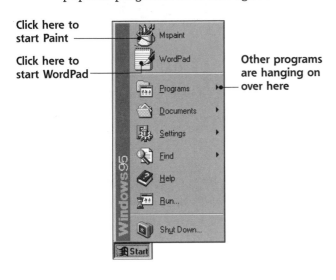

Other programs are hanging on over here

Figure 5-1 Popular programs can sit squat on top of the Start Thing command totem pole.

Follow these steps to place a program on the Start menu:

1. Start by opening My Computer, then open drive (C:), open the Program Files folder, and then look inside the Accessories folder. WordPad's program icon should be there. (You may have to scroll the window around to find it.)

2. Drag the program icon to the Start button on the Taskbar. Figure 5-2 shows how it works.

3. To verify that a shortcut copy of the program is now on the menu, activate the Start Thing; click on the button, or press CTRL+ESC. You'll see your program's icon living high and mighty on top of the pile.

You haven't really moved the program or its icon. Instead, you've created a shortcut to it. This way you can remove the icon later if you like, without worrying about deleting the original program.

X-REF See Chapter 4 for a discussion of Windows' shortcuts and how they work.

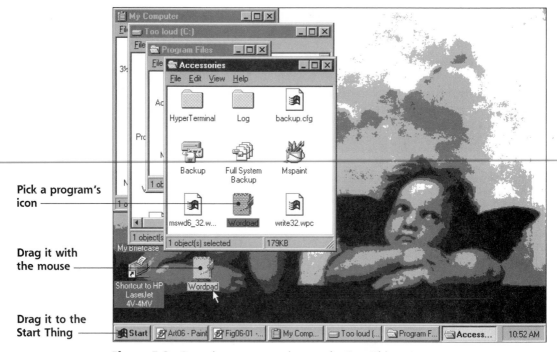

Pick a program's icon

Drag it with the mouse

Drag it to the Start Thing

Figure 5-2   Dragging a program icon to the Start Thing menu

Adding a Program to a Start Thing Submenu

New software you install on your computer is automatically placed onto the Start Thing menu. Older stuff you install, or software already on your computer, must be manually added to the Start Thing menu.

Follow these steps to add a program to the Start Thing menu:

1. Pop up the Start Thing menu.

2. Choose   Settings → Taskbar . This brings up the Taskbar Properties dialog box.

3. Click the *Start Menu Programs* panel. This brings it forward, looking a lot like Figure 5-3.

4. Click the Add button, which brings up another dialog box, Create Shortcut.

5. Click the Browse button. A Browse dialog box is displayed. It enables you to scour your disk drives and folders for the program you want to add to the Start Thing menu.

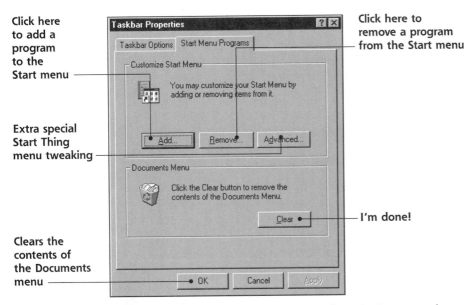

Click here to add a program to the Start menu ──

Extra special Start Thing menu tweaking ──

Clears the contents of the Documents menu ──

Click here to remove a program from the Start menu

I'm done!

Figure 5-3 You add or remove programs from the Start menu here.

6. Find your program. For example, suppose you want to add the Welcome program to the ⟨Accessories⟩ → ⟨System Tools⟩ submenu. (Welcome is actually the silly little program that displays the Welcome dialog box when you first start Windows.) To do that, you'd hunt down the Welcome program.

7. Choose drive (C:) from the *Look in* list box. Welcome lives in the Windows folder on your (C:)drive.

8. Double-click the Windows folder.

 Welcome

9. Use the scrollbar at the bottom of the window to scroll right until you see the Welcome program's icon.

TIP You can add documents and folders to the Start menu as well as programs. It works the same, but you must choose All Files from the *Files of type* drop-down list box near the bottom of the Browse dialog box.

10. Click the Welcome icon once. This highlights it, selecting the icon for further action.

11. Click Open. This closes the Browse dialog box and puts the program's geeky pathname into the Create Shortcut dialog box. Ugly isn't it? For the Welcome program it may look something like this: C:\WINDOWS\ Welcome.exe.

12. Click Next. Now you select a Start Thing submenu for your program. All of the submenus are shown in a list, each represented by a little folder (see Figure 5-4). Just click the folder you want your program shoved into. For this example, click the System Tools folder to stick the Welcome program there.

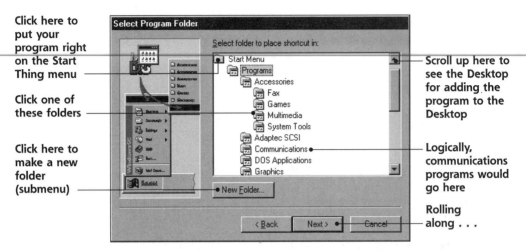

Figure 5-4 The Start Thing menu setup wizard asks you where to stick your program.

13. Click the Next button again. If you like, you can type in a nifty name for the shortcut/menu item you've created. Presently, Windows suggests a simple one, such as **Welcome** for the Welcome program. You can type in something more descriptive if you like, such as **Welcome to the nightmare that is Windows.**

14. Click Finish. This closes the wizard dialog box, returning you to the Taskbar Properties dialog.

15. Click OK and you're finished.

Now check out the Start Thing menu for the program you just added. The program will be there, which is a lot handier than having to fumble through My Computer for it every time.

Zapping a Program from a Start Thing Submenu

I believe the best way to work the Start Thing is to fill its menus with those programs you use the most. As Windows comes out of the box, it puts several of its own programs on various submenus of the Start Thing. However, if you're like me, you only use a few programs in Windows and rarely need to start any others, so it makes sense to clear out some of the deadwood.

Before following the steps to remove a program from a Start Thing submenu you should remember this: Deleting a program from the Start Thing menu doesn't delete the program from your hard drive. Instead, you're only deleting its shortcut. For example, in the following practice steps, you're going to delete the *Welcome to the nightmare that is Windows* item added on the previous page. The Welcome program will not be deleted, however.

Follow these steps to remove a program from the Start Thing:

1. Whip out the Taskbar Properties dialog box. You can choose Settings → Taskbar from the Start Thing menu. This brings up the Taskbar Properties dialog box.

2. Click the Start Menu Programs panel to bring it in front if it isn't already. (See Figure 5-3 because I'm too lazy to reproduce it here.)

3. Click Remove. The Remove Shortcuts/Folders dialog box appears, looking eerily similar to Figure 5-5. It details a common Windows element — the *collapsible tree structure* — which you can use to find the program you want to remove from the menu.

4. Double-click a folder to open it and see its menu items. Any items on the main start menu appear at the bottom of the list by themselves. Yes, you can remove these things, too. For this example, open Accessories and then the System Tools folder to find the Welcome to the nightmare that is Windows program.

5. Click once on *Welcome to the nightmare that is Windows.* This selects the program, and it appears highlighted on the screen.

6. Click the Remove button. *Thwoop!* The program is gone from the menu. (Remember, the program itself hasn't been deleted, only its menu item.) If you're itching to remove more programs from the menu, repeat Steps 4 and 5 again.

7. Click the Close button. The Remove Shortcuts/Folders vanishes.

8. Click the OK button. You can check the Start Thing menu to confirm your changes. Programs you've removed will no longer be there.

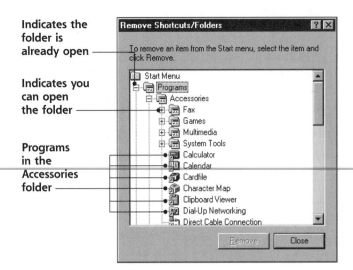

Indicates the folder is already open

Indicates you can open the folder

Programs in the Accessories folder

Figure 5-5 The Remove Shortcuts/ Folders dialog box, where you surgically alter the Start Thing menu.

Applications That Start Automatically (Amazing!)

Windows has the capability to start a given program or set of programs automatically each time you turn on your computer. Ideally these should be programs you either start yourself every day (the manual approach) or programs you just like to have handy, humming along and ready when you need them.

Adding and Moving Programs to the StartUp Submenu

A special submenu in the Start Thing is named StartUp. It contains a list of programs, just like any other menu. The difference is that Windows goes through this menu, automatically starting every program listed every time you start Windows.

To add a program to the StartUp menu, follow the steps for adding a program to any menu as outlined earlier in this chapter, in the section "Adding a Program to a Start Thing Submenu." Just choose the StartUp folder for your programs.

If the program you want to add to the StartUp menu lives in another Start Thing menu, you can move it. In fact, you can move any program from one menu to another.

Follow these steps to move a menu item to the StartUp menu:

1. Summon the Taskbar Properties dialog box. The completely *keyboardy* way to do this is: CTRL+ESC, S, T.

2. Click on the Start Menu Programs panel to bring it to the front. (Gaze at Figure 5-3 to see what it should look like.)

3. Click Advanced. A mini Explorer window appears, which enables you to manipulate Start Thing menu items as you would work with files on a disk drive (see Figure 5-6).

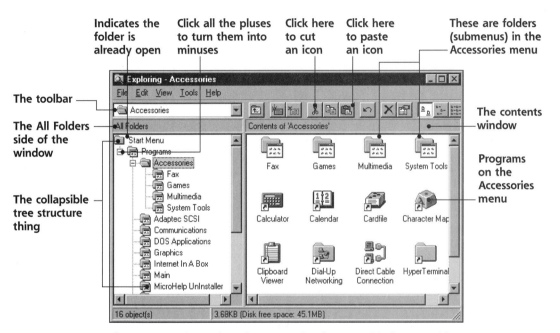

Figure 5-6 The Explorer lets you seriously mess with the Start Thing menu.

4. Find the file you want to move. Use the scrollbars to move the window around if its contents aren't displayed all at once. Double-click a folder icon to open that folder — which is really a submenu. Keep double-clicking to open folders, just as you would choose items from a menu, until you locate the menu item you want to move.

X-REF See Chapter 26, "The Collapsible Tree Structure Thing," for more information about using the collapsible tree structure thing.

5. Click on the file's icon to highlight the file.

6. Choose [Edit] → [Cut]. After cutting the program, you'll notice its icon appears dimmed. This means it's been cut and hasn't yet been pasted. No biggy.

7. Choose the StartUp folder/submenu. Click the StartUp menu in the left side of the Exploring-Accessories window. That's where you want to paste the program you're moving. (You could paste it into any folder/menu, but this exercise moves things to the StartUp menu.)

8. Choose [Edit] → [Paste]. The icon has been pasted. Its original faded icon was moved up to the new folder, and it appears in the new folder or submenu on the Start Thing menu. Oh, just you wait and see. . . .

9. Close the Exploring-Accessories window. Click the X in the window's upper-right corner. Zoom! It goes away.

10. Click the OK button in the Taskbar Properties dialog box. Now you can check the Start Thing menu to ensure that the icon/program name/shortcut was moved. (Don't worry, it was.)

Running a Program *Minimized* When It Starts

When you start a program in Windows, it normally appears full-blown, big on the screen, and massive to deal with. This may not be the case with the programs you want started automatically in the StartUp menu. For example, you may want to start your Rolodex, but because you don't need it right away, it would be nice to run it minimized, out of sight.

Follow these steps to minimize a program that starts automatically in the StartUp menu:

1. Choose [Settings] → [Taskbar] from the Start menu. This displays the Taskbar Properties dialog box.

2. Click the Start Menu Programs tab to bring that panel forward.

3. Click on the Advanced button. This displays a mini Explorer window you can use to work with the programs and submenus on the Start Thing.

4. Double-click the Programs folder to open it. The Programs folder is in the left box under All Folders.

5. Open the StartUp folder.

6. Locate the program you want to run minimized. It will be listed on the right side of the Explorer window under Contents of Start Up.

7. Right-click on the program's shortcut icon. This displays the program's shortcut menu.

8. Choose **Properties** from the shortcut menu. The program's Properties dialog box appears.

9. Click the Shortcut tab. This brings the Shortcut panel up front (see Figure 5-7).

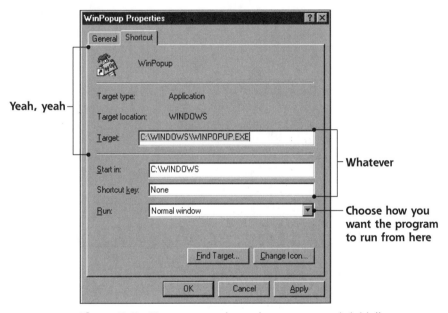

Yeah, yeah

Whatever

Choose how you want the program to run from here

Figure 5-7 Here you can choose how a program is initially run.

10. Near the bottom of the dialog box is a list box with the word *Run* by it. Click the arrow by that list box. This displays three options for the program's window when it starts. Click the mouse on the word Minimized.

11. Click OK. This closes the Properties dialog box. If you want to configure more programs to run minimized, repeat Steps 2 through 5 for each of those programs. Choose Minimized in their Properties dialog box and those programs will start unobtrusively as buttons on the taskbar instead of as full-blown programs.

12. Close the mini Explorer. Click the X in the upper-right corner of the window. This makes that window go away.

13. Click OK in the Taskbar Properties dialog box. It goes away as well.

MAXIMIZING YOUR PROGRAMS IS ALSO POSSIBLE

Just as you may want to run some of your StartUp applications minimized, you'll probably want to run most of your other programs maximized to fill the screen. You can do this when the program starts by clicking its maximize button, or you can preset the program to always do that by altering the steps in this section.

Start in Step 1 by locating the program you always want to start maximized in its own folder/submenu. (It probably won't live in the StartUp menu, which is what Step 1 helps you find.)

Change Step 10 so you choose Maximized from the list, not Minimized. This ensures that Windows will start the program full-screen, which is the way I recommend running most of your major applications.

Continue with the rest of the steps as necessary. This saves you a few mouse clicks when you start a program, because Windows starts it full-screen automatically.

BONUS

Some Cool Programs to Add to the StartUp Submenu

It makes sense to add any program you first start up when you run Windows to the StartUp submenu.

For example, if you always start the day by dialing up Prodigy, just stick a copy of its icon into the Startup submenu. That way, your computer will always start and Prodigy will be up there, waiting for you to make your first call.

Prodigy

Cardfile is a handy little Rolodex of sorts, one you can use to store names, phone numbers — even graphical images. I use it as a Rolodex myself, shunning those other sophisticated programs that take too long to use.

Cardfile

Another cool networking tool to use is the Winpopup program. This program can be found in your Windows folder. Use the steps detailed in the section "Adding a Program to a Start Thing Submenu" earlier in this chapter for information on adding that program to the StartUp submenu.

Winpopup

Other ideas for handy things to add to the StartUp menu include: a day planner, contact or "tickler" program (so you can have your names, dates, and contacts ready every time Windows starts); some folks like starting the Explorer every time Windows starts; and if you always plan on starting some other, major application, consider copying that program from its submenu in the Start Thing over to the StartUp menu.

A Really Nerdy Way to Add a Program

I f you're really smart and know exactly where a program lives on your computer, you can just type its name into the dialog box. For example, typing **WELCOME** into the dialog box starts the process of adding the Welcome program.

For some programs, you'll need to type a full MS-DOS pathname into the box. This is for programs that live in out-of-the-way places. For example, if WordPerfect is in the WP62 folder on drive (D:), you would type:

D:\WP62\WP

into the box. This is called a pathname (which is covered in Chapter 13, in the section "Beating a Pathname to a File's Door"). If the idea of using it drives you nuts, just stick with the steps for finding files as outlined in this section.

Summary

This chapter was dedicated to the Start Thing. It told you what you'll find in the Start Thing and how to change stuff to personalize it just for you.

Did you learn any of this stuff from Chapter 5?

- ☐ The stuff that lives on the main Start Thing menu.
- ☐ How to place a program on the Start menu.
- ☐ How to add a program to the Start Thing menu.
- ☐ How to remove a program from the Start Thing.
- ☐ How to add and move programs to the StartUp submenu.

GETTING TO KNOW THE TASKBAR

IN THIS CHAPTER YOU LEARN THESE KEY SKILLS

USING THE TASKBAR   PAGE   75

DEALING WITH TOO MANY BUTTONS ON THE
TASKBAR   PAGE   76

FINDING A LOST TASKBAR   PAGE   78

HAVING FUN WITH THE "LOUD TIME"   PAGE   79

The *taskbar* is Windows' home base. It's the place where the Start Thing lives, and the spot you'll return to time and again to do something new or to revive something old. (Boy, would this make great copy for a travel brochure or what?) The taskbar ties into much of what Windows does. In addition to starting new tasks with the Start Thing, the taskbar is the main tool you use to switch among tasks in the fun game of *multitasking*, or the art of running more than one program at a time. Plus the taskbar has controls for setting the PC's speaker volume and time. It's just chock full o' excitement.

Buttons and Windows Galore

For every window open on the desktop, a corresponding button exists on the taskbar. Open a window, grow a button. Open lots of windows, grow lots of buttons. And when you close the windows, the buttons go away.

The main reason for connecting a window on the screen with a button is the taskbar helps you to find this window quickly. Figure 6-1 shows several buttons on the taskbar. Each button represents a window, either somewhere on the desktop or on a window that's been minimized.

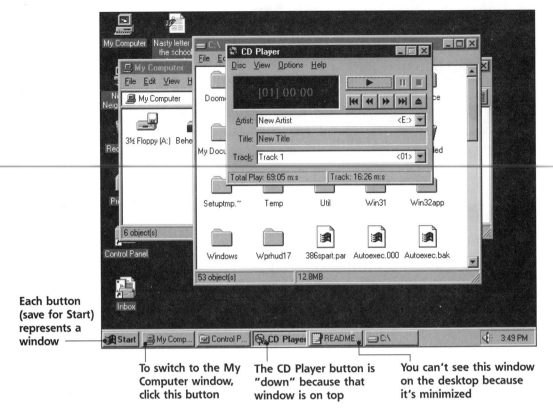

Each button
(save for Start)
represents a
window

To switch to the My
Computer window,
click this button

The CD Player button is
"down" because that
window is on top

You can't see this window
on the desktop because
it's minimized

Figure 6-1 Quickly find a window in this mess by using the taskbar.

 TIP Clicking a taskbar button to display a window comes in especially handy when all windows are "zoomed," or *maximized*, to fill the entire screen. In that case, you can't see any other windows on the desktop and clicking a button on the taskbar is one of your only other options.

Too Many Buttons on the Taskbar!

Figure 6-2 shows what a normal button looks like on the taskbar. Ahhh. . . . Figure 6-3 shows the nightmare that happens when there are too many buttons on the taskbar. The icons go away. The names get butchered. Pretty soon it gets so ugly it almost looks like DOS.

**Program or
window's name**

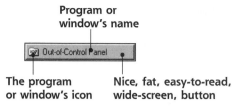

**The program   Nice, fat, easy-to-read,
or window's icon   wide-screen, button**

Figure 6-2 A nice, fat, healthy button
on the taskbar

**A mere fragment of text   Buttons closer together than houses
"describes" the button   in a San Diego housing tract**

Figure 6-3 A messy, over-buttoned taskbar

A taskbar with too many buttons doesn't make any fashion sense. For those times when the taskbar has too many buttons, your only solution is to stretch the taskbar and make it fatter.

Follow these steps to stretch the taskbar:

1. Hover the mouse over the top edge of the taskbar. The mouse pointer changes to an up-down pointing arrow thing. That means the mouse is set to drag and move something.

2. Press and hold the mouse's left (main) button.

3. Drag the mouse up, making the taskbar fatter. The line drags up in given increments, each time making the taskbar's outline appear fatter on the screen. If you don't notice the taskbar's outline getting fatter, keep dragging the mouse upward.

4. Release the mouse button when the taskbar is twice as large. Or maybe even release the button when the taskbar is three times as large. What you'll see looks something like Figure 6-4 — a fat taskbar, where the buttons are legible.

You can use the same steps to restore the taskbar to normal size; just drag the taskbar's top edge down instead of up.

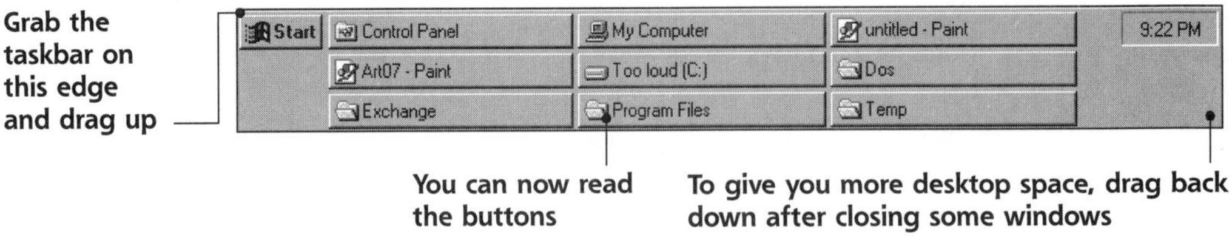
Grab the taskbar on this edge and drag up
Start
Control Panel
My Computer
untitled - Paint
9:22 PM
Art07 - Paint
Too loud (C:)
Dos
Exchange
Program Files
Temp
You can now read the buttons
To give you more desktop space, drag back down after closing some windows

Figure 6-4 With a fatter taskbar, you can see all the buttons.

"My Taskbar Is Gone!"

This is perhaps the biggest problem (or annoyance) with Windows 95: The all-important taskbar disappears. Forget about using the mouse to get it back. You need the keyboard.

Follow these steps to restore a vanished taskbar:

1. Press CTRL+ESC. This pops up the Start Thing menu — no matter what. It may make the taskbar appear, but the darn thing doesn't stick around.
2. Press ALT+SPACEBAR. This displays the taskbar's control menu, which replaces the Start Thing menu.
3. Press S for size. You may not see it, but an up-down arrow thing appears on the screen where the taskbar lives.
4. Press the ↑ key on the keyboard. Each time you press the ↑ key, the taskbar grows in size. Keep pressing the ↑ key until you can see the taskbar. If this doesn't work (which is rare), try pressing the ↓ key repeatedly, and then the ← key, and then the → key.
5. Press ENTER. This restores the taskbar to the size you see on the screen.

You should also check with the taskbar's properties to see if, by chance, someone set up your taskbar's auto-hide.

Follow these steps to look at your Taskbar Options:

1. Right-click the mouse on a blank spot on your taskbar. A menu should pop up.
2. Click Properties.
3. Click the Taskbar Options tab to bring this screen forward. Look at the

options on the bottom of the screen. Make sure the option, *Auto hide*, does not have a ✔ check mark in it.

4. Click the ✔ check mark next to *Auto hide* to delete the ✔ check mark. This will make certain your taskbar won't hide from you.

Having Fun with the *Loud Time*

Off to one end of the taskbar, playing teeter-totter with the Start Thing, is what I call the *loud time*. (Its real name is the system tray, but that's boring.) Its a graphic of a megaphone, apparently shouting the current time of day (see Figure 6-5).

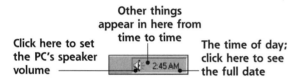

Click here to set the PC's speaker volume

Other things appear in here from time to time

The time of day; click here to see the full date

Figure 6-5 The loud time shouts that it's 2:45 A.M., way past the author's bedtime.

The loud time area shows you several things, depending on how your computer is set up and what it's doing. See Table 6-1 for details.

TABLE 6-1 "Loud Time" Stuff

Icon	Name	Description
	The volume button	This enables you to adjust the PC's speaker volume (providing you have a sound system installed).
	The printer dude	This icon appears whenever you're printing something, and then immediately disappears.
	The modem guy	He appears when you're connected to an online service or the Internet.

(continued)

TABLE 6-1 "Loud Time" Stuff (*continued*)

Icon	Name	Description
	The fax guy	The fax guy, or rather *guys*, only appear when you're messing with faxes — sending or receiving. Sending a fax is a lot like printing, which is why all that information is conveniently located in the same place, Chapter 17.
	The mail guy	When you're connected to a network and mail awaits you, you see the little happy mail guy.
1:50 PM	A.M. or P.M.	The last goodie you'll see there is the current time.

Other little "guys" may show up in the loud time area, depending on what type of software you have installed and other complex factors known only to Einstein.

> **TIP** To find out more information on any item that shows up in the loud time area, hover the mouse pointer over it. A pop-up bubble appears, telling you more than you need to know about what your computer is doing.

If you click on one of the little taskbar guys, something interesting happens; either you get more information about what the little guy does or you see a dialog box where settings can be adjusted.

Setting the PC's Speaker Volume

If you click the mouse on the taskbar's volume button, a volume slider pops up (Figure 6-6). This is where you can adjust the PC's speaker volume, making the noise your computer squawks louder, softer, or turning it off altogether.

If you click twice on the volume button, you'll see a multimedia Volume Control panel. Strange stuff. Close that window if it bothers you.

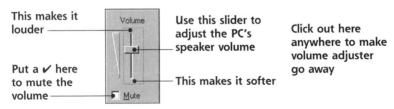

This makes it louder

Use this slider to adjust the PC's speaker volume

Click out here anywhere to make volume adjuster go away

Put a ✔ here to mute the volume

This makes it softer

Figure 6-6 The volume button helps adjust the PC's speaker volume.

The clock isn't a fixed part of the taskbar; in fact, nothing on the right side of the taskbar is there permanently. To see the clock (or to hide it), follow these steps:

1. Click the Start button or press CTRL+ESC. Either way, the Start Thing menu pops up.

2. Choose `Settings` → `Taskbar`. The Taskbar Properties dialog box appears.

3. Click in the box by *Show Clock.* If a ✔ check mark appears in the box, then the current time appears on the taskbar. If the box is empty, the clock won't show up. Click the mouse once in the box to change from the ✔ check mark to nothing or back again.

4. Click OK. The Taskbar Properties dialog box is retired, and you now have a clock (or not) on the taskbar.

Hanging Out with Printer Dude

The little printer icon will come and go as quickly as you print. When printing stops, he goes away. Sometimes, if you have a fast printer, you'll never see him. Nope, not ever.

If you hover the mouse over printer guy, you'll see information on which printer is printing and who's printing what. For example, it may say something like:

1 document(s) pending for Mary Munchkin

TIP You can always get information on what's printing by checking out the printer icon associated with your PC's printer. Chapter 17 discusses how this works.

Messing with the Modem Guy

The modem guy on the taskbar tells you when you're online and sending or receiving information. When you click on him, a dialog box appears telling you what the modem is doing (see Figure 6-7).

"BUT I DON'T SEE THE VOLUME CONTROL!"

If you don't see the volume control, you either don't have a PC that can bleep or, somehow, your computer wasn't set up properly. To see the volume control, follow these steps:

1. Open My Computer.

2. Open the Control Panel. It's a folder with a hammer and some other tool on it.

3. Locate the Multimedia icon, located in the Control Panel's window.

4. Double-click the Multimedia icon.

5. Click the Audio panel to bring it in front.

6. Click the *Show volume control on the taskbar* box. This puts an (in the box, which causes Windows to display the volume button.

7. Click OK in the Multimedia Properties dialog box to close it. The volume button appears on the taskbar when the window disappears.

8. Close the Control Panel window and My Computer's window if you like. Get back to work.

This is an external modem

The number of bytes sent

The number of bytes received

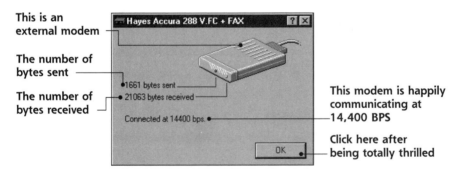

This modem is happily communicating at 14,400 BPS

Click here after being totally thrilled

Figure 6-7 The dialog box you see when you click the taskbar's modem guy

If you hover the mouse pointer over the modem guy when you're connected to another computer (or *online*), you'll see the bytes sent and received appear in a little bubble. Major whooptidoo factor there.

X-REF The modem guy on the taskbar lets you know your modem is on and working, which can be beneficial if you have an internal modem. On external modems, you can see the reassuring blinking lights. For more information on the fun world of computer communications, flip the pages to Chapter 9.

Remember, the modem guy shows up only when your computer is talking to another computer with the modem.

Fooling with the Time (Setting the Time on Your PC)

Forget the date? Point your mouse at the time in the taskbar and a bubble pops up displaying the current date and time in its full format. This way you can find out if it's Saturday so you can stop working.

If you double-click the time, a dialog box appears (see Figure 6-8), enabling you to set the current date and time for your computer. This comes in handy for those times when your computer has lost track of the time.

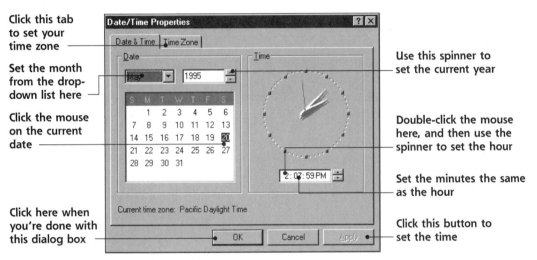

Figure 6-8 Set your PC's date and time in this dialog box.

 TIP Set the time in the Date/Time Properties dialog box to about a minute from now. Set the seconds to zero-zero. Then dial the time on the phone (sorry, I don't have the number). When the nice lady says it's blah-blah o'clock and blah minutes *exactly*, click the Apply button. This sets the PC's time to whatever time you've entered.

The Time Zone panel in the Date/Time Properties dialog box enables you to set the time zone in which your computer lives. Click that tab with the mouse to bring that panel forward in the dialog box. It shows a global map with the current time zone highlighted (see Figure 6-9). To set a new time zone, click the mouse on the part of the map where your computer lives.

Know your geography? Click your house on this map

Click here if your part of the country obeys daylight saving time. A ✔ appears in the box when this option is set (optional in some parts of Indiana)

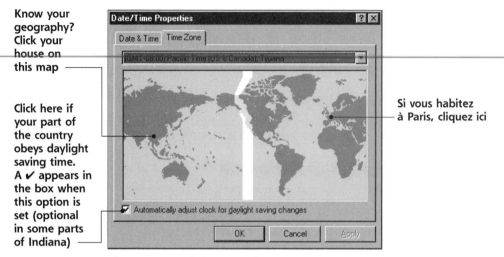

Si vous habitez à Paris, cliquez ici

Figure 6-9 Windows must know the time zone or else it zones.

Click the OK button in the Date/Time Properties dialog box when you're done messing with it.

SIDE TRIP

DAYLIGHT SAVING TIME

If you live in one of those parts of the country that celebrates daylight saving time, make sure you click the mouse in the *Automatically adjust clock for daylight saving changes* box on the Time Zone panel (see Figure 6-9). When the time changes from Standard to Daylight time, Windows will pop up a little message letting you know it's adjusted the computer's clock accordingly. This is one of those amazing things computers should have done all along but are only now coming around to doing.

BONUS

Other Taskbar Stuff

Like everything else in Windows' universe (or almost everything else), the taskbar has its own pop-up shortcut menu. Figure 6-10 shows what it looks like.

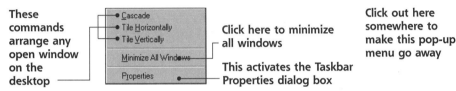

These commands arrange any open window on the desktop

Click here to minimize all windows

This activates the Taskbar Properties dialog box

Click out here somewhere to make this pop-up menu go away

Cascade
Tile Horizontally
Tile Vertically
Minimize All Windows
Properties

Figure 6-10 The Taskbar's shortcut menu

You need to right-click the mouse on a blank area of the taskbar to see the shortcut menu. This can be tricky. Finding a blank area on a taskbar full o' buttons is like finding a parking space at the mall during Christmas. If you can't find a blank spot, however, click the current time at the far-right side of the taskbar. This displays the Time Thing shortcut menu, which is identical to the taskbar's, with the addition of one specific item on top.

The Envelope, Please

Seeing the wee little envelope guy on the taskbar means you have mail waiting somewhere, either from your computer network, the Internet, or an online service, such as CompuServe or the Microsoft Network.

Hover the mouse over the envelope guy and he says, "You have new mail."

To read your mail, double-click the little "you have mail" envelope guy. This starts the Microsoft Exchange program, which enables you to read and compose mail.

X-REF Obviously, you must connect to an online service before you can get mail; see Chapter 9.

Summary

Yep, the taskbar's pretty cool. You can make it fatter, thinner, adjust the volume, mess with the modem guy, check your mail. There's a lot to do there. If this is news to you, then go through the list and make sure you learned the following:

- ☐ How to stretch the taskbar.
- ☐ How to restore a taskbar that's left the screen.
- ☐ How to find the Taskbar Options.
- ☐ How to set the PC's speaker volume.
- ☐ How to see or hide the clock.
- ☐ How to set the current date and time.

INTRODUCING THE APPLETS

IN THIS CHAPTER YOU LEARN THESE KEY SKILLS

USING THE PAINT PROGRAM   PAGE 88

USING WORDPAD   PAGE 94

AVOIDING NOTEPAD   PAGE 99

FIGURING OUT THE CALCULATOR   PAGE 99

HANGING UP WITH THE PHONE DIALER   PAGE 100

No, the applets weren't a rock band from the '50s. *Applet* is Windowspeak for a miniapplication, a little program, something handy that comes free with Windows. Basically applets are feeble versions of much better stuff you could get if you paid real money. But for handling basic tasks, such as drawing and writing, they're pretty adequate. In fact, you may never need anything more than these little programs that come with Windows.

Secret Background Information on the Applets

Windows comes with a dozen or so applets, or miniapplications. Nearly all of them can be found in the Start Thing menu; choose `Programs` → `Accessories` and you'll see all the applets nestled there.

TIP   By the way, you may notice your copy of Windows doesn't have all the applets. Pity, but a way exists to install them all. Refer to Chapter 11 on installing software; the section "Adding the Rest of Windows" will tell you how.

Making Purty Pictures with Paint

Windows comes with its own drawing program, officially called *Paint*. You can use it to create graphical images, doodle, to make artwork for your documents or new desktop wallpaper patterns, and to edit graphic images. It's actually quite handy and will suit most of your needs most of the time. (I created most of this book's artwork using Paint.)

I think that I shall never see something as beautiful as a tree drawn using the Windows Paint program, as shown in the following tutorial. Now, stay with me here. You're going to start this a little backward, so don't be confused. This will give you another way to start a program. You know, variety and all.

Follow these steps to make a purty tree in the Paint program:

1. Double-click on *My Computer*.

2. Double-click on your (C:) drive.

3. Double-click on *My Documents*. (What you are doing is finding a place for your new Paint document.)

4. Choose ⌑File⌑ → ⌑New⌑ → ⌑Bitmap Image⌑ from the menu. This is one way to create a new Paint document.

New Bitmap
Image

5. Rename the New Bitmap Image document. Type **Tree** over the old cruddy name, New Bitmap Image, and then press the ENTER key to lock in the new name.

6. Open the document. Double-click the document's icon, or just press the ENTER key if it's still highlighted on the screen. This starts the Paint program with your new document ready for editing (which looks like Figure 7-1, but with a blank canvas).

7. Your first job is to set the size of the image. Click **Image** → **Attributes**. The Attributes dialog box appears (see Figure 7-2). In this box, you can set the image size, or dimensions, of the electronic canvas on which you're about to draw. Normally, Paint gives you an area about half a sheet of paper in size. But this tree should appear on a canvas maybe two inches square.

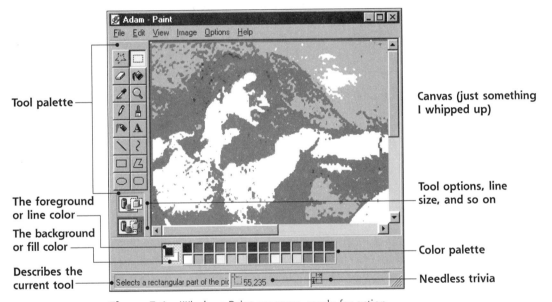

Tool palette

Canvas (just something I whipped up)

The foreground or line color

Tool options, line size, and so on

The background or fill color

Describes the current tool

Color palette

Needless trivia

Figure 7-1 Windows Paint program, ready for action

TIP A *bitmap* document is basically anything Paint creates. Why it isn't called Paint in the menu is just a stupid nerdy mistake Microsoft made. It should be called Paint.

8. Enter a value of **2** for both the *Width* and *Height* of the canvas. Be sure to click the *Inches* option button, so you're creating a 2 × 2 inch canvas, and not some silly 2 × 2 centimeter canvas or a 2 × 2 pixel canvas (which would be really teensy).

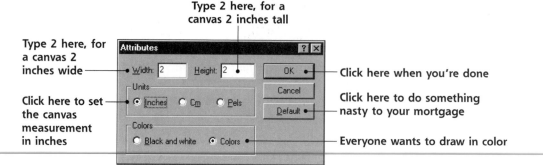

Type 2 here, for a canvas 2 inches tall

Type 2 here, for a canvas 2 inches wide

Click here to set the canvas measurement in inches

Click here when you're done

Click here to do something nasty to your mortgage

Everyone wants to draw in color

Figure 7-2 The Attributes dialog box

9. Click OK. This closes the Attributes dialog box, returning you to the Paint program, but with a smaller canvas (provided the Attributes were set at higher numbers to start). That's okay; you're making a tiny tree.

10. Click the Polygon tool button. This selects that tool for drawing.

11. Click the filled and outlined style, which means the polygon will be drawn as both an outline and a filled middle. (It's the one in the middle.)

12. Pick the colors. Click on black. That's the outline color. Right-click a brown, tree-like color. That's the fill color, the one that will fill the inside of the polygon.

13. Draw the tree. Look at Figure 7-3 and use this as a reference. Start by dragging a line from point A to point B. This must be a drag; everything else is a click. Then click the mouse at the remaining points, from C to J in order. Here, you're creating the "branches" of the tree. Yes, this is a lot like connect-the-dots when you were a kid. Finally, double-click point K. This finishes the polygon, which will look something like Figure 7-4.

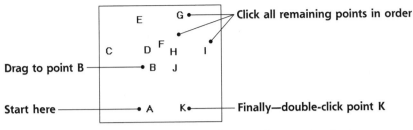

Figure 7-3   Points to drag to when creating the tree

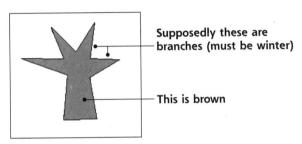

Figure 7-4   The finished polygon

14. Time to spray paint the leaves. For leaves, you'll use the spray paint can tool and just dapple the leaves in an assortment of colors. Choose the spray paint can tool. It's actually called the Airbrush tool, but it looks like a spray can to me.

15. Click the biggest spew pattern.

16. Click a color for the leaves. Be creative: Use a green for spring, use a yellow-brown for fall, use purple for the apocalypse.

17. Click and drag the mouse a few times around the tree's branches. Click to put down a light smattering of leaves. Drag the mouse around to make a more full, leafier look. Lay down a layer of leaves on the branches and fill out the tree.

18. Repeat Steps 15 and 16 a few times to build up layer of leaves. Choose a subtly different color each time. Then, one time, choose a bizarre color, like red or blue. Use this color sparingly.

19. The tree is done. Figure 7-5 shows what my tree looks like following these directions. It's quite lovely, as you can see. Choose File → Save to save your Tree document to disk.

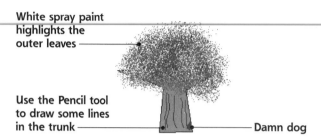

White spray paint highlights the outer leaves

Use the Pencil tool to draw some lines in the trunk

Damn dog

Figure 7-5 A fine proud tree

20. Quit the Paint tutorial. Click File → Exit. Don't completely forget about your tree because you'll use it again in the next chapter.

I don't have the space to show you how all the tools in Paint work. The most fun you can have in Paint is just goofing around with the tools. Remember to tell the boss this isn't exactly "goofing around"; it's scientific experimentation, of course. Take a look at Table 7-1 for a description of some of the Paint tools.

TABLE 7-1 Tool Time

Art	Tool	Description
	SELECTION TOOLS	Use the Selection tools to select graphics on the screen for dragging, copying, or cutting. Use the star-shaped Selection tool to drag around unusual shapes and to select them; the rectangle Selection tool selects only rectangular shapes (duh).
	COLOR ERASER	If you click the right mouse button while using the Eraser tool, you're actually using the *color eraser*. In that mode, only the selected foreground color will be erased, replaced by the current background color. This is a handy tool for erasing only certain parts of your image without the need for precision.

Art	Tool	Description
	PAINT BUCKET	The Paint bucket fills an area on the screen with a specific color. Click with the left mouse button to fill with the foreground color; click with the right mouse button to fill with the background color.
	EYEDROPPER	The Eyedropper tool is used to choose a color from the canvas's image. For example, click a weird-looking puce with the Eyedropper tool and that color is selected as the current foreground color.
	PENCIL	The pencil is used to draw a thin line. It's best used when you zoom in to a graphic for tight or tiny work. Press CTRL+PAGE DOWN to zoom in; press CTRL+PAGE UP to zoom out.
	BRUSH	The brush draws a thicker line than the Pencil using one of the shapes chosen from the tool options palette.
	TEXT TOOL	Text tool allows you to type in graphical text. Choose View → Text Toolbar , so you can choose the font, size, and style for the text. Note, the text is drawn in the current foreground color; if you don't see the text, it's probably because you've selected white as the foreground color.
	LINE DRAW	Line draw enables you to draw a straight line from one point to another. You do this by dragging the mouse. If you press the SHIFT key while you drag, the line is drawn at a right, or 45-degree, angle from its origin. Choose a line width from the tool options palette.
	SHAPE TOOLS	Shape tools draw their respective shapes. The width of the line is chosen by clicking the Line Draw tool and setting a width. Then you can choose how the shape will be filled by clicking in the tool options palette (see the previous tutorial). If you press and hold the SHIFT key while drawing an oval or rectangle, you'll actually draw a perfect circle or square, respectively.

GENERAL PAINTING INSTRUCTIONS

Whenever you paint an image, you need to choose three things, in this order:

The tool. This is one of the 16 different tools that appears on the left side of the screen (see Figure 7-1).

The tool's options. Choose the line style, width, and other options from the options area.

The colors. Set the line and fill colors, which determine how your object will be colored when it's drawn.

Let WordPad Bring Out the Shakespeare in You

WordPad is Windows' freebie text editor, though it's more than just a program for writing text. With WordPad you can format your text and add some fancy effects. While it lacks features like a spelling checker, page numbering, footnotes, and so on, it does have features that make it a handy, if somewhat limited, writing tool. You can see WordPad in Figure 7-6.

This is WordPad, editing the document saved as Jerry's Hunt

Choose View → Toolbar to see this handy toolbar

Choose View → Ruler to see Queen Elizabeth, er, this thing here

Choose View → Format Bar to see this toolbar

Here is where you write, la-di-da

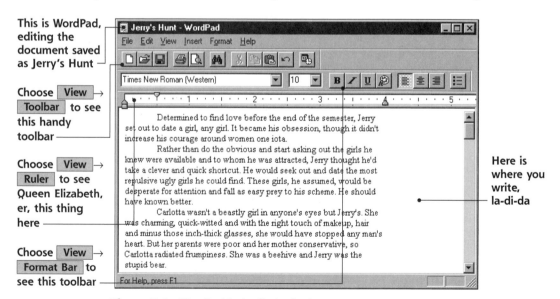

Figure 7-6 WordPad in its (limited) glory

Figures 7-7 through 7-9 describe various aspects of WordPad and its toolbars and ruler. The main purpose of WordPad is to write, which is demonstrated in the following tutorial to prepare the EnviroGeeks newsletter (or at least part of it), which is also used in the multitasking tutorial in Chapter 8.

Standard New, Open, and Save shortcut buttons

A shortcut to the Find command

Inserts date and time into the document in a number of different formats

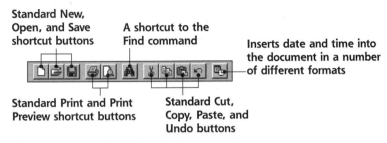

Standard Print and Print Preview shortcut buttons

Standard Cut, Copy, Paste, and Undo buttons

Figure 7-7   WordPad's handy shortcut toolbar

Choose a size here

Left, Center, and Right justify buttons

Pick a font here

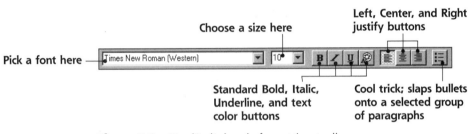

Standard Bold, Italic, Underline, and text color buttons

Cool trick; slaps bullets onto a selected group of paragraphs

Figure 7-8   WordPad's handy formatting toolbar

Drag this to set the indent for the first line of a paragraph

Click anywhere in here to set a tab stop

Right margin dragging doojobbie

Drag this to set the left margin for a paragraph

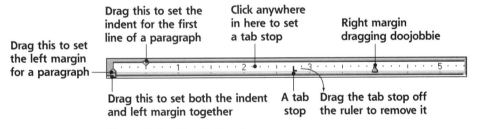

Drag this to set both the indent and left margin together

A tab stop

Drag the tab stop off the ruler to remove it

Figure 7-9   WordPad's ruler

Follow these steps to practice using WordPad:

1. Start WordPad. Summon the Start Thing's menu by pressing CTRL+ESC. Then choose Programs → Accessories → WordPad . WordPad explodes on the screen. (Well, maybe *explodes* is an improper verb here.)

TIP   **If WordPad becomes one of your favorite word processors, consider slapping it down right atop the Start Thing menu. See Chapter 5, "Sticking Something on the Main Start Thing Menu."**

2. Choose ⟨New⟩ from the File menu, or click the New icon on the handy toolbar. Either way, you'll see the New dialog box (see Figure 7-10), which allows you to pick the type of document you want to create.

Good for exchanging files with alien word processors (formatting remains intact)

Use this one most of the time

Choose this only when directed by a user manual or someone bigger and meaner than yourself

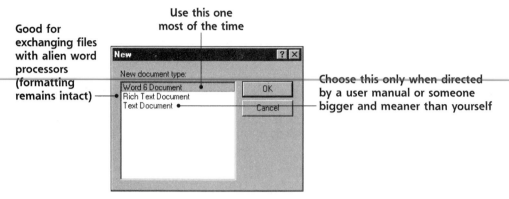

Figure 7-10   Choose which type of document you want to create.

3. Choose *Word 6 Document*, click OK. This is WordPad's standard modus operandi.

4. Type the newsletter's title. Without regard to formatting anything, type the following four lines, pressing the ENTER key after each one (if you make a mistake, press the BACKSPACE key to back up and erase):

the

EnviroGeeks

Newsletter

Making our PCs more PC

5. Select the first line of text. Do this by moving the mouse pointer to the document's left margin, just before the word *the*. When it's positioned correctly, the mouse pointer will point to the NE instead of the NW (or instead of the straight cursor line). Click. This highlights the entire line.

6. Format the text. Change the font to Arial MT Black (Turkish) (or something Arial-similar if you don't have that font). Choose this option from the Font drop-down list on the formatting toolbar. Change the text size to 12; choose 12 from the Size drop-down list. Center the line by clicking on the Center formatting button.

7. Select the second line and format it. Follow the instructions in Step 5 for selecting the second line of text. Change the font to Arial MT Black (Turkish) or whatever. Change the text size to 36. Center the line.

8. Select the third line and format it. Heed the instructions in Step 5 to select the third line of text. Change the font to Arial MT Black (Turkish). Change the text size to 18. Center.

9. Select and format the fourth line. Arial MT Black (Turkish) at 22 points, centered.

10. Press the ENTER key to add a blank line. This goes after the last line in the title and before the table of contents. (It's where you'll paste in the trees in the other tutorial.)

11. Set the formatting for the table of contents. Because you're formatting before any text is written, there's no need to select anything. Choose the Courier font from the Font drop-down list on the formatting toolbar. The font may also be called Courier New or Courier New (Western). Choose 10 as the size.

12. Click the Left justification button to slam the text against the left side of the page.

13. Adjust the left margin for a "hanging indent"; Drag the lower pointer on the ruler to a position ³/₄ inches from the left margin. Use Figure 7-11 for help.

Drag the lower pointer to about this position

A line of ants shows you how text will line up in the window

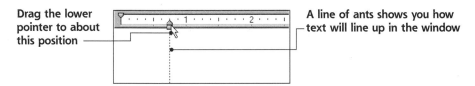

Figure 7-11   Creating a hanging indent in WordPad

14. Type the first table of contents entry. Type **Page 1:** Don't press ENTER just yet. After the colon, press the TAB key. This tabs you over to the hanging indent thing. Continue by typing the rest of the line: **Solar-powered PC Experiment Fizzles in Seattle!** (The reason for pressing the TAB key after the colon — and the weird hanging indent format — will become apparent in a moment.)

15. Press ENTER to end the line.

16. Type the second line. Type **Page 2:** Press the TAB key after the colon. Type **Larry has a heart attack on pedal-powered PC!** and press ENTER to end the line of text.

17. Type the third line. Enter the following line, pressing TAB after the colon and the ENTER key to end the line: **Page 3: Samantha claims her opinion on clean air shouldn't conflict with her personal smoking habit.** (Note, this text is longer than a single line. Watch what happens as you type the line. Nifty, eh?)

18. Enter the last two lines, pressing the TAB key after the colon in each and ENTER after the period: **Page 4: Vern's do-it-yourself all-wood PC. Page 5: Message from our president.** Figure 7-12 shows how the final letter should look, provided you used the same fonts I used.

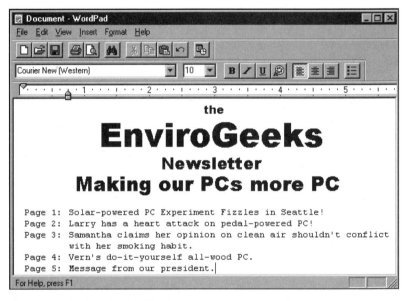

Figure 7-12 The finished EnviroGeeks newsletter (so far)

19. You can continue writing if you like but, in any case, you should save your work first. Choose File → Save As . Find a proper folder for your work. (When in doubt, use My Documents.) Give the file a name, **EnviroGeeks.** Click the Save button.

20. Quit WordPad by clicking its Close button. It's time to move on.

Notepad, Windows Feeble Text Editor

Lesser than WordPad is the *Notepad*, which is Windows text editor. Notepad is not a word processor at all; it even lacks some of the features of WordPad. No, with Notepad you can only work on and create plain, boring text documents. No formatting, nothing fancy. In fact, few people even use it as a notepad. Personally, I keep a green steno pad by my computer for taking notes. It's just handier.

Notepad is ideally suited for working on short, text-only documents. This is actually an anachronism because few of the things you do in Windows require a plain text file. Anyway, Notepad hangs around for whenever you need it.

To start Notepad, press CTRL+ESC to fire up the Start Thing menu, choose
| Programs | → | Accessories | → | Notepad |. Figure 7-13 shows what it may look like. Kinda boring, really.

Feeble menu commands —

Text would appear here —

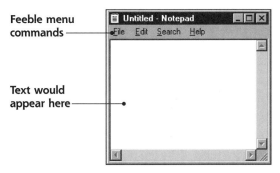

Figure 7-13 The Notepad sits alone and waiting.

Figure It Out Yourself (the Calculator)

Windows has a calculator, but don't throw away that solar-powered one you got as a freebie from your title company. Windows Calculator enables you to make all sorts of calculations; you can even Copy and Paste the results between Calculator and other applications.

To start the Calculator, press CTRL+ESC to pop up the Start Thing menu, then choose | Programs | → | Accessories | → | Calculator |. The Calculator splashes all over the screen, which may look like Figure 7-14.

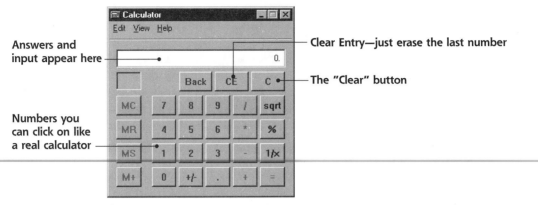

Answers and input appear here

Clear Entry—just erase the last number

The "Clear" button

Numbers you can click on like a real calculator

Figure 7-14   A Calculator to make Einstein happy

A nerdier version of the Calculator is available. Choose View → Scientific from the menu and the left side of the dialog box explodes with mind-numbing calculator keys for doing complex scientific-like things.

BONUS

Is This the Party to Whom I'm Speaking? (the Phone Dialer)

The Windows phone dialer enables you to make phone calls using the convenience of your computer, modem, and mouse — which comes in especially handy when you feel it's too much effort to dial the phone using your fingers. *A-hem!*

To display the phone dialer, press CTRL+ESC to pop up the Start Thing menu, then choose Programs → Accessories → Phone Dialer . The Phone Dialer appears, as shown in Figure 7-15. It's neither visually impressive nor threatened with any type of creativity; that is, it could have looked like a phone or had some clever elements, but being creative on a deadline is hard.

X-REF   Obviously, to make use of the Phone Dialer, you need a modem. Your modem needs to be on, ready, and connected before you can dial out. See Chapter 9 for more information on modems.

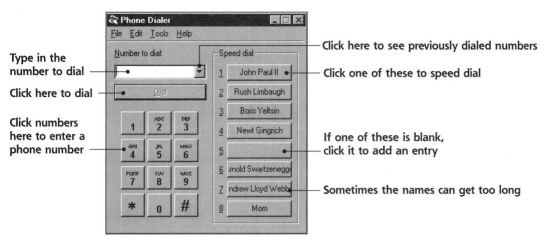

Type in the number to dial ————

Click here to dial ————

Click numbers here to enter a phone number ————

———— **Click here to see previously dialed numbers**

———— **Click one of these to speed dial**

If one of these is blank, click it to add an entry ————

———— **Sometimes the names can get too long**

Figure 7-15 The Phone Dialer is ready to ring up some killer phone bills.

Making the Call

To use the Phone Dialer, type in a number or click it in using the mouse and the phone keypad. Click the big *Dial* button to dial.

When the other party answers, click the *Talk* button in the Call Status dialog box.

You should type the person's name in the Active Call dialog box for the phone log (providing the name isn't entered automatically, such as when you use the Speed dialer).

Click the Hang Up button in the Active Call dialog box when the phone call is over. This way the call's duration will be kept in the handy Call Log. Hmmm, that deserves its own little section.

Keeping Track of Who You Call

One interesting feature of the Phone Dialer is it keeps a log of your phone calls. This can be incredibly handy if you work in one of those busybody offices where they insist you keep phone logs. To see the log, choose Tools → Show Log .

The log shows who you called (providing you typed in the person's name), the number called, and the date and time. It also shows the call's duration.

Hold on for Speed Dialing

The Speed dial entries enable you to press and click to dial someone immediately. To create a Speed dial entry, click a blank button, and then type in the name and number in the dialog box provided.

You can edit, change, or delete speed dial entries later by choosing Edit → Speed Dial from the menu. To delete an entry, just erase its name and number.

Summary

Applets are what I consider the fun part of a computer — the miniapplications. The Paint program and Calculator are tools that make life a little more fun.

In this chapter, you should have learned this fun stuff:

- ☐ Where the Applets are located.
- ☐ How to make a picture in Paint.
- ☐ How to navigate around WordPad
- ☐ Where to find the Notepad and Calculator.

MULTITASKING — SHARING AND LOVING

IN THIS CHAPTER YOU LEARN THESE KEY SKILLS

USING THE TASKBAR TO SWITCH BETWEEN TWO APPLICATIONS PAGE 104

UNDERSTANDING HOW THE ALT + TAB "COOL SWITCH" WORKS PAGE 106

SHARING INFORMATION WITH CUT, COPY, AND PASTE PAGE 107

UNDERSTANDING OLE PAGE 111

M ultitasking is a scary computer term. Honestly, it really means "I can do more than one thing at a time." I remember watching a home movie where I was fishing and chewing gum. My mother jibed, "See, you can do two things at once!" Ever since then, I've remembered that multitasking is fishing and chewing gum at the same time.

Windows can multitask quite well. It can run dozens of programs at once. You never really have to quit one to start another. Aside from that, Windows also ensures that each program remains friendly to any others running at the same time. It does this by enabling you to copy or cut and then paste information between two programs, even two programs of different natures. It's all part of sharing and loving, which plays in well with Windows' multitasking motif.

An Episode in Multitasking

Multitasking is one of those "how did you do that?" tricks. It's something a seasoned Windows user will casually do before you and it pops your eyeballs out. "I didn't know you could do that!" Yet it really isn't a big deal to do and can save you hours of time and dozens of steps once you know how it works.

TIP The only part of multitasking madness you must remember is you don't really have to quit one program to start another. Try minimizing occasionally. For more information, see Chapter 4, the section "Done for the Day? to Quit or Put Away?"

Switching Applications with the Taskbar

Each button on the taskbar represents a window on the screen. Most of the time, windows on the screen represent programs. One window equals one program. In Figure 8-1, which shows only the taskbar, you can see two programs are currently running in Windows: Paint and WordPad.

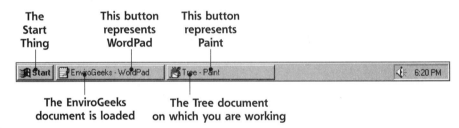

The Start Thing **This button represents WordPad** **This button represents Paint**

The EnviroGeeks document is loaded **The Tree document on which you are working**

Figure 8-1   The taskbar shows you both Paint and WordPad are running.

To switch from one program to the other, simply click on its button on the taskbar. Click on Paint, go to Paint. Click WordPad, go to WordPad. You never really need to quit one program and start another.

If the program has been minimized, then clicking on that button automatically unminimizes the program's window, zooming it back up to the size it was before. Windows calls this restoring your program. If the program is full-window, or maximized, then clicking on the button is about the only way to get to other windows or programs on the desktop.

A Multitasking Tutorial Involving Paint and WordPad

Figure 8-2 shows the WordPad document you worked on in the previous chapter. But if you remember, you didn't quite finish your project. Your tree is finished, but you need to add it to your WordPad document.

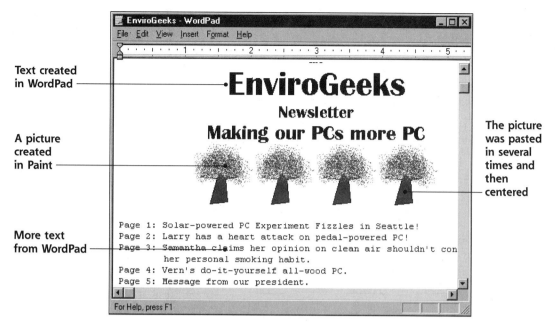

Text created in WordPad ————

A picture created in Paint ————

More text from WordPad ————

The picture was pasted in several times and then centered

Figure 8-2 A nifty WordPad document with a Paint picture in the middle

Follow these steps to practice multitasking:

1. Start your Paint program. You want to find your Tree document you worked on in Chapter 7. Click on `Start` → `Programs` → `Accessories` → `Paint`. And thar she blows! Paint is all over your screen.

2. Click `File` → `Open`. You're looking for your Tree file you created in Chapter 7. Remember the pretty tree? If you followed the instructions, your tree will be in the My Documents folder. Also, if it's one of the last four files you created, you can find it at the bottom of the File menu.

3. Double-click on the Tree folder. And there's your tree. My, hasn't it grown since you last saw it?

4. Put the Paint program aside by clicking on the minimize button. You'll find this button at the top-right corner of your screen. Clicking the minimize button shrinks a window down to a button on the taskbar. The Paint program is still "on," but you've set it aside while you work on something else.

5. Start your EnviroGeeks WordPad document. From the Start Thing menu, choose `Programs` → `Accessories` → `WordPad`. This starts WordPad with a fresh document for you to edit.

6. Click on File → Open . Inside the Open dialog box, find the folder where your EnviroGeeks sits. Remember, you put it in My Documents, which is in the (C:) drive. You should see EnviroGeeks listed with your other folders on which you've already worked.

7. Double-click on EnviroGeeks. And there it is! EnviroGeeks spread all over your screen.

8. Minimize WordPad. Put WordPad away. Don't quit. There's no need to quit.

9. Switch to Paint by clicking on the Paint button on the taskbar. The Paint program's window zooms out to fill the screen. Everything is as you left it.

10. Switch back to WordPad. Don't bother minimizing Paint this time. Just click on the WordPad button on the taskbar. Voom! WordPad fills the screen, just as you left it.

Using the Cool Switch to Switch Applications

Another option for switching windows is to use the *cool switch*, the ALT+TAB key combination. This enables you to change quickly from one application to another and also to see which applications are running without being boggled by buttons on the taskbar.

To use the cool switch, press and hold the ALT key on the keyboard. (Most people use the left ALT key, because it's close to the TAB key.) Tap the TAB key once. You'll see a pop-up window, displaying all the programs Windows is currently running, similar to what's shown in Figure 8-3.

The highlight box tells you which program you'll
switch to when you release the ALT key

The name of the
currently
highlighted
program,
document
name first

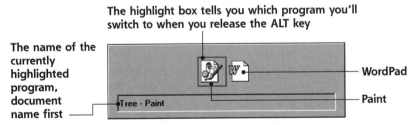

WordPad

Paint

Tree - Paint

Figure 8-3 The ALT+TAB cool switch displays a list of running programs.

Keep your finger on the ALT key! Tap the TAB key again. The highlight box moves from left to right, each time you tap the TAB key. This highlights a different program.

To switch to a program, release both keys. Windows instantly brings up whichever program you've highlighted.

Sharing Information — the Three Amigos

Besides sharing a common look and feel, all Windows programs can also share information. This is done with the Cut, Copy, and Paste commands — the three amigos, as I call them — which appear in almost every Windows application in the Edit menu.

In an application, you use the Cut, Copy, and Paste commands to move around bits and pieces of the stuff on which you're working. For example, you can copy your name and address from the bottom of one letter to another in a word processor. You can cut a graphic of the sun and move it to the other side of a picture to change from a morning to an evening mood. Or you can cut a picture of a tree from one program and move it to a document in a different program. This is all cinchy Cut, Copy, and Paste stuff.

The two items you'll be cutting, copying, and pasting most often are text and graphics. Most programs enable you to paste in either text or graphics. But be aware, some programs only let you paste in text or graphics stuff, not both. If you *swear* you just copied a graphic but the Paste command doesn't seem to work, then the program you're working with won't accept graphics. This is just one of those tough parts of Windows life you must deal with. Table 8-1 lists the three amigos common to all Windows programs that help you share information.

TIP Even if they don't appear, you can use the Cut, Copy, and Paste commands nearly anywhere in Windows, especially if you're working with text. For example, you can copy and paste information inside fields in a dialog box. This is done by selecting the text and using the CTRL+X, CTRL+C, and CTRL+V key command shortcuts for the Cut, Copy, and Paste commands, respectively.

TABLE 8-1 Cut, Copy, and Paste Commands

Toolbar Button	Command	Menu	Keyboard Shortcut
	CUT	Edit → Cut	CTRL+X
	COPY	Edit → Copy	CTRL+C
	PASTE	Edit → Paste	CTRL+V

The Cut, Copy, and Paste commands are also found on shortcut menus when you right-click the mouse on something into which you can cut, copy, or paste. For example, right-click on an icon in My Computer and you'll see the Cut and Copy commands in a shortcut menu.

Notice these three keys are clustered together on your keyboard. This explains CTRL+V for Paste. CTRL+X for Cut is okay because cutting something is like deleting it or crossing (X'ing) it out. CTRL+C for Copy is obvious, which only leaves CTRL+V for paste. Maybe it means vomit?

To copy something or to make a duplicate, you Copy and then Paste. First the original material is selected, and then it's copied and pasted.

To move something, you Cut and then Paste. Cutting appears to delete but, in fact, it's merely copying the information to a special storage place in Windows called the *Clipboard* (see the next section). From there, you can paste the information elsewhere in the same application or in another application.

You can paste and paste and paste the same image over and over. Whatever you last cut or copied can be repasted until you cut or copy something else or shut off your computer.

Sharing Between Paint and WordPad

Using the three amigos — Cut, Copy, and Paste — in any program is old hat. Cutting and pasting a block of text in a word processor is called a *block move*. Copying and pasting is a *block copy*. And a neighborhood coming together for fun is called a *block party*. You can do the same thing in a graphics program with images, making one tree into a forest or removing Uncle Ed's head and pasting it into Aunt Bessie's purse. Easy stuff.

What is new is using cut, copy, and paste between documents. This can be done and comes in quite handy when creating complex-looking documents.

SIDE TRIP

THE FOURTH AMIGO: UNDO

Another common editing command is Undo, which is also found in the Edit menu and is assigned the shortcut key CTRL+Z (right next to the Cut key, CTRL+X). The Undo command undoes whatever you just did in Windows. If you deleted a file and want it back, use the Undo command. Undo will recover from about any other Windows command, restoring things to the way they just were. You must use the Undo command quickly, however; the more you work, the less likely Windows will remember what to undo.

Follow these steps to practice using cut, copy, and paste:

1. Use the tree-making tutorial you did in Chapter 7. Switch to Paint. Click on the Paint program's button on the taskbar to bring its window up front and center.

2. Select the tree.

3. Click on the rectangular selection tool.

4. Select the entire tree by dragging a rectangle around it. Click on a spot somewhere to the northwest of the tree, and then drag the mouse down to the southeast. Release the mouse button. The area within the line of ants is selected (see Figure 8-4). If you can't quite get all of the tree, try the operation over again with a new starting point. Drag the mouse farther down or to the right to lasso more of it.

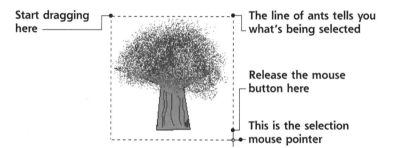

Start dragging here → The line of ants tells you what's being selected

Release the mouse button here

This is the selection mouse pointer

Figure 8-4 A graphical tree has been selected.

5. Copy the tree by choosing [Edit] → [Copy] (or CTRL+C). This places a copy of the image inside the line of ants into Windows' Clipboard. You'll have to trust it was copied because nothing will give you a hint it worked.

6. Switch over to WordPad by clicking WordPad's button on the taskbar. This zooms that application back out to its full-screen glory.

7. Click the blank line between the "Making our PC's more PC" and "Page 1: Solar......" Clicking a text document moves the flashing toothpick cursor to that spot. This is not only where any new text you type will appear, but also where anything you paste will appear.

8. Paste the tree by choosing [Edit] → [Paste] (or CTRL+V). There is a tree in your document!

Remember, you don't have to run two programs at once to cut and paste between them. You could just quit one program, play a game of Solitaire, and then start another program and paste. Windows enables you to do this because the cut or copied image stays in the Clipboard until you cut or copy something else or turn the computer off.

The tree appears as a graphic object inside WordPad, like a big letter of the alphabet. You can select it for cutting or copying again, or you can resize the tree using the wee thumb tabs located on the corners and edges.

X-REF **Resizing is covered in Chapter 28, "Basic Messing with Graphics Stuff (Stretching)."**

Ending the Tutorial

Suppose all your work is done on the EnviroGeeks newsletter. If so, it's time to print it, save it one last time, and get on with things.

Follow these steps to finish your tutorial:

1. Bring up WordPad one last time. Click WordPad's button on the taskbar to move it up front on your screen. (This is technically referred to as "moving an application into the foreground," if you care to know.)

2. Print the EnviroGeeks document (optional). Choose `File` → `Print`. You'll see WordPad's Print dialog box. Click the OK button to start printing. If you want, you can click the Print button on the toolbar. WordPad will print without bothering you with a dialog box. Cherish that hard copy.

3. Save the EnviroGeeks document. Choose `File` → `Save`. Because you've already saved the document to disk, this step saves it one final time.

4. Quit WordPad. Choose `File` → `Exit`. Quick as a wink, WordPad is gone. No struggle. No fuss.

5. Bring up Paint one last time. Click the Paint program's button on the taskbar. This brings it up front and center, ready for action.

6. Quit Paint. Choose `File` → `Exit`. This quits the Paint program and also saves your art to disk one last time if you haven't done this recently. Click the Yes button if you're asked to save the document. Paint is gone!

An Episode with OLE

You must know two things about OLE. First, the acronym stands for *Object Linking and Embedding*, which is a much fancier way of copying and pasting information. Second, it's pronounced *oh-lay*, as in what you would say at a bullfight if you were politically opposed to the way bulls treat human beings.

The O part of OLE means object. What you copy and paste is more than a mere image or text. It's an *object*, like a separate piece of another program. For example, one part of OLE is you can choose an `Insert` → `Object` menu command and it will cause another program to run right inside of the program you're already running. So instead of starting a drawing program and then copying and pasting into your word processor, you merely insert a drawing object and create it smack dab in the middle of your word processor.

The L part of OLE means link. Some programs have a `Paste Special` command in their `Edit` menu. When you choose this command, you can paste an object with a link back to the original object created in another application. When that original object is updated or changed, the paste-linked copy in your document changes with it. So if you update your spreadsheet with new year-end numbers, the linked copy in your annual report document reflects those changes instantly.

The E part of OLE means embed. The object you create or paste into another document remembers which document created it. If you want to reedit the pasted object, you merely double-click it. This runs the program that created the object, enabling you to tweak, tweak, tweak to your heart's content. Normally pasted objects? You cannot double-click on them and expect anything exciting to happen.

Not every program is capable of OLE. WordPad can do it, which you can determine by the give-away Insert menu with its Object command. You can choose that menu item to see a list of other OLE-friendly applications you may have on your PC.

OLE-friendly applications can also copy and paste chunks of information to the desktop; just drag the selected item to the desktop to save it like a scrap pile of information. This can come in handy for saving often-used bits of text or graphics, such as your company logo or address at the end of a letter. To reuse the scraps, just drag them back into another OLE-friendly application.

And now, the ugly truth: Although quite a few programs use OLE, fewer users bother with it. While choosing the `Insert` → `Object` is a great shortcut, most people just copy and paste between applications the old-fashioned way. This doesn't mean you must be stuck in the past. If you remember you have OLE, you can be one of the few who actually use it.

BONUS

Everything Goes to the Clipboard

Whenever you cut or copy something, it's placed into the Clipboard. What the Clipboard is isn't important. What is important is your cut or copied whatever stays in the Clipboard until you cut or copy something else. This is because the Clipboard can only hold one thing at a time.

The Paste command automatically inserts whatever is in the Clipboard into whichever application you're using. This works for text and graphics objects, as well as programs, sounds, and other whatnot you can cut or copy in Windows.

If you'd like to, you can see what's in the Clipboard by using the Clipboard Viewer program. The only trick here is the Clipboard Viewer isn't normally installed with Windows 95. You have to add it yourself, which isn't tough, but it's covered later in Chapter 11.

Run the Clipboard Viewer by popping up the Start Thing menu and choosing `Programs` → `Accessories` → `Clipboard Viewer`. The Clipboard Viewer program appears on the screen, looking similar to the one shown in Figure 8-5. Whatever is "in" the Clipboard, having been cut or copied there, appears in the Clipboard Viewer's window just as it would in the program that created it.

Figure 8-5 The Clipboard Viewer program shows you the last thing cut or copied.

TIP The Clipboard Viewer may occasionally contain a filename or a list of filenames, shown in the cryptic MS-DOS pathname format. This means a file or group of files has been cut or copied in My Computer or the Explorer, probably to be pasted elsewhere. See Chapter 14 for more information on this type of file management.

Summary

Multitasking? Easy stuff. Did you learn how to Multitask? Find out...

- ☐ How to switch between various programs (multitasking).
- ☐ How to use the ALT+TAB key to switch between programs.
- ☐ How to cut, copy, and paste.

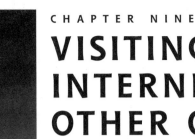

CHAPTER NINE

VISITING PLANET INTERNET AND OTHER ONLINE STUFF

9

IN THIS CHAPTER YOU LEARN THESE SKILLS

GETTING A GRIP ON YOUR MODEM   PAGE 115

PREPARING YOUR PC FOR THE INTERNET   PAGE 116

FINDING AN INTERNET SERVICE PROVIDER   PAGE 117

INSTALLING YOUR INTERNET SOFTWARE   PAGE 118

CONNECTING TO THE INTERNET   PAGE 119

USING HYPERTERMINAL   PAGE 124

RECEIVING (DOWNLOADING) AND SENDING (UPLOADING) FILES   PAGE 131

To end your computer's loneliness and despair, you can buy a modem and hook it up. This gives your computer access to phone lines, the Internet, and all sorts of other computers. It's the Information Age! With a modem you can waste hours of time surfing the World Wide Web (the Web), chatting on America Online, dialing local systems and Bulletin Board Services (BBSs), playing online games, and all sorts of technologically advanced things. You'll never need to leave your house again!

Internet Folderol

Windows 95 is not the Internet. And the Internet is not a program you run. Instead, it's a service. The Internet is something you use your computer, software, and a modem to access. You already have the computer. You'll need a modem. And Windows 95 comes with some software to help you get started. But, honestly, using the Internet has nothing to do with Windows 95. I'm just writing about it here because it's trendy and I'm in a good mood.

The Internet is a collection of computers, all networked together, which exchange and store information. It's also the current "in" thing with computers. Everyone is talking about the Internet. If you aren't on the Internet or (heaven forbid!) you don't have an Internet e-mail address, you might as well be using DOS in a cave. *You just gotta have this Internet thing!*

To use the Internet — to "get on" the Internet — you need four things:

* A modem
* Internet programs (software)
* An Internet Service Provider (ISP)
* Money, money, money, money

FORMER COMPUTER "IN THINGS" BEFORE THE INTERNET

The Rage	The Truth
Multimedia	Just before the Internet became, oh, all the rage, there was multimedia. Multimedia was a mystery to everyone, but something you definitely had to be doing or attempting to do or at least trying to understand if you were anyone in the computer biz. If you weren't doing multimedia, you were living in the past! Multimedia was simply an evolutionary step in computers, like having a disk drive or a printer. A Multimedia PC is one with a CD-ROM drive and sound card — which is the way nearly every computer is sold today. And multimedia software was software that used sound and animation, which most of the new stuff does. But magazines and books on CD-ROMs — "the end of the printed page" — never came to pass.
Networking	Prior to the multimedia spasm came networking. "The Year of the LAN" or the year all PCs were put on a local area network (LAN) was supposed to be the greatest thing, don't miss it! Networking was another evolutionary step, though a slow one to gain acceptance.

FORMER COMPUTER "IN THINGS" BEFORE THE INTERNET (continued)

The Rage	The Truth
Networking	Windows 95 has built-in networking. Just add a network adapter to two or more PCs, connect them with a cable, and you have a network. No big deal.
Multitasking	Computers have the ability to do several things at once. Alas, the old DOS operating system wasn't designed to do that. So other solutions popped up — literally, there were pop-up programs you could run simultaneously on a DOS computer. This was really a work-around and not a true solution, but it pointed out how people really needed their computers to do more than one task at a time. Multitasking was a real problem for which a solution was needed. The surviving solution is Windows, which runs several programs at once without so much as showing a bead of sweat.

Modem Mayhem

Your computer can't dial the Internet unless you have two vital pieces of hardware: a modem and a phone line. If your PC already has a modem, great. If not, buy the fastest modem you can afford. Try to avoid cheapy, no-name modems, any modem that does not come with a warranty, and modems sold by guys in tank tops at the swap meet.

X-REF If you just bought a modem, go to Chapter 21 and learn how to install it.

The second thing you need is a separate phone line for your computer. While you can use your main line, a dedicated line for the modem makes sense. The most important reason is you don't have to worry about someone else picking up an extension and disconnecting you. Also, you can't receive any calls while your computer is using the phone, so having a second line means people can still call your house while you're off using your modem.

You don't pay any extra for using a computer on your phone lines. There is no toll or extra tax involved (at least not yet). You still pay for long distance and if you pay per call, then each call the computer makes gets racked up like any other call.

Modems must also be connected to a COM or serial port. If you have an external modem, it hooks up to one of the ports located on your computer's rump. Internal modems plug inside of your computer, though they still use a COM port.

X-REF The COM port your modem uses was configured by Windows when you first installed your modem. If not, see Chapter 21 on installing new hardware. Everything should be set and ready to go after you've fully informed Windows about your modem.

Internet Software

A modem just doesn't do it by itself. You also need Internet software. Two parts exist to Internet software. There is a dialing program (a *dialer*), which dials the modem and connects to the Internet. Then there are programs you use to access the vast vault of information stored on the Internet.

The dialer program you need to connect to the Internet comes with Windows 95. It's built into something called Dial-Up Networking — one of those mystery folders that lurk in the My Computer window.

The other software, the programs you actually use on the Internet, you must get separately. You'll need something that can do all of the following:

* View the World Wide Web (a Web browser)
* Send and receive electronic mail (e-mail)
* View and post to newsgroups

These are the biggies, the primary things you'll do on the Internet: browse the Web, read and send mail, and view the newsgroups. (You can do other things on the Internet as well. After you get comfy with it all, you can search out individual applications to deal with each of those tasks.)

Two main applications handle all three of those tasks: Netscape's Navigator and Microsoft's Internet Explorer.

In my humble opinion, the one you should get is Netscape's. You can find a free version or get a copy of the Netscape evaluation program at most computer stores. It's a give-away. But if you want the latest, best version, you'll have to pay for it. My advice: Buy the latest version. It's really the best software for working the Web.

Microsoft's Internet Explorer is another program you can use to conquer the Internet. You probably have a copy already, because Microsoft gives it away with Windows 95. This is the cheap, instant way to get on the Internet.

TIP The copy of Internet Explorer that comes with Windows is *not* the latest version. While it will connect you to the Internet, you still have to upgrade to the latest version of Internet Explorer.

Whichever way you go, Navigator or Internet Explorer, you can use that program to start your exploration of the Internet.

Get Yourself an Internet Service Provider

Internet access is provided by various companies, some big and national, some small and local, which connect you to the Internet. These companies are referred to as ISPs or Internet Service Providers. I call them simply "providers" because it's easier to say (and type).

The Internet provider offers access to the Internet, plus some additional services. Among the services they should offer are:

* An e-mail account, for sending and receiving Internet mail
* Access to newsgroups — the more the better
* Personal disk storage space for a personal Web page
* A Web page (which isn't important, but can be fun)

Even if you live in the sticks, you'll probably find a local or national Internet provider. (We have three Internet providers in our tiny village of 24,000 people up here in northern Idaho.) Make sure they offer the above services. Make sure they're nice and understanding, maybe even offering classes to help you get started. Remember: Internet providers are offering a *service*. If they don't want your business, go elsewhere.

Where? You can ask in local computer stores, at user group meetings, or find Internet providers advertising in the paper or maybe a local computer magazine. At some point, they'll probably be listed in the yellow pages. Until then, you may have to hunt for them.

TIP The best thing an Internet provider can offer you is a handy booklet and start-up disk (maybe even Navigator itself). That's better than having them just take your money and give you a phone number.

Get Important Information from Your Provider

Part of what your Internet provider should provide you with is technical information about connecting to the Internet. Alas, in the (relatively) simple era of Windows 95, there are still complex numbers to know and hoops to jump through to get on the Internet. Your Internet provider should give you that information, preferably in a helpful booklet. You cannot access the Internet without it.

Gotta Have the Cash

Money. Access to the Internet is usually paid for monthly. It runs anywhere from $5 to over $50, depending on what you're getting from your provider.

Instances exist where you can get on the Internet without paying for it yourself. If you're a student at a major university, you probably have a computer account and, therefore, Internet access. If you work for the government or military, you probably have Internet access as well. And many large companies have Internet access.

In these cases, you can get on the Internet using your work (or school) PC just as you would at home. Refer to the Head Guru In Charge for more information about Internet access at work or school. Some restrictions may exist, but at least you won't be paying through the nose like normal people.

Installing Your Internet Software

After you get your Internet software, you install it. This copies the program to your hard drive, as well as configures the Dial-Up Networking thing for you. (Software other than Navigator and Internet Explorer may not configure the Dial-Up Networking, which is another reason I recommend them and not something else.)

For Netscape, install the program according to the instructions that came in the box, as well as the instructions in Chapter 11.

Setup for
Microsoft
Internet
Explorer 3.01

The Internet

For Internet Explorer, locate the installation icon on your desktop, (the icon of the globe with the magnifying glass with the words, *The Internet)* and open it to start installation. If you don't see the installation icon, just click the Internet Explorer icon to start installation.

In either case, you'll be taken through installation and Internet setup. Have the information from your Internet provider handy so you can fill in the various numbers and other information as required.

Here is a short list of some of the more important tidbits of information you may be asked. Get this information from your Internet provider and copy it here as a handy reference.

Your log-in name and e-mail name may be different, as might your two passwords. The Dial-Up Networking dialog box will ask for your log-in name and password (see the next section). Your e-mail program will want to know your e-mail log-in and password.

You may be asked other, specific questions. Your Internet provider or their handy booklet should give you all the answers. If not, phone them and ask. That's why you pay them.

Installation is done!

The end result of installation will be an icon in the Dial-Up Networking folder that connects you to the Internet. How this works is covered in the next section.

Primary DNS (Data Name Server) number: ____ . ____ . ____ . ____

Secondary DNS number (optional): ____ . ____ . ____ . ____

Primary DNS name: _____

Secondary DNS name: _____

STMP name: _____

(or STMP number: ____ . ____ . ____ . ____)

POP3 name: _____

(or POP3 number: ____ . ____ . ____ . ____)

News server (NNTP) name: _____

(or NNTP number: ____ . ____ . ____ . ____)

Your host's domain name: _____

(For example, the domain name for IDG Books Worldwide is IDGBOOKS.COM.)

Do you need a Static or Dynamic IP address?

STATIC — the same address every time: ____ . ____ . ____ . ____

DYNAMIC — the Internet provider gives you a different address (most of them are set up this way).

Enter your log-in name: _____

Your log-in password: _____

(you don't have to write this here).

Your e-mail name: _____

(just the name, not the @ or whatever follows it)

Your e-mail password: _____

(you don't have to write this here).

Your full e-mail address:_____

(for example, dang@idgbooks.com is Dan's e-mail name; Sandy's is sandyg@iea.com).

Connecting to the Internet

Before you can run your Internet software, you must connect your computer to the Internet. This is done by dialing your Internet provider's computer, having both your computers' modems sing at each other, and then become magically connected and ready to go.

Your Internet software should have set up everything for you. It should have placed in your Dial-Up Networking folder an icon you'll use every day to connect to the Internet.

Follow these steps to connect to the Internet:

1. Double-click My Computer.

Dial-Up
Networking

2. Double-click the Dial-Up Networking folder. The Dial-Up Networking window contains icons for connecting to remote networks, which is exactly what the Internet is.

CompuTech

3. Open the icon representing your Internet provider. This is NOT the Make New Connection icon. It's the other one with your provider's name on it. Mine says *CompuTech*.

4. The Connect To dialog box appears (see Figure 9-1).

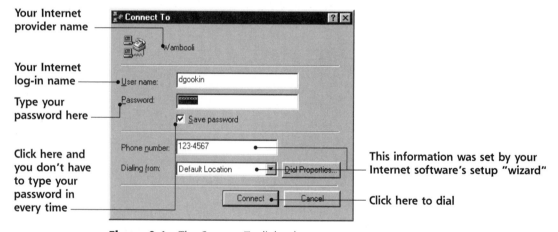

Figure 9-1   The Connect To dialog box

5. Type in your password (if you need to).

6. Click the Connect button. Windows dials your modem, connecting with your Internet provider.

7. If a connection is made, you'll see the Connected dialog box appear, as shown in Figure 9-2.

8. You can now start using your Internet software.

TIP Don't let the modem speed ("Connected at 28800") item bother you. Sometimes your modem may connect faster than other times. Your modem is trying to do the best job it can, which sometimes means you'll connect at a slower speed than normal.

Your modem's speed —

The total time you're connected to the Internet —

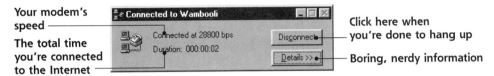

Click here when you're done to hang up

Boring, nerdy information

Figure 9-2 The Connected dialog box

Connecting to the Internet is only half the job. After the connection has been made, then you can run your Internet software.

TIP You can use the Connected To dialog box to help you keep track of how much time you've spent online. The Duration figure tells how long you've been connected to the Internet. It's a good idea to check that value occasionally, to make sure you don't get carried away (which happens).

Running Your Internet Programs

After being connected, you can run any (or all) of your Internet programs. Start the Internet Explorer by double-clicking *The Internet* icon on the desktop. Same with starting Netscape. The programs work only after the Internet connection has been made.

Figure 9-3 shows the Netscape Web browser visiting a Web page. You can also use Navigator to read e-mail and view newsgroups.

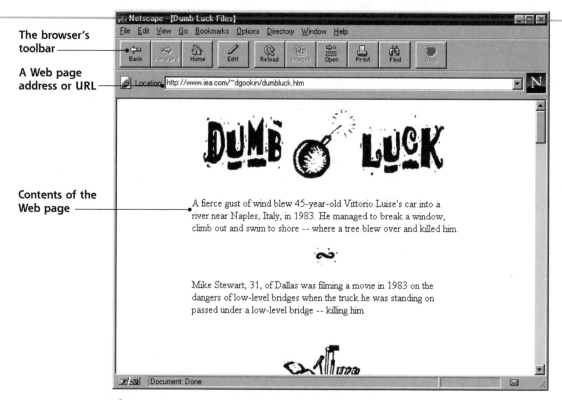

The browser's toolbar

A Web page address or URL

Contents of the Web page

Figure 9-3 Netscape browses the Web.

What you do online and how you do it is really the subject of an entire book — maybe even two books. I can't go into much detail here because this chapter is big enough already. The best advice I can offer is to buy another book, one specific to getting started with the Internet. My favorite is Dan Gookin's *Web Wambooli*, which you can pick up at any bookstore near you.

PLACES TO GO ON THE WORLD WIDE WEB

The Web is the most exciting part of the Internet. You can use your Web browser software to visit various pages on the Web, finding information, trivia, wasting time, or doing research. It's vast.

To get anywhere on the Web, you need to know a Web page's address or Uniform Resource Locator (URL). Type that address into the Web browser's address box, press the ENTER key, and that Web page loads into your browser for viewing (as shown in Figure 9-3).

Here are some Web pages you can visit if you're looking for something different to do on the Internet:

http://www.yahoo.com	The Yahoo catalog of the Internet
http://www.whitehouse.gov	The White House's Internet page
http://www.idgbooks.com	IDG Books home page
http://www.microsoft.com	Microsoft's home page
http://www.wambooli.com	The Wambooli home page
http://www.moviedatabase.com	The Internet Movie Database

Disconnecting from the Internet

Any time you use the phone — even with a computer — you need to say good-bye properly. For the Internet, you need to say good-bye in several steps, as shown in the following.

Follow these steps when you're done (for today) with the Internet:

1. Quit all your Internet software. Close all the program windows.

2. Find the Connected dialog box. It may be lurking as a button on the taskbar. If so, click that button to see the Connected dialog box.

3. Click the Disconnect button. This officially hangs you up from the Internet, ending your Internet session.

Some Internet providers may hang up on you if you sit idle for too long. Typically, they'll wait for 15 minutes before assuming you've walked away or fallen asleep at the keyboard. Other Internet providers — primarily the ones who charge you by the hour — don't mind if you stay on all day!

A Shortcut to the Internet on the Desktop

f you plan on calling the Internet often, then it helps to make the connection icon handy. When you open the Dial-Up Networking folder, right-click the connection icon and drag it (using the *right* mouse button) out onto the desktop. When you release the mouse button, a pop-up menu appears. Choose Create Shortcut(s) Here from the menu. That pastes a shortcut copy of your connection icon to the desktop, where it will be much handier for you to start than having to open all those windows.

The Joys of HyperTerminal

f you would like to do the online thing, but hate to go through the hassle of getting an Internet provider, you need a modem, a phone line, and a special program to control your modem, aka *communications software*. One such program is included "free" with Windows: HyperTerminal, which, as communications software goes, really isn't that bad.

Then again, coffee isn't that bad but it does take time to get used to it.

Follow these steps to start HyperTerminal:

1. Pop-up the Start Thing menu by clicking the Start button or — the guaranteed way — press CTRL+ESC.

2. Choose Programs → Accessories → HyperTerminal. This opens HyperTerminal's window (see Figure 9-4).

Open the HyperTerminal program to start a new session

Open a session icon to dial that system

Companion program files — to hide these, choose View → Options, click the View tab, and put a dot by Hide files of these types

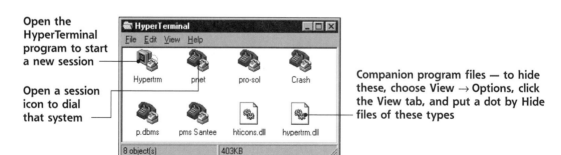

Figure 9-4 A typical HyperTerminal window

Grazing Through the HyperTerminal Window

Unlike other applications, HyperTerminal struts its stuff in a window, such as the one in Figure 9-4. You have two choices:

Hypertrm

Open a session icon, which dials a specific computer.

Create a new session by opening the HyperTerminal program itself. The session is then saved in the window, so you can run it again to access that same computer.

The details of how you do these things are covered in the next two sections.

Creating a New Session in HyperTerminal

A session is something you dial using your modem. The session contains all the information for calling another computer, its phone number, technical communications junk, and other information. Once assembled, you can then click that session's icon in the HyperTerminal folder to connect with that system at any time in the future.

The following steps show you how to create a session for the Microsoft Downloads computer, a massive system at Microsoft corporate HQ that contains all sorts of freebie files and updates. This is a handy system to have in your group of sessions.

Follow these steps to create a session for the Microsoft Download computer:

1. Open the HyperTerminal program by double-clicking its icon in the HyperTerminal folder. The Connection Description dialog box appears (see Figure 9-5), which is sort of a wizard for telling HyperTerminal about the other computer you plan on dialing.

Hypertrm

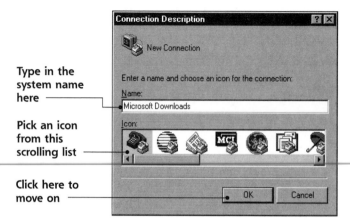

Type in the
system name
here

Pick an icon
from this
scrolling list

Click here to
move on

Figure 9-5 The Connection Description dialog box

2. Type in a name for the system you're calling. For this tutorial, it's the Microsoft Download system, so type **Microsoft Download** into the box (see Figure 9-5).

3. Pluck out a handy icon for the session. Me, I always pick the first icon because I lead a boring life. But you can choose any of the icons listed, including some predestined for such systems as AT&T Mail, MCI Mail, Genie, and the Radioactive Yellow Phone.

4. Click on the OK button. The Connection Description dialog box goes away and the Phone Number dialog box appears, where you type in the number you're dialing.

5. Enter the country code of the computer you're dialing. For the Microsoft Download system, enter the numbers listed in Figure 9-6: **United States of America (1)** is the country code; **206** is the area code (always enter the area code, even if it's the same as your own area code); **637-9009** is the phone number.

6. Don't mess with the *Connect using* box, which tells Windows what modem you're using (or where you can choose from more than one modem connected to your PC).

7. Click on the OK button.

8. The Connect dialog box is displayed. Now you're ready to call the other computer, which is covered in the next section.

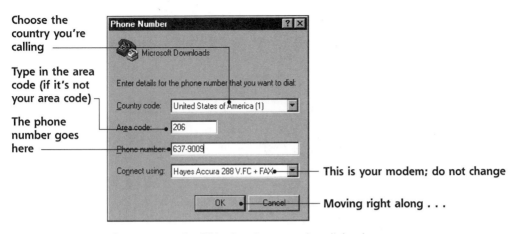

Choose the country you're calling

Type in the area code (if it's not your area code)

The phone number goes here

This is your modem; do not change

Moving right along . . .

Figure 9-6 The fill-in-the-phone number dialog box

Dialing a Something You Already Created

After you create a session, you can dial it at any time simply by opening its session icon in the HyperTerminal window. For example, after saving the Microsoft Download session to disk, you need only double-click its icon to display the Connect dialog box and dial that computer.

Follow these steps to connect to another computer:

1. In the Connect dialog box, click on the *Dial* button. This directs Windows to dial your modem. (If you're continuing from the previous tutorial, you will connect to the Microsoft Download computer, located somewhere near Seattle.) You'll hear your modem dial the number. You'll hear the other computer answer the phone. Finally, you'll hear the modems sing to each other in glorious harmony as a connection is made. If a human answers the modem's call by mistake, click the *Cancel* button. If the other phone doesn't answer or it's busy, click the *Dial Now* button to try dialing again.

2. When you're online and connected, you'll see the terminal screen displayed (see Figure 9-7). It shows you text sent from the other computer, as well as text you typed in yourself. Your first task is to log in, just as you logged in to Windows. Type your name or ID for the system you called. Then you're usually asked for a password. Some systems, such as Microsoft Download, merely want your name and location.

Some systems won't let you in until you've officially registered. Messages displayed on the screen will give you more information, or you may have to search for a menu of options to register yourself as a member.

TIP If you don't see anything after you've connected, try pressing the ENTER key once.

You are connected to Microsoft Download

Text sent by the other computer, the "host"

Text I typed in

This tells you how long you've been online; it's great for gauging long distance charges

Use this scrollbar to see text that has wandered past

You can adjust the size of the window

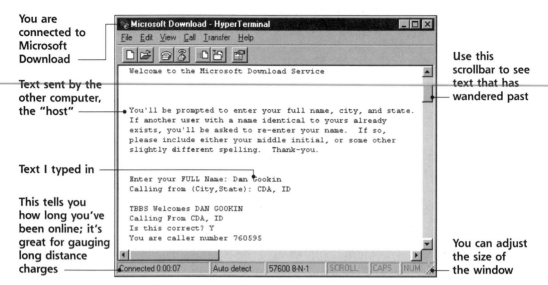

Figure 9-7 The terminal screen

Doing the Online Thing

What you can do when you're online is usually up to whatever computer you've called. Usually a menu of options is available. Figure 9-8 shows the menu for the Microsoft Download system. Type a number at the prompt to see more choices or a list of files to retrieve.

Generally speaking, when you're connected to another computer, you can do several things. The most popular thing is to download software, which means you copy it from the other computer to your own computer. The Microsoft Download system lives to download software.

Aside from downloading software, you can also upload software (send it from your computer to another computer), chat, or read your mail and news bulletins or messages. Doing one or more of these depends on what the computer you're dialing offers. For example, the Microsoft Download computer only enables you to download; you can't do anything else.

These are menu choices ———

This gets you to the files available for downloading

Type E to hang up when you're done ———

The prompt, where you type your commands

Figure 9-8 The menu on the Microsoft Download system

Hanging Up

You can stay online, download another file, chit-chat, do whatever. Just remember to hang up properly when you're done, just as you'd hang up on Aunt Mildred when she eventually stops talking.

How you hang up depends on which computer you call. Always use a menu command you see in the terminal screen; never just unplug the modem. For example, in Figure 9-8, you would type the E command to exit or hang up from the Microsoft Download computer.

TIP You can check the box at the lower-left corner of the status bar to determine whether you're still connected. It says Disconnected when you're finally, well, disconnected.

After you hang up, you still must quit HyperTerminal. Choose the File → Exit command as you would any other program in Windows.

Other Modem Programs You May Have

Most of the sophisticated online systems have their own software. This makes it a heck of a lot easier to get around than having to deal with a text-based communications program such as HyperTerminal. Here's a quick run-down of what you may encounter:

CompuServe

CompuServe is the granddaddy of online networks. Heck, I bought my CompuServe account back in 1982! It's gotten a lot better since then, with a Windows-based program that makes sending mail and reading news messages a snap. Of all the online services, this is the one from which you can get the most. It can also be the most frustrating.

Prodigy

Prodigy, often viewed as the dumb person's online network (which is how they used to advertise it), has come a long way. It's a lot more fun and family oriented than any other service, but its graphics and splashy looks make it appear slow. Also its mail system is probably one of the worst out there. Still, it's much easier to find stuff in that slow graphical interface than it is on other systems.

America Online

America Online (AOL) is popular, especially among Macintosh users. It has a graphical interface and lacks Prodigy's stodginess. My main complaint with AOL is the proliferation of the chat rooms. Now, you may like chatting with different people and having fun with your modem. If so, AOL is your cup of tea. For me, it always feels like I'm walking in on some 22-year-old's birthday party instead of visiting the library.

Finally, there's the Internet, which isn't an online service as much as a ganglia of online things, UNIX computers, major corporations, and millions of people who think being "on the Net" is just the coolest thing. Granted, many fun and interesting things are on the Internet. But the Internet is anarchy. No one is in charge. As a result, things are often nonprofessional and clumsy. Still, a few jewels are out there (see "Places to Go on the World Wide Web" in this chapter).

BONUS

What About the Speed, Data Word Format, and All That?

In Windows 95, you no longer need to mess with the trivial aspects of setting up your modem in a communications program. This is done instead using the modem's Properties dialog box.

In HyperTerminal, click the Properties button on the toolbar to see the session's Properties dialog box. Click the *Configure* button located near the bottom of the dialog box. This brings up your modem's Properties dialog box.

In the modem's Properties dialog box, set the maximum speed your modem can handle in the Maximum speed drop-down list box. For a 28.8 modem, choose 57600; for a 14.4 modem, choose 19200; all other modems choose their top speed as rated.

In the Connection panel you can set the *data word format*, but I wouldn't bother. Keep everything set at 8, None, and 1.

Click OK to exit the various dialog boxes, and then don't bother with this stuff ever again.

Uploading and Downloading

Sending and receiving files (uploading and downloading) is complex, something that makes first-time users fill with fear. It's nothing difficult, just the art of coordinating two computers to talk and listen in harmony.

Either way you're going, sending or receiving files, your job is first to tell the *other* computer of your intentions. For example, if you want to download a file from the Microsoft Download computer, you tell it which file you want to send and how you want it sent.

For HyperTerminal, all files should be sent via the Zmodem protocol (which is a question the other computer will ask you). When the other computer finally says it's ready to send, you choose `Transfer` → `Receive File` from the menu. Click the Receive button and the file should start coming your way. You'll see a dialog box, such as the one shown in Figure 9-9 displayed, detailing your progress.

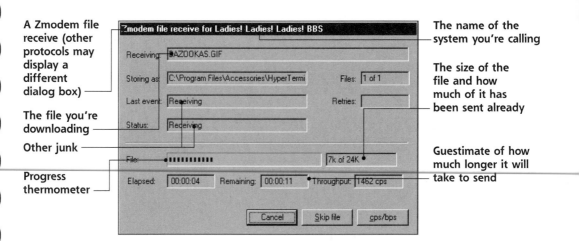

A Zmodem file receive (other protocols may display a different dialog box)

The file you're downloading

Other junk

Progress thermometer

The name of the system you're calling

The size of the file and how much of it has been sent already

Guestimate of how much longer it will take to send

Figure 9-9 A file is being received via Zmodem.

When the dialog box disappears, the file has been received safe and sound, and stored on your hard drive.

Sending a file works the same way; you tell the other computer to receive a file and wait until it says it's ready before you start sending. Then choose Transfer → Send File from the menu.

Summary

Are we all clear now? The Internet is not a program. It's a service. But you do use your computer, software, and modem to access the Internet. If you don't have any of those things, you're not on the Internet.

☐ What are the four things you need to get on the Internet?

☐ How to connect to the Internet

☐ How to disconnect from the Internet

☐ How to start HyperTerminal.

☐ How to connect to another computer.

☐ You should buy a copy of *Dan Gookin's Web Wambooli* if you really want to understand the Internet.

CHAPTER TEN

DEALING WITH ANCIENT DOS APPLICATIONS

IN THIS CHAPTER YOU LEARN THESE KEY SKILLS

USING DOS PROGRAMS IN WINDOWS   PAGE 134

SHARING INFORMATION BETWEEN DOS PROGRAMS
    AND WINDOWS   PAGE 137

MESSING WITH A DOS PROGRAM'S
    PROPERTIES   PAGE 139

D OS isn't dead, only the smart people are using it now. Why? Because, though it may be ugly, it's simple. There's nothing to get you frustrated. DOS doesn't claim to multitask or offer a common look and feel for all its programs. And DOS is fast. Very fast. DOS smokes on a Pentium computer. Me a DOS fan? Well, maybe. . . .

Like myself, you may be hanging on to some fond old DOS applications, including jewels such as WordPerfect 5.1, Magellan, dBASE, the die-hard 1-2-3, or a host of other programs — solid software — good applications you still need to use and you still enjoy. If so, you can use them under Windows. Maybe not as fast as they'd run if you were still running DOS by itself, but you can use them nonetheless.

Starting Your Old, Favorite DOS Program

I f you upgraded to Windows 95, your hard drive kept any memory of your older DOS programs you used with your previous version of Windows. They should all be there, sitting as menu items off the Start Thing menu.

Follow these steps to work with DOS programs:

1. Pop up the Start Thing menu. Press CTRL+ESC or click on the Start Thing if you see it loitering off on one end of the taskbar.

2. Choose **Programs**, and then choose any submenus where your DOS program is located.

3. Click on your DOS program to start it. It will start in its own graphical window on the screen, which is covered in the next section.

If you don't see your DOS program on the menu, start the MS-DOS Prompt program, which lives on the main Programs menu (see Figure 10-1). This starts a DOS window, which you can use like the old DOS prompt you loved.

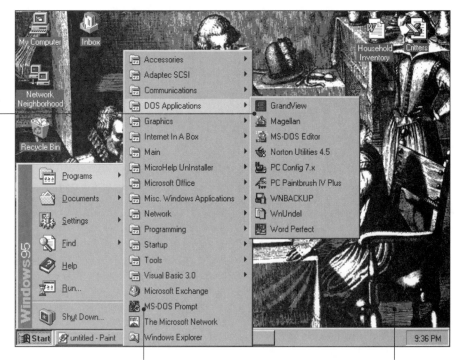

Here they are (most of them, anyway)

The DOS prompt is right here on everyone's computer; you can always start any DOS program from here

You don't have to live with a boring background

Figure 10-1 All DOS programs nestled into their own Start Thing menu

X-REF If you really must, you can start your computer in the MS-DOS mode. It will come up with the DOS prompt — CONFIG.SYS, AUTOEXEC.BAT, all that — just as it did before. The secret is divulged in Chapter 24, in the section "DOS Games? Forget Windows!"

Messing with a DOS Window

DOS programs run inside a graphical window on the screen, which is shown in Figure 10-2. This is how all your DOS programs look in Windows, but you're not stuck with exactly what you see on the screen.

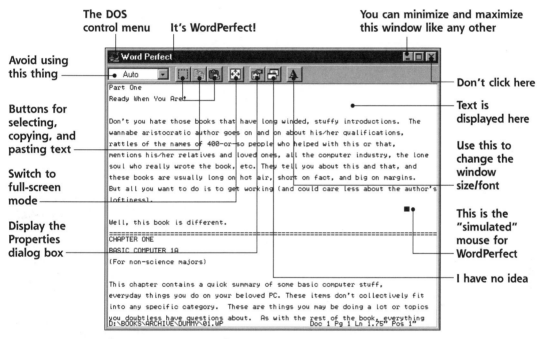

Figure 10-2 WordPerfect 5.1 looking sad and bored in a Windows window

You can change the DOS program's window size in a number of ways:

As with any window, you can minimize it to a button on the taskbar.

Or you can maximize the window. When you do, it may not fill the screen; Windows tries to keep the DOS text proportional, so the window may not be full size.

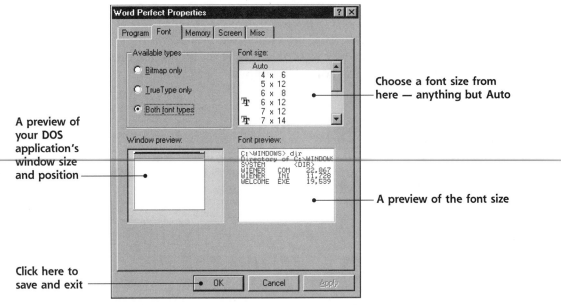

A preview of your DOS application's window size and position

Choose a font size from here — anything but Auto

A preview of the font size

Click here to save and exit

Figure 10-3 A DOS program's Properties dialog box — Font panel forward

Perhaps the best way to resize the window is to click on the Font button — the A button — on the toolbar. In addition to setting a new font size, the dialog box displayed helps you gauge the DOS window's size on the screen.

Figure 10-3 shows what you see when you click the Font button. It's really the DOS program's Properties dialog box, Font panel forward. In addition to selecting a font (see Figure 10-3), you get to preview how the DOS window will size up on your screen.

After toying around with the Font panel in the program's Properties dialog box, click the OK button. This returns you to the DOS application, where you can keep working.

A final DOS window trick you can employ is to see your DOS program the way it oughta be: text only, no graphics. To do this, you can click on the way it oughta be button or press the ALT+ENTER key combination (which normally brings up a Properties dialog box, but not here).

To return from full screen to Windows mode, press ALT+ENTER again. Remember this! You don't want to forget and think you're using only DOS again. The joy would kill you.

Copying and Pasting Between DOS Programs

DOS isn't as friendly as Windows when it comes to sharing and loving between programs. But under Windows, you can get your DOS programs to share text with each other and with Windows programs when text has been copied. You can select and copy text in a DOS program's window, and then paste that text into another DOS program's window or into a Windows program. The key is the Selection tool.

When you click on the selection tool, your DOS application changes modes. What you see on the screen freezes and the title bar changes to tell you you're in Text Selection Mode (see Figure 10-4). You can use the mouse to block out a large chunk of text for copying.

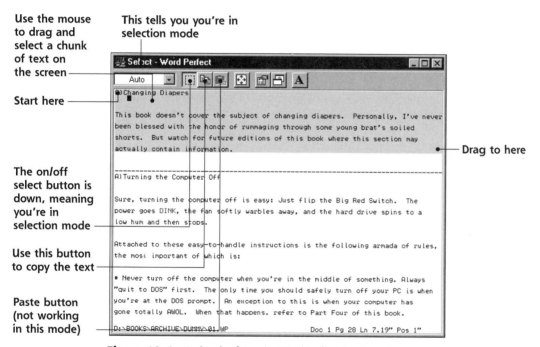

Figure 10-4 A chunk of text in WordPerfect is selected.

After roping off a section of text, click on the Copy button. This returns you to normal mode, where you can use your DOS application again. But the text you selected is now stored in Windows' Clipboard. You can paste it into any Windows program that can accept text, you can paste it into any DOS program, you can even paste it into the DOS program you're working on right now.

To paste, first position the cursor in your DOS program and click on the Paste tool. The text flows into your DOS program just as if you typed it at the keyboard.

Granted, you cannot cut and paste graphics this way; Windows doesn't understand DOS graphics and severe beatings won't help. The pasting is rather inelegant, as the text seems to spew everywhere, but at least you can do it. Sort of.

Also, you can't pull this trick when you run your DOS program full-screen (as God intended). You'll need to press the ALT+ENTER key combination to switch back to window mode to play with Copy and Paste.

 You can run several DOS programs at a time in Windows — multitasking them just as in Windows' own applications. See Chapter 8 for more information on multitasking programs and switching between them. Everything there applies to DOS programs run in Windows, as well.

Quitting a DOS Program

This is very special: You should quit your DOS programs the same way you did under DOS. Use whatever command you used before to quit the DOS prompt. For example, in WordPerfect, it's the F7 key. Use this command *first*.

If you absolutely must, you can close a DOS program by clicking its Close button. When you do, you'll probably see a warning dialog box (see Figure 10-5). Click No and go back to close the program properly.

The program
you tried to
sneak out of

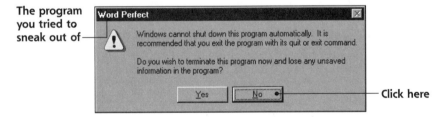

Click here

Figure 10-5 Oops! Can't close a DOS window that way

One exception to this rule is the DOS prompt. When you're at the DOS prompt, you can click on the Close button to close the window. But this only happens at the DOS prompt, not when you run a program.

TIP   Never, ever quit a DOS application by pressing CTRL+ALT+DELETE. This may have worked under DOS, but it's taboo under Windows. See "The Drastic Way to Quit" in Chapter 3 for an explanation of why you should avoid this.

Installing DOS Software (Is a Pain)

Oh, if you have Windows software, it can just be so beautifully installed using the Add/Remove Programs icon in the Control Panel. Alas, that probably won't help you install your DOS software.

To install DOS software, run a DOS prompt window as described in the next section. Then follow the instructions for installing the software according to the installation manual. This will get things running.

TIP   Beware of DOS programs that insist on resetting the computer after they install. In all cases, answer No to the *Do you want to reset?* question. If your program does try to reset the computer without asking, then only your DOS window will close. Shut down Windows properly and reset if you must.

Messing with a DOS Program's Properties

Just like witches have warts, everything in Windows has a Properties dialog box attached. DOS programs are no exception. Of course, what passes as a Properties dialog box for a DOS program is really the Universal DOS Properties sheet; it isn't specific to whichever program you're running, just to DOS.

To see a DOS program's Properties dialog box, click on the Properties button on the toolbar. If you can't see the toolbar, click on the window's control menu and choose Properties (the last item). Figure 10-6 shows the Properties dialog box for a DOS program.

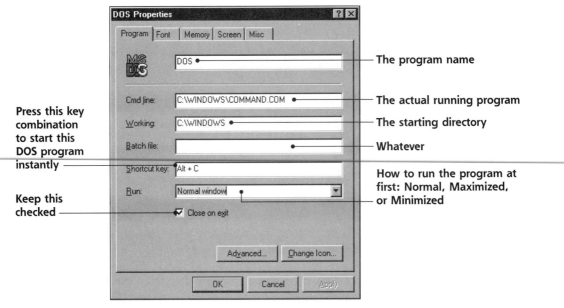

The program name

The actual running program

The starting directory

Whatever

Press this key combination to start this DOS program instantly

Keep this checked

How to run the program at first: Normal, Maximized, or Minimized

Figure 10-6 A DOS program's Properties dialog box

Several different panels are in the dialog box, but don't waste your time on them. Highlights for the Program panel are shown in Figure 10-6. The Font panel was discussed in the section "Messing with a DOS Window" earlier in this chapter.

The Screen panel has a few interesting items in it. Click on the Screen tab to bring that panel forward. What you see will look similar to Figure 10-7.

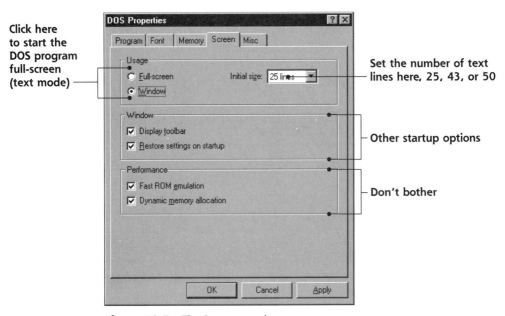

Click here to start the DOS program full-screen (text mode)

Set the number of text lines here, 25, 43, or 50

Other startup options

Don't bother

Figure 10-7 The Screen panel

If you prefer to run your DOS program full-screen, click the Full-Screen item. This way everything will start as it did in the old days. Of course, when you quit, or if you switch away from the full-screen DOS program, everything will switch back to graphical Windows.

The *Initial size* drop-down list enables you to set the number of lines that appear on the screen. Pick 25 for a traditional DOS screen, though many programs (including WordPerfect) adjust themselves nicely to 43 or even 50 lines.

All these settings are remembered by Windows, so the next time you start your DOS program, things will look similar to when you used it last. Of course, you can still dink with things later, which is one of the things about which Windows is passionate.

BONUS

Troubleshooting MS-DOS Program Problems

Trouble looms for some DOS programs, especially those stubborn ones that refuse to behave or some programs that are, honestly, startled to find themselves running under Windows. When the cloud of doom rolls in for your DOS programs, you can try your hand at the MS-DOS Troubleshooter, which is part of the Windows help system.

Follow these steps to use the MS-DOS Troubleshooter:

1. Choose Help from the Start Thing menu. Press CTRL+ESC, H.

2. Click on the Index tab if this panel isn't forward already.

3. Type the word **Installing** into the number one box on the Index panel. This scrolls the index list to the word *Installing*. You'll see various items listed under that heading, one of which is *MS-DOS programs*.

4. Click MS-DOS programs once to highlight this item.

5. Click the Display button. You'll see the MS-DOS Program Troubleshooter on the screen (see Figure 10-8). It lists several situations that arise when running a DOS program under Windows.

Click here and
choose Print
Topic from
the menu to
get a hard
copy of these
instructions

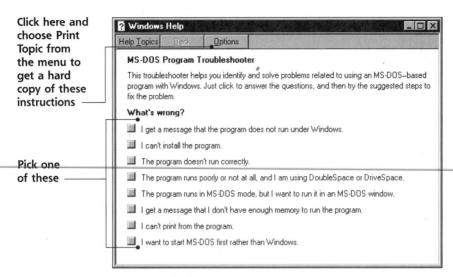

Pick one
of these

Figure 10-8 The MS-DOS Troubleshooter

6. Choose the item that bugs you. For example, *The program doesn't run correctly.* This covers a wealth of problems. Click on the little button by that item and you'll see another dialog box either explaining a solution or asking more questions.

Keep answering questions and trying solutions as you work through the Troubleshooter. Eventually, the problem will be solved.

TIP Sometimes it pays to get a hard copy of the detailed instructions offered by the Troubleshooter. Click on the Options button and a special menu appears. Choose the *Print Topic* item to print the instructions. This way, you'll have them for a reference as you dig through the bowels of your DOS program to fix something.

Summary

Back to DOS. Wow! Who would of thought? Yes, DOS is still alive, even in Windows. Don't be shy about working with DOS because it really is fun (once you get use to it). Here is the stuff you should have learned in this DOS Chapter:

- [ ] How to work with DOS programs.
- [ ] How to copy and paste between DOS programs.
- [ ] How to quit a DOS program.
- [ ] How to find the DOS Properites box.
- [ ] If you want to learn more about DOS, buy *DOS For Dummies* by Dan Gookin.

INSTALLING NEW SOFTWARE

IN THIS CHAPTER YOU LEARN THESE KEY SKILLS

INSTALLING NEW SOFTWARE   PAGE 143

INSTALLING EXTRA WINDOWS
   COMPONENTS   PAGE 146

UNINSTALLING SOFTWARE   PAGE 149

REMOVING WINDOWS COMPONENTS   PAGE 150

UPDATING TO THE NEXT VERSION
   OF WINDOWS   PAGE 151

B uying a computer is only half the cost of owning one. The other half is software, the programs you buy for your computer. That's an ongoing purchase. Even if you already have an all-encompassing program such as Microsoft Office, you'll still need to buy other software to make your PC go. And then there's the whole ordeal of updates and upgrades. Fortunately, it's all handled in a sane, central place in Windows, which is the core of this chapter.

And Now for Something New

C omputer software comes on disks, either floppy disks or compact discs (CDs). To get that software off those disks and on to your computer's hard drive, it must be installed. That process not only involves copying the programs, it also involves customizing the new software to work with your computer, letting Windows know about the software, and setting other options along the way.

Follow these steps to practice installing software:

1. Double-click on My Computer.

2. Double-click on the friendly Control Panel. There's also a copy of the Control Panel nestled in the Settings menu right off the Start Thing main menu.

Control Panel

3. Double-click on the Add/Remove Programs icon. The Add/Remove Programs icon is the computer software equivalent of Chicago's O'Hare airport; this is where your computer software arrives or departs, depending on your schedule. Figure 11-1 shows the Add/Remove Programs Properties dialog box.

Add/Remove
Programs

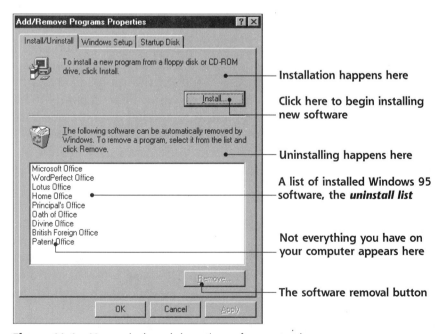

Figure 11-1 New arrivals and departing software start here.

4. Click on the Install/Uninstall tab if that panel isn't up front already. What you see will look something like Figure 11-1.

5. Click on the Install button.

6. Stick the installation disks into the drive. If it's a CD, put it into your CD-ROM drive (typically the D: drive). If you're installing from floppy disks, put the first floppy disk (#1) into your computer's (A:) drive.

7. Click Next. Windows will ferret out your installation diskettes. Eventually it will locate your software's installation or setup program, displaying technical information such as you see in Figure 11-2.

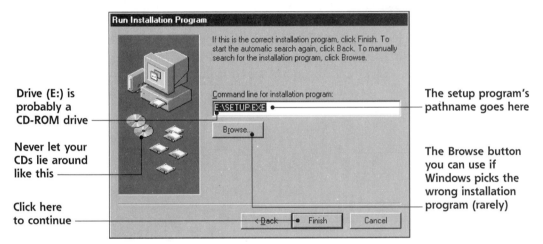

Figure 11-2   Windows has found your installation program.

8. Click Finish (or Install).

You're not really done; only the Windows setup part is finished. At this point, your new application's Setup or Install program will take over, completing the task of copying and configuring the new software. Your job is to read the screen where you may be asked a variety of questions. Don't worry, you'll know the answers (maybe).

What happens next? Generally, every application will set itself up differently. You may be given several options for installation: Custom or Advanced, Minimum, and Express or Typical.

Express or Typical installation. Choose this option first. It's not the *stupid* option; you will be able to make some decisions here. A lot of the nerdier details are just left out, that's all.

Custom installation. Only fussy users should bother with the Custom setup options. These options usually include every minute detail and pages and pages of setup options. Most of this stuff is standard for all PCs, so there's no need to bother (I don't).

Minimum setup options. Use the Minimum setup for laptops or other computers where disk space can be tight. A working version of the application will be installed, but no options, bells, whistles, and the like will get in your way. And you can usually add them later, if you like, by rerunning the installation program.

Now you wait; watch your screen and it will tell you what's happening. You'll probably have to restart Windows, but your program will tell you when to do this. When Windows starts again, your new program will be installed.

Adding the Rest of Windows

Windows comes with tons of stuff, most of which wasn't installed when you first got Windows. This may come as a shock, but remember, there was probably a reason for it; some stuff isn't installed because your computer lacks the proper hardware. For example, sound files don't work well on a computer without sound abilities; networking programs can't help you on a nonnetworked computer; no modem means no communications software; and so on.

SIDE TRIP

How to Exit any Other Programs Carefully While You're Installing

You may see an alert dialog box appear when you're setting up new software on your computer, asking you to shut down, or *carefully exit,* any other programs you may have running. This is a wise idea, because some unruly program may barge in and spoil your installation.

Follow these steps to quit other running programs:

1. Press ALT+TAB. This switches you to the next running program if you're running more than one program.

2. If you've switched back to the Setup program, then you're done. It's okay to install now. If not, keep working the next two steps.

3. Close the application by clicking on the Close button in the upper-right corner of the window.

4. Go back to Step 1. Continue looking for and closing programs.

The idea here is to keep switching programs using the ALT+TAB key combination. When there are no more programs to switch to, you've closed everything down and the Setup program can proceed safely.

Sometimes programs may not have been installed because there wasn't enough room on your hard drive. Windows tries its best not to be disk-piggy, but if you're swimming in spinning megabytes, you can install some of the programs Windows forgot later. Or you can install the rest of Windows right now.

Follow these steps to install the rest of Windows:

1. Wrastle up the Add/Remove Programs Properties dialog box. Follow along with Steps 1 through 3 in the previous section "And Now for Something New."

2. Click the *Windows Setup* tab. You'll see the Windows Setup part of the dialog box, as shown in Figure 11-3. It displays a scrolling list of Windows components and options. Those items without a ✔ check mark or with a ✔ check mark in a gray box are only partially installed; you can add the other components at this time. Some items have a gray check mark in their box. That means only one of several options has been selected. You can click on the *Details* button to select among the options available (covered in Step 3).

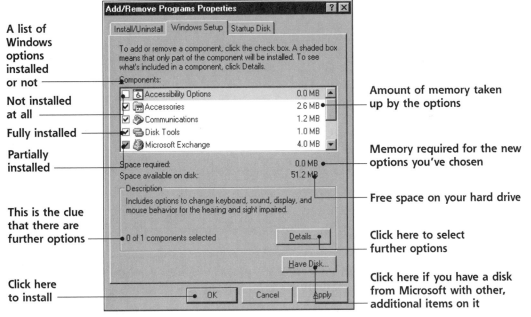

Figure 11-3   Here is where you add or remove bits and pieces of Windows.

3. Put a ✔ check mark in the box by those items you want to add to Windows. For example, if you want to install the WinPopup program (for networking), look for that item in the list and put a ✔ check mark in its box.

4. Click on the Details button if the item has more than one option. You'll see another, similar dialog box that lists individual components (see Figure 11-4). Click in the box next to those items you want to add. (There is yet another Details button, just in case even more options are available. This can get hairy.)

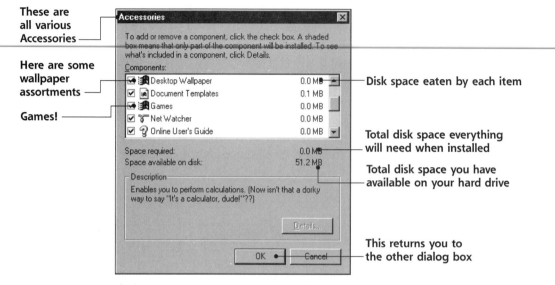

These are all various Accessories

Here are some wallpaper assortments

Games!

Accessories

To add or remove a component, click the check box. A shaded box means that only part of the component will be installed. To see what's included in a component, click Details.

Components:

☑ 🎨 Desktop Wallpaper	0.0 MB
☑ 📄 Document Templates	0.1 MB
☑ 🎨 Games	0.0 MB
☑ 🖧 Net Watcher	0.0 MB
☑ 🎯 Online User's Guide	0.0 MB

Space required: 0.0 MB
Space available on disk: 51.2 MB

Description

Enables you to perform calculations. (Now isn't that a dorky way to say "It's a calculator, dude!"??)

Details...

OK   Cancel

Disk space eaten by each item

Total disk space everything will need when installed

Total disk space you have available on your hard drive

This returns you to the other dialog box

Figure 11-4 Adding individual components

5. Click on the OK button when you're ready to add your stuff. You may be asked here to quit any other programs you're running. (See the sidebar "How to Exit any Other Programs Carefully While You're Installing.")

6. Stick the Windows setup disk into your disk drive. Either put the CD into your CD-ROM drive or put whichever disk it begs you for into your (A:) drive. If you're using floppy disks (and I really feel for you), you'll probably be asked to remove one disk and insert another. These things take time. (An argument for upgrading your PC with a CD-ROM drive, in my opinion.)

7. You're done. Eventually the changes will be made. Windows may inform you that it needs to reset. If so, do it right now; don't put it off. Enjoy your new toys!

The Subtle Art of Uninstalling

Sometimes it happens. You install some program on your computer, and then you don't like it. Or it could be you really need the space and suddenly notice the 14MB spreadsheet you installed eight months ago doesn't get any use. In that case, you can uninstall the software, safely peeling it from your hard drive.

Uninstalling is better than just dragging something off to the Recycle Bin. When you uninstall, you also remove secret pockets of programs hiding in various unobvious places. Not removing those hidden bits could lead to trouble later, so it's always best to uninstall stuff officially.

Officially Uninstalling Stuff

Some Windows 95 programs can be uninstalled the same way they were installed.

Follow these steps to uninstall stuff:

1. Incant the spell that summons the Add/Remove Programs Properties dialog box. Work Steps 1 through 3 in the section "And Now for Something New."

2. Click the mouse on the application you want to remove in the uninstall list. Look through the list for your application (see Figure 11-1).

3. Click on Remove. You'll see a Confirm File Deletion dialog box, asking if you're really sure you want to remove the program from your hard drive.

4. Click Yes. *Chugga-chugga.* You'll hear the hard drive chipmunks chirping away as your program is removed. Actually what happens is the program's special uninstall or antisetup program is run. It's this program that actually removes your application from disk; just as the Add/Remove Programs Properties dialog box only starts the setup program from an installation disk, here it only runs the uninstall program. (I hope that doesn't disappoint you.)

5. Resume your deinstallation. Continue with the unsetup program that appears on your screen. For example, if you're removing the Microsoft Office, click on the Remove All button to uninstall all of its components.

An off-chance may exist that Windows will want to reset after uninstalling. If so, do it right then.

Uninstalling Bits and Pieces of Windows

Just as you can "add the rest of Windows" you can also remove bits and pieces of Windows, stuff you don't use, to free up disk space. To do so, work through Steps 1 through 3 in the section "Adding the Rest of Windows" earlier in this chapter.

When you get to the Windows Setup panel in the Add/Remove Programs Properties dialog box, simply remove a ✔ check mark by an item. When you click the OK button, Windows will carefully delete whatever it was from your computer, freeing up that much disk space.

Unofficially Uninstalling Stuff

Not every application on your computer will be listed in the uninstall list in the Add/Remove Programs Properties dialog box. Even so, those programs may sport their own uninstall program.

The first way to find out if your program has an uninstall feature is to browse through its help file. Use the Index to look up Setup or Install. Then check under that heading to see if there is an uninstall procedure.

Sometimes the uninstall program is located on the disk from which you installed the program. In those cases, it may be necessary to rerun the application's setup program and then choose an uninstall option.

Always remember to try these options first. Never just wantonly delete a program from your hard drive.

X-REF   See Chapter 4 for more information on using Help in Windows, "Finding a Specific Topic Using the Index."

SIDE TRIP

"But My Programs Don't Appear in the Uninstall List!"

Only certain Windows 95-approved software appears in the ready-to-uninstall list. In Figure 11-1, the only real program that appears there is Microsoft Office — the 95 version. The other programs I just made up (in case it wasn't obvious). Older software you already had on your computer, and any and all DOS programs, won't appear on the list. See the section "Unofficially Uninstalling Stuff" for some suggestions on how to uninstall software that doesn't appear on the list.

Updating Windows

Every so often an update to Windows will appear. These may be called *maintenance releases* or *updates* or even *patches*. Whatever, they're some additions and improvements to Windows that will be made available every so often. As long as you registered your copy of Windows with Microsoft, you should be alerted to when these updates are available and where to get them.

Updating Windows works like adding any new software: You just stick the CD into your CD-ROM drive or the first diskette into your (A:) floppy drive. Then run the Add/Remove Programs tool as described earlier in this chapter. Windows will update itself to the latest, most improved version, and you'll be off and running in a few minutes.

As a general rule of advice, I usually wait a few months before updating my software. I apply this rule to any software, not just Windows. After a few months you can get feedback from other users and the major computer magazines. That way you can judge whether the update is worth the risk and expense. For most minor Windows maintenance releases, this shouldn't be a problem. But keep an ear to the ground anyway.

Summary

This chapter may be one you keep referring to as you find more programs you just can't live without. Rather than referring to this chapter, why don't you just learn this stuff:

- [ ] How to install software.
- [ ] How to install the rest of the Windows programs.
- [ ] How to uninstall programs.

DISKS, FOLDERS, FILES, AND WHATNOT

THIS PART CONTAINS THE FOLLOWING CHAPTERS

CHAPTER **12** WHAT DRIVES YOUR DISK DRIVES

CHAPTER **13** ORGANIZING FOLDERS AND FILES

CHAPTER **14** MANIPULATE THEM FILES

CHAPTER **15** THE POLITICALLY CORRECT RECYCLE BIN

Late in the afternoon, Eurystheus came to the small room in his palace where Heracles toiled at the imperial Windows 500 B.C. Pentium computer.

Heracles had managed to clean up. Eurystheus asked the big man about this. Heracles said, "I noticed I had Cerberus' blood and soot and stuff from Hell pasted on my body like a wicked frosting. So I took a bath. Did it while I defragged the hard drive."

Eurystheus smiled faintly. "You did what to my hard drive?" he asked.

"*Defragged* it. It was getting sluggish. Probably all that rearranging I did earlier this morning," Heracles said, his left hand dancing on the keyboard, and his right hand thrusting the mouse to-and-fro like some wiggly little kid.

"So this was a good thing?"

Heracles nodded. "You see," he explained, "files just accumulate. Like all that, uh, dung in the stables of Augeias. You know: doo-doo here, doo-doo there. You may think you know where everything is, but after a few weeks you have a disk full of doo-doo."

Eurystheus missed the connection between the foul stables of Augeias and his brand new 4-gigabyte IDE hard drive. He smelled the air to see if the machine had any doo-doo odors about it. After a few moments of no odor, he concluded Heracles had done a good job — whatever it was.

"So I put all your files into folders to keep everything organized. You can see it's all spiffy now," Heracles said, proud of himself.

"Then I'm happy you're doing well," Eurystheus said, certain he would one day figure it out himself. Or, he could make Heracles' fourteenth task writing a book on Windows 500 B.C.

Eurystheus stared at the screen, amazed. After a time, he began to make sense of it. He could see folders with dates on them and names of war campaigns. Some folders contained records of harvests and names of certain special priestesses in the temple of Artemis. There was even a folder named "Naughty GIFs." He asked Heracles about it.

"Oh, that's nothing. Just something I got from the Internet," Heracles said.

"Let me see," Eurystheus begged.

"No," Heracles said, closing the folder. "Now don't you have something else to do while I toil here? Can't you see this is hard work? Go do whatever it is you do. Do something kingly. Dress up in your armor. Throw a banquet. Execute someone."

Eurystheus left, dispelled, but pleased Heracles would soon finish his task and then Eurystheus, himself, could sit at his computer and explore the depths of folders in its hard drive.

Especially that Naughty GIF folder.

CHAPTER TWELVE

WHAT DRIVES YOUR DISK DRIVES

IN THIS CHAPTER YOU LEARN THESE KEY SKILLS

UNDERSTANDING DISK DRIVES   PAGE 155

GIVING YOUR DISK DRIVES NAMES   PAGE 158

DETERMINING DISK USAGE   PAGE 159

FORMATTING FLOPPY DISKS   PAGE 160

PLAYING A MUSICAL CD WITH YOUR
   COMPUTER   PAGE 163

12

The typical PC hardware tour starts off with the disk drives. Oh, some may start with the keyboard and monitor. But they're boring. Disk drives, they offer 'round the clock excitement. This is because they spin wildly, some hard drives reaching dizzying speeds of 3,600 RPM or even faster. That's enough centrifugal force to more than flatten Silly Putty. It's more centrifugal force than you get when Grandma's driving and she thinks the "Slow to 25 MPH" sign on the off-ramp is merely a suggestion. It's fast.

The Big Spinnin' Deal with Disk Drives

Three basic types of disk drives dwell in any given PC, maybe even yours:

* Floppy drives, with removable disks
* Hard drives, without removable disks
* CD-ROM drives, with removable disks

Almost every computer has one floppy drive, some have two.
Almost every computer has one hard drive, some have two.

Most computers also have one CD-ROM drive.

 X-REF This chapter offers only a get-acquainted session with your disk drives. Chapter 16, on the other hand, deals with maintaining and tuning your disk drives. Refer there for regular maintenance chores.

All disk drives store information. However, you can only read information from a CD-ROM disk; the RO in ROM means "read-only." So CD-ROMs are used for information storage only, not for saving files. Other than that, you need to know how the disk drives are recognized by your computer, which means understanding their uncreative letter names.

Disk Drive (A:), (B:), (C:)

Every disk drive living in your computer has two names. First comes the letter name, then a more creative name. The letter name you can't change. The other name is yours to play with. This whimsy is probably granted because the letter names are so boring.

Disk drives are given letter names, one for each letter in the English alphabet. The first disk drive is (A:), the next one (B:), and then (C:) on up until you hit drive (Z:).

The letter name ends in a colon (see Table 12-1). Further, in My Computer and the Explorer, the letter and colon are put in parenthesis. After all, the more characters you have in addition to the letter, the more cryptic and scary it looks.

TABLE 12-1 Drive Letters, Drives, Icon, and Fun

As Seen in My Computer	Type	Letter	Comments
	FLOPPY	(A:)	First floppy drive
	FLOPPY	(B:)	(Second floppy, maybe a $5\frac{1}{4}$-inch disk)
	HARD DISK	(C:)	First hard drive
	HARD DISK	(D:)	(additional hard drive)

As Seen in My Computer	Type	Letter	Comments
	CD-ROM	One letter after the last hard drive	The CD-ROM drive
	RAM DRIVE	One after previous drive	Fast memory drive
	NETWORK DRIVES	Assigned their own letter, not in order	Drives on someone else's computer

Traditionally, drives (A:) and (B:) are floppy drives. Drive (A:) is your computer's first floppy drive. If you have a second floppy drive, it's drive (B:).

Your first hard drive is given the letter C. This is true whether you have one or two floppy drives. So if you're missing your second floppy drive, (B:), your first hard drive is still named drive (C:).

Any additional hard drives in your computer are named (D:), (E:), and on up for every hard drive.

If you have any other types of disk drives in your computer, such as a CD-ROM drive, they're given the next letters right after your last hard drive.

The typical PC has the disk drive arrangement pictured in Figure 12-1, one floppy drive and one hard drive. The floppy is drive (A:), the hard drive is drive (C:). Figure 12-2 shows a PC with one floppy drive, two hard drives, and a CD-ROM drive.

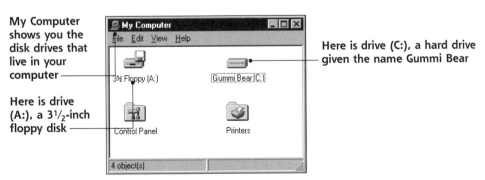

My Computer shows you the disk drives that live in your computer

Here is drive (A:), a 3½-inch floppy disk

Here is drive (C:), a hard drive given the name Gummi Bear

Figure 12-1   Drives (A:) and (C:) as seen by My Computer

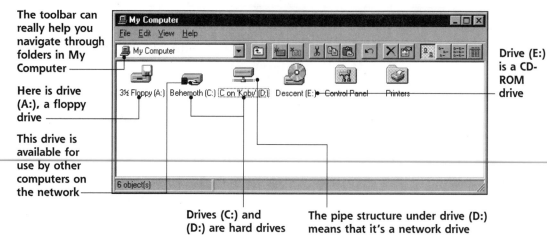

The toolbar can really help you navigate through folders in My Computer

Here is drive (A:), a floppy drive

This drive is available for use by other computers on the network

Drive (E:) is a CD-ROM drive

Drives (C:) and (D:) are hard drives

The pipe structure under drive (D:) means that it's a network drive

Figure 12-2   Drives (A:), (C:), (D:), and (E:) as seen by My Computer

Giving Your Disk a Proper Name

In addition to the letter, you can give the hard drives in your computer clever names, which you can use your imagination creating. That name appears before the boring drive letter when listed by My Computer or the Explorer.

Follow these steps to create or change the name of your disk drives:

1. Double-click My Computer. This is where your disk drives live.

2. Locate the hard drive you want to give a new name. Your choice! Pick which drive you want to name. (You cannot rename CD-ROM disks, and floppy disks can only be renamed when there is a diskette in the drive.)

3. Right-click on the disk drive icon to bring up its shortcut menu.

4. Click on Properties .

5. Click on the General tab to bring that panel forward if it isn't forward already. (Figure 12-3 shows you what you should see on your screen.)

6. Look for the Label input box (see Figure 12-3). It contains the name currently given to the disk drive, all highlighted and ready for editing. If your drive isn't named, the box will be empty.

7a. If you don't want any name for your disk drive, press the DELETE key to erase the current name, and then skip up to Step 8.

7b. If you want to type in a new name, do so. However, you can only use letters, numbers, and spaces when naming the disk. You cannot use any other special symbols or be creative in any way. Also, the name can be no more than 11 characters long.

8. Click on OK. This closes the disk drive's Properties dialog box, adjusting the name as you saw fit in Step 7. You'll see the new name appear in My Computer, the Explorer, and in any of the number of collapsible tree structure things that infest Windows.

X-REF If the label name isn't highlighted, double-click the mouse in that box, click-click. This selects the old name for editing, enabling you to replace it easily with a new name. You can also refer to Chapter 26 on working in a dialog box for more hints on how all those doodads work; see "Input Boxes."

Checking on Disk Usage, or "Fills up Fast, Doesn't It?"

To help you keep an eye on disk usage, Windows has a special pie chart you can view, showing you how much disk space is used and how much remains for every disk drive in your computer (see Figure 12-3). You can use the chart, maybe not to prevent a disk from filling up, but to prepare you for when it does.

Here is where you type a new disk drive label ——

This number tells you how many bytes of junk you have stored on your hard drive ——

Grape ——

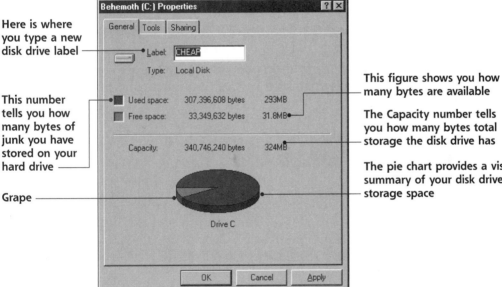

This figure shows you how many bytes are available

The Capacity number tells you how many bytes total storage the disk drive has

The pie chart provides a visual summary of your disk drive's storage space

Figure 12-3 The Properties dialog box for drive (C:), General panel forward

To see the chart, follow Steps 1 through 4 in the previous section. (Even if it's a CD-ROM disk you're looking at, though, I can promise you the disk will be "full.")

X-REF When a disk gets full, you should start removing files and uninstalling programs you no longer use. Files, like junk in your closet or garage, tend to accumulate. See Chapter 14 for information on deleting excess files and Chapter 15, "Reducing Disk Space the Recycle Bin Hogs Up." Chapter 11 discusses uninstalling software.

The Thrill of Formatting a Floppy Disk

All floppy disks must be formatted before you can use them. It's the law. Some disks will come formatted out of the box. Hallelujah! But you may, one day, need to erase all their data and start over with a fresh disk.

Follow these steps to format a disk:

1. Place a floppy disk into drive (A:) (your computer's first floppy drive). If you want to format a disk for drive (B:), put a disk in there instead. Make sure the disk you use matches the size of the floppy drive. Only put a 5 ¼-inch disk into a 5¼-inch drive, the same for 3½-inch disks. Also make sure you're using high-density disks, unless you have an older computer that can only use the lower-density disks. For 5¼-inch disks, make sure you close the drive door latch before proceeding.

 TIP Only format an old floppy disk, one you want to erase completely, or a new disk straight from the box. Formatting erases any information already on a disk.

2. Double-click on My Computer.

3. Right-click the mouse on drive (A:) to display its shortcut menu. Or right-click drive (B:) if you're formatting a disk in that drive.

4. Click *Format*. The Format dialog box appears, looking similar to the one shown in Figure 12-4. This is where you can set various options for formatting your disks. However, all of them are probably preset the way you want them, so it's safe to move up to Step 5.

5. Click on Start. The formatting operation starts a-hummin'. Graphics in the bottom of the Formatting dialog box will keep you occupied while you wait. When the operation is done, a summary dialog box appears (see Figure 12-5). It tells you all sorts of interesting and barely useful information about the disk just formatted and blah, blah, blah.

6. Click on Close in the Formatting dialog box. You're done.

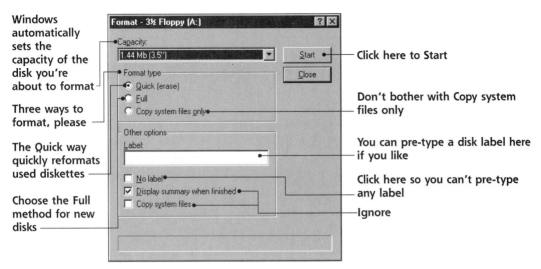

Windows automatically sets the capacity of the disk you're about to format

Three ways to format, please

The Quick way quickly reformats used diskettes

Choose the Full method for new disks

Click here to Start

Don't bother with Copy system files only

You can pre-type a disk label here if you like

Click here so you can't pre-type any label

Ignore

Figure 12-4 The Format dialog box in all its glory

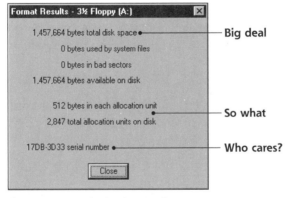

Big deal

So what

Who cares?

Figure 12-5 The boring results

7. Remove the formatted disk from the drive. Label the disk right now! Write the disk's name or contents (or both) on a sticky label, and then peel and stick that label to the disk. Don't use a Post-it note because those flit off and will sometimes do so right inside your disk drive. And don't put the label over the silver part of the disk. Again, make the label right now! Unlabeled disks are a pain.

8. If you want to format another disk, start over again with Step 1.

TIP **Never format a hard drive.** Hard drives should be installed and initially formatted according to the instructions that came with the drive. After that, you should never ever format a hard drive — even though there is a *Format* command on the hard drive's shortcut menu, don't use it.

Creating a Disk to Start Your Computer: The Fun Yet Useful Emergency Boot Disk

One of the options in the Format dialog box is to copy system files to the new disk. This creates a DOS boot disk, one you can use to start your computer and run MS-DOS Version 7 as opposed to Windows. Whoop-de-do. That probably won't come in handy anytime soon.

Boot disks can be useful, however, especially when you have hard drive trouble and need some way to start your computer. When that happens, you should create a system disk, or a special boot disk you can use to start and troubleshoot Windows.

Follow these steps to make a special Windows Emergency Boot disk:

1. Double-click on My Computer.

2. Double-click on the Control Panel.

3. Double-click on the Add/Remove Programs tool inside the Control Panel. The Add/Remove Programs icon is used to install new software on your computer, to add or remove Windows components, and to make a special Windows startup disk. Double-click on that icon to open its exciting dialog box. The Add/Remove Programs Properties dialog box appears.

4. Click on the startup Disk tab to bring that panel forward. The special Startup Disk contains special Windows startup files plus tools you can use to recover a damaged or flaky hard drive.

5. Click the Create Disk button. Windows hums and whirls. At this point, you may be asked to insert a few of your original Windows distribution disks, or the CD-ROM if you installed Windows that way. Obey! Windows needs special files.

6. Read the Insert Disk dialog box. It basically tells you to stick a sacrificial disk into drive A. It must be drive A, by the way, so get a disk that fits into drive A.

7. Click on OK. More whirling. Doh-dee-doh. Takes a while, don't it?

8. Whoops! All of a sudden, you're done. The disk is created. Not much fanfare. It's now ready for use.

9. Click on the OK button. This step closes the Add/Remove Programs dialog box.

10. Close the Control Panel's window. You can do this by clicking on its Close button in the upper right corner.

Remove the disk from the drive and properly label it. Give it a name, such as Windows Emergency Boot Disk (yeah, real creative). If you have more than one computer, label the disk for whichever computer created it, and keep that disk close to its computer. Also, date the disk. You'll want to make a new disk every year because disks get old and can wear out.

Playing a Musical CD

Windows is very smart when it comes to knowing the difference between a CD-ROM with computer information and a music CD. If you stick a music CD into your CD-ROM drive, Windows will recognize it and — in an amazing feat of intelligence for a computer — start playing the music.

When you insert a musical CD disk, you'll see the music-is-playing CD icon in My Computer, and the CD Player program will run (see Figure 12-6). If that doesn't happen, you can manually start the CD Player program; press CTRL+ESC to bring up the Start Thing's menu, and then choose Programs → Accessories → Multimedia → CD Player . (Whew!)

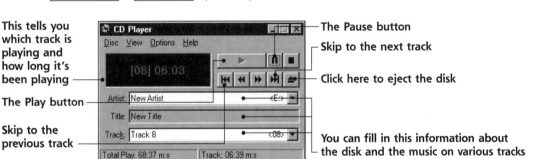

Figure 12-6 The CD Player program starts whenever you shove a musical CD into your CD-ROM drive.

If you can't hear the CD, or the neighbors are pounding broomsticks on the ceiling, adjust the volume. Use the Volume thing as described in Chapter 6, "Setting the PC's Speaker Volume." If all else fails, you can always adjust the volume knobs on your speakers — if you have the kind you can adjust.

BONUS

RAM Drives Belong in the Past

N o one needs a RAM drive with Windows 95. It's a waste of memory that would be put to use better by Windows itself.

To see if you already have a RAM drive in your computer, look for a RAM drive icon in My Computer. If you find one there, you have a RAM drive and it would be a good idea to remove it.

Follow these steps to remove your RAM drive (if you have one):

1. Choose the *Run* command from the Start Thing menu.

2. Type the following line exactly: **notepad c:\config.sys.**

3. Double-check what you typed.

4. Press the ENTER key. The Notepad program will load CONFIG.SYS, a special startup file from disk (see Figure 12-7).

CONFIG.SYS is a special startup file used by Windows, but mostly by DOS

These lines contain commands used to configure your computer, plus start special programs called device drivers

Click the mouse here to insert the word REM, which disables the RAM drive. You want to type REM and then a space

The RAMDRIVE.SYS device driver creates a RAM drive on your system. This is the type of line you need to remove

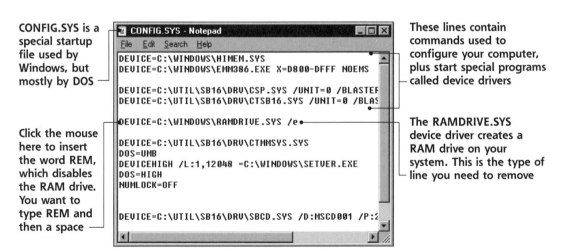

Figure 12-7 The CONFIG.SYS file is ready for editing in the Notepad.

4. Look for the line of text in the CONFIG.SYS file that starts the RAM drive. The line looks somewhat like the following:

```
device=c:\dos\ramdrive.sys 1024 /e
```

or maybe:

```
device=c:\windows\ramdrive.sys
```

or possibly:

```
device=c:\dos\vdisk.sys
```

It might also say *devicehigh* instead of *device*.

5. Edit the line by sticking the word REM at the start. The line should look something like this when you're done:

```
REM device=c:\windows\ramdrive.sys
```

Double-check to make sure there is a space after the word REM.

6. If your computer has more than one RAM drive, disable it as well; insert the word REM at the start of each line.

7. Choose File → Save .

8. Close Notepad.

9. Eventually, reset your computer.

For some reason, Windows doesn't obey the instructions in CONFIG.SYS until *after* you start or restart your computer. If you're able to do that now, go ahead. When the computer restarts, the RAM drives will be gone. Bye-bye.

Summary

Keep Table 12-1 handy. You'll find that you'll refer to it for drive information. Before you continue, make sure you understood the following:

- ☑ What the three basic types of disk drives are.
- ☐ How to create or change the name of your disk drive.
- ☐ How to format a disk.
- ☐ How to play a musical CD.

CHAPTER THIRTEEN

ORGANIZING FOLDERS AND FILES

IN THIS CHAPTER YOU LEARN THESE KEY SKILLS

GETTING TO KNOW THE FOLDERS   PAGE 167

CREATING A NEW FOLDER   PAGE 169

WORKING WITH THE FOLDER TREE   PAGE 171

ORGANIZING FOLDERS   PAGE 174

When it comes to using a computer, a certain portion of your sanity is at risk. Unfortunately, few people accept this notion: It's a person's laziness that makes using a computer so frustrating. The problem is *organization*. Using a computer requires effort. It requires a plan of attack. It requires making new folders on your computer and putting files into them according to some Grand Organizational Scheme. It's being neat and tidy with the desktop. It's ending up with a computer that's much more fun to use.

But organizing folders only once isn't enough; you must be vigilant in this effort, constantly arranging your files and folders to maintain order. The end result is a (what else?) logically organized computer with a sane human attached.

How Folders Helped Tame the Wild West

A hard drive can be a big, wild, and unforgiving place. The problem is the massive amount of storage space. While this seems ideal because space is always at a premium, great care must be taken to use the storage space wisely. Imagine a huge closet the size of an Olympic swimming pool. Then imagine putting all your stuff into the closet, no hangers, no drawers, no

California Closet Organizer. Just use a dump truck and load it all in. You'd have a mess! The same thing can happen on a hard drive, if you don't organize.

Hi! I'm just a happy little storage bin for your stuff in Windows!

Organization of files and programs on a hard drive is done by shoving everything into its own unique storage bin. In Windows, these storage bins are called *folders*. They used to be called directories, but that was deemed too technical because it has four syllables and folder only has two.

A folder is merely a place to put files and programs on a hard drive. All those files and programs live by themselves, not seeing or touching any other files or programs elsewhere on the disk.

Folders can also contain more folders, which means organization is carried one level deeper. For example, on drive (C:) you can have a *Games* folder. Inside this, you may have an *Arcade* folder. And inside the *Arcade* folder may live a *CapMan* folder. Inside the *CapMan* folder is your *CapMan* game program and all its files. That's organized.

Without organizing folders you get cosmic mess. Who knows where the *CapMan* game is? Or worse, imagine 2,000 files and programs all stored sloppily in one place. Even if the files are all well-named with pretty icons, it would still be a major bother to find anything.

The only drawback to this scheme is Windows, frankly, doesn't care how you organize folders. There are no rules, no regulations. It's up to you to be the sheriff and organize the wild, untamed, hard drive territory. This isn't as hard as you might think. And you don't even need a gun.

What's up with the Root Folder?

No matter what, every disk has one main folder called the *root* folder. You see this folder's contents each time you open a disk drive for viewing. That first window displays the contents of the root folder for that drive. Figure 13-1 shows the root folder for drive (C:) in My Computer.

Of all the folders in your computer, the root is the one most likely to be called a *directory*. Old habits die hard, and calling this folder the *root directory* is a PC tradition. Just know it means the first folder on a disk, the one you see when you peer into a disk drive's icon in My Computer or the Explorer.

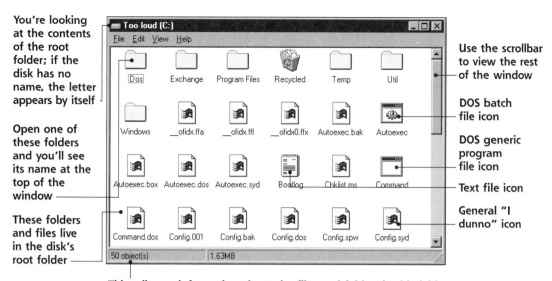

You're looking at the contents of the root folder; if the disk has no name, the letter appears by itself

Open one of these folders and you'll see its name at the top of the window

These folders and files live in the disk's root folder

Use the scrollbar to view the rest of the window

DOS batch file icon

DOS generic program file icon

Text file icon

General "I dunno" icon

This tells you information about the files and folders in this folder

Figure 13-1 The root folder on drive (C:)

Crazy Folder Terminology

Folders should be everywhere on your computer. Windows is in its own folder, surprisingly named *Windows*. Inside this folder are other folders where Windows has organized all its various pieces' parts (take a look sometime).

The folders in the Windows folder are its *children*. This isn't biological, this is just the term used. (Some nerds will call them subfolders.) The root folder, of which the Windows folder is a child, is said to be Windows' parent folder.

A folder in a folder is a *child*.

A folder "above" the current folder is the *parent*.

There are no brother, sister, aunt, uncle, cousin, or grand-anything folders.

Observe Figure 13-2, which illustrates this concept.

Conjuring Up a New Folder

Making a new folder is a part of computer life, something you shouldn't be timid about and something required, if you're to keep your hard drive organized. Finding a place for the new folder is the first step, but this depends on your hard drive organization. New folders can be placed anywhere, however. But before you make the new folder, you must open its parent's window. For this example, you are going to create a *My Documents* or *Work* folder for your future projects.

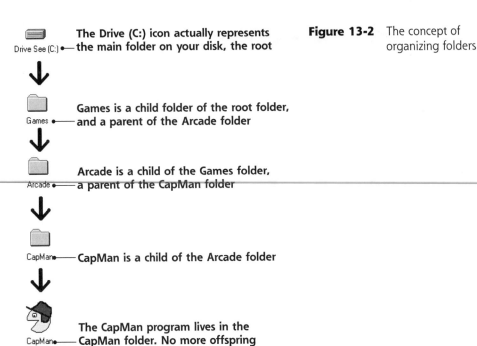

The Drive (C:) icon actually represents the main folder on your disk, the root

Figure 13-2 The concept of organizing folders

Games is a child folder of the root folder, and a parent of the Arcade folder

Arcade is a child of the Games folder, a parent of the CapMan folder

CapMan is a child of the Arcade folder

The CapMan program lives in the CapMan folder. No more offspring

Follow these steps to create a new folder:

1. Start in the root folder. Go to My Computer and open drive (C:). The window you'll see is the root folder, the parent of your new folder baby.

2. Choose **File** → **New** → **Folder** from the menu. The new folder appears in the window, similar to what you see in Figure 13-3.

3. Type a new name for the new folder. Remember, the name should reflect what it is, but it should also be short and sweet. For example, you can name the folder *Projects* or *Work*; it can be your main project folder.

4. Press the ENTER key when you're done, which locks in the new name. You can always rename the folder at a later time if you realize *Stuff* was a bad title.

Creating a New Folder as You Save Something to Disk

The Save As dialog box you use when first saving a file to disk has a special button you can use to create a new folder. Clicking on this button plops a new folder down in the current window, the same as working through Steps 1 and 2 in the previous section.

After creating the new folder, you should type in its name. Then, go on and save your file to disk.

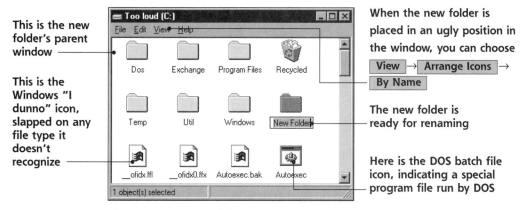

This is the new folder's parent window

This is the Windows "I dunno" icon, slapped on any file type it doesn't recognize

When the new folder is placed in an ugly position in the window, you can choose

View → Arrange Icons → By Name

The new folder is ready for renaming

Here is the DOS batch file icon, indicating a special program file run by DOS

Figure 13-3   A new folder is hatched.

Climbing the Folder Tree

With all its folders and files, a disk drive is organized like a tree, which is one way to look at it. At the base of the tree is the main folder, the root. (Ahhh — a pun. Get it?) Then come more folders, branching [sic] off into other folders, and eventually, you have files and programs, which are the leaves. Figure 13-4 shows one way you can look at this.

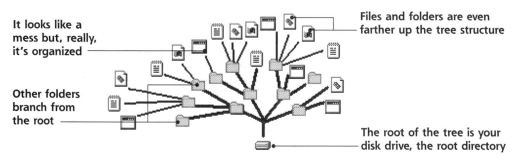

It looks like a mess but, really, it's organized

Other folders branch from the root

Files and folders are even farther up the tree structure

The root of the tree is your disk drive, the root directory

Figure 13-4   The folder tree structure of a hard drive

With all this negotiation comes the job of going from one folder to another, sort of like climbing a tree. For example, you may have your projects in a *Tahiti* folder that lives inside your *Work* folder. The report you just scammed from the Internet, though, is in your *Internet Stuff* folder, which lives in your *Communications* folder. That's being organized, but it presents a problem in getting information from one place to another.

Fortunately, climbing the folder tree doesn't require hairy arms, feet with thumbs, or a long tail. All you must know is how to manage a collapsible tree structure, which is the graphical doojobbie Windows uses to represent folders on your disk drives. The main tool for this is the Explorer.

Let's Go Explorering

The Explorer displays files in a more nerdy fashion than My Computer. You can use either one or both, but for looking at your hard drive's folder structure, the Explorer is best.

Follow these steps to explore the bowels of the folder tree on your (C:) drive:

1. Open My Computer.

2. Right-click the mouse on your (C:) drive icon. This displays drive (C:)'s shortcut menu.

3. Choose *Explore* from the shortcut menu.

The Explorer starts. It appears in a window with many elements similar to those in My Computer (see Figure 13-5). The main difference is you only have two windows with which to work. The one on the left, *All Folders*, shows the folder tree on your hard drive (actually for your entire computer); the window on the right, *Contents*, shows the contents of a specific folder.

The general approach to using the Explorer is as follows:

1. Use the All Folders side of the window to locate the disk drive you want to examine. (You can even look on other computers using the Network Neighborhood icon.)

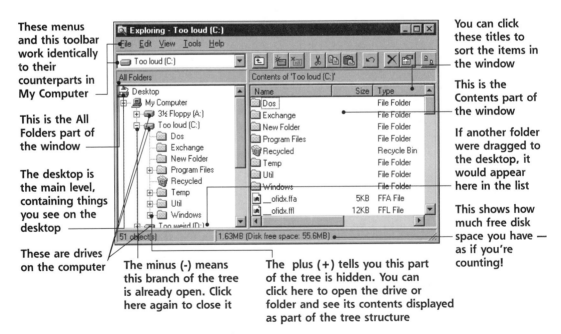

These menus and this toolbar work identically to their counterparts in My Computer

This is the All Folders part of the window

The desktop is the main level, containing things you see on the desktop

These are drives on the computer

You can click these titles to sort the items in the window

This is the Contents part of the window

If another folder were dragged to the desktop, it would appear here in the list

This shows how much free disk space you have — as if you're counting!

The minus (-) means this branch of the tree is already open. Click here again to close it

The plus (+) tells you this part of the tree is hidden. You can click here to open the drive or folder and see its contents displayed as part of the tree structure

Figure 13-5 The Explorer

2. Open the folders on that disk drive until you get to the one you want.

3. Look in the Contents window for the icons or files you want.

X-REF For information on working the collapsible tree folder thing in the Explorer, refer to Chapter 26, the section "The Collapsible Tree Structure Thing."

TIP When you're ready to close the Explorer, choose File → Close or click the Close button in the window's upper-right corner.

Working with Folder Trees in the Save As, Open, and Browse Dialog Boxes

Most Windows programs use the Save As dialog box to help you save a file in a proper folder on a specific disk drive. Three tools are in that dialog box to help you do so:

* A *Save in* or *Look in* drop-down list
* An Up One Level button
* Folders that appear in the dialog box's main window

The Save in or Look in drop-down list enables you to jump to another hard drive or another computer on the network.

The Up One Level button enables you to move to a parent or even a grand-parent folder somewhere on the current hard drive.

 Look in me!

 No! Look in me!!

And you can open folders visible in the dialog box's window to go "down one level" and store files there.

This all makes perfect sense, providing you have a good organizational strategy to start.

See Figure 13-6 to identify these three items in a typical Save As dialog box. In the Open or Browse dialog boxes, the *Save in* drop-down list is called *Look in*.

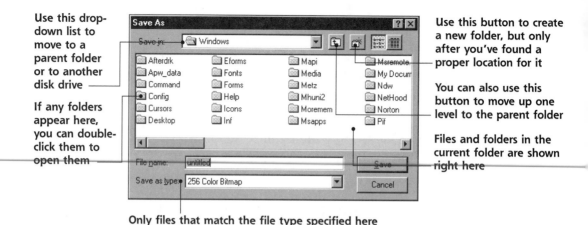

Use this drop-down list to move to a parent folder or to another disk drive

If any folders appear here, you can double-click them to open them

Use this button to create a new folder, but only after you've found a proper location for it

You can also use this button to move up one level to the parent folder

Files and folders in the current folder are shown right here

Only files that match the file type specified here appear in the window, along with any folders

Figure 13-6 The Save As dialog box

Setting Up Folders Just So

Windows, and most of its applications, know you hate to organize folders on your computer. That's nice, because most of these programs do some form of organization for you. For example, inside Windows' own folder, you'll find dozens of other folders, each of which contains some aspect of Windows, all organized neat and tidy. The same thing happens with Microsoft Office, which also organizes itself into a clean branch of folders. But your own stuff? That organization job is up to you.

The Useful *Work* Folder Organizational Strategy

The best way to organize your stuff is to create one, central folder. Call it *Projects*, *Work*, what have you. (Microsoft Office creates a folder called *My Documents* for the same reason.) This folder, created right off the root of your (C:) drive, will contain all the stuff you do on your computer.

My personal preference is a *Work* folder. Figure 13-7 illustrates how the Work folder works on my computer.

You should set up something similar on your PC, a place where you can store other folders related to other projects on your computer.

Below the *Work* folder, you should have other folders. Each of them should contain information pertaining to one of your projects. And if your project has different elements, you can create separate folders for each element.

Above all, never be afraid to create a new folder. When I start a new book, I immediately make a new folder for it in my *Work* folder.

Sometimes material for a new folder comes from a *Misc* or *Temp* folder. I just pull together all related files and move them over to the new folder.

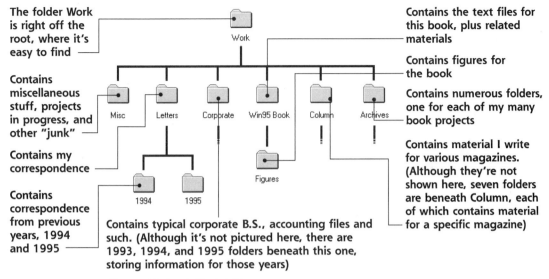

The folder Work is right off the root, where it's easy to find

Contains miscellaneous stuff, projects in progress, and other "junk"

Contains my correspondence

Contains correspondence from previous years, 1994 and 1995

Contains the text files for this book, plus related materials

Contains figures for the book

Contains numerous folders, one for each of my many book projects

Contains material I write for various magazines. (Although they're not shown here, seven folders are beneath Column, each of which contains material for a specific magazine)

Contains typical corporate B.S., accounting files and such. (Although it's not pictured here, there are 1993, 1994, and 1995 folders beneath this one, storing information for those years)

Figure 13-7 A Work folder strategy

X-REF Refer to "Deeply Moving Files" in Chapter 14 for more information on moving files.

Random Folders for Random Stuff

In addition to a *Work* folder for your projects — or a *Projects* folder for your work — you should have a random folder for "junk" you collect. Call it *Misc*, call it *Temp*, call it *Junk*, whatever. Creating such a folder off the root is ideal for storing ne'er-do-well files and other information that doesn't seem to have a place elsewhere on your disk.

My junk folder is called *Temp* and I put it right off the root. This is where I put new files I download or steal from the Internet, plus other stuff that just doesn't go anywhere else. Refer to "Conjuring up a New Folder" earlier in this chapter for information on how to make a new folder.

Don't forget to clean out your *Temp* or *Junk* folders! Make liberal use of Cut and Paste to put files you want to keep in a more permanent location. And don't forget the Delete command for scrubbing off files you didn't want to keep in the first place. Both commands are detailed in Chapter 15.

Beating a Pathname to a File's Door

Pathname is an ugly computer term you'll encounter all too often. It's used to describe the exact location of a file in your computer, on which disk drive and in which folder(s) the file happens to live. In a way, it's a path to a file's door, which is sort of where the term originates.

The following is a typical pathname:

```
C:\WINDOWS\SYSTEM\PASSWORD.CPL
```

This is broken into several parts:

C:	is the drive on which the file lives.
WINDOWS	is the name of a folder, here a folder right from drive (C:)'s root.
SYSTEM	is the name of a folder in the WINDOWS folder.
PASSWORD.CPL	is the name of the file or program inside the SYSTEM folder.

The backslash (\) characters are used to separate the various folder names and the final filename. Be careful not to confuse this character with a forward slash (/).

Summary

If you didn't catch the subtle hints throughout this chapter, you need to keep your hard drive organized. Use your folders! Give them descriptive names! Put proper things in them. You know, a file named MOM works if it's in the AUGUST folder in the LETTERS folder in the MY STUFF folder. Make sure that you walk away from this chapter knowing this too:

- ☐ The folder terminology (i.e. root, child, parent).
- ☐ How to create a new folder.
- ☐ How to use the Explorer.
- ☐ How to set up new folders to keep organized.

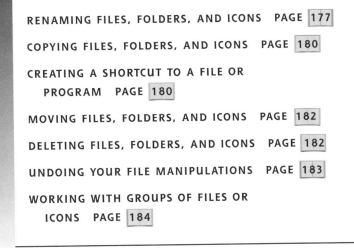

CHAPTER FOURTEEN

MANIPULATE THEM FILES

IN THIS CHAPTER YOU LEARN THESE SKILLS

RENAMING FILES, FOLDERS, AND ICONS   PAGE 177

COPYING FILES, FOLDERS, AND ICONS   PAGE 180

CREATING A SHORTCUT TO A FILE OR
   PROGRAM   PAGE 180

MOVING FILES, FOLDERS, AND ICONS   PAGE 182

DELETING FILES, FOLDERS, AND ICONS   PAGE 182

UNDOING YOUR FILE MANIPULATIONS   PAGE 183

WORKING WITH GROUPS OF FILES OR
   ICONS   PAGE 184

You can do four basic things to files: You can rename them, you can copy them, you can move them, and you can delete them. You can do all this using My Computer or the Explorer and various commands to manipulate the file icons you see.

By the way, all the commands in this chapter apply to folders as well. You can rename, copy, move, or delete a folder if you like, just as easily as you can delete a file. You should be more careful, though, because folders typically contain lots of files and maybe other folders with even more files.

Blessing a File with a New Name

When you first save a file to disk, you give it a name. Maybe not the best name because you can't always be creative and maybe the file's contents change, warranting a name change. When this happens, Windows blesses you with the ability to change a file's name.

Follow these steps to change a file's name:

1. Click on the icon once. This highlights the icon, selecting it.

2. Press the F2 key. F2 is one of your keyboard's function keys. Press this key and the icon's name becomes selected, ready for editing or replacement.

3. Type in a new name for the icon.

4. Press ENTER when you're done. The new name is now in place.

If you change your mind and you don't want to rename the file, press the ESC key.

Don't rename any file, icon, or folder you didn't create yourself — especially program files.

Don't rename folders, especially Windows' own folder or any folders or files inside this folder.

Another rename warning: You cannot rename a file with the same name of another file in the same folder. If you try, Windows displays an ugly warning dialog box. Press the ENTER key to close the dialog box, and then rename your file again.

On the other hand: You can give two files of different types the same name. It's possible, for example, to have both a WordPad and Paint file named Airplane Food in one folder. But two WordPad files named the same? No way.

Airplane Food Some Art

SIDE TRIP

BASIC FILE-NAMING RULES AND REGULATIONS

You can name a file just about anything. Primarily you should concern yourself with being brief and descriptive. For example:

Matt 14

This filename describes the 14th letter I've written to Matt. It could have been "Letter to Matt 14," but the file lives in my Letters folder, so I already know it's a letter.

BASIC FILE-NAMING RULES AND REGULATIONS (continued)

Other than being short and descriptive, these are the technical rules for naming a file:

✳ A filename can be any number of characters long, from 1 to 255. A 256 character filename is one character too many and probably ridiculous, as well.

✳ A filename can contain letters, numbers, and spaces.

✳ Uppercase and lowercase letters look different on the screen, but Windows doesn't notice any difference. So you can save a file as "May Schedule" and Windows will still find it when you type in "may schedule" or even "MAY SCHEDULE."

✳ A filename cannot contain any of the following characters:

" * / : < > ? \ |

✳ The naming rules for files also applies to folders. But with folders I urge you, even more so, to be brief and descriptive. It's just easier to read the names under the icons and to navigate the various directory collapsible tree structures.

ANCIENT HISTORY ON THE OLD DOT-THREE FILENAME EXTENSIONS

Windows 95 no longer requires you to type in the optional filename extension when you name a file or save something to disk. For example, in the old days, you might have saved a document to disk with the following name:

PORB.DOC

You type the dot-D-O-C to flag the file as a WordPad "document." Whatever. In Windows 95, this is no longer necessary because Windows does it automatically. When you save a file, such as document, you're given the chance to save it as a certain *type* in the Save As dialog box. When you choose a type, Windows automatically assigns the file the proper extension. You'll never have to type dot-DOC or dot-TXT or anything like that again.

Windows does its best to hide the filename extensions from you. But if you want to see them in My Computer or the Explorer, follow these steps:

1. Choose View → Options . This displays the Options dialog box.

2. Click on the View panel to bring this forward.

3. Click on the box by *Hide MS-DOS file extensions for registered file types*. If a ✔ check mark appears in the box, the extensions are hidden. If the box is empty, you can see the extensions.

4. Click OK to close the Options dialog box.

Copying Files

Copying a file in Windows 95 is done with the Copy and Paste commands — just like you'd copy and paste text between two windows. Other methods exist, but copying and pasting is best.

Follow these steps to copy or duplicate a file:

1. Click on the file once to select it. The file becomes highlighted on the screen.

2. Choose Edit → Copy . Or you can even press the CTRL+C key combination.

3. Go to the destination. Open the folder to which you want to copy the file.

4. Choose Edit → Paste . Or press the CTRL+V key combination.

If you paste a file into a directory and a file already has a file by that name, then your copy is given a new title: "Copy of" and then its original name. This way you can tell which file was originally there and which file was just copied into the directory. The new name does not change the file's contents.

Taking a Shortcut Instead of Copying Files

Copying files takes up disk space. For example, a 32K file copied from one place to another takes up 64K of disk space, 32K for each file copy. Egads! A better solution is to create a shortcut to the original file instead of a copy.

A shortcut is essentially a finger pointing elsewhere on the disk. It looks like the original file, except for a little box with an arrow in it — the shortcut tattoo. A shortcut also works like the original; double-clicking on a shortcut merely redirects Windows' attention back to the original file. This way, you can keep a copy of a file convenient — in another folder, on the desktop, wherever — without bothering with the original. You can also delete a shortcut without the guilt, because the original file isn't touched when the shortcut is eliminated.

Making a New Shortcut

Several ways exist to make a shortcut to a file. The best way is to copy a file as you normally would, and then paste the file as a shortcut. This is a special version of the Paste command, not the one you'd normally use.

Follow these steps to make a new shortcut:

1. Find the file for which you want to make a shortcut.

2. Copy the file; choose **Edit** → **Copy** from the menu or press the CTRL+C keyboard combination.

3. Move to the location where you want to paste the shortcut. This can be any folder or even the desktop, if you want.

4. Choose the **Edit** → **Paste Shortcut** command. On the desktop, right-click the background and choose **Paste Shortcut** from the pop-up menu.

 TIP You might also consider renaming the shortcut; each shortcut icon is given the new name *Shortcut to* plus the original icon's name. Renaming is fine because the little arrow guy on the icon will always let you know what's a shortcut and what's not.

Don't Make a Shortcut This Way

The worst way to create a shortcut is to choose **New** → **Shortcut** from the various File menus in My Computer or the Explorer, or from a shortcut menu. When you do this, you're faced with a dialog box that forces you to type in manually the original file's pathname (barf!) or to use a Browse dialog box to hunt down the original file.

What a colossal waste of time!

Use the methods outlined in the previous two sections instead of bothering with this hackneyed approach.

Deeply Moving Files

Just as you copy and paste to duplicate a file, you cut and paste to move a file. This should happen frequently as you organize your hard drive: You'll realize your *Misc* folder contains a lot of doodles you draw while you're on the phone. So you move them out of that folder and into a special *Doodle* folder, where you keep them until one day they're published and you're famous (but this will happen after you're dead, so you'll never see any money from it).

Follow these steps to move a file:

1. Click on the file's icon once to select it.

2. Choose Edit → Cut . Or use the keyboard-friendly CTRL+X shortcut key. The Cut icon appears dimmed on the screen. This lets you know it's been "cut," though it actually won't be moved until you paste it somewhere. (You can cancel the whole Cut/Move operation now by pressing the ESC key.)

3. Open the folder to which you want to move the file.

4. Choose Edit → Paste . Or press the CTRL+V Paste command shortcut key.

5. The file now lives in the new folder.

Before you repeat these steps a dozen times for a dozen files, know you can cut and paste a whole gaggle of files at once. Refer to the section "Crowd Control, or Working with Groups of Files" later in this chapter.

Some Files Just Hafta Go, or Deleting Files

It may seem like a scary proposition, but deleting files is part of computer life. You delete files because you no longer need them, to free disk space, or because they're old and useless. This is all a part of routine file maintenance which, like sweeping the floor, is something you'd rather have someone else do.

Follow these steps to delete a file:

1. Click on the file's icon to select it.

2. Choose File → Delete . Or you can just whack the DELETE key in a malevolent fit of vengeance.

3. The Confirm File Delete dialog box appears (see Figure 14-1), questioning your sanity as to whether you really want to delete the file. Click Yes.

This dialog box only appears if you've configured Windows to alarm you every time you delete a file

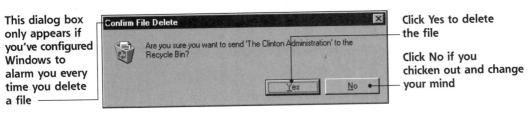

Click Yes to delete the file

Click No if you chicken out and change your mind

Figure 14-1 The Confirm File Delete dialog box

 X-REF Dragging stuff into the Recycle Bin is kind of a bold move. But, if you want to refresh your memory about warning dialog boxes, deleting files (tons more severe than the Recycle Bin), or restoring stuff from the Recycle Bin, head to Chapter 15.

Undo Thy File Manipulation Sins!

Almost anything you do to a file can immediately be undone. Simply choose Edit → Undo from the menu. This will undo a copy, move, delete, or even a rename command.

You can also use the handy CTRL+Z keyboard shortcut, if your hands happen to be there.

Don't be confused by some rogue dialog boxes that may appear after you undo something. For example, if you undo a file copy, Windows may ask if you really want to delete a file. What it's asking is whether you want to delete the file's *copy*, not the original. Click Yes in all these instances to finish the Undo operation.

Not everything can be immediately undone. You cannot undo a SHIFT+DELETE command. See "The Super Deadly Delete Command" sidebar in this chapter.

THE SUPER DEADLY DELETE COMMAND

When you delete a file, Windows places it into the Recycle Bin. This doesn't mean the file is really deleted because you can recover it later if you like — just like pulling that old black banana out of the dumpster when you change your mind and decide to make banana nut bread. You can utterly erase a file from your disk, though, avoiding the Recycle Bin altogether. This is done by pressing SHIFT+DELETE (see previous Step 2) to delete the selected file. But be careful here: No possible recovery exists.

Why use this command? The Recycle Bin doesn't delete things as much as it stores them. So if you're deleting files to free disk space, you might consider SHIFT+DELETE instead of dragging icons to the Recycle Bin. Or you can consider moving the files to a floppy drive or backing them up instead of deleting.

Crowd Control, or Working with Groups of Files

Everything that can be done to a single file can also be done to a group of files. The only difference is you need to select more than one file in the first step. This way, you can treat the files as a group for a gang-copy, gang-cut, or gang-delete. Obviously this is much more efficient than doing things one file at a time.

The Best Way to Select a Rag-Tag Rogue Group of Files

Many ways exist to select more than one object on the screen.

The best way is CTRL+click:

1. Point the mouse at the icon you want to select.

2. Press and hold the CTRL key on your keyboard.

3. Click each file you want to select (keeping the CTRL key held down the whole time).

4. Repeat Step 3 for every file you want to select in the group. Just keep CTRL+clicking. Every file you select appears highlighted on the screen (see Figure 14-2).

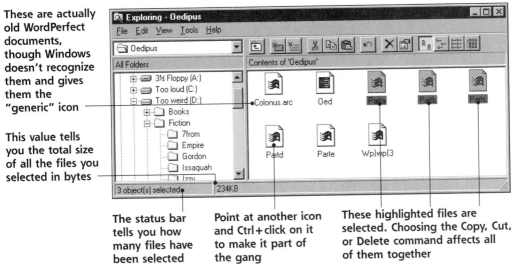

These are actually old WordPerfect documents, though Windows doesn't recognize them and gives them the "generic" icon

This value tells you the total size of all the files you selected in bytes

The status bar tells you how many files have been selected

Point at another icon and Ctrl+click on it to make it part of the gang

These highlighted files are selected. Choosing the Copy, Cut, or Delete command affects all of them together

Figure 14-2   Several files are selected in this window.

You can use the scrollbars to scroll the window and select more files. You don't need to press the CTRL key for this; only hold down the CTRL key while you're clicking to select files.

You cannot, unfortunately, select files in more than one window at a time.

After the gang of files has been selected you can manipulate them as a group. Refer to the sections in this chapter on copying, cutting, and deleting for the details. Those steps apply to groups of files you select, as well as individual files.

You cannot rename a group of files; Windows only lets you rename files one at a time.

Calf Ropin' Files

A wholly graphical way to corral a bunch of files into a group is to drag the mouse around them (see Figure 14-3). Start by clicking above and to the left of the group of icons, and then drag the mouse down and to the right. Dragging creates a line of ants outline and all the files inside the outline will be tagged and selected for copying, cutting, or deleting.

Often times you're not blessed with having all your file's icons in a neat and nifty group. If this is the case, rope as many files as you can, and then you can still CTRL+click other rogue icons to make them part of the group.

Selecting Scads of Files with SHIFT+Click

In the Details view, files can still be clicked one a time, CTRL+clicked, or calf-roped. But another trick you can try is the SHIFT+click. This selects a whole lotta files in a row, which can be handy in a Details view.

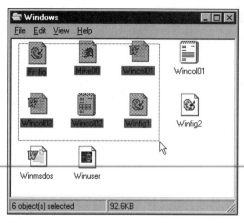

Figure 14-3 A group of files is selected at once.

Follow these steps to select a group of files:

1. Select the first file in the group. For example, suppose you're selecting bitmap image files from Figure 14-4. You'd click on the first file in the list, *samicon*, to select it.

2. SHIFT+click on the last file in the list. In Figure 14-4, the last file is *Straw Mat.* You can use the scrollbars to move the window if you can't see it on the screen. This selects that file and all the files between it and the first file you selected.

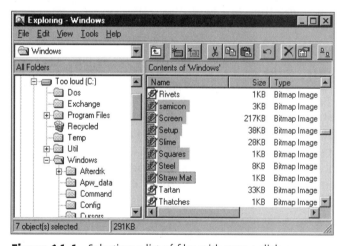

Figure 14-4 Selecting a list of files with SHIFT + click

TIP If you're trying to tag files of a similar type, sort the Details view first by this type. Click on the *Type* heading with the mouse. This sorts all the files by their type. (Click a second time to sort in reverse alphabetical order.) That way, you can find groups of similar files in a Details view window. See "The Details View (Nerds Love This)" in Chapter 2.

Selecting the Whole Dang Doodle

If you're not discriminating about which files you select, it's possible to select them all — the whole dang doodle — all the files in a folder or window on the screen. Here's how you do this:

1. Go to the window containing the hoard of files you want to select.

2. Choose Edit → Select All . Or you can press the handy CTRL+A shortcut key combo. Whatever, everything in that window is selected.

Suppose you choose Edit → Select All but, in addition to all the files in the window, some folders and other whatnot are also selected. If so, you can deselect various items by CTRL+clicking on them. When you CTRL+click on a selected item you unselect it without affecting anything else selected in the window. Refer to the previous section "The Best Way to Select a Rag-Tag Rogue Group of Files" for more information on CTRL+clicking.

TIP Here's a fancy way to select all but one file in a window. First, click on the one file you *don't* want to select. Click on the file's icon once to highlight it. Then choose Edit → Invert Selection . This causes all deselected files to become selected and vice-versa. The end result is your only selected file becomes the only unselected file.

BONUS

More Stuff on File Manipulation

J ust when you thought you had learned all you could about files (or perhaps all you wanted to know), we come up with even more stuff. The following section will give you some tips on renaming files (because we don't always get the names right the first time), go over duplicating a file in the same folder, and a lovely way to move or copy a file quickly.

File Renaming Tips

You can rename files in the Open and Save As dialog boxes if you like. Just point the mouse and click on a file listed in the dialog box, then press the F2 key. You can type in a new name for the file, just as if you were in My Computer or the Explorer.

You can also rename a file by clicking it twice with the mouse. This is *not a* double-click; just click once, wait, and click again. The file's name becomes selected and you can edit the name or type a new one.

Creating a File Copy in the Same Folder

To duplicate a file in the same folder, press and hold the CTRL key and drag the file down to the bottom of the file list in the folder. This creates a duplicate of the file quickly, though you can also just select the file, press CTRL+C, and then CTRL+V to do the same thing.

An *occasional* bug occurs in Windows, where it won't let you duplicate a file in the same folder. You'll see the universal "NO" icon displayed, meaning you can't duplicate the file. Restarting Windows fixes this problem (see Chapter 1).

The Old Drag-and-Drop

A quick way to move or copy a file is to take advantage of that graphical user interface and use the mouse to move the file's icon. The only limitation is you must see both folders' windows before you move or copy anything.

To move a file, drag its icon from its current folder's window to a new folder's window. Behold! The file has been moved.

To copy a file using the drag-and-drop method, you must first press and hold the CTRL key, and then drag. (If you don't hold down the CTRL key before you click the file's icon, you'll be moving the file, not copying.)

TIP If you drag-and-drop an icon with the right mouse button, you'll see a nifty pop-up menu appear when you release the mouse's button. This enables you to select how you want the file manipulated: copied, moved, or pasted as a shortcut.

Summary

File manipulation in Windows 95 is done by your friends and mine, the three amigos: Copy, Cut, and Paste.

This chapter is chock full of good stuff. Make sure you got it all:

- [ ] How to change a file's name.
- [ ] How to copy files.
- [ ] How to make shortcuts, move, and delete files
- [ ] How to undo something you did.
- [ ] How to select a group of files.

THE POLITICALLY CORRECT RECYCLE BIN

IN THIS CHAPTER YOU LEARN THESE KEY SKILLS

USING THE RECYCLE BIN   PAGE 189

TOSSING OUT PROGRAMS   PAGE 190

DELETING FILES, FOLDERS, WHATNOT   PAGE 191

RESTORING A DELETED FILE   PAGE 192

EMPTYING THE RECYCLE BIN   PAGE 194

STEALING BACK DISK SPACE FROM THE RECYCLE
    BIN   PAGE 196

The Recycle Bin is where you throw things away. It's an icon that lives on the desktop, but also is used when you delete icons from My Computer, the Explorer, or any of a number of places where the urge to destroy becomes uncontrollable (this happens frequently). But the advantage of the Recycle Bin over, say, a Trash Can, is your discarded stuff sits there so you can *undelete* later if you desire. This may not sound like a big deal but, if you've ever tossed something out and wished you had it back just as it was, the Recycle Bin can be a blessing.

15

How to Find a Recycle Bin Near You

There is a Recycle Bin icon on the desktop, but other ways are available to find it. For example, a copy of the Recycle Bin exists for each disk drive on your computer. It's found in the topmost folder, the *root* (the first window of files and folders on any disk drive).

Recycle Bin

Most of the time you'll toss away files and whatnot by dragging them to the Recycle Bin icon on the desktop. The details of this were covered in Chapter 14 under "Some Files Just Hafta Go, or Deleting Files."

If you can't get to the Recycle Bin icon on the desktop, you can always dispose of unwanted files, folders, or icons using the `File` → `Delete` command. Or, if you like the keyboard, you can press the DELETE key to shuffle select files over to the Recycle Bin.

TIP **You can delete a whole gaggle of files at once by selecting a bunch of them as a group, and then either dragging them to the Recycle Bin or choosing the `Delete` command. See Chapter 14, "Crowd Control, or Working with Groups of Files."**

"But the File *Whatever* Is a Program!"

Whenever you delete a file, Windows confronts you with an appropriate dialog box. *Are you sure you want to move it to the Recycle Bin?* When you delete a program, Windows wants to make extra sure (see Figure 15-1). Are you sure?

A warning dialog box does not appear, however, when you drag a group of icons or a folder to the Recycle Bin. Because you're dragging the stuff to the trash, Windows assumes you must deliberately want to delete it and no warning is given. Beware!

The program's name ———

Click here to delete the file — probably not a wise move

Click here to be safe

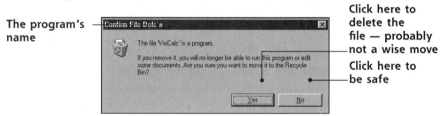

Figure 15-1 This dialog box pops up when you try to delete a program.

Well, you may or may not be sure. If you're deleting a *copy* of a program, go ahead. Otherwise, go ahead. You can *recover* things you accidentally delete from the Recycle Bin later, although this should not be an excuse for being cavalier about wantonly deleting anything.

TIP You may also see a warning if you delete a folder that is *shared*, or being used by others on the network. Just as your parents told you, you can't share something you're about to destroy. Better think twice about it, or just delete the folder's contents instead of the folder.

X-REF Also check out Chapter 20, which goes into more detail on sharing and network stuff.

Using the Recycle Bin Just Once to See How It Works

To see how the Recycle Bin works, follow these steps. You won't actually be deleting anything important from your computer's hard drive because the final steps here recover the item you've deleted.

Follow these steps to practice using the Recycle Bin:

1. Open My Computer if you haven't opened it already.

2. Double-click on drive (C:).

3. Double-click on the My Documents folder

4. Click once on the My Address document. This selects the document, letting Windows know you want to do something with it. My Address is a WordPad document, created in Chapter 4. Its icon should live in your My Documents folder and look like the icon pictured nearby.

My Address

X-REF If you can't locate My Address, and you really did create it in Chapter 4, turn to Chapter 29, the section "File? File? Here File! C'mon, Boy! Where'd You Go?" for information on hunting down that lost file.

5. Drag the My Address document over to the Recycle Bin. Do this by clicking on My Address, keep the mouse button down and drag the icon over the Recycle Bin, then release the mouse button. If you can't see the Recycle Bin, then choose `File` → `Delete` from the menu, or just press DELETE on the keyboard.

6. Are you sure? Click Yes.

This is the part where Windows wants to make absolutely sure you know what you're doing. The dialog box *doesn't* appear, however, when you drag an icon to the Recycle Bin on the desktop.

When you delete a file, a dialog box appears showing that file being "tossed" into the Recycle Bin (see Figure 15-2). The more stuff you delete, the more papers fly into the Recycle Bin. You may not see this dialog box when you delete My Address, but it shows up when you delete large or multiple files. This just gives you something to watch while you twiddle your thumbs.

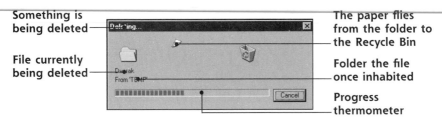

Something is being deleted

File currently being deleted

The paper flies from the folder to the Recycle Bin

Folder the file once inhabited

Progress thermometer

Figure 15-2   A file document is being deleted.

Okay, so you tossed it. Now it's gone; hence, the blank space where it used to be. If you want it back, you'll have to keep reading the next section.

A Quick, Odorless Peek into the Recycle Bin to Restore Something

Deleting files is a fact of life, something you'll be doing frequently. But those times will occur when you delete something and want it back. That's why Microsoft made the Recycle Bin. Unlike a garbage disposal, it's easy to recover something tossed into a Recycle Bin.

Follow these steps to restore a document from the Recycle Bin:

1. Double-click the Recycle Bin on the desktop. If you can't see the Recycle Bin icon, minimize all the windows on the desktop, as described earlier in this chapter. The Recycle Bin contains a list of all the files you've deleted (see Figure 15-3). Deleted files stay in the Recycle Bin for a given amount of time, enabling you to recover them if you eventually change your mind. (But after a time, everything will be deleted for good; see the next section, "Tweaking the Recycle Bin," for more info.)

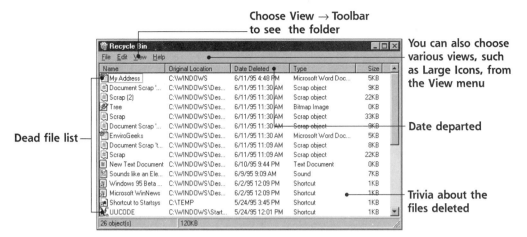

Choose View → Toolbar
to see the folder

You can also choose various views, such as Large Icons, from the View menu

Date departed

Dead file list

Trivia about the files deleted

Figure 15-3 The stuff in the Recycle Bin doesn't smell all that bad.

2. Look for a file to recover and restore, such as My Address. If you have to, use the mouse to scroll through the list of files.

3. Click once on the file you want to recover and restore using the mouse. Clicking once on the file's icon highlights the icon, letting you know it's selected.

4. Choose File → Restore from the menu. The file is removed from the Recycle Bin and put back on disk, in the exact folder from which it was deleted.

5. Click its little Close button in the window's upper-right corner to close the Recycle Bin. Or you can click on File → Close .

TIP A quick way to find a file in a long, long list is to type the first letter in its name. So for My Address, you would type an *m*. This tells Windows to display the part of the window with the m icons in it. From there, it's relatively easy to find the file.

6. You should confirm your file has been restored by checking the My Documents folder window in My Computer and seeing if the My Address file has been restored.

TIP To find files easily that you just hacked-off, open the Recycle Bin, choose View → Arrange Icons → by Delete Date . This will show you the most recently deleted files first.

Flushing the Recycle Bin Empty

Normally no need exists to venture into the Recycle Bin to delete files completely; Windows takes care of this for you. But times occur when you may need to delete sensitive files, stuff you may not want anyone else snooping into or recovering. Like the history of your weight loss or all the love letters from your ex-boyfriend. In those instances, you can permanently remove all or some of the files stored in the Recycle Bin. Remember, this is permanent. No going back once you take these steps.

To flush empty the entire Recycle Bin, choose the Empty Recycle Bin command, found in the Recycle Bin window's File menu and also on the Recycle Bin's shortcut menu. This is one command you shouldn't take lightly. After choosing Empty Recycle Bin, Windows will whirl through the Recycle Bin like a tornado through a trailer park, smiting everything and laying all files to waste. Yes, Empty Recycle Bin deletes everything. For good. Bye-bye.

If you don't want to be drastic about it, you can selectively delete files from the Recycle Bin. For example, during a normal fit of organizational frenzy, you may decide to purge some old and utterly useless files from the Recycle Bin.

Follow these steps to delete files selectively from the Recycle Bin:

1. Click the file(s) you want to delete. You can hold the CTRL key down while clicking to select more than one file, or you can "drag-lasso" a group of files. (See Chapter 14 for more information on these concepts.)

2. Click File → Delete . The Delete command in the Recycle Bin zaps files for good. The Confirm File Delete dialog box appears (see Figure 15-4), telling you the files will really be gone if you click Yes.

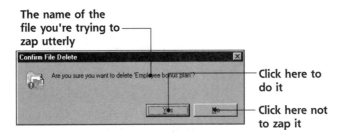

Figure 15-4   The files will seriously be deleted
if you click the Yes button.

3. Click the Yes button. The files are gone. A graphic dialog box may appear, showing the files as bits of paper flying from the Recycle Bin off into the electronic ether. Whoosh!

Tweaking the Recycle Bin

The Recycle Bin, like almost everything else in Windows, has a special *Properties* command that controls how it works.

Follow these steps to work the Recycle Bin's Properties command:

1. Right-click the Recycle Bin icon or somewhere inside the Recycle Bin's window.

2. Left-click Properties from the menu. The Recycle Bin Properties dialog box (see Figure 15-5) helps you set up how the Recycle Bin works. Basically, you set the size of the Recycle Bin, telling Windows how much to throw away before it starts deleting anything.

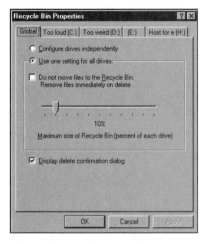

Figure 15-5   The Recycle Bin
Properties dialog box

SIDE TRIP

DISPLAYING THOSE WARNING BOXES FOR THE TIMID FILE-DELETING PERSON

If you prefer to be constantly warned whenever you throw anything into the Recycle Bin, whip out the Recycle Bin Properties dialog box (as described in the previous section) and click the mouse in the box by *Display delete confirmation dialog.* This tells Windows always to ask if you're sure before anything is put into the Recycle Bin. The check mark in the box lets you know your request has been granted.

BONUS

Reducing Disk Space the Recycle Bin Hogs Up

The way Windows comes out of the box, it sets aside 10 percent of your total hard disk drive space for throw-away stuff. This is a good number, though it may be a little big. For example, on my 600MB disk drive, Windows sets aside 60MB of space for throw-away stuff. That's way too much space, which I'd rather have available to store stuff I don't want to throw away.

It's possible to change the setting using a *slider* in the Recycle Bin Properties dialog box. You can change the amount of disk space the Recycle Bin uses from 10 percent to something like 5 percent, or maybe even 1 percent.

Follow these steps to change the setting on the Recycle Bin:

1. Bring up the Recycle Bin's shortcut menu. Click the right mouse button on the Recycle Bin's icon to bring up the shortcut menu. If you're inside the Recycle Bin, right-click inside the Recycle Bin's window.

2. Click the **Properties** command.

3. If you only have one hard drive, skip up to Step 7.

4. Click on the Global panel to bring it up front if it's not in front already.

5. Click the *Configure drives independently* option button. This puts a black dot in the button, meaning each of your hard drives can be adjusted separately, setting aside a different amount of space for the Recycle Bin for each drive.

6. Click on the panel associated with a particular drive, such as drive (C:) or (D:) to set the space for one of those drives.

7. Use the slider to set the amount of disk space the Recycle Bin uses. Point at the slider with the mouse and drag it to a new percentage value. For example, I'll set my drive to 1 percent, meaning the Recycle Bin will take up only 6MB of disk space, giving me back 54MB of space to use for storing programs, graphic files, games I play way too often, and whatnot.

8. Click on the OK button. Windows will make the proper adjustments to the Recycle Bin. This may take some time (of course), especially if your Recycle Bin is already full. Have a little patience.

TIP   If you'd rather not bother with the Recycle Bin at all, open up the
Recycle Bin Properties dialog box as described in the section "Reducing
Disk Space the Recycle Bin Hogs Up" above, and click the mouse in the
box by *Do not move files to the Recycle Bin. Remove files immediately on
delete.* This means the files will instantly be munched up by Windows
without any easy possibility of recovery. Do this only if you're very bold
or just plain foolish.

Summary

The Recycle Bin is like a temporary deletion holding bin. Remember, what
you place in the Recycle Bin will eventually be deleted for good if you
leave it there too long. Think of the Recycle Bin as a trial commitment. Unlike the severe DELETE key, you can go back and remove things from
the Recycle Bin if, by chance, you were too quick to judge the demise of your
document.

You should have picked up these skills from Chapter 15:

- [ ] How to find the Recycle Bin.
- [ ] How to use the Recycle Bin.
- [ ] How to restore a document from the Recycle Bin.
- [ ] How to selectively delete files from the Recycle Bin.
- [ ] How to work the Recycle Bin's Properties dialog box.

PART FOUR

DINKING

THIS PART CONTAINS THE FOLLOWING CHAPTERS

CHAPTER **16** KEEPING MR. DISK DRIVE HEALTHY AND HAPPY

CHAPTER **17** MESSING WITH YOUR PRINTER

CHAPTER **18** DINKING FRENZY AT THE CONTROL PANEL

CHAPTER **19** FUN WITH FONTS

CHAPTER **20** WINDOWS AND EVERYONE ELSE'S PC (THE JOYS OF NETWORKING)

CHAPTER **21** INSTALLING NEW HARDWARE

"Hi, Dave," Heracles said to Eurystheus. He didn't turn from the computer to acknowledge the king's presence.

A servant girl had just ducked out after delivering Heracles his evening meal. It consisted of three baked pheasants, a dozen apples, and a roast pig. Heracles ate everything with his knife. A small candle burned yellow against the pale blue light of the computer monitor.

Eurystheus stepped closer, trying to see what Heracles was doing. "Dave?" he asked.

"Yes, I changed your name in the computer. Dave is much easier to type and remember than Eurystheus. Nothing personal, but your name has that annoying *s-th* sound combination in it. The spelling checker keeps suggesting *euthanasia* or *urethra*."

"But . . . *Dave?*"

Heracles spun around on the little stool and faced Eurystheus. He said, "It's now your log-in name, your Highness."

"Log-in name?" Eurystheus asked.

Heracles grunted and turned back to the computer. He stabbed at the roast pig and tore off a chunk with his knife. "Loin?" he asked, presenting the strip of meat to Eurystheus.

"No thanks," Eurystheus said. "My wife and I had some baked Brie and wine for dinner. I'm stuffed."

Heracles smiled and stuffed the pork into his mouth. He continued to talk as he chewed. "This is for the network," he said, bits of pig flying from his mouth during the F, T, and K in the sentence. "I installed a network card in here today. You're now part of a WAN that includes all of northern Greece."

Eurystheus watched as Heracles clicked the mouse and windows appeared on the screen.

"See this thing here?" Heracles said, pointing to a picture of a tiny computer on the screen. "That's King Creon's computer over in Thebes. You can open it to see what kind of files he's hiding."

Eurystheus leaned in a bit closer. Political intrigue was one of his specialties. He asked, "Anything interesting?"

"Nope," answered Heracles. "A lot of stuff from the Internet, though."

KEEPING MR. DISK DRIVE HEALTHY AND HAPPY

IN THIS CHAPTER YOU LEARN THESE KEY SKILLS

FINDING THE DISK TOOL PROGRAMS   PAGE 202

USING THE BACKUP PROGRAM   PAGE 203

ELIMINATING DISK ERRORS WITH
    SCANDISK   PAGE 209

DEFRAGMENTING YOUR HARD DRIVE   PAGE 211

There are three common disk chores you must occupy yourself with occasionally. They are: Backup, Defragment, and ScanDisk. All are necessary, and each is universally proclaimed as a pain in the rear. It's true: It takes *effort* to keep your system up to speed. And though I've been writing about disk chores for more than ten years (and each time is more clever), most people still don't practice what I call *disk housekeeping*. This is sad because the benefits offered by these cute little programs far outweigh any inconvenience they may cause you.

Some Mild Ranting

Somewhere out there, out in the electronic ether, are several unique programs that may someday, sometime in the future, really save your butt. They are listed in Table 16-1.

16

TABLE 16-1 Butt-saving Disk Tools

Program ("Utility")	How It Saves Your Keister
Backup	Creates a second, emergency copy of the stuff on your hard drive. Even if your hard drive goes *poof,* the second copy will help you get your stuff back.
ScanDisk	Detects and fixes any errors that creep into your hard drive. A must.
Defragment	Removes nasty fragments from your disk, greatly speeding disk access. A boon to mankind.

Each of the special disk tools — or *utilities* — does something to your hard drive, fixing some problem you may have. Isn't that wonderful? The problem is, you must motivate yourself to use them. That back up copy won't be any good to you if it's three months old. You need to backup, defragment, and scan your disk on a regular basis for any of these handy tools to be effective.

Enough finger wagging!

Finding the Disk Tools Tool Shed

The three tools most central to your hard drive's health can be found right in your hard drive's Properties dialog box.

Follow these steps to locate your hard drive's Properties dialog box:

1. Open the My Computer icon on the desktop. This displays a window in which you see all your PC's disk drives.

2. Right-click a disk drive, such as drive (C:). The drive's shortcut menu is displayed.

3. Choose ⬚ Properties ⬚. The Properties dialog box appears.

4. Click the Tools tab to bring that panel forward. You'll see three tools (see Figure 16-1): ScanDisk, Backup, and Defragment. The buttons are just shortcut links to those programs.

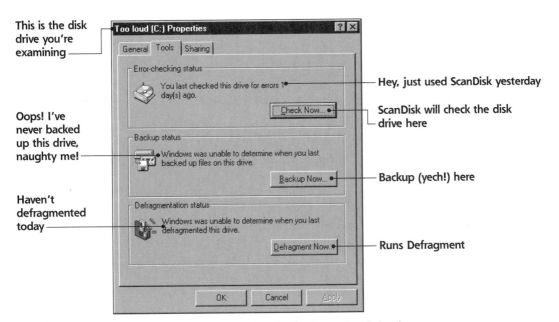

This is the disk drive you're examining

Oops! I've never backed up this drive, naughty me!

Haven't defragmented today

Hey, just used ScanDisk yesterday

ScanDisk will check the disk drive here

Backup (yech!) here

Runs Defragment

Figure 16-1   Disk tools galore in the Properties dialog box

Another nice thing about this dialog box is that it tells you when you last used the tools on your hard drive (the hard drive indicated at the top of the Properties dialog box). That way you can get a gauge on whether you need to run the program again.

How often should you run these tools? For Backup, it should be done at least once a day, if only to back up your working projects. ScanDisk should be run every few weeks or so and always right after a system crash or accidental reset. Defragment needs to be run every few months, though you don't need to defragment your disk unless the tool tells you it's necessary.

Backup Drudgery

Backing up your hard drive is underrated. You *need* that backup copy just in case something happens: a file is mangled or overwritten, you lose a file that was there yesterday, some doofus reformats your hard drive, or the hard drive walks out of the back of your computer and goes on a skiing vacation in the Alps. Whatever, backing up is a good thing.

The problem? If you don't have a tape backup unit, it takes a lot of floppy disks, elbow work, and time to back up.

The solution? Buy a tape backup unit. It's a snap to back up your files to the little cassette tapes. You don't even need to sit there and watch. And if you keep the tape in the drive all the time, you can back up every day without ever having to fuss over it. That's what we do around my office. No one complains.

What to Back Up and When to Do It

You should have a backup schedule that works like this:

* ✸ Back up the work you do every day.

* ✸ Every week, back up your entire hard drive.

The first backup is called an *incremental* backup. It only backs up those files that have been changed or created since the last time you backed up.

The second backup is a *full* backup. This takes a bit longer, but it keeps that valuable second copy of your information current.

TIP I always keep my backup tapes in a fireproof safe. It's not a real safe, just a thick box with a locking lid. Supposedly whatever's inside stays nice and comfy while outside there can be 1,200 degrees of flames. In fact, you should get a fireproof safe for every member of the family. It's the ultimate way to keep everything safe.

How It's Done

Whether it's a daily backup or a weekly backup, you follow the same steps. Here they are in an abbreviated manner, because I don't know exactly what you're backing up.

Follow these steps to back up your computer:

1. Start the Backup program. (See "Finding the Disk Tools Tool Shed" earlier in this chapter.) Click the Backup Now button.

2. Read the Welcome screen. It outlines the process (see Figure 16-2).

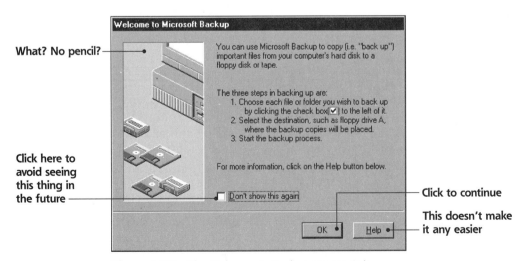

Figure 16-2 The Welcome to Backup screen. Rah.

3. You might see a dialog box saying, "Backup has created the following full backup set for you." If so, click the OK button. You can optionally put a ✔ check mark in the box so you won't see that screen again.

4. The main Backup screen appears (see Figure 16-3). It looks a lot like a typical Explorer window, with a collapsible tree structure thing on the left and a list of files on the right. This is where you pick files to back up.

Click here to move on to the next step

Collapsible tree structure thing

Item selected for backup

Put a ✔ in here to back up this item

Files and such

Each of these folders and files are selected for backup

Trivia about the files you selected

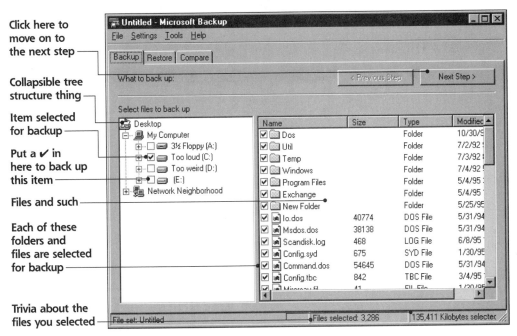

Figure 16-3 The main Backup screen

5. Select disk drives, folders, or files to back up. Pick one or more items by clicking the mouse in its box. This selects that drive (and all its files) or a folder (and all its files) or an icon for backing up.

 TIP To back up all your files, you probably only need to click the mouse by drive (C:). That puts a ✔ check mark in the box, flagging all those files for backup.

If you don't want to back up files in a certain folder, find that folder and remove the ✔ check mark from its box. If only part of a disk drive or folder's files is selected, the ✔ check mark appears inside a gray box.

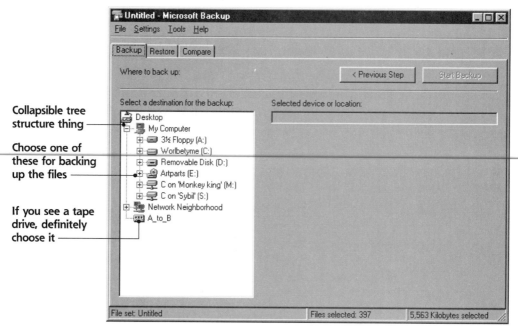

Collapsible tree structure thing —

Choose one of these for backing up the files —

If you see a tape drive, definitely choose it —

Figure 16-4 The Backup destination screen

6. In the next screen, you'll tell Windows where to back up your files (see Figure 16-4). You can choose a floppy drive or another disk drive on your computer (or elsewhere on the network), or you can choose any tape drives that Windows has found.

TIP If you have a tape backup drive, it appears at the bottom of the list (see Figure 16-4). Choose it as your backup destination.

7. Click on the start backup button.

8. Type in a Backup Set Label. Try to describe the backup here. Type in something such as: **It's Friday and it's time to back up the whole hard drive.** Or you can be nerdy: **Friday, 10/18, full backup of (C:).** Click the OK button when you're done.

9. Make sure the disk or tape is ready in the drive, formatted, and willing to receive backup copies.

10. Click on OK. The backup begins. You'll be entertained while this happens (see Figure 16-5).

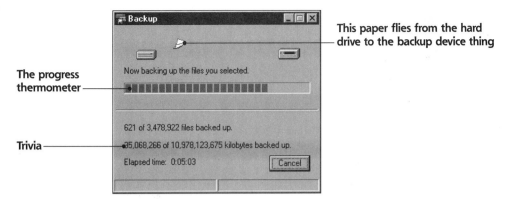

This paper flies from the hard drive to the backup device thing

The progress thermometer

Trivia

Figure 16-5 Backing up is hard to do.

11. If the disk already contains files, you'll see a warning dialog box. Oops! Better use another disk. There's no sense in erasing a disk that may hold important files.

12. You might be asked to switch disks. If you're backing up to floppy disks and, face it, one floppy disk doesn't hold a whole hard drive's worth of information, you'll need to switch disks. You'll see a message displayed (see Figure 16-6).

13. Remove the current disk. Yank it from your disk drive and set it aside. Insert the next disk. Close the drive door latch if it's a 5¼-inch drive.

Click here after removing the old disk and inserting a new one

Well, do it!

Figure 16-6 Feed me, Seymore!

TIP When you set aside the disk, number it. Write the disk's number on the sticky label. This will keep your backup disk set organized. You might also want to write the date, time, your name, company name, astrological sign, and blood type.

14. The backup is complete. Close stuff. A dialog box appears, congratulating you for completing your hard disk backup (see Figure 16-7).

It's about time!

It's OK

Figure 16-7 A happy dialog box to see

15. Remove and number the final disk. If you did a tape backup, remove it and label it as well.

16. Click on OK to close the Backup Complete dialog box.

17. Click on OK to close the other dialog box.

18. Close the Microsoft Backup application window.

Whew! You're done.

Restoring Something You Backed Up

Backing up is pretty useless without its other counterpart, Restore. You use Restore to take the files stored on backup disks and recopy them to your hard drive.

Follow these steps to restore something you backed up:

1. Start the Backup program.

2. Click the Restore tab to bring that panel forward. The Restore panel is where you pluck out files from a backup set of diskettes to be restored to your hard drive (see Figure 16-8).

3. Put your first backup disk or tape into the proper PC orifice. *Kee-lunk!*

4. Click that backup device in the Restore panel. For example, if you backed up to floppy drive (A:), you'd click on drive (A:). In a few moments, you'll see your backup set appear in the right half of the window, along with the time you last backed up (see Figure 16-8).

5. Choose the files you want to restore. Just like backing up, the next screen details all the files saved on your backup set. Go through the collapsible tree structure and put a ✔ check mark into all those files you want to restore. To restore the whole hard drive, put a ✔ check mark in its box.

6. Click the Start Restore button. Windows flies the file from the backup disks back to your hard drive.

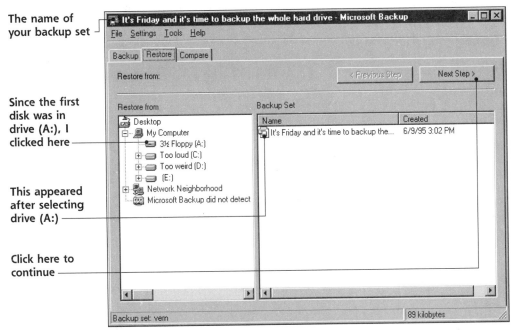

The name of your backup set

Since the first disk was in drive (A:), I clicked here

This appeared after selecting drive (A:)

Click here to continue

Figure 16-8   The Restore panel, ready to recover files

7. Swap disks if necessary. This is the boring step. Windows will let you know if you need to switch disks.

8. And suddenly . . . you're done.

Weaseling Out Errors with ScanDisk

Disk errors happen. It's ScanDisk's job to look for and fix them where it can. While it doesn't work miracles, ScanDisk can patch up a lot of problems and fix things such as broken long filenames and errant shortcuts. Because of this, you should run ScanDisk at least once a week, and more often if it always reports a few errors.

Follow these steps to run ScanDisk:

1. Start the ScanDisk program. Follow the directions posted earlier in this chapter, "Finding the Disk Tools Tool Shed." In the disk drive Properties dialog box it's the Check Now button (see Figure 16-1).

2. When ScanDisk starts, you'll see its window displayed, similar to Figure 16-9.

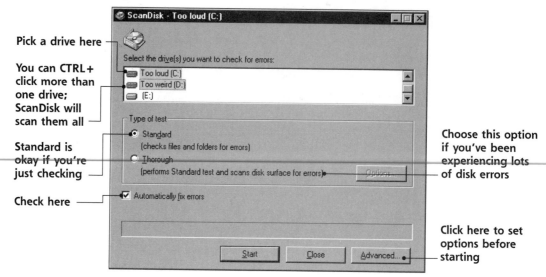

Pick a drive here

You can CTRL+ click more than one drive; ScanDisk will scan them all

Standard is okay if you're just checking

Check here

Choose this option if you've been experiencing lots of disk errors

Click here to set options before starting

Figure 16-9 ScanDisk is about to go error hunting.

3. Pick a drive to scan from the scrolling list. You can drag through all of them with the mouse to select every drive, or you can CTRL+click only those drives you want to check.

4. Make sure the *Standard* option is chosen (as shown in Figure 16-9). The Advanced option does a longer, more detailed check.

5. Make sure the *Automatically fix errors* item is checked (again, see Figure 16-9).

6. Click the Advanced button. (There's nothing really "advanced" there, not like the advanced section of the Math SAT you skipped.)

7. Use Figure 16-10 as a guide to show you which options you should click. This enables ScanDisk to do a proper job without any extra bother on your behalf.

8. Click on OK to close the Advanced Options dialog box.

9. Click the Start button. ScanDisk examines all sorts of technical things about your hard drive. It checks this. It checks that.

10. If you encounter any errors, ScanDisk should fix them automatically. If not, a dialog box may be displayed explaining the problem. Just click on the OK button and everything will be fixed.

11. ScanDisk is done.

You can go back and repeat these steps to scan another drive, or you can close ScanDisk now by clicking its Close button.

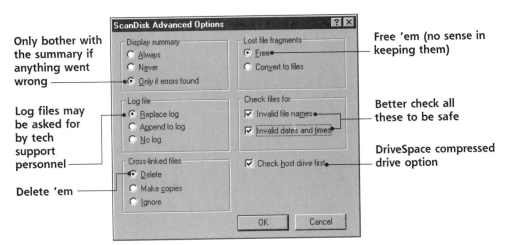

Only bother with the summary if anything went wrong

Log files may be asked for by tech support personnel

Delete 'em

Free 'em (no sense in keeping them)

Better check all these to be safe

DriveSpace compressed drive option

Figure 16-10   Save yourself some time with these options.

Removing Those Nasty Fragments from Your Disks

File fragmentation is a blessing and a curse. It's a blessing because without it your hard drive would fill up faster than an unattended litter box. The problem is all those little file fragments take time for Windows to manage. Too many of them turn your hard drive into a frozen slug pig.

Follow these steps to end the fragmentation curse:

1. Start the Defragment program. Click the Defragment Now button if you're running the Defragment program from a disk's Properties dialog box.

2. Decide whether you really need to do this. The cool thing about the Disk Defragmenter is that it immediately lets you know whether you're wasting your time. Figure 16-11 shows you the first screen. When the fragmentation level of a drive is low, there's no point in going on. Just click the Exit button and you're done.

3. If Windows suggests you defragment your drive, or if you'd like to do it for the heck of it, click the Start button. If you choose *All Hard Drives* from the Select Drive button's list, then Windows will immediately go ahead and defragment all your hard drives — whether they need it or not — skipping the "press the Start button" step.

Windows moves into defragmenting mode. While this is going on, I'd advise you not to do anything else with the computer. Sure, you can. But defragmenting will move a lot quicker if you just sit and watch until it's done. While you wait, a progress dialog box entertains you (see Figure 16-12).

The drive currently being examined

Good advice

Go ahead and defragment

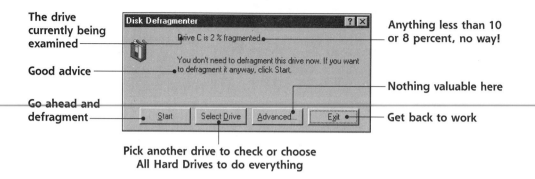

Anything less than 10 or 8 percent, no way!

Nothing valuable here

Get back to work

Pick another drive to check or choose All Hard Drives to do everything

Figure 16-11 To defragment or not to defragment, that is the question.

Pretty graphics to entertain you while you wait

Stop defragmenting now

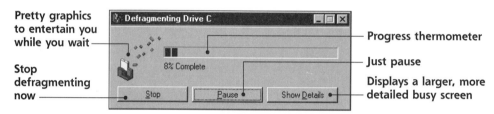

Progress thermometer

Just pause

Displays a larger, more detailed busy screen

Figure 16-12 I'm defragmenting now.

If you click Pause, Windows will temporarily halt defragmentation.

If you click Stop, Windows will first ask if you really want to stop, then it will stop if you claim to be serious.

4. Wait. If your screen saver kicks in, just press the CTRL key or wiggle the mouse to get rid of it. Or you can take a nap, because this does burn up a bit of time.

5. You're done!

Windows will announce that defragmentation is complete and will ask if you want to defragment another drive.

If you click Yes, pick a drive from the drop-down list and then return to Step 2. If you click No, you're really done.

TIP   Windows disk tools can also be found on the Start Thing menu. Choose
Programs → Accessories → System Tools . In addition to the three big tools covered in this chapter, you may also find some network tools and other helpful programs.

BONUS

Doing It All Automatically

Windows 95 comes with a special program called the *System Agent*. It's a tiny program that, like many employees at your office, just sits around and watches the clock. But when a given time passes, System Agent jumps up and performs some preassigned task. Those tasks can include backing up your PC, checking for errors, and defragmenting your hard drive. In fact, System Agent is preconfigured to do those things, typically in the wee hours of the morning.

To see if you have System Agent installed, check the loud time area on the taskbar. Double-click the System Agent icon to see a list of the tasks it performs, the times they're scheduled to run, and the results of the last operations. Because System Agent does its thing automatically, there's nothing else you need to do!

All About Disk Compression

Windows also comes with a disk compression program called *Drive Space*. Don't use it. Drive Space is a solution for a problem that no longer exists. In the old days, hard drives were too small for the new, bloated applications. For those small hard drives (under 100MB), Drive Space offered a solution that gave your PC more disk space. It was handy, but only in the past.

With today's PCs you probably don't need Drive Space. In addition to slightly slowing down your PC's performance, Drive Space is incompatible with many programs. Also, it's often a better and more reasonable solution to buy your PC a second hard drive instead of messing with compression nonsense.

Summary

The three common disk chores are: Backup, Defragment, and ScanDisk. All of these are necessary, but it's up to you to decide if they are a pain in the rear. As you become more familiar with Windows, you'll find these housekeeping tools will really benefit you.

You really don't want to mess up while doing disk chores, so make sure you got all of this:

☐   How to find your hard drive's Properties dialog box.

☐   How to back up your computer.

☐   How to restore something you backed up.

☐   How to run ScanDisk.

☐   How to defragment your drive.

CHAPTER SEVENTEEN

MESSING WITH YOUR PRINTER

IN THIS CHAPTER YOU LEARN THESE KEY SKILLS

FINDING THE PRINTERS FOLDER PAGE 215

USING THE PRINTERS FOLDER PAGE 217

SELECTING AND CONFIGURING A MAIN PRINTER
  PAGE 217

USING THE PRINT QUEUE PAGE 219

UNDERSTANDING FAXING PAGE 222

One of the major joys of Windows is it takes care of all the printing hassles for you. In the olden days of DOS, you had to muss with each program to get it to work with your printer. In Windows, you muss only once. And because Windows itself is in charge of printing, there is no more waiting for a slow printer. Windows sits and *spools* information out to the printer while you're off doing something else. This is truly one of the miracles of the twentieth century.

This chapter discusses using your printer, but it doesn't mention how to print something in Windows. That subject is covered in Chapter 4 in the section, "Printing Your Stuff."

Where the Printer Lurks

Obviously, the printer lurks somewhere nearby your computer, tethered by some sort of printer cable. Or there's an off-chance the printer is down the hall and you print on a network. But this is only where the printer *physically* lives. Mentally, you can find your printer by looking for its handy icon located somewhere in the bowels of Windows.

My li'l LaserJet

To find your printer's icon, you can always look in the Control Panel. Open My Computer to find the Control Panel's folder, or you can choose `Settings` → `Control Panel` from the Start Thing menu.

Control Panel

After opening the Control Panel, look for the folder named Printers. Open this folder by double-clicking on it and you've found your printer or, more accurately, you've found the Printers folder, which may contain your printer, network printers, faxes, and other goodies, all related to printing (see Figure 17-1).

The add-a-printer wizard (see Chapter 21, "Installing a Brand New Printer")

A fax something

Another fax something

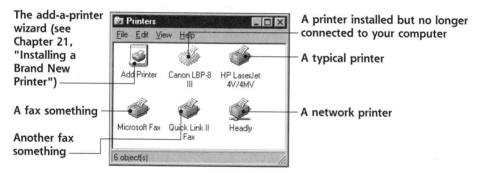

A printer installed but no longer connected to your computer

A typical printer

A network printer

Figure 17-1 Treasures in the Printers folder window

TIP A more direct route to the Printers folder is through My Computer, where it sits as a folder along side the Control Panel. Just double-click to open it and you'll see something similar to Figure 17-1.

Another place to find the Printers folder — an almost guaranteed instant abduction — is off the Start Thing menu. Choose `Settings` → `Printers`. Voilà, instant Printers folder (see Figure 17-1).

Peeping at the Printers Folder

The Printers folder is merely a waiting room for anything to do with printing in Windows. Honestly, you can't do much there. Most of the real action happens in your own printer's window, something called the *queue*, which the section "Playing with the Queue" later in this chapter discusses in detail.

Yo, My Main Printer

Odds are you have only one printer. If so, it's your main and only printer. But if your PC is hooked up to two printers (which is possible) or you have printers available on a network, then you must choose one of them as your main printer.

Follow these steps to pick a main printer:

1. Mosey on over to the Printers folder. Use any of the paths to the Printers folder as described in the first part of this chapter.

2. Point the mouse at the printer you want to choose as your main printer. Make sure it's a printer and not a fax machine thing.

3. Bring up the printer's shortcut menu. Right-click the mouse. The shortcut menu appears.

4. Choose Set As Default. If a ✔ check mark is already by this item, then this printer is your main printer. If not, choosing *Set As Default* makes it your main printer. This will now be the printer Windows uses whenever you print.

It's possible to change your main printer at any time; just repeat the previous steps. You can also change "on the fly," though, whenever you print something. This is done by choosing an alternative printer in the standard Print dialog box (see Figure 17-2). Use the drop-down list to pluck out another printer. Windows will print using this printer from then on as your main printer; you must repeat these steps to reestablish your original main printer.

Printer Setup and Properties Nonsense

Like almost everything else in Windows, your printer has its own Properties dialog box, chock-full of interesting options and gizmos. Honestly, I can tell you most of it is pretty useless. The following illustrates some of the highlights.

Display your printer's Properties dialog box by finding your printer (see the start of this chapter), right-clicking it, and choosing Properties from the shortcut menu. In the Print dialog box you can click the *Properties* button to bring up your printer's Properties dialog box, looking something like Figure 17-3.

Choose a new
printer from this
drop-down list

How the
printer feels

The printer's
brand name

Where the printer
sits (this is a
network printer)

Rude comments
(optional)

Click here to see the
printer's Properties
dialog box

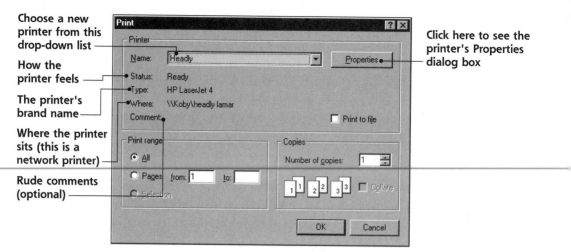

Figure 17-2   The standard, boring Print dialog box

Not all these
tabs appear for
every printer

Set the paper
type here

Set which way
the paper
prints here

These tabs are specific
to this HP printer

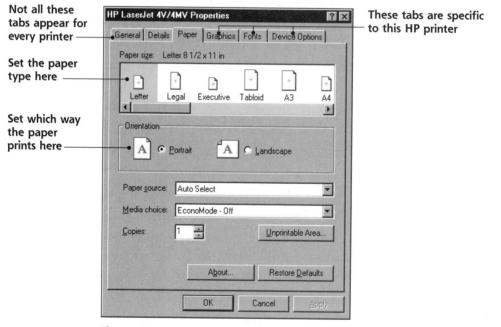

Figure 17-3   Any old printer's Properties dialog box

TIP   You must choose the Properties command from the printer's icon itself,
not from a shortcut. When you choose the Properties command for a
printer shortcut, such as one that may live on your desktop, you see the
Properties dialog box for that shortcut and not for the original printer.

Some printers have a special configuration button, located in the Details panel. Click the Details tab to bring this panel forward and look for the Setup button in the lower-left corner. Click on that button to run special setup software for your printer. Figure 17-4 shows what happens when you click the Setup button for an HP DeskJet 500 C, a color printer.

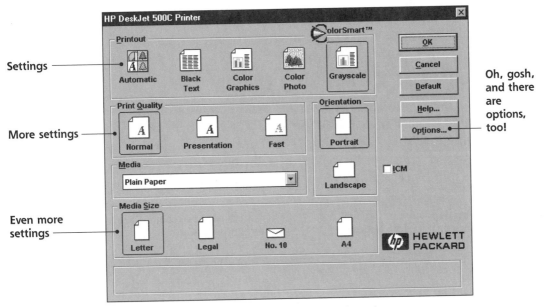

Figure 17-4 A cool Setup dialog box for a color printer

Network printers may lack certain control features in their Properties dialog box. In some cases, you can only set specific printer options at the computer directly connected to that printer.

Playing with the Queue

The word *queue* means a waiting line. When you're waiting to buy tickets in Britain, you're standing in a queue. In America, you stand in a line. Queue (pronounced "Q") is actually correct; compare its definition in the dictionary with that for *line* and you'll see what I mean. And this does have something to do with printing in Windows.

The Theoretical Hockey Puck of a Printing Queue

When you print something in Windows, the application sends it off to a special place in memory. There it sits, waiting to be printed. When the time comes, Windows prints a little bit of your document at a time, sending small bits out to the printer so nothing else you're doing in Windows is disturbed. This is known as *spooling;* spooling is what enables you to keep working while Windows prints. (Often times, your stuff prints quickly but, relatively speaking, Windows doesn't give printing a high priority.)

So you could, theoretically, print 100 documents and, while they're printing, be off playing the Minesweeper game. The 100 documents sit and wait in the printing queue (British), which is a line (American) of documents waiting to be printed. To see the line, open a handy printer icon near you.

Looking at the Printing Queue

To see the printing queue, you need to open your printer's icon. Double-click on it and the queue appears. Of course, if you have a quick printer, you may never see anything there (see Figure 17-5). But print several complex documents in a row and you may see them lurking in the queue: The document at the top of the list is printing; the others are waiting in the queue.

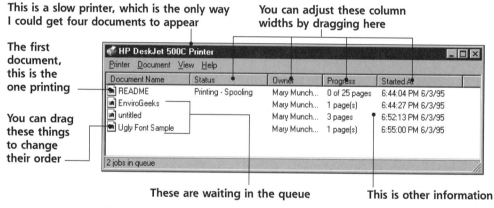

Figure 17-5 A typical printing queue

Pausing Your Printing

If you need to get at the printer or you want to pause printing for any reason, choose Printer → Pause Printing from the menu in your printer's dialog box (the queue box). I've done this a few times to change paper or to keep things inside the queue waiting until I had a whole boatload of things to print at once.

Note, while pausing printing stops Windows from sending something to the printer, your printer has its own memory and will continue to print a little bit after you've paused printing. Sometimes this may be half a page and, sometimes, six pages will print before things are "paused."

You can pause individual documents by clicking on them in the queue and choosing Document → Pause Printing from the menu.

Moving Documents in the Queue

Things print in the order you printed them. This makes sense; the people who ordered food ahead of you in the line, er, queue at McDonald's get their food before you. But if you're really hungry, or you want one document to print before another, simply move it up toward the top of the queue: Click on the document's icon and drag it up. Just as you would elbow your way to the front of the line at McDonald's. Easy enough.

Killing Documents in the Queue

Sometimes you may not want something to print. For example, you just pounded out a steamed letter to your department head about what an incompetent twit she is and then she phones to say you got that big raise. Oops.

Immediately, you can open your printer's windows to see the queue. Locate the offending document and click on it once with the mouse to highlight it. Then choose `Document` → `Cancel Printing`. *ZAP!* The document is gone.

If you choose `Printer` → `Purge Print Jobs` from the menu, every print job is purged.

You should be quick with this one. Only if something is waiting to print can you yank it back. Otherwise, like words uttered, no way exists to stop it.

TIP **If you cancel a document that's printing, you may end up with part of it stuck in the printer. To clear the document from the printer, press your printer's Page Eject or Form Feed button. This will spit that final page from the printer and clear the document completely from memory.**

SIDE TRIP

NAME YOUR PRINTER

You can name your printer anything. Just click on the printer's icon and press the F2 key — just as you would rename a file. And there's no reason for a dull printer name. In fact, consider these clever printer name examples:

* Eventually
* Firecracker
* Gutenberg
* Jammer
* Kinko

* Mr. Slug
* Shredder
* Smudgy
* The Hammer

BONUS

Basic Fax

Faxing should be similar to printing. If you think of a fax machine as another type of printer, but one that's miles away and you have to dial a phone to get it to print, then the image holds. Alas, this image didn't hold at Microsoft. To them, faxing is an event, one that's dealt with in a strange manner. I recommend you forget Microsoft and get a third-party faxing program and use it instead of Windows. If you do this, you'll use the Print command to send a fax; choosing the fax modem as a printer instead of your normal printer. Now, if you really, really want to, you can use Win95's fax thing, but it's not the most pleasant experience. It's kinda up there with getting a root canal.

Follow these steps to send a fax:

1. Create the document to fax. Unlike printing to fax, you must create the document you're faxing separately. You don't have to quit your program to send the fax, but the document must be created and saved to disk before you can fax it.

2. Choose Start Thing → Programs → Accessories → Fax → Compose New Fax. This fires up the Microsoft Fax program, which may or may not work on your computer. If it works, then you'll see the Fax Wizard, as shown in Figure 17-6.

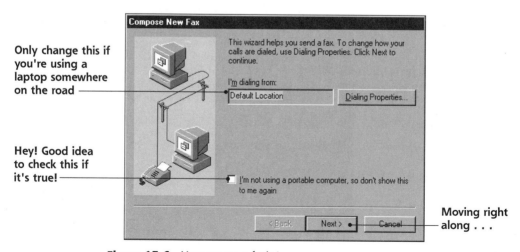

Only change this if you're using a laptop somewhere on the road

Hey! Good idea to check this if it's true!

Moving right along . . .

Figure 17-6 Here we go a-faxin'.

3. Click Next. Now it's time to type in the phone number. For example, if you're sending a fax to the Pope, you'd type in his private fax machine number, which is CENSORED BY PUBLISHER. Figure 17-7 describes the current Fax Wizard dialog box in more detail.

Type the recipient's name here

Windows suggests you put your current area code here

You can click this button to send the fax to multiple recipients

You can select their info from your address book here

Type the phone number here

Multiple recipients appear here

Moving right along

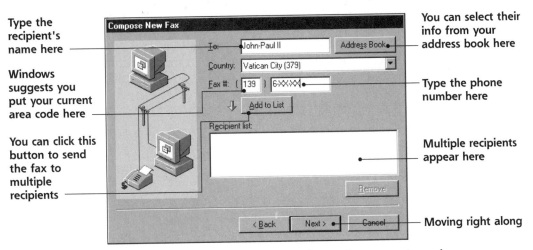

Figure 17-7   The Fax Wizard wants to know where to send your fax.

4. Click Next. The next dialog box in the Fax Wizard suggests a cover page (see Figure 17-8). Pick one from the list. It will be filled in according to the information you've already given this dialog box.

Click here for no cover page

Click here and then . . .

. . . select a cover page here

Don't bother

Moving right along

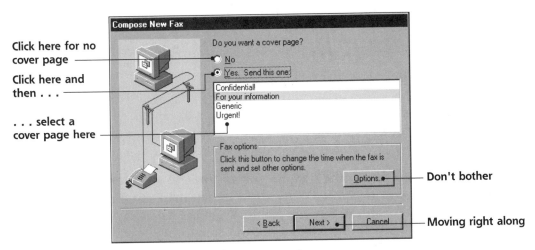

Figure 17-8   Pick a fax cover page here.

TIP You can use a program called Cover Page Editor to modify or create your own fax cover pages. Cover Page Editor is located off the Start Thing menu: choose `Programs` → `Accessories` → `Fax` → `Cover Page Editor`. It's too complex to describe in this paragraph, but you can use it to view, modify, or create your own interesting fax cover letters.

5. Click Next. The next dialog box enables you to fill in additional information about the fax, info that will be stuffed into the cover page (if you elected to send one).

6. Fill in the *Subject* field.

7. Fill in a *Note* if you want. Make sure a ✔ check mark is in the box by *Start note on cover page*.

8. Click Next. Ah ha! You're done.

9. Click Finish. The little "I am printing" dialog box appears; Windows assembles your document and prepares to send it.

You'll see a Microsoft Fax Status dialog box appear (see Figure 17-9).

You'll hear the modem dialed.

The other fax will pick up.

Tension builds. . . .

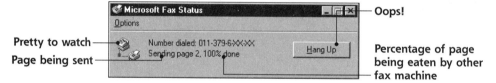

Figure 17-9 Fax sending dialog box

Your fax has printed. No fanfare. Nothing really special. Your modem has sent the fax — along with your cover page — to a fax machine elsewhere on the planet.

TIP Reactivating the Print dialog box at this time to reset your main printer may be a good idea: Press CTRL+P to bring up the Print dialog box, then choose your original, favorite printer from the *Name* drop-down list. This way, the next time you go to print something, it will print out on the printer and Windows won't try to send another fax.

Summary

When it comes to your printer, Windows is truly master of the universe. Windows will take care of all the printing hassles for you.

Are you leaving this chapter knowing the following?:

- ☐ How to pick a main printer.
- ☐ How to pause your printer.
- ☐ How to stop a document from printing.

IN THIS CHAPTER YOU LEARN THESE KEY SKILLS

FINDING THE CONTROL PANEL   PAGE 227

USING ACCESSIBILITY OPTIONS   PAGE 229

USING THE JOYSTICK ICON   PAGE 230

USING THE KEYBOARD ICON   PAGE 231

USING THE MODEMS ICON   PAGE 233

LOOKING UP OTHER ICONS IN DIFFERENT PARTS OF THIS BOOK   PAGE 235

he Control Panel is the dinker's paradise. It's where you have direct access to tweak, twiddle, or tangle with any or all of Windows' various settings and options. You could spend weeks there. You may have already. This chapter discusses the various icon/programs in the Control Panel, how they work, and why bother.

The Great Control Panel Hunt

he Control Panel lives as a special folder icon. You can find it right in the main My Computer window or you can pluck it out from the Start Thing menu: choose Settings → Control Panel .

Control Panel

X-REF If dinking is your passion, you might consider pasting down a shortcut copy of the Control Panel on the desktop. Chapter 14 tells you how.

Open the Control Panel folder by double-clicking on it — just as you'd open any folder. Its window appears looking something like Figure 18-1. What you see may be different; certain programs may add their own icons to the Control Panel, and you may not see some specialty items, such as the Accessibility Options, as shown in Figure 18-1.

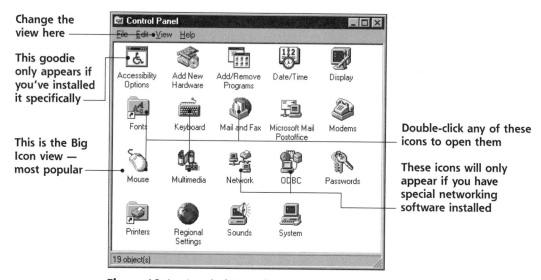

Change the view here

This goodie only appears if you've installed it specifically

This is the Big Icon view — most popular

Double-click any of these icons to open them

These icons will only appear if you have special networking software installed

Figure 18-1 A typical Control Panel window

The way the Control Panel works is just like any folder: You double-click on an icon to run a special control gizmo. The icon usually opens a window or dialog box where additional settings are made.

If you want a detailed list of what each icon in the Control Panel is for, then choose View → Details from the menu. The icons are then listed with a brief description listed for your convenience. If you want the icons the way they were, then choose View → Large Icons .

The remaining sections in this chapter detail the functions of the various components in the Control Panel.

Working the various icons in the Control Panel presents you with a smorgasbord of various dialog box options, gizmos, and gadgets.

X-REF **See Chapter 26 for more information on how these various options, gizmos, and gadgets work.**

Items Not Covered Elsewhere in This Book

The following sections outline various Control Panel icons and their functions. This group consists of icons covered only in this chapter, which you can probably interpret as their function isn't crucial or what they do isn't exciting enough to appear elsewhere.

Accessibility Options, or Making Windows Friendly to Everyone

The Accessibility Options icon is used to assist handicapped or physically impaired folk with using Windows. It contains options for using a keyboard with one hand, having visual clues instead of sounds appear, a keyboard-simulated mouse, and other settings to make using a computer more pleasurable.

Accessibility
Options

You must install this icon as an optional extra. Refer to the section "Adding the Rest of Windows" in Chapter 11.

Double-click on the Accessibility Options icon to open its window. The Accessibility Properties dialog box appears with several tabs and panels for making various adjustments to the way Windows works. I won't tread through each one here because most are pretty obvious in function and use. Here are some highlights:

✳ If you must use the keyboard with only one hand, consider turning on the Sticky Keys option. This allows you to press SHIFT, CTRL, or ALT key combinations one key at a time. So you can type CTRL+P by pressing the CTRL key and then the P key, one after the other. To set this up, go to the Keyboard tab and put a ✔ check mark in the *Use Sticky Keys* box, and then click on the Settings button for more options and information.

* The Sound Sentry option can be used to have Windows offer visual clues when it would normally bleep the speaker. (I like this option because loud computers annoy me.) Go to the Sound panel and put a ✔ check mark in the *Use Sound Sentry* box. Then click the Settings button to make more adjustments and get an explanation of what's happening. The *Show Sounds* option is also pretty cool.

* If you're visually impaired, you might want to check out the Display panel. There you can set up Windows to splash things on the screen in high-contrast mode. A bizarre key combination sets this up: Left ALT+Left SHIFT+PRINT SCREEN. I suppose they don't want anyone accidentally falling into this mode.

X-REF Also check out Chapter 22 for information on changing Windows' color scheme in other ways. Chapter 23 discusses how you can make the mouse pointer larger and easier to find.

As usual, after making any changes here, Windows may beg that it wants to restart your computer. Click Yes, because it's better to do this now than dawdle around and forget about the changes.

Happy, Happy, Joystick

The Joystick icon only appears if you have a joystick attached to your Windows computer. This is silly because most Windows games use a mouse. And DOS games that use a joystick typically require you to calibrate them when you start the DOS game. Even so, you can double-click the Joystick icon to do some in-Windows calibration.

Joystick

Supposedly, Microsoft has included splendid Windows game technology that's supposed to allow for nifty Windows games in the future. This is why the Joystick icon was included in the Control Panel. But I wouldn't hold your breath if I were you.

 TIP Your Joystick may have come with its own Control Panel icon for making adjustments or it may have a separate utility you can run from the Start Thing menu. In all cases, using that program is better than using the generic Joystick icon.

Spicing Up a Keyboard

The Keyboard icon allows you to make minor adjustments to your keyboard. Nothing major can be done there — like rearranging the keys to a more proper pattern or speeding up your fingers. And this is where you can set up a foreign language keyboard, if typing in French is your thing.

Keyboard

To display the Keyboard Properties dialog box, double-click on the Keyboard icon. You'll see something similar to Figure 18-2. Honestly, unless you're having trouble with your typing, don't bother with anything there.

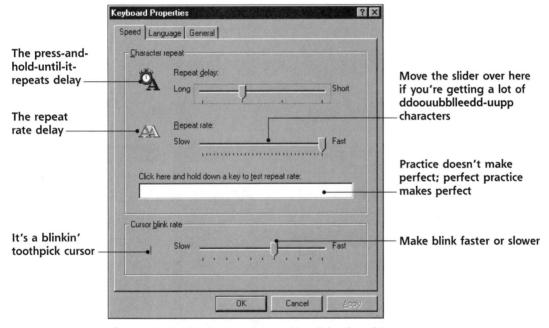

The press-and-hold-until-it-repeats delay

The repeat rate delay

Move the slider over here if you're getting a lot of ddoouubblleedd-uupp characters

Practice doesn't make perfect; perfect practice makes perfect

It's a blinkin' toothpick cursor

Make blink faster or slower

Figure 18-2 The Keyboard Properties dialog box thing

The Language panel can be used if you ever plan to use your keyboard to type in a foreign language, such as English. Seriously, if you, for example, occasionally type letters to French people, you can configure Windows to have a French keyboard ready for you, complete with various French letters.

Follow these steps to change the language on your keyboard:

1. Follow the steps in this chapter for locating the Control Panel, then double-click on the Keyboard icon to open it.

2. Click the Language tab to bring that panel forward. If you already have two or more languages selected, skip to the last step (but don't click on OK).

3. Click on the Add button. The Add Language dialog box appears.

4. Choose *French (Standard)* from the drop-down list.

5. Click on OK. You're returned to the Keyboard Properties dialog box. You'll notice you now have two languages listed, plus the *Switch Languages* region is activated. This means you can now use the key combination marked with a dot to switch keyboard language layouts. For example, to switch to a French keyboard (with special French characters available) as set up in Figure 18-3, press the CTRL+SHIFT key combination. *Voila! Vous pouvez maintenant taper des mots doux à votre chère Française secrète.*

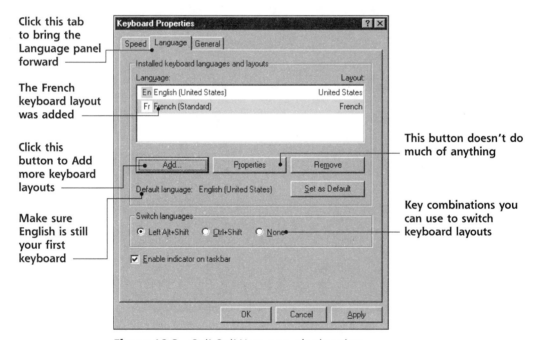

Click this tab to bring the Language panel forward

The French keyboard layout was added

Click this button to Add more keyboard layouts

Make sure English is still your first keyboard

This button doesn't do much of anything

Key combinations you can use to switch keyboard layouts

Figure 18-3   Oui! Oui! Vous avez selectionné un clavier français!

6. Click on OK to exit the Keyboard Properties dialog box.

You'll be asked to insert your Windows setup disk(s) to copy over the files for the new keyboard layout — so be prepared when asked! (You don't have to reset your computer, though.)

With this option set, you'll see a little icon in the Loud Time area, letting you know which keyboard is selected. It's really boring: En for English, for example.

When you can press the proper key combination to switch to French, for example, the En changes to Fr for French. Boring, but informative.

No, I'm sorry, switching to a French keyboard doesn't mean you'll instantly become a master of the French language.

Hey! And you'll need to look up the French (or whatever) keyboard layout in your Windows manual. This will tell you where all the funny frank keys are located.

Merry Modems

The modem guy in the Control Panel gives you access to a configuration panel for your modem. You can also get there by choosing Modem Setup from any of a number of other places: in a communications program, the Phone Dialer, or from the little modem guy who appears in the taskbar's Loud Time when you're using your modem. Whatever, when you open the Modems icon in the Control Panel you see the Modems Properties dialog box similar to the one shown in Figure 18-4.

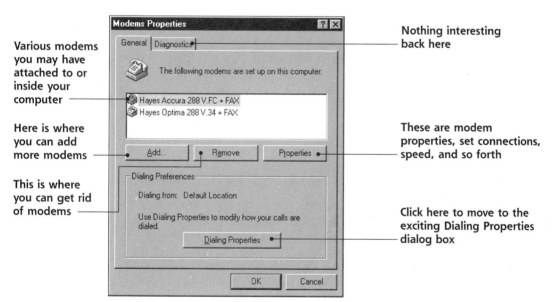

Figure 18-4 The illustrious Modems Properties dialog box

Nothing of radical importance in the Modems Properties dialog box; don't be seduced into wasting any time there.

You may want to configure the Dialing Properties information. If you don't do it now, you'll be asked about it later, when you use your modem. Click on the *Dialing Properties* button to see the Dialing Properties dialog box (see Figure 18-5). This will help your modem programs dial numbers; it also comes in handy when faxing. The information in the figures will help you get around.

Modems

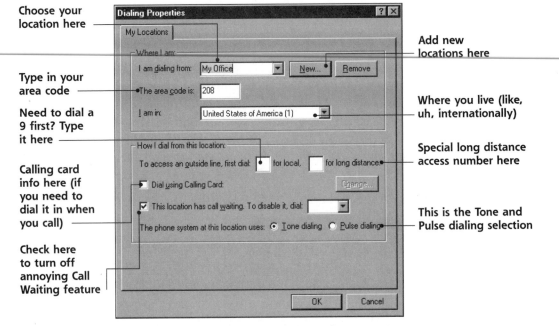

Choose your location here

Type in your area code

Need to dial a 9 first? Type it here

Calling card info here (if you need to dial it in when you call)

Check here to turn off annoying Call Waiting feature

Add new locations here

Where you live (like, uh, internationally)

Special long distance access number here

This is the Tone and Pulse dialing selection

Figure 18-5   The even more exciting Dialing Properties dialog box

TIP   If you want to know bunches and bunches more about modems, buy *Modems For Dummies* by Tina Rathbone. Tina does an excellent job of explaining the whole modem thing.

WEB PATH   You can also go on the Web, to

http:\\www.dummies.com

and search for *Modems For Dummies*.

Other Strange and Wonderful Goodies

No limit exists to the madness you may encounter in the Control Panel. Often lots of interesting things will be available to tweak and dink there, each of which controls something interesting in Windows or in some hardware attached to your computer.

My best advice is *be careful*. You shouldn't mess with some settings. Always be sure to read the Help file or any documentation before setting various options. Also, be aware of this: Choosing a new option may require your computer to reset. It's best to do all your dinking at once. Keep your dinking time separate from your work time.

Items Covered Elsewhere in This Book

A lot of the dinking that takes place in the Control Panel is covered elsewhere in this book, in chapters devoted to the subject at hand. Table 18-1 will tell you where to look for various Control Panel icons.

TABLE 18-1 Dinking Stuff

Icon	Name	Description
Add New Hardware	ADD NEW HARDWARE	This icon opens the Add Hardware wizard. Use this thing any time you add new hardware to your computer. The wizard will examine your system and discover what you've installed. It's all part of Windows' Plug & Play feature, which supposedly saves you setup time. See Chapter 21 for more information on installing new hardware and setting up your printer.
Add/Remove Programs	ADD/REMOVE PROGRAMS	This icon is used to help you install software (though all it really does is hunt for the Setup or Install program on a floppy disk or CD-ROM drive). Anyway, it's an improvement over the way things worked in the olden days. See Chapter 11 for more information on adding new software. Removing old software is also covered there.
Date/Time	DATE/TIME	This icon fires up the Date/Time Properties dialog box, which you can also get to from the Loud Time on the taskbar. Chapter 6 gives you information on how to work the Date/Time Properties dialog box.

(continued)

TABLE 18-1   Dinking Stuff (*continued*)

Icon	Name	Description
Display	DISPLAY	This icon in the Control Panel is a shortcut to the Display Properties dialog box, which you can get to directly from the desktop as well: Bring up the desktop's shortcut menu and choose Properties. See Chapter 22 for information on the Display Properties dialog box. Also, look into Chapter 23 for information on the screen saver, also located in the Display Properties dialog box. See "Saving the Screen from Boredom."
Fonts	FONTS	The fonts folder opens to reveal all the fonts (or most of them, at least) installed on your computer. There you can look at the fonts, print previews, delete fonts, or install new fonts. See Chapter 19 for more information on fonts (it's just a barrel of fun).
Mouse	MOUSE	The mouse icon opens the Mouse Properties dialog box where you can mess with the mouse, change its pointer, adjust the buttons, speed, and so on. Eek! Eek! See Chapter 23, "A More Lively Mouse Pointer" for some pointers on mouse pointers.
Network	NETWORK	The Network icon in the Control Panel is something you probably don't want to mess with at all. Network stuff is such voodoo, no one should really bother. This icon only appears if you're using Windows on a network. Chapter 20 discusses the network and the areas you can mess with a bit.
Passwords	PASSWORDS	This icon is where you change your password. To be honest, Windows doesn't rightly care about your password; just type in a new one if you forget the old one and Windows will, do-de-do, change it right like that.

Icon	Name	Description
Printers	PRINTERS	This folder in the Control Panel opens a special window where your printer(s) live, along with their cousins, the fax machine and a special icon for installing new printers. See Chapter 17 for anything to do with your printer . . . except for the actual task of printing, of course, which is covered in Chapter 4, "Printing Your Stuff."
Sounds	SOUNDS	Obviously, you need a sound card to make sounds really happen, but the Sounds icon still appears in the Control Panel whether or not your PC has sound equipment. Using the Sounds Properties dialog box is covered in Chapter 23, in the section "A More Euphonious PC."

X-REF One piece of the Passwords puzzle covered elsewhere is the capability of Windows to configure itself differently for different users. Mosey on up to Chapter 20 for more information.

If you're using a screen saver, it can also be password-protected, which essentially locks your entire computer (and no way exists to regain your password if you forget). See "Shhh! Using the Password Option" in Chapter 23.

BONUS

Items You Just Don't Need

Some stuff is too hairy to mess with at all. The following list includes several items you may find lurking in the Control Panel, ones I'd never bother changing, either because they're too complex or changing them just isn't done by us mere mortals.

The Mail and Fax icon contains various advanced and confusing settings to use the Microsoft Exchange. While it wouldn't kill you to wander through that dialog box and ogle at the settings, it all seems like a colossal waste of time.

Mail and Fax

The Microsoft Mail Postoffice icon doesn't need messing with unless you plan on tweaking the network mail system. This is a job best left for those who know how mail works; while the Mail Wizard that runs when you open this icon seems friendly enough, I'll bet your network administrator would rather not have you tweak it.

Microsoft Mail
  Postoffice

The Multimedia icon is a locus for various multimedia things in your computer, all of which you don't really need to bother. These settings were either customized by Windows when it was installed or by the Add New Hardware wizard when you upgraded your PC. No reason exists to tread those waters now — unless you're directed to do so by some hardware or software manual that makes *specific* suggestions.

Multimedia

Who really knows what ODBC means or what it does? You'd think, in their efforts to make Windows easy to understand, Microsoft would come up with something a bit more pleasant for this item. Alas, it just has "don't touch me!" written all over it.

ODBC

The Regional Settings icon opens an interesting dialog box, which is kind of fun to examine. Options exist for changing various cultural and national settings for different parts of the world. Weird and wacky, but not worth frustrating yourself.

Regional
Settings

The System icon opens the System Properties dialog box, which is the same dialog box you'd see if you chose Properties from My Computer's shortcut menu. The items there are complex and should not be disturbed.

System

If you don't have the Telephony icon, you're lucky. This one is a fine example of something average folk shouldn't mess with. Heck, filling out the income tax form is a lot easier than understanding how this sucker goes about its business.

Telephony

(You may not have this icon in your Control Panel; it's only available with certain Windows configurations.)

Summary

The Control Panel is not for serious, goal-oriented people. It's for dinking, pure and simple. This is where you have direct access to tweak, twiddle or tangle with any or all of Windows' various settings and options.

So that you can appropriately dink, make sure you learned the following:

☐ How to find the Control Panel.

☐ How the various icons in the Control Panel are used.

☐ How to change the language on your keyboard.

FUN WITH FONTS

IN THIS CHAPTER YOU LEARN THESE KEY SKILLS

FINDING THE FONTS FOLDER   PAGE 241

VIEWING FONTS   PAGE 243

INSTALLING NEW FONTS   PAGE 245

DELETING FONTS   PAGE 246

USING THE CHARACTER MAP PROGRAM   PAGE 246

There really isn't anything fun about fonts. They're basically different styles of type you can see on the screen, use in documents, and send to the printer. Hub caps are more interesting (especially when they pop off on the freeway and transform themselves into spinning metal disks of death).

Fonts add pizzazz, but that's not the subject of this chapter. With Windows 95, fonts have collected themselves in one location. Now working with and organizing fonts is easier and more sane than it ever was. It's all worthy of a good look.

Where the Fonts Folder Lurks

All Windows fonts (well, almost all of them) are kept in their own Fonts folder. It's a special folder sitting right beneath the Windows folder on your hard drive. But you don't have to wade through My Computer or the Explorer to get there; a handy shortcut to the Fonts folder lives inside the Control Panel.

Follow these steps to find the Fonts folder:

1. Open a handy Control Panel near you. You can find a Control Panel icon located in My Computer's main window. There's also one you can grab from the Start Thing menu: Press CTRL+ESC, S, C.

Control Panel

2. Double-click on the Fonts folder to open it. You'll see its contents displayed, similar to Figure 19-1. That's the Big Icon view in the figure; like any other My Computer window, you can change the view to something else.

Fonts

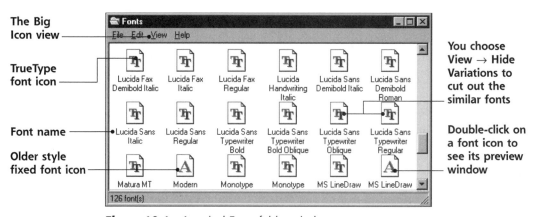

Figure 19-1 A typical Fonts folder window

MISSING AND **AWOL** *FONTS*

Only Windows TrueType fonts live in the Font folder. Other types of fonts, such as those supplied by Adobe for use with their ATM software, will probably live in another folder. This chapter doesn't cover using ATM fonts or the ATM software.

Playing with the Fonts Folder

The Fonts folder is the center of font activity on your computer. I know, big deal. But it's extremely nice to have a central place for fonts, especially to have a way to preview and print them before you use them. That's what the Fonts folder offers, which makes it handy for those times you sit and agonize over fonts (which is a lot more often than you'd think).

Here a Font, There a Font, Everywhere a Font Font

Fonts in Windows are used to form the text you see on the screen and the text that's printed. Primarily, there is one type of font, the TrueType font. These fonts are earmarked by the T-T icon in the Fonts folder (see Figure 19-1).

Matura MT

Another type of font is the screen font or fixed font. This type of font, marked by the letter A (see Figure 19-1), is an older style font primarily used by old Windows applications.

Modern

Both the TrueType and fixed fonts appear on the screen as they do on your printer. The TrueType font is best, because it can be any size, big or little, and still look good. The fixed fonts only look good in a handful of sizes; when you try to make the font too big or too little, it looks terrible.

A third type of font is the printer font, which is a font your printer can produce with ease. In most cases, your printer will come with a disk full of TrueType counterparts you can see on the screen — but not all printers come with such a disk. An older Canon printer of mine has a beautiful set of fonts, but on the screen they all look strange. Because Windows doesn't know about the printer fonts, it *substitutes* what it thinks is a similar font on the screen. The result is kind of maddening, so most people (obviously) tend to avoid printer fonts, except for those that have TrueType counterparts for the screen.

Figure 19-2 shows a typical *Fonts* drop-down list in a word processor. There you can get some kind of clue as to which type of font you're using; in addition to the font's name, a small icon appears next to the font, telling you which type it is. There are three: TrueType, printer, and fixed font (no icon).

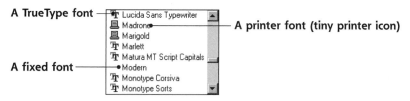

A TrueType font ——— *Lucida Sans Typewriter*

A printer font (tiny printer icon)

A fixed font ———

Figure 19-2 A typical Fonts drop-down list thing

TIP Use TrueType fonts instead of other fonts when you can. TrueType fonts will look good at any size and on any printer.

My Font's Uglier than Your Font!

To see what a font looks like — the sneak preview — double-click on its icon in the Fonts folder. You'll see a special Quick View window displaying all sorts of details, as shown in Figure 19-3.

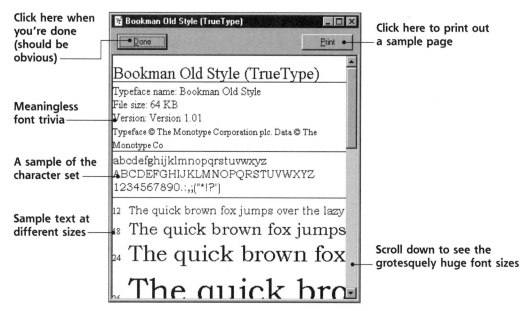

Click here when you're done (should be obvious) ———

Click here to print out a sample page

Meaningless font trivia ———

A sample of the character set ———

Sample text at different sizes ———

Scroll down to see the grotesquely huge font sizes

Figure 19-3 A sneak peek at the Bookman Old Style font

When you examine a font, look for certain special characters. Admittedly, every font uses the Roman alphabet, but subtle differences appear in the letters. Pay close attention to the lowercase G, for example. Also look at the capital W and the capital Q.

X-REF For more exact font differences and some suggestions on how to use them, you'll need to refer to a desktop publishing and design book. My favorite is anything by Roger Parker. His *Looking Good in Print* is a classic for any budding desktop designer.

Adding Fonts to Your Collection

New fonts are added to your system using a special command in the Fonts window — a command that doesn't appear in any other My Computer window.

Follow these steps to add new fonts to your system:

1. Open the Fonts window. See "Where the Fonts Folder Lurks" earlier in this chapter.

2. Choose File → Install New Font . The Add Fonts dialog box appears (see Figure 19-4).

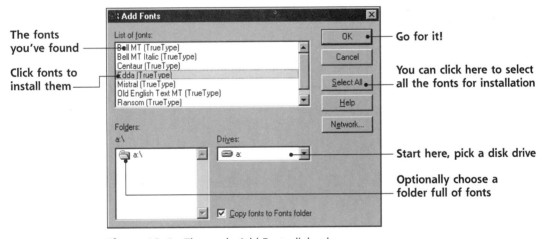

The fonts you've found — Click fonts to install them

Go for it!

You can click here to select all the fonts for installation

Start here, pick a disk drive

Optionally choose a folder full of fonts

Figure 19-4   The crude Add Fonts dialog box

3. Use the *Drives* and *Folders* windows to locate your font files. For example, if you have a disk full of fonts, stick it into drive (A:) and choose that drive from the Drives drop-down list. It will take Windows a while to read the font names and such. Be patient. You can also look in any folder on your hard drive for the fonts; use the Folders window for that.

4. Choose the fonts you want to install from the *List of fonts* list. You can select groups of fonts at a time to install. The method here is the same as for selecting a group of files. (Refer to "Crowd Control, or Working with Groups of Files" in Chapter 14 for the how-tos.)

5. Click on OK. *Chugga-chugga.* Soon the fonts are copied to the Fonts folder window, where they'll live safely on your hard drive. There's no need to reset; the fonts are ready to use.

Removing an Old Cruddy Font

Font glut happens. Fonts can sprout up on your computer thicker than a clump of Canadian Thistle. While this gives you endless variety, there are many fonts you will never really use. Also, font glut tends to slow down you and your computer. And it can take days to scroll through a heavily laden *Font* drop-down list.

Follow these steps to kill off old unused fonts:

1. Open the Fonts window.

2. Select the font(s) you want to kill off by clicking that font. The font is selected and ready for action. (Follow the instructions in Chapter 14, "Crowd Control, or Working with Groups of Files" for information on selecting a group of fonts.)

3. Choose File → Delete . A warning box appears asking if you're sure you want to delete the font.

4. Click Yes. The font is deleted.

 Although the *Undo* command isn't available, you can undelete the font. See Chapter 15, "A Quick, Odorless Peek into the Recycle Bin to Restore Something" for the details.

BONUS

Weeding Out Cool Characters with the Character Map Program

While you can preview what a font will look like in the Fonts folder, you really can't get at any of the interesting characters it offers. I'm not talking about the regular alphabetic characters. I mean the strange and wonderful characters included with special fonts such as Wingdings and Zapf Dingbats. These fonts contain all sorts of fun stuff you may want to use to spice up dull documents. You need the Character Map program to get at those fun characters.

Start the Character Map program. From the Start Thing menu, choose `Programs` → `Accessories` → `Character Map`. The Character Map program appears, looking similar to Figure 19-5.

X-REF On the off-chance the Character Map isn't installed on your computer, see the section "Adding the Rest of Windows" in Chapter 11 for information on getting it.

Choose a font here —

Click a character to see it magnified —

Double-click to paste the character —

Characters are pasted here for copying

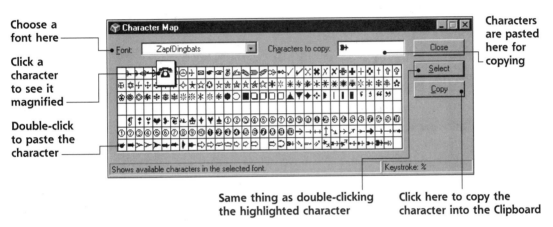

Same thing as double-clicking the highlighted character

Click here to copy the character into the Clipboard

Figure 19-5 The Character Map program

Start by choosing a font from the drop-down list. This displays all the characters available with that font, especially the bonus characters in addition to the standard alphabet.

To enlarge a character for better viewing, click the mouse on that character but keep the mouse button down (see Figure 19-5).

If you double-click on a character, it's sent up to the paste zone. You can double-click on any number of characters from any number of fonts. Click on the Copy button to copy them to the Windows Clipboard. From there, you can paste them into any application capable of receiving pasted text.

Remember to close or minimize the Character Map window when you're done playing.

TIP Microsoft Word has a special command that works just like the Character Map program. If you choose `Insert` → `Symbol` from Word's menu, you'll see a dialog box similar to the Character Map. You can use that dialog box to insert special characters right into your document; just click on the Insert button.

X-REF If you find yourself using the Character Map often, consider making it one of those programs Windows automatically starts each time you turn on your computer. See Chapter 5, "Applications That Start Automatically (Amazing!)."

Unfortunately there's no way in Windows to display a list of all your fonts and what they look like — not all at once. But you can open font icons to see individual fonts and you can print those images on your printer. In fact, I recommend you print all your fonts, or at least those you plan on using most of the time. Keep them in a little folder or a three-ring binder by your computer. This will help you pick out a proper font for your designs.

Summary

Okay, now you know the truth. I lied! Even though this chapter is called Fun With Fonts, fonts really aren't that fun, even though they do add pizzazz to your work.

To make you feel like you learned something, go over the list and see if you know the following:

- ☐ Where is the Fonts folder located?
- ☐ How do you add a new font to your computer?
- ☐ How do you get rid of unused fonts?

WINDOWS AND EVERYONE ELSE'S PC (THE JOYS OF NETWORKING)

IN THIS CHAPTER YOU LEARN THESE KEY SKILLS

UNDERSTANDING NETWORKING
   (VERY BRIEF)   PAGE 250

WORKING IN THE NETWORK
   NEIGHBORHOOD   PAGE 250

DOING STUFF ON ANOTHER COMPUTER   PAGE 253

SHARING STUFF ON THE NETWORK   PAGE 253

GETTING FRUSTRATED WITH WINDOWS
   MAIL   PAGE 262

USING WINPOPUP INSTEAD OF MAIL   PAGE 266

20

Happiness is a network that works. When they work, networks can be a joy. For example, I have three computers hooked up to one printer. Not all the computers are even in the same office, yet they all *share* one printer. That's the joy of networking. It's all about sharing, offering your disk drives up for use by others, and, likewise, stealing things from their disk drives.

This chapter goes into light detail on using Windows' built-in network to get your work done. There's just too much technical stuff to bother with anything more complex.

Networking Nonsense

If your computer is hooked up to some type of network, then Windows saw it when it was installed and everything is set up for network activity. Windows saw your network card. It saw the network hose leading out the back of your computer. Everything is done. Now you need only worry about using the network to get work done.

TIP Your office should have a networking guru in charge of configuring your PC's networking hardware and software. All you need to know is that you're on the network and you can use Windows 95 to access other computers and those other computers can access your PC.

Bonus: Your computer should have a network name. Make sure the networking guru tells you the name. (It might be found taped to the top of your monitor.)

It's a Beautiful Day in the Network Neighborhood

The Network Neighborhood is simply the name Windows gives the doorway into other computers on your network. Other than the fact you're looking at other computers, it all works the same as My Computer. There are windows, My Computer's toolbar, different views, and so on.

Prowling Around the Network Neighborhood

Open the Network Neighborhood icon on the desktop. You'll see a window appear, looking something like Figure 20-1. That shows you all the computers up, running, and on the network in your workgroup. Figure 20-2 shows a different view of the Network Neighborhood.

Network
Neighborhood

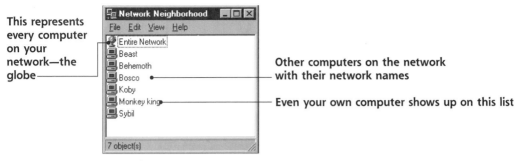

This represents every computer on your network—the globe

Other computers on the network with their network names

Even your own computer shows up on this list

Figure 20-1 Other computers lurking in the Network Neighborhood

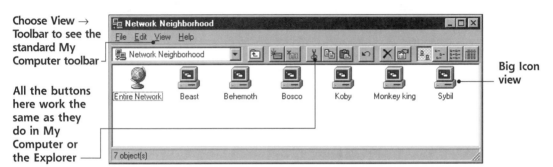

Choose View → Toolbar to see the standard My Computer toolbar

All the buttons here work the same as they do in My Computer or the Explorer

Big Icon view

Figure 20-2 Network Neighborhood — different view

Browsing Other Computers à la My Computer

To find out more about a computer on the network, open it; double-click on the network computer's icon and you'll see another window displaying what that computer has to offer. Again, everything appears as it would in My Computer (see Figure 20-3).

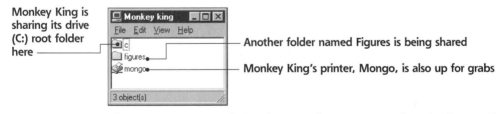

Monkey King is sharing its drive (C:) root folder here

Another folder named Figures is being shared

Monkey King's printer, Mongo, is also up for grabs

Figure 20-3 A view of what the network computer Monkey King has to offer

Anything you see in another computer's window is up for grabs. You can open folders, copy files, paste files, run programs, make shortcuts on your desktop — just about anything.

If a computer doesn't share anything, then its window will be blank when you open it.

Some computers are password protected; before you can peer into their shared folders you must enter the proper password. When you try to open such a folder, you'll see a dialog box similar to the one shown in Figure 20-4. Carefully type in the password, cross your fingers, and click the OK button. If you guessed correctly, you'll be able to use the computer.

This is what you're trying to access, drive (C:) on the computer named Behemoth ———

Type the password here ⌐

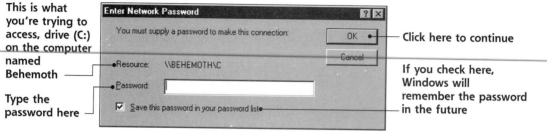

Click here to continue

If you check here, Windows will remember the password in the future

Figure 20-4   You must enter a password before you can access some network goodies.

There are two types of passwords: A read-only password, which gives you access merely to browse through another computer's folders, and a full password, which gives you full access. See the section "Surrendering Your Hardware to the Network" for information about setting the passwords.

Spanning the Globe

If you open the globe icon in Network Neighborhood, you'll see a window displaying all the different workgroups on your entire network (Figure 20-5). This enables you to browse through them, though that's probably not a good idea because you were assigned to one workgroup for a reason and network managers hate browsers.

Entire Network

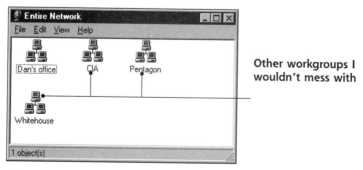

Other workgroups I wouldn't mess with

Figure 20-5   Open the globe to see various workgroups in your network.

Using the Explorer/Network Neighborhood Connection

The Network Neighborhood also appears in the Explorer and in those little tree structures that appear in various drop-down lists. Using the Network Neighborhood there is no different than using other items on the Explorer, though you're opening other computers to see what they have to offer instead of opening disk drives and folders on your own computer.

Figure 20-6 shows how the Explorer shows an open Network Neighborhood with the computer named Koby being examined. To continue investigating various items attached to another computer, keep exploring them using the collapsible tree structure — just as you would when exploring your own computer.

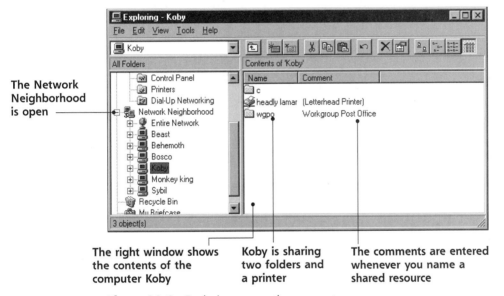

The Network Neighborhood is open

The right window shows the contents of the computer Koby

Koby is sharing two folders and a printer

The comments are entered whenever you name a shared resource

Figure 20-6   Exploring some other computer

Messing with Someone Else's Computer

When you're on a network, you're not limited to using only those goodies attached to your computer. You can save and open files on other computers, and use another computer's printer. This is a lot easier than you may think.

Saving Files Elsewhere

Saving files is pretty universal in Windows; just about every application uses the same steps (outlined in Chapter 4) for saving just about anything to disk. Saving your file on another computer is no different.

Follow these steps to save a file on another computer:

1. Open a file you would like to save elsewhere. Your EnviroGeeks newsletter is probably a good one to use.

2. Choose File → Save As from the menu. The standard Save As dialog box appears.

3. Use the Save in drop-down list and choose *Network Neighborhood.* Windows displays a list of other computers available on the network (Figure 20-7).

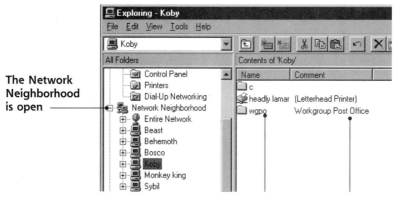

The Network Neighborhood is open

Figure 20-7 The Network Neighborhood is chosen for saving a file.

4. Open the computer you want to save to by double-clicking on the computer's icon. This displays any folders shared on that computer. If no folders appear, then that computer hasn't made its disk drives available for sharing. Oh well. Try another computer if you're desperate.

5. Double-click on the folder you want to open (you'll notice it's not really a folder but an icon of an itty-bitty computer). This displays that folder's contents in the window, just as if that folder were opened on your own PC.

6. You may be asked to enter a password here. Note, some folders have two passwords attached. You need the *full access* password to save a file on another computer. The read-only password will not let you save.

7. Continue double-clicking on folders until you find the one where you want to save your file.

8. At this point using the Save As dialog box works exactly as it would for your own computer. In fact, it's often hard to tell the difference.

9. After finding the proper folder, type in a filename next to the *File name* box. Do this just as you would on your computer.

10. Choose a file type.

11. Click the Save button. The file is saved on another computer.

 TIP **Watch your filenames here. Windows 95 is a little more forgiving on filenames than the older version of Windows. So if you're saving a Windows 95 document to an older version of Windows, you may have to shorten the name a bit.**

Some computers will share their root folder; for example you see drive (C:)'s root folder up for sharing in Figure 20-3.

Sometimes you may find an individual folder up for sharing. For example, in Figure 20-3, the folder *Figures* is shared on the Monkey King computer. Incidentally, that's the computer on my network where this book's figures are kept. Sharing a folder like that means you have instant access to it from any other computer.

Opening Files Elsewhere

You can open any file anywhere on the network, provided the other computer will grant you access to its disk drives. One of the best ways to find out is just to dive into an Open dialog box and browse the Network Neighborhood. See if your Personnel Department has their Employee Evaluations hooked to the network. Now *that* would be fun reading!

Follow these steps to open a file:

1. Choose File → Open from the menu. One of those typical Open dialog boxes appears.

2. Choose Network Neighborhood from the *Look in* drop-down list. A list of other computers available on the network appears in the Open dialog box. (It looks like Figure 20-7, but the dialog box says Open instead).

3. Find the computer on which you want to open a file and double-click its icon. Any folders available on that computer are then displayed. If you don't see any folders, then none are available. Try another computer.

4. Double-click on a folder to open it. The folder's contents are then displayed in the window. Type in a password if you're asked.

5. Continue opening folders until you find that file you want.

6. Eventually you'll find what you're looking for, a document, file, program, whatever. Double-click it to open it. The file then appears in your application ready for editing or, if it was a program, the program runs.

If you open a file on another computer and then choose the Save command, the file will be saved again on that computer.

X-REF If you want to save it elsewhere, use the Save As command as described in Chapter 4, in the section "Saving Your Stuff."

SIDE TRIP

THE ORDEAL OF MAPPING A NETWORK DRIVE

In Chapter 12, Figure 12-2, you can see an illustration of a mapped network drive. That's a drive on someone else's computer that shows up just like one of the drives on your computer. To get one of these to appear, you have to go through the ordeal of mapping the drive, which is an about-face from the graphical ease of using something like the Network Neighborhood; to map a drive you must know its cryptic network pathname. Yikes!

The only way to map a drive is to click on the Map Drive button on the toolbar in My Computer or the Explorer (so you must choose View → Toolbar first, and then click the button). This displays a dialog box where you pick a drive letter for your computer (easy) and then type in the network pathname for the networked drive (not so easy).
A network pathname looks like this:

`\\computer\resource`

That's two backslashes, the name of the network computer, another backslash, and finally the shared resource. For example, in Figure 20-6, the network computer *Koby* is seen in the Network Neighborhood sharing its folder named C. Here is how that would look:

`\\koby\c`

That's the network path you'd type into the Path input box to map drive C on Koby.
Click in the *Reconnect at logon* box if you want to have the mapped network drive always appear when you start your computer. A ✔ check mark appears in the box. Whew! Like I said, this is no easy task. Maybe in a future version of Windows it'll be simpler to map a network drive.

Using an Alien Printer

Your computer may not have its own printer. No problem — just steal someone else's from the network. Anyone who uses a computer with a printer attached, and who is dopey enough to share it, makes that printer available for anyone to use. In fact, you can even use that printer and use your own; just make shortcuts to both printers on the desktop and drag-and-drop stuff to print to either printer. It can really be quite swell.

Follow these steps to add a network printer to your hoard of printers:

1. Double-click on My Computer.

2. Double-click on the Control Panel.

3. Double-click on the Printers folder to open it. You'll see the Printers window, where all sorts of printers and faxes live.

4. Double-click on the Add Printer icon. This opens a hardware wizard thing, which enables you to set up a printer on your computer. It's basically a step-by-step thing with lots of *purty* pictures.

5. Click on the Next button.

6. Choose the *Network printer* option and click on the next button.

7. Next you'll see a dialog box asking you to find the network printer (see Figure 20-8). Use the Browse button to hunt down an available computer on the network. Follow the instructions in the previous section "Opening Files Elsewhere" for details on hunting down a shared printer; open various network computer icons until you find a printer. Click that printer, and then click OK. After choosing your network printer, its ugly network name will appear in the *Network path or queue name* box. For example:

   ```
   \\Koby\headly lamar
   ```

   Be thankful you didn't have to type that from memory and click Next.

8. Now you get to tell Windows which brand and model of printer you have. There's quite a list to choose from. Pick *Manufacturers* first, something like HP — which stands for Hewlett Packard. If your printer isn't on the list but came with an installation disk, stick the disk in drive (A:) and click the Have Disk button. (You may have to hunt down someone else in the office who has the disk.)

9. Pick the model number second. This is under the *Printers* column. You may need to ask someone in your office or in your IS department for hints of a manufacturer and model number.

10. Click on the Next button.

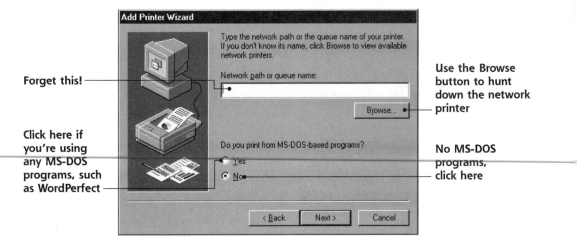

Forget this!

Click here if you're using any MS-DOS programs, such as WordPerfect

Use the Browse button to hunt down the network printer

No MS-DOS programs, click here

Figure 20-8   Where are you, O network printer?

11. Choose how the printer is connected to your computer. Normally you'll be picking *LPT1*, your computer's first printer port. This option is, thankfully, already highlighted on the screen for you.

12. Click on the Next button.

13. Now you get to give your printer a name. Already entered in the *Printer name* box is the printer's brand name. Bor-ing. Just type in a cute name for your printer in that box. Also, Windows lets you have several printers installed, but you can only choose one as your main printer (the — ugh! — *default* one). Refer to "Yo, My Main Printer" in Chapter 17 for more information on setting your main printer from a gaggle of other printers.

14. Click on the Next button.

15. Would you like to print a test page? This can be fun. Make sure there's a dot in the Yes option button, and then do the next step. (The test page ensures that your printer is hooked up properly and working just fine.)

16. Click on the Finish button. If you've chosen to print a test page, it will print now wherever the printer you just installed is located. A dialog box announces that the page printed. Click the Yes button if everything was okay. If not, click the No button to run through some troubleshooting.

Surrendering Your Hardware to the Network

If you want to be nice, you can have others use your PC's hardware, offering up your disk drives and printer for sharing on the network. There's really nothing to it, though you do have the option of slapping on various passwords and (my favorite) making your disk drives *read only* so no one can alter or (gulp) accidentally erase anything on your system.

All the stuff you share on your computer will be tagged with the little sharing hand guy. He'll appear under disk drives, folders, or printers you've elected to share with your networking neighbors.

Sharing Hard Drives and Folders

Sometimes you may want to let everyone else play with your entire hard drive. If so, just surrender the entire thing by sharing the disk drive itself. Other times, it's better just to share a folder or two. Not only does this limit the access others have to your computer, but it makes it easier for them to find those folders because they appear right there when your computer is opened in the Network Neighborhood.

Follow these steps to offer up any hard drive or folder onto the net:

1. Locate the disk drive or folder you want to share by using My Computer or the Explorer. Remember, when you choose a disk drive, you're sharing the entire drive.

2. Click the folder or disk drive once to select it.

3. Choose `File` → `Sharing`. This brings up the Sharing panel properties dialog box, as shown in Figure 20-9.

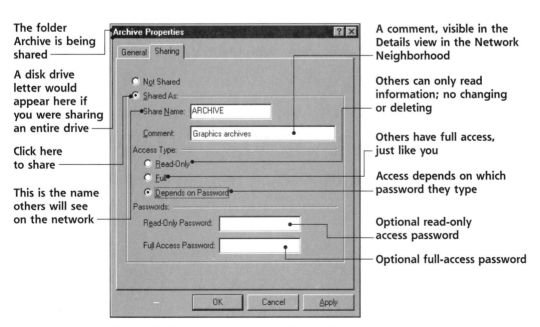

Figure 20-9 Surrendering something to the network gods

4. Click *Shared As.* This surrenders the disk drive or folder for sharing.

5. Click OK. *Humma-humma-humma.* Eventually you'll see the sharing hand appear under whatever you shared. It's now up and on the network.

That's really it. Anything else you set in the dialog box is optional at this point. The disk drive or folder is shared and everyone else will have full access when you click OK. But . . .

Click *Read Only* to permit others only to browse your disk drive, not allowing them to add, change, or delete anything. This is a safe bet. You can even limit access further by typing a password in the *Read-Only Password* input box. This way, they can access the drive only if they type in the proper password, and they still can't change anything.

Click on *Full* only to give everyone else the same access you have. You can optionally enter a password in the *Full Access Password* input box. This way, they can only have full access if they type the proper password.

Click *Depends on Password* to grant access depending on which password they type. In this case you need to enter a password in each input box. Whoever tries to play with your computer will have either read-only or full access depending on which password they guess correctly.

You can still access your disk drives from your own computer, no matter what the password.

TIP The name you type into the *Share name* text box is the name others will see attached to that folder in the Network Neighborhood. Normally this should be the name of the disk drive or folder shared, but you can type anything you like. And if you stick a dollar sign character ($) at the end of the name, that folder will not appear in the Network Neighborhood — even though it's still shared. For example, type C$ instead of C to share drive (C:) secretly.

By the way, you can reverse this process at any time. All you need to do is repeat the previous steps and choose *Not Shared* from the dialog box in Step 4.

Sharing Your Printer

Surrendering your printer to everyone else on the network is almost as much a cinch as sharing a disk drive.

Follow these steps to be a good kid and share your printer:

1. Find a Control Panel near you and open it up. Or choose it from the Start Thing menu: CTRL+ESC, S, C.

Control Panel

2. Double-click on the Printers folder to open it. You'll see the Printers window where all sorts of printers and faxes live.

Printers

3. Select the printer you want to share by clicking once on your printer's icon.

4. Choose File → Sharing . This brings up the printer's Properties dialog box with the Sharing panel up front and ready for action, similar to what you'll see in Figure 20-10.

Click here to stop sharing a printer

Click here to share a printer

The printer's name as others will see it on the network

Optional rude comments

Optional pointless printer access password

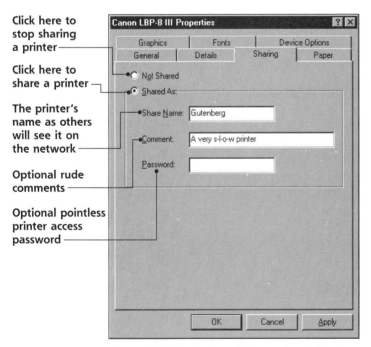

Figure 20-10 A printer's Properties dialog box

5. Click on the *Shared As* option button. This shares the printer. That's really it, though you can toy around with the other options in the dialog box.

6. Click on OK. You're done. The printer is up on the network and soon you'll see the little sharing hand guy under it, meaning it's all cozy and ready to go.

TIP **My advice is not to password-protect any printer. Having to enter a password every time you print is a major pain in the butt. If there's any reason to give your printer a password, then just don't share it on the network.**

If, for any reason, you want to stop sharing your printer on the network, just choose *Not Shared* in Step 5. Be sure to let others on the network who might have been using your printer know it's no longer available.

X-REF **Check out Chapter 17, which discusses using a printer on your PC in depth. Everything that applies to a local printer also applies to a network model.**

Stop! Oh, Yes, Wait a Minute, Mr. Postman!

There are really only two things you want to do with mail: Read any mail you get and send mail to other people. But, before doing this, you need to get acquainted with the *Exchange* program, which is Windows' mail manager program.

TIP **Odds are real good you'll have a different mail program from the Exchange provided "free" with Windows. You should consult with your office's network manager for tips on using your mail system.**

X-REF **If your office is small enough, I'd recommend using WinPopup for most of your messaging. WinPopup is covered in the section "The Joys of Winpopup" at the end of this chapter.**

Fussing with the Exchange (i.e., Mail) Program

Windows mail is brought to you by the Exchange program. I hate that name. It sounds like those little booths in international airports where they overcharge you to swap money. I suppose they can't call it *mail* because you can't copyright that name. *C'est la guerre.*

The mail you send and receive here is to the other people who are on the network. So if you want to send a message to the new guy in the office:

```
"Hi, I met you in the elevator this morning. If you really want a
  great career in this company, stop wearing so much Brut!"
```

If you want to send a message to your Aunt Margie in Arkansas, you'll have to use the post office (unless you have an Internet account, but that's something different).

Exchange can be found off the Start Thing menu; choose <kbd>Programs</kbd> → <kbd>Microsoft Exchange</kbd>. You may also see the *Inbox* icon on your desktop, in which case you can click it to start Exchange.

Inbox

Once you start Exchange, you'll probably want to minimize it; click the minimize button in the window's upper-right corner. You can keep Exchange as a button on the taskbar until you're ready to compose new messages or read your mail.

The following sections assume you've started Exchange and it sits waiting as a button on the taskbar.

 Exchange is a great program to have start automatically each time you start Windows. Refer to "Applications That Start Automatically (Amazing!)" in Chapter 5 for more information.

Checking Your Mail

When new mail arrives, your computer will beep and you'll see the friendly mail guy appear near the loud time on the taskbar. Double-click him to pop up the Exchange and read your new mail (see Figure 20-11).

Any unread mail you have appears in your *Inbox* mail list in bold type; double-click it to read it. This displays the mail reader, where you can view the message, reply, or forward it to someone else. Figure 20-12 shows where the buttons are to push.

Click here to compose a new message

Your mail folder list

The Inbox is highlighted

Click here to delete a message (move it into your Deleted Items folder)

Messages in your Inbox

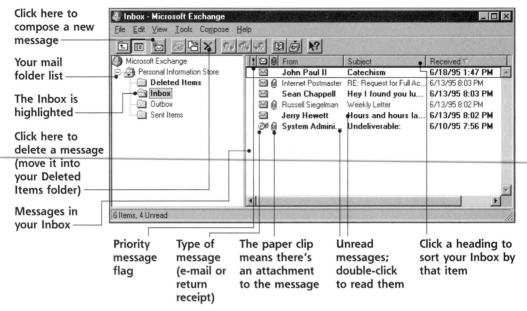

Priority message flag

Type of message (e-mail or return receipt)

The paper clip means there's an attachment to the message

Unread messages; double-click to read them

Click a heading to sort your Inbox by that item

Figure 20-11   The joys of getting new mail in the Exchange program

Print the message

Reply to the sender

Forward this message to someone else

See the previous message in your Inbox

See the next message in your Inbox

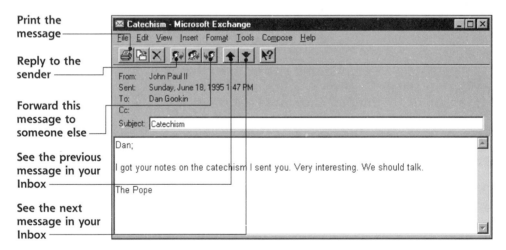

Figure 20-12   The mail reader window

Sending Mail

Sending mail in Windows is easy.

Follow these steps to send a new mail message:

1. Choose [Compose] → [New Message] from the Exchange menu. Or you can click the wee little New Message button on the toolbar. This starts a text editor for you to type your message (or it may start a special version of Microsoft Word if you have Word). The New Message editor is shown in Figure 20-13. (If you have Microsoft Office installed, you'll see a different dialog box displayed, but they both accomplish the same thing.)

2. Fill in the *To* and *Subject* input boxes, and, optionally, the *CC* (carbon copy) box.

3. Fill in the message text.

4. When you're done, choose File → Send to send your message, or click the wee little Send button on the toolbar.

Click here to send the message

Click here to pull a name from your personal address book

Or just type the name in here

Carbon copies are entered here

The message subject

Body of the message

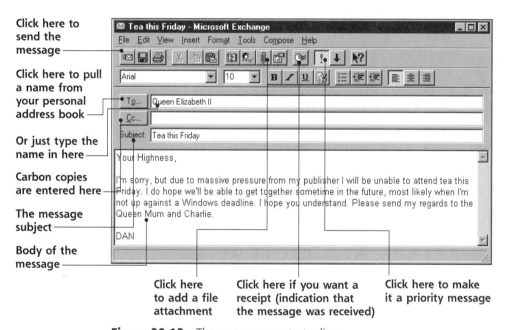

Click here to add a file attachment

Click here if you want a receipt (indication that the message was received)

Click here to make it a priority message

Figure 20-13   The new message text editor

TIP   Fill in the body of the message just as you would when writing a letter. Remember, most people tend to write e-mail casually, yet people tend to take e-mail just as seriously as any business letter. Try not to be clever or quirky when it can easily be misinterpreted. Save the humor for the phone.

The Joys of WinPopup

WinPopup can be really handy and is a lot simpler to use than a full-on mail program. In a two-person office, it's about all you need. The only thing you can't do with it is send files back and forth. WinPopup is shown in Figure 20-14.

 X-REF You may not be blessed with WinPopup's presence on your computer. If so, you'll need to install it manually. Refer to "Adding the Rest of Windows" in Chapter 11 for information on adding WinPopup.

If you can't find WinPopup, refer to Chapter 29 for information on tracking down lost programs. When you find WinPopup, add it to the Start Thing StartUp submenu as described in Chapter 5, "Adding and Moving Programs to the StartUp Submenu."

Click here to send a message ⟶

Trashes the current message ⟶

Who sent what ⟶

The message ⟶

⟵ See the previous message

⟵ See the next message

When WinPopup is active, you'll be alerted when network printing jobs print

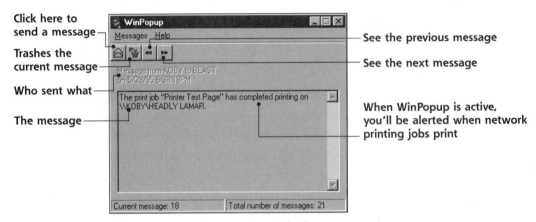

Figure 20-14 WinPopup is used for instant messaging.

Follow these steps to use your WinPopup:

1. Start WinPopup by choosing it from the Start Thing menu. It should be in the Programs → Accessories submenu.

2. To send a message, click on the little envelope button.

3. Type in the user's name (how they're logging in to their computer) or type in the computer name.

4. Press the TAB key and then type the message (see Figure 20-15).

5. Click on OK to send it.

6. A dialog box pops up that says your message was successfully sent.

7. Click on OK.

8. You are now ready to send another message.

Unlike a real mail program, there's nothing fancy with a WinPopup message. You can't send files, you can't schedule mail, you can't get your mail at another computer, and you can't pass go and collect $100. But it's not a big hassle to install or use, either.

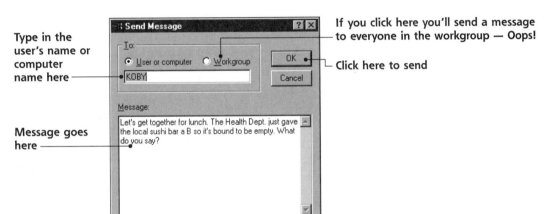

Figure 20-15 Sending a message in WinPopup

TIP Remember to minimize WinPopup when you're done; don't quit. If you quit you can't get any new messages. WinPopup will warn you of this if you do try to quit.

BONUS

Strange Filenames on Older Windows Computers

Windows 95 can network easily with other computers running the Windows for Workgroups or MS-DOS for Workgroups operating systems. You can use these computers just like any Windows 95 computer on the network. The only difference is long filenames cannot be saved on them; instead of a long name, the older operating system will save the file using a *truncated name.*

The truncated name is merely the first six letters of the long name — no spaces — plus a tilde and a number. For example, `Potato Salad` becomes `POTATO~1` on the non-Windows 95 computer. Unfortunately, when you go to open the file, it will have that same name; the original, long name will be forgotten.

My advice is to use only eight or fewer characters when saving a file on a non-Windows 95 computer. Further, limit the filename to only letters and numbers; don't try any spaces, periods, or other fancy characters. That's easy enough to remember.

Summary

Networking is all about sharing. Sharing disk drives and printers, stealing things from others' disk drives, and printing all your stuff on someone else's printer so they run out of paper and you don't.

If you're working with a network, it's important that you learn these skills:

- [ ] How to find open the Networking icon and use the Network Neighborhood.
- [ ] How to save and open a file on another computer.
- [ ] How to add a network printer and share your printer.
- [ ] How to check and send network mail.
- [ ] How to use the WinPopup.

CHAPTER TWENTY-ONE

INSTALLING NEW HARDWARE

IN THIS CHAPTER YOU WILL LEARN THESE KEY SKILLS

SETTING UP NEW HARDWARE (THE SOFTWARE SIDE)   PAGE 269

CONFIGURING FOR A NEW PRINTER   PAGE 273

REMOVING AN OLD PRINTER   PAGE 277

Installing new hardware isn't really a hassle. Anyone with a screwdriver, a few minutes, and a good book of instructions can add any component to a PC. No problem. What used to be a problem, though, was getting that *new something* to work properly with your software. This isn't a problem because Windows now comes with a hardware installation wizard that automatically does the software part of your hardware setup for you.

This chapter does not go into detail on the hardware side of installation. It assumes you've already set up, screwed in, or attached some new hardware gizmo to your PC and have just replugged it and turned on the power. Only after doing this do you need to follow the instructions in this chapter.

Adding a *New Something* to Your Computer

Pretty much anything you add to your computer can be detected by Windows and configured automatically. This is all part of the new *Plug and Play* standard, a feature of Windows that enables it to scrutinize, identify, and set up your software properly to work well with your hardware.

TIP If you've just set up an external piece of hardware, such as a modem, external CD-ROM drive, whatever, turn it on before you go through the following steps. Windows can't find your hardware unless you turn it on first.

Follow these steps to complete your hardware installation:

1. Restart Windows (if you haven't already).

2. Close all open programs. When you get into the Add New Hardware Wizard, it will tell you to close all programs. So, you might as well do it now.

3. Double-click on My Computer.

4. Double-click on the Control Panel.

Control Panel

5. Double-click on the Add New Hardware icon. This starts the Add New Hardware Wizard. Because this chapter is brief, I'm going to show you all the steps with figures attached. The opening dialog box is shown in Figure 21-1, though it's truly boring.

Add New
Hardware

6. Click Next in the Add New Hardware Wizard box. Windows next asks if you want do this manually or automatically. No masochists here, so keep the dot in the Yes option button (see Figure 21-2). If you click No, then Windows merely presents you with a list of new items that *could* have been installed. You pick one, and then pick the brand name and model number in additional dialog boxes. Eventually, Windows confirms your choices and sets things up. But because this is a computer, and they're *supposed* to make life easier, you should stick with the Yes option.

Why is there always a pencil?

Yeah, yeah

Click here to move forward

Figure 21-1   The boring opening dialog box

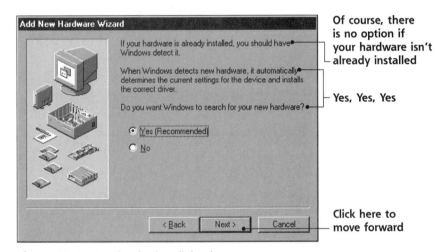

Of course, there is no option if your hardware isn't already installed

Yes, Yes, Yes

Click here to move forward

Figure 21-2   Another boring dialog box

7. Click Next. Windows warns you it might seize on you while it's looking for your new hardware and you should close all your open programs before you begin. Hey! If you want perfection, you should have bought a Macintosh. Figure 21-3 echoes these sentiments.

8. Click Next. It's the detection stage, similar to the last stage, but with a progress thermometer along the bottom of the dialog box (see Figure 21-4). Now Windows is searching high and low for any hardware changes you've made. If your hard drive is beside you, don't be surprised at the buzzing noises coming from the box. Your computer is working really hard now and is kinda grunting.

This will take a few hundred moments. Like the instructions say, if your computer stops working for a while — meaning you don't see the thermometer move or the hard drive chipmunks seem to have died — then you'll need to reset your computer. Please wait an *extra* two minutes after you've made this decision before you really do reset.

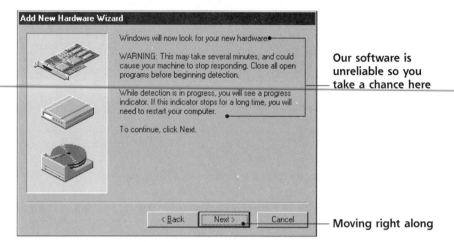

Our software is unreliable so you take a chance here

Moving right along

Figure 21-3   Nothing to do here

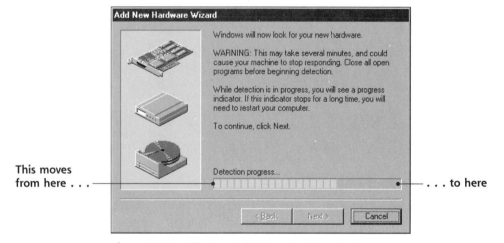

This moves from here . . .

. . . to here

Figure 21-4   Windows is looking, looking, looking.

 TIP   If you need to reset: Turn off your computer. Wait about 40 seconds. Then turn on the computer again. Start over with your installation procedure, but do it manually and choose No in Step 6.

9. Windows found your hardware! The next dialog box (see Figure 21-5) shows Windows has found and set up something new. To see the new something(s) displayed, click the Details button, as shown in the figure.

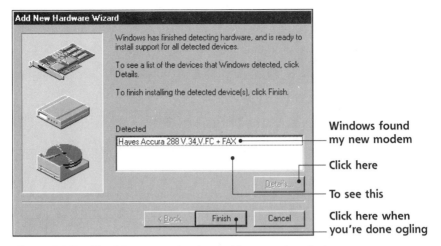

Windows found
my new modem

Click here

To see this

Click here when
you're done ogling

Figure 21-5   Alors! Some new hardware thingy was installed.

10. Click on the Finish button and you're done.

Well, not really. Depending on what was installed, there may be additional verification or configuration. What happens next depends on what was installed. For example, with my modem, Windows next went through verification of the modem (whatever that means; the dialog box said "OK" and that was it). Your hardware may require additional setup depending on what it does.

Just keep working your way through the end of the wizard. When the wizard disappears from the screen, or in those rare instances where you may need to reset, you'll be ready to start using your new hardware.

If you've just installed a modem and faithfully rebooted your computer as you were told, look on your desktop. You'll see a new and amazing icon, *Setup for Microsoft Internet Explorer 3.01.* Now you can go back to Chapter 9 and hook up to the Internet.

X-REF   **If you have any trouble with your new hardware, you can use Windows' hardware troubleshooting wizard. This is covered in Chapter 29.**

Installing a Brand New Printer

Windows probably asked you a dozen questions about your printer when it was installed. Great. But when you add a new printer, you have to tell Windows about it. This is a must! Once Windows knows about your printer, you can print anything you can see on the screen.

Follow these steps to add a new printer:

1. Double-click on My Computer.

2. Double-click on the Control Panel.

Control Panel

3. Double-click on the Printers folder to open it. You'll see the Printers window, where all sorts of printers and faxes live.

Printers

4. Double-click on the Add Printer icon. This opens a hardware wizard thing, which enables you to set up a printer on your computer. It's basically a step-by-step thing with lots of purty pictures. (The steps here point out the highlights only, no sense in echoing all those splendid graphics.)

Add Printer

5. Click on the Next button. The *How is this printer attached to your computer?* panel appears, as shown in Figure 21-6.

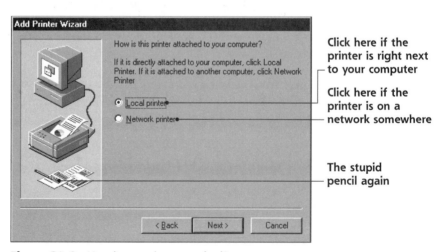

Figure 21-6 How is my printer attached?

6a. If your PC has its own printer, choose *Local printer*.

6b. If your PC doesn't have its own printer, but must share a printer elsewhere on the network, choose *Network printer*.

7. Click on the Next Button.

8a. If you're installing a network printer, click the Browse button to find the printer to which you want to connect and click the printer's name. Then click OK. The Printer Wizard will then confirm your choice of printer. Click Next.

8b. If you chose *Local printer*, click the Next button.

9. Now you can tell Windows which brand and model of printer you have. There is quite a list to choose from (see Figure 21-7).

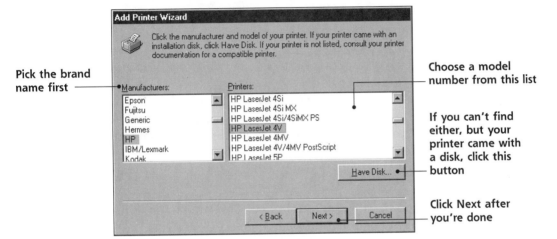

Pick the brand name first

Choose a model number from this list

If you can't find either, but your printer came with a disk, click this button

Click Next after you're done

Figure 21-7 Pick your printer from the list.

10a. Pick *Manufacturers* first, something like HP — which stands for Hewlett Packard.

10b. If your printer isn't on the list but came with an installation disk, stick the disk in drive (A:) and click the Have Disk button.

11. Pick the model number second. This is under the Printers column. You may need to look at your computer for hints of a manufacturer and model number.

12. Click the Next button.

13. Choose how the printer is connected to your computer. Normally you'll be picking *LPT1*, your computer's first printer port. This option is, thankfully, already highlighted on the screen for you.

14. Click the Next button.

15. Now you get to give your printer a name. Trudge through Figure 21-8.

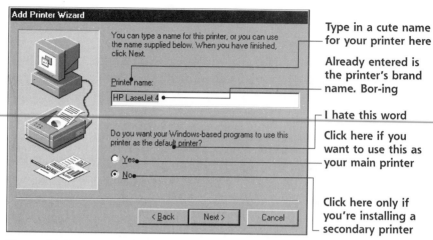

Type in a cute name for your printer here

Already entered is the printer's brand name. Bor-ing

I hate this word

Click here if you want to use this as your main printer

Click here only if you're installing a secondary printer

Figure 21-8 Name that printer!

X-REF Windows lets you have several printers installed, but you can only choose one as your main printer (the, ugh, *default* one). Refer to "Yo, My Main Printer" in Chapter 17 for more information on setting your main printer from a gaggle of other printers.

16. Click the Next button.

17. Would you like to print a test page? This can be fun. Make sure there's a dot in the Yes option button, then do the next step. (The test page ensures your printer is hooked up properly and working just fine. Frame it as the first thing you printed in Windows on your printer. Or, better yet, send it to your mother. She'll be so proud!)

18. Click the Finish button. If you've chosen to print a test page, it will print now. A dialog box announces the page printed. Click the Yes button if everything was okay. If not, click the No button to run through some troubleshooting.

If you've installed a network printer, the page will print elsewhere on the network. Run around madly looking for it and, when you find it, hold the test page up over your head and grin with glee.

BONUS

"There's a Stupid Printer Installed Here and I Want to Get Rid of It"

If you've just changed printers, then you'll probably want to get rid of the old one. This is just too silly; to get rid of the old printer, simply delete it from your Printers folder in My Computer. Poof! It's gone.

TIP My advice is: Do not delete the old printer. You can leave it hanging around "just in case." For example, suppose your new printer breaks and goes back to the shop, or maybe someone else (some manager doodoo-head) in the office steals your newer printer and gives you back the old one. Then it's merely a matter of switching your "main printer" in the Printers window; no reinstallation is required.

It's a Drag to Drag-and-Drop to a Printer

One of the virtues of Windows (or so they say) is you can print any document by dragging that document to a printer icon. While this is true, it's also not the most elegant solution. First, you must copy and paste a shortcut to your printer icon, usually on the desktop. Second, you need to drag the file from a window in My Computer or the Explorer to the printer. Third, Windows fires up the program that created your document and, finally, fourth, the document prints. It would be easier just to double-click on the document to open the application, then print by clicking on the Print tool or pressing CTRL+P.

Summary

Because Windows comes with a hardware installation wizard that automatically does the software part of your hardware setup for you, everything about installing new hardware really is cinchy.

Don't go on to Chapter 22 unless you understand the following:

☐ How to complete your hardware installation.

☐ How to add a new printer.

PART FIVE

HAVING FUN

THIS PART CONTAINS THE FOLLOWING CHAPTERS

CHAPTER **22** CHANGING THE LOOK OF WINDOWS

CHAPTER **23** INTERESTING, WEIRD, AND NEAT STUFF

CHAPTER **24** FUN, GAMES, AND FRIVOLITY

THE THIRTEENTH LABOUR (PART V)

On the third day of Heracles' thirteenth labour, he discovered Solitaire.

On the tenth day, King Eurystheus became concerned. He hadn't seen Heracles in seven days. He slid food under the door. Hours later an empty plate slid back. No answer came when Eurystheus knocked.

Eurystheus summoned the Oracle at Delphi. The wise seer Teiresias came to consult with King Eurystheus.

Old, blind Teiresias was the greatest of the wise men. But he was cursed. He told the future to those who asked, but they did not believe him. Teiresias had the knowledge of the gods, but the reputation of a weatherman.

"I have news for you, King Dave!" Teiresias announced upon entering the palace.

"O, great and wise Teiresias. Truly Apollo blesses this house by sending us your presence," Eurystheus said, bowing.

"Yeah, yeah, yeah," Teiresias answered. "Go ahead and kiss up to the gods, Dave. They have a nice juicy one planned for you when all this Hercules stuff falls through."

"It's *Heracles*," Eurystheus corrected the blind old man, "he prefers that name. And I am only Dave on the computer. Call me Eurystheus. So, tell me Teiresias, what do you see?"

"Nothing," he answered. "I see nothing. I'm blind."

"Forgive me, O great one," Eurystheus said. "I was referring to Heracles and my computer. Heracles, what news?"

"Hearken!" Teiresias said, a word he used to instill terror. "I shall tell you the future, O King of Labours, but you will neither like nor believe it because you didn't earn this job — you inherited it."

Eurystheus nodded.

"I can't see you nod, boy. Speak up!"

Eurystheus said, "Yes! I understand I won't believe."

Teiresias stepped closer. "Heracles is setting the standard for all computer-using employees of the future. He's having fun. He's changing the colors of his monitor. And he's playing games instead of working."

Then Teiresias began to shout: "You want to know the future, King Dave? I'll tell you in a word: Tetris! They'll play it for hours. Don't expect anything to get done!"

"I don't understand," Eurystheus said.

"I know. No one ever believes me," Teiresias said. "I could say, 'Hey! A grand piano is about to fall on your head,' and they'd scoff. Then there's that horrid 88-key sound."

"But what about Heracles?" Eurystheus asked.

"I told you," Teiresias answered, turning to leave the palace but instead, heading toward the kitchen. "He is no longer your problem. Heracles is owed something from the gods. And he will get it in Part VI of this story."

A loud crash came from the kitchen. Eurystheus heard Teiresias' voice shouting in the distance: "Baklava!"

C H A P T E R   T W E N T Y - T W O

CHANGING THE LOOK OF WINDOWS

IN THIS CHAPTER YOU LEARN THESE KEY SKILLS

DINKING WITH THE DESKTOP PROPERTIES DIALOG
   BOX   PAGE 283

ALTERING THE SCREEN RESOLUTION   PAGE 286

CHOOSING A NEW COLOR SCHEME   PAGE 288

MESSING WITH THE TASKBAR   PAGE 290

Windows has some basic parts that don't change: The gizmos on a window and gadgets in a dialog box are pretty much there for good. But you can change certain aspects of Windows, primarily the way it looks. Specifically, you can change the screen resolution, color scheme, and the graphics you see in the background. You can also move around the taskbar if you want to be different. All of this is covered here. All rather tastefully, too.

22

Background Information

The background you see when you work in Windows is called the *desktop*. But how the desktop looks can be changed. You can either choose an exciting pattern for the desktop or an interesting graphical image appropriately called *wallpaper*. Figures 22-1 through 22-3 show several examples of background wallpapers and patterns.

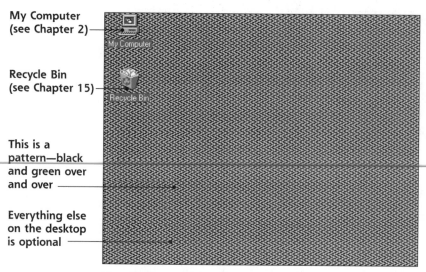

My Computer
(see Chapter 2)

Recycle Bin
(see Chapter 15)

This is a
pattern—black
and green over
and over

Everything else
on the desktop
is optional

Figure 22-1 The "Dizzy" pattern (as if using a computer wasn't annoying enough)

See Chapter 20
for more
information
on this

The Microsoft
Network

See Chapter 14
for information
on pasting a
printer on the
desktop

This wallpaper file is named Win95 and
it comes on the Windows installation CD

Scrap files dragged or
pasted to the desktop

Figure 22-2 The Windows 95 background (Microsoft loyalist)

Figure 22-3   Simon and Jonah flying over to Grandma's and Grandpa's house

The First Step to Change the Look of Windows

To change the way Windows looks you need to access the Display Properties dialog box.

Follow these steps to change the way Windows looks:

1. Right-click on a blank part of the desktop. This makes the desktop's shortcut menu appear.

2. Choose Properties from the shortcut menu. The Display Properties dialog box appears (see Figure 22-4).

The preview window shows you how your Pattern and Wallpaper choices affect the screen

Choose a pattern from this list to give the display a cheap look

You must first choose the (None) option at the top of this list to select a pattern (on the other side of the dialog box)

Click here to edit patterns or create new ones

Various graphics bitmap files in the Windows folder; choose one to preview how it will look on the little screen above

Click here to scope out a bitmap image file elsewhere on your hard drive

Smaller graphical patterns should be tiled so that they fill the entire screen

Larger images and those that look better in the middle of the screen should be centered

Click here to preview how the screen will look without making any permanent changes

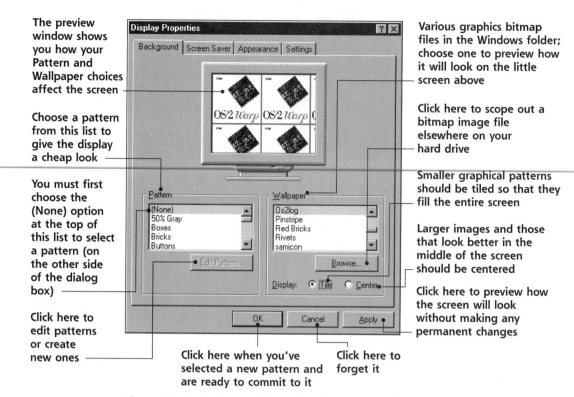

Click here when you've selected a new pattern and are ready to commit to it

Click here to forget it

Figure 22-4 The Display Properties dialog box; Background panel in the foreground

3. Click on the proper tab to bring whichever panel forward. Each of the four panels can adjust something clever with the screen or desktop background.

The only panel that's not covered in this Chapter is *Screen Saver*. Refer to Chapter 23 — the section "Saving the Screen from Boredom"— for more information on screen saver settings.

Choosing One of Them Fancy Desktop Patterns

Desktop patterns are boring — but quick. They're basically two-color graphic images that yawn with excitement. In fact, the only true advantage to picking a pattern for your desktop background is it takes up less memory than wallpaper and it's faster to draw on the screen. So if you have a PC low on memory or with an ancient, sluggish graphics system, or even if you're just tired of Windows taking forever to draw the desktop, then pick a pattern.

Follow these steps to select a pattern:

1. Bring up the Display Properties dialog box, as discussed in the previous section.

2. Click on the Background tab to bring that panel forward.

3. In the Wallpaper area, make sure the *(None)* option is selected.

4. Choose a pattern. Scroll through the list to find a pattern that thrills you. Tulip is nice. It matches my paper towels. I don't understand Field Effect. Cargo Net is cool. Pick whatever pleases you. (Guys, you can always pick Daisies and tell your macho male friends they're U-boat propellers.)

5. Click on the pattern once with the mouse to preview it in the monitor preview window.

6. Click on OK. This locks in your pattern selection and returns you to the desktop to view your choice with pride.

 TIP **If you don't like the black and slate colored background, you can change the slate color to something else. In the Display Properties dialog box Appearance panel, choose a new pattern color from the Color drop-down list.**

Wallpaper Without the Glue

Wallpaper is much more exciting and colorful than the desktop patterns. Windows comes with a whole museum full of them, though you can use any bitmap graphic image—even one you create yourself using Paint — as wallpaper. This means you can let your creative juices flow to make your own, download an image by Michelangelo from the Internet, or use a scanner to scan in pictures of your kids to have as wallpaper.

 WEB PATH **Visit the Louvre museum on the Internet at:**

`http://mistral.culture.fr/louvre`

Follow these steps to pick out wallpaper for the desktop:

1. Summon the Display Properties dialog box. (Refer to the section "The First Step to Change the Look of Windows" for directions.)

2. Click on the Background tab to bring that panel forward if it isn't already.

3. Make sure the *(None)* option is selected in the Pattern area.

4. Choose a Wallpaper image. Scroll through the list and click on each image name using the mouse.

5. Experiment with the Tile and Center buttons to see which method displays your image better. If you don't see your graphic-listed file here, click the Browse button to find it elsewhere on your computer.

6. Click on OK. Your newly selected background image appears on the screen, ready to impress the neighbors.

The Screen Resolution Revolution

ere's a tip you'll never hear about on those infomercial real estate shows: It's possible to increase the size of your desktop without buying a larger monitor. Imagine your cozy 640 X 480 pixel lot enlarged to an 800 X 600 or even a 1024 X 768 pixel ranch, all without buying a new monitor! This can be really nice, enabling you to see more windows on the screen, more icons on the desktop, more of everything without losing a penny.

Follow these steps to change your screen-size real estate:

1. Conjure up the Display Properties dialog box.

2. Click on the Settings panel to bring it forward. This panel appears in Figure 22-5.

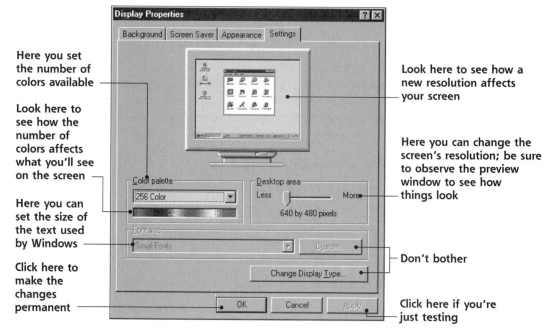

Figure 22-5   The Display Properties dialog box — Settings panel front and center

3. Goof around in the Settings panel all day if you like, using the preview window in the dialog box to see how the changes affect your system. Just click the Cancel button to chicken out and leave.

4. Choose a new resolution from the *Desktop area*. Don't slam the slider all the way up to the highest value right away. Instead, settle on the next-highest resolution first. For example, drag the slider until you see 800 X 600 pixels displayed.

5. If you choose a higher resolution, you may also want to choose *Large Fonts* from the *Font size* area. Or you can skip this option, run through the rest of the steps, and do it later if you like.

6. Choose a new color value from the *Color palette*. Click the arrow to drop down the drop-down list. (For kicks, change this value to 16, then to 246, and then to any higher values available.)

7. Pluck out a new color value. Don't pick 16! It's too stupid. Besides, it looks truly gross. The 256 value is okay. Anything higher is great for working on high-end graphics applications such as Adobe Illustrator, those "morphing" programs, and seeing computer video.

8. Click OK. Depending on the options you selected, Windows may want to restart itself now. Normally, if you change only the resolution, Windows won't balk; skip to Step 10. But if you change the font size or number of colors, Windows may request a reset. If so, click the Yes button when asked if you want to reset now. Windows restarts to test the new display options. Don't panic at anything you read on the screen! Log in. Read your tip-o-day. Enjoy your new screen resolution. Of course, you can't chicken out now. You'll have to begin again if you want to change back.

9. Read the Info dialog box. What it means is Windows will try out the new resolution. After switching over, it will give you 15 seconds to say "yeah this is cool." Otherwise it will switch back. If the new resolution doesn't work, you won't see anything on the screen, so just sit tight.

10. Click OK. Psychedelic, eh?

11. You resized the desktop. Do you want to keep this setting? Click Yes if it looks okay. Click No if not. Or just sit stunned and, after 16 seconds, Windows will switch back. Click OK in the dialog box displayed if Windows switches back on you.

If you give up, be sure to close the Display Properties dialog box by clicking on its Close button.

By the way, you may notice the text is teensy tiny in those large resolutions. Better rework the preceding steps and choose *Large Fonts* where I indicated.

Making Windows' Color Scheme Match Your Office

I f you've just done up your office or computer room in trendy earth tones (which are coming back, by the way), you may want Windows' drab onscreen colors to match. This is entirely possible. Just about every element on the screen can be changed to another color, font, size, whathaveyou.

Follow these steps to change the color of your Windows screen:

1. Muster the Display Properties dialog box. (Review the information in the section "The First Step to Change the Look of Windows" for how this is done.)

2. Click the Appearance panel to move it center stage. The Display Properties dialog box Appearance panel looks something like Figure 22-6. It shows several of Windows' onscreen elements, colors, fonts, and whatnot. Each of these items can be changed, either individually or all at once, by using some predefined schemes — like in a Miss Marple novel.

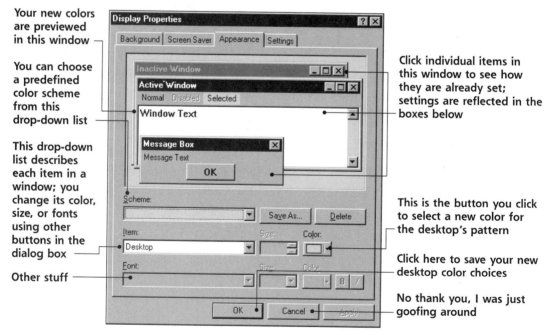

Your new colors are previewed in this window

You can choose a predefined color scheme from this drop-down list

This drop-down list describes each item in a window; you change its color, size, or fonts using other buttons in the dialog box

Other stuff

Click individual items in this window to see how they are already set; settings are reflected in the boxes below

This is the button you click to select a new color for the desktop's pattern

Click here to save your new desktop color choices

No thank you, I was just goofing around

Figure 22-6   The Appearance panel in the Display Properties dialog box

3. Preview a bunch of color schemes. Use the drop-down list box below *Scheme* to display some of the color patterns dreamt up by the overly creative boys and girls at Microsoft — but don't do this if you need to

drive or operate any heavy equipment later. The options aren't too exciting. After choosing an option, you'll see in the preview window how it would affect things. If you find a color arrangement you like, move on to Step 4.

4. Click the Apply button. Unlike OK, the Apply button resets Windows with your changes, but it lets you change your mind if you don't like what you see. That way you can preview how things will look without fully committing.

5. If everything looks fine, click OK to lock in your choices. If it looks horrid, go back a step and reset your choices. Then click Cancel and be done with it.

Funky Items You Can Change

Three icon entries appear in the *Item* drop-down list. These aren't related to anything you can click on in the preview window, and they don't control colors or fonts. Choose each item listed as follows and click the Apply button to see how they affect your desktop.

Icon	This option sets the size of Windows icons, which means you can make them appear larger or smaller. For example, change the value in the *Size* spinner to 48. Then click the Apply button to see what happens to the icons on your desktop. (They get huge!) Be sure to set the value back to 32 if you want things normal before you click OK.
Icon Spacing (Horizontal)	This value sets the distance that icons are placed away from each other, left and right. When you arrange icons on the desktop, Windows normally spaces them 43 pixels apart. You can make this value smaller to line things up more snugly, or make it larger to give yourself a wider icon grid on the desktop.
Icon Spacing (Vertical)	This value sets the distance between icons up and down. You can set the value larger or smaller than 43 to make your desktop's icon grid taller or shorter.

You can preview your selections by clicking on the Apply button. But be sure to reset these values before you click OK or Cancel, especially if you're just goofing around.

Messing with the Taskbar

The taskbar is definitely a part of Windows' look. It's not the desktop. No, it's more like an annoying fat lip on the face of Windows. You can make some minor tweaks to that fat lip, moving it, stretching it out, or even putting it away. But, remember, most people don't mess with the taskbar much. In fact, all Windows documentation, articles in magazines, and whatnot show the taskbar the way it was when you first started Windows. Any changes you make will leave you on your own.

 Chapter 6 has lots and lots of information on the taskbar, primarily stuff that doesn't pertain to the way the taskbar looks. Flip back there to get the rest of the story.

Whipping About the Taskbar

The taskbar isn't glued to the bottom of your screen. You can flip it to either the right, left, or top edges of the screen, whichever you prefer.

Follow these steps to whip that taskbar around:

1. Point the mouse at a blank part of the taskbar. If you can't see a blank part, then point it at the loud time. And if you can't see the loud time, see Chapter 6, "But I Can't See the Clock!"

2. Using the left mouse button, the main one, press and hold the button as if you're starting a mouse-drag operation — which is exactly what you're about to do. When you press and hold the mouse's button, you'll see a fuzzy outline appear around the taskbar.

3. Drag the taskbar elsewhere. You can drag it to the left side of the screen, the right, bottom, or top. When you drag, the outline shows you where the taskbar will end (see Figure 22-7).

4. Release the mouse button. Behold! The taskbar lives in a new place on the screen. Funky, huh? Now you'll have to remember when this book or other documentation says "The Start Thing's button is in the lower-left corner of the screen," they're not talking about you because you've moved the taskbar.

To change the taskbar's location back to where it was, just repeat the preceding steps and move the taskbar back to the bottom of the screen — primary fat-lip position.

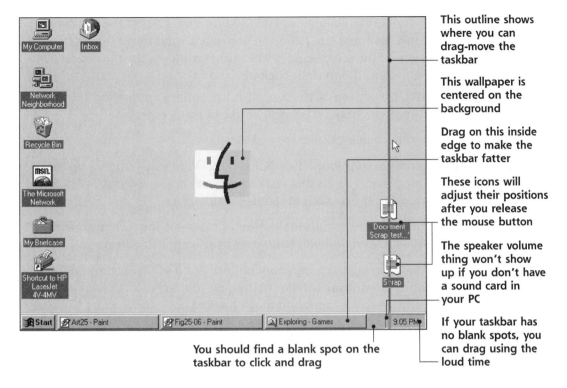

This outline shows where you can drag-move the taskbar

This wallpaper is centered on the background

Drag on this inside edge to make the taskbar fatter

These icons will adjust their positions after you release the mouse button

The speaker volume thing won't show up if you don't have a sound card in your PC

If your taskbar has no blank spots, you can drag using the loud time

You should find a blank spot on the taskbar to click and drag

Figure 22-7 General taskbar messing

Stretching the Taskbar

You can adjust the taskbar's width by dragging it out to a larger size. Just click the mouse on the taskbar's inside edge to *s-t-r-e-t-c-h*. This comes in especially handy when the taskbar has too many buttons, or if you choose a vertical taskbar orientation.

 X-REF The fine details on performing this task can be found in Chapter 6, in the section "Too Many Buttons on the Taskbar!"

Tweaking the Way the Taskbar Works

You can change the taskbar's operation in only two ways:

✻ Force the taskbar to be always on top or treated like any other window on the screen. Normally the taskbar is always on top, always visible. You can change this option so the taskbar is covered by new windows as you open them.

✳ Employ the auto-hide option. The taskbar moves out of the way when something new pops up. However, you can always move the mouse to the bottom of the screen and it will (rather annoyingly and often when you don't want it) pop right back up.

My personal preference is to turn off both options, removing the little ✔ check mark from their check boxes. You're free to think otherwise.

Follow these steps to change the way the taskbar works:

1. Call up the taskbar Properties dialog box. Do this by popping up the Start Thing menu (press CTRL+ESC), and then choose Settings → Taskbar . This brings up the taskbar Properties dialog box.

2. Click the Taskbar Options tab to bring that panel forward. It probably already is forward, but you can never trust computer software.

3. Click *Always on top* to change that option. Put a ✔ check mark in the box if you always want the taskbar on top, no matter what. Click again to remove the ✔ check mark and make the taskbar behave more like any other window. If you leave this option blank, you can always summon the taskbar by pressing CTRL+ESC. While that does pop up the Start Thing menu, you can see the taskbar and poke at any buttons or tweak it, if you like.

4. Click *Auto hide* to change that option. Click once to put a ✔ check mark in the box, again to remove the ✔ check mark. If this item is checked, the taskbar will always sulk out of the way when something pops up over it. Dragging the mouse to the bottom edge of the screen pops it back up, however. Sometimes, having this option on can be annoying. For example, any time you move the mouse to the bottom of the screen, the taskbar will pop up — "Here I am!" — like a lonely puppy dog wanting attention. You have to move the mouse subtly away from the taskbar a bit to make it hide again. Major pain.

5. Click the OK button in the taskbar Properties dialog box to lock in your changes.

BONUS

Make Up Your Own Color Scheme

T he *Item* drop-down list on the Appearance panel in the Display Properties dialog box (see Figure 22-6) contains all the different elements of Windows you can tweak. However, it's easier to change your screen's appearance by just clicking the mouse on the element you want to change in the window in the top of the dialog box. For example, click Active Window to change its colors, fonts, or size. If you toil a lot here, click the Save As button to give your new color scheme a name. This way you can retain your choices for later. You can use the gizmos in this dialog box to adjust the various parts. Still, note this is one complex dialog box.

X-REF **Refer to Chapter 26, "Trapped in a Dialog Box," for information on using the various gizmos and deeleebobs herein.**

If you need help figuring out what anything in the dialog box does, click the question-mark button in the upper-right corner. Then click the mouse on whatever is making you curious. For example, the button with the "/" on it is used to make text appear *italic*. I wouldn't have known that had I not question-mark clicked on it. See the sidebar "The Weird "?" Button on Some Windows" in Chapter 4 for more information.

Create Your Own Desktop Pattern and Wallpaper

I f you tire of the patterns that Windows has preset for your desktop, then create your own. Right-click the desktop, choose the Properties menu item, and then click on the Edit Pattern button in the Background panel. A Pattern Editor dialog box appears. It's pretty easy to figure out. Type in a new name and click Add to retain your new pattern. And tell your overlord's boss this is really "work" if he asks.

You can create your own wallpaper lickety-split using the Windows Paint program. In fact, when you use Paint, you'll see two items in the File menu, *Set as Wallpaper (Tiled)* and *Set as Wallpaper (Centered)*. Save your image in Paint, and then select either item to have your masterpiece appear as wallpaper. See Chapter 7 for more information on Paint; keep reading in Chapter 23 for information on Tiled and Centered wallpaper.

Summary

This chapter taught you how to change the screen resolution, color scheme, and the graphics you see in the background.

This chapter should have also taught you the following:

- [ ] How to change the way Windows looks.
- [ ] How to select a pattern for your desktop.
- [ ] How to pick out wallpaper for the desktop.
- [ ] How to change the size of the desktop.
- [ ] How to change the color of the Windows screen.
- [ ] How to move the taskbar around.
- [ ] How to change the way the taskbar works.

CHAPTER TWENTY-THREE

INTERESTING, WEIRD, AND NEAT STUFF

IN THIS CHAPTER YOU LEARN THESE KEY SKILLS

SETTING UP A SCREEN SAVER   PAGE 295

MAKING A DIFFERENT MOUSE POINTER   PAGE 298

ADDING SOUND TO WINDOWS   PAGE 299

TOYING WITH COMPUTER VIDEOS   PAGE 305

A Windows that's all work and no play would be almost as dull and boring as DOS once was. I'm not talking about games; DOS has plenty of clever games to rule your days. Windows, on the other hand, dishes up tasty treats such as animated mouse pointers, screen savers, sounds, videos, and a host of other interesting and sweetly charming goodies — what I call the interesting, weird, and neat stuff.

Saving the Screen from Boredom

A *screen saver* is nothing more than a toy. It's a tool originally intended to save the phosphor on older black-and-white (monochrome) monitors; if you left those monitors on too long, an image "burned" into their phosphor permanently. The screen saver prevented this by periodically darkening the screen or providing constant movement to prevent the burn-in.

Today's color monitors no longer need screen savers to prevent phosphor burn-in. Even so, the screen saver remains a fun toy. It's neat to have your computer's monitor turn blank and then see, for example, Mickey Mouse march across and start painting something. (For Mickey Mouse, you'll have to buy a third-party screen saver; he doesn't come with Windows.)

Has Your Screen Been Saved?

Screen savers also offer a form of security. First, with your screen darkened, someone can't wander by your office and see what you're doing when you're not there. Second, screen savers also offer a form of password protection because only by typing the proper password can you return to Windows from the screen saver.

Follow these steps to activate a screen saver for your monitor:

1. Summon the Display Properties dialog box (right-click the desktop).

2. Click on the Screen Saver tab. This brings the Screen Saver panel forward, similar to what you see in Figure 23-1. Work this box to set a screen saver for your monitor.

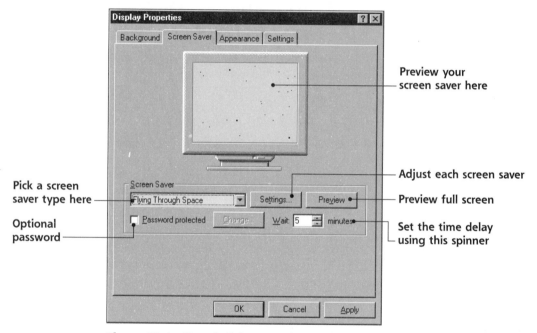

Pick a screen saver type here

Optional password

Preview your screen saver here

Adjust each screen saver

Preview full screen

Set the time delay using this spinner

Figure 23-1   How shall the screen be saved?

3. Pick a screen saver. Several are offered in the drop-down list (see Figure 23-1). Each turns your screen black with some type of busy graphic. Pick one to see what it does in the Preview screen. For each screen saver, click on the Settings button to see what kind of adjustments you can make. Nothing serious is there, just fun. For the *Scrolling Marquee* screen saver, click on the Settings button to type in your own special text. If you do this, click on the Preview button on the Display Properties dialog box to see how your text will look. This way you can make editing changes right away, adjust the formatting, color, and so on. To have no screen saver, choose (*None*) from the list.

4. Set the *Wait* time. The screen saver will appear on your screen after a certain interval of laziness, anywhere from 1 to 60 minutes after you last touch the keyboard or move the mouse. Set the interval using the spinner in the dialog box. I prefer a time delay of about five minutes. This means the screen saver snaps on automatically after I sit there looking at the screen, drooling for five minutes. It keeps me busy.

5. Click OK.

Your screen saver is set in motion. The next time you return to your computer after a break, you'll see the screen saver on the screen instead of the overdue project in Excel. Just move the mouse a little bit and the screen saver will flee.

Your computer will still work while the screen saver is on. If your computer is on a network, the screen saver will not interfere with anything. (Heck, the network interferes with itself enough; it doesn't need a screen saver for that.)

Shhh! Using the Password Option

To set a password for your screen saver, click in the *Password protected* box, putting a ✔ check mark there. The Change button enables you to enter a screen-saver password.

Follow these steps to use the password option:

1. Click the Change button. The Change Password dialog box appears.

2. Type your new password into the *New password* box. Make it brief. This is one password you don't want to forget casually.

3. Type the same password again into the *Confirm new password* box.

4. Click OK. Windows will tell you the password has been successfully changed. Rah.

The screen will be blank just as it was before, but when you try to reactive it (by moving the mouse or pressing a key on the keyboard), you'll be greeted with a password box (see Figure 23-2). Type in the proper password and press the ENTER key. Only then can you get back into your computer.

Type in the proper password here ——

—— Click here to gain entry

Figure 23-2 Knock, knock. What's the password?

If you forget the password, you're seriously screwed. You'll have to reset your computer, and then run through the steps in this section to reassign a password before the screen saver kicks in. (See, it's not good security, but it will keep snoopers out of your PC.)

A More Lively Mouse Pointer

Nothing will make someone's jaw drop like seeing a mouse pointer that looks like a flapping Windows flag. "How'd you do that?" they'll wonder. The trick is quite cinchy, because all you must do is switch mouse pointers from the cruddy old stationary models to something new and potentially different.

Follow these steps to change your mouse pointer:

1. Open a handy control panel near you. If you don't see the Control Panel's folder, press CTRL+ESC, S, C.

Control Panel

2. Double-click on the little mouse guy. This opens the Mouse Properties dialog box.

Mouse

3. Click on the Pointers tab to bring it forward. You'll see the Pointers panel, as shown in Figure 23-3. This is where you can choose new mouse pointers to replace the standard ones used in Windows.

4. Click on a pointer to change it. For example, click on the Busy pointer, the hourglass.

5. Click on Browse. This brings up a standard Browsing dialog box, where you can hunt down a new pointer. Windows will automatically show you pointers in the Cursors folder (under your Windows folder). You might want to browse elsewhere, for example, if you've just downloaded a batch of new cursors from CompuServe or the Internet.

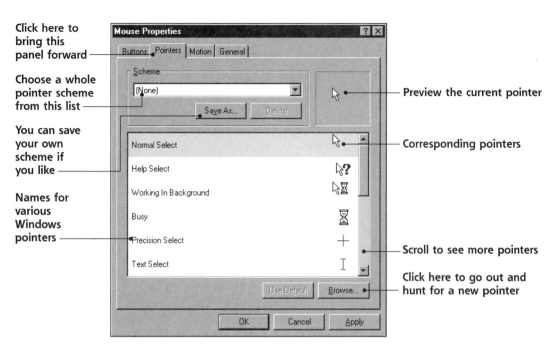

Click here to bring this panel forward

Choose a whole pointer scheme from this list

You can save your own scheme if you like

Names for various Windows pointers

Preview the current pointer

Corresponding pointers

Scroll to see more pointers

Click here to go out and hunt for a new pointer

Figure 23-3   The Mouse Properties dialog box, Pointers panel

6. Double-click on a new pointer in the Browse dialog box to select it and return to the Mouse Properties dialog box. If you don't like your new pointer, click the Default button to restore the old pointer.

7. Repeat Steps 4 and 5 for each pointer you want to change. Or, if you really want to make an impact, choose a pointer scheme from the Scheme drop-down list. A *scheme* is merely a preset collection of pointers, all following some theme. For example, the Tarzan scheme has all sorts of jungle pointers in it. Unfortunately, Windows doesn't come with the Tarzan scheme.

8. When you're done making changes, click OK.

You can click on Apply first, if you like. This way, you can try out some of the cursors, but remember, you can always change them later.

A More Euphonious PC

Equipped with the proper hardware, your PC can really hoot it up. That feeble little speaker can do a lot more than beep or twitter every time Windows tries to communicate with you. When your PC has the proper sound equipment, Windows can make wonderful music. Heck, just plowing through menus and opening windows can induce it to make symphonic rhapsodies. Granted, this has nothing to do with getting work done, but that would go against the theme of this part of the book.

Making Windows Noisy

Windows enables you to associate any one of a number of things it does with a specific sound. Open a window, hear a bleep. Start a new program, hear a splat. Quit Windows and hear a dozen people cheering. Windows makes it almost too much fun.

You need to fire up the Control Panel and play with the sounds icon.

Follow these steps to make noise:

1. Open the Control Panel, which lurks in My Computer's main window, or you can snatch it from the Settings submenu off the Start Thing's main menu.

Control Panel

2. Double-click on the Sounds icon to open it up and mess with sound on your computer. The Sounds Properties dialog box appears, looking something like Figure 23-4.

Sounds

3. Pick a Windows event from the *Events* list. A number of events are associated with Windows and several other programs. The events are fairly descriptive. Click on the event you want to have make a sound.

4. Choose a sound to associate with that event from the drop-down list by picking a sound from the *Sound* list.

5. You may want to use the Browse button to look for a specific sound on your hard drive. Any standard "wave" sound file will work, such as those you can create yourself using the Sound Recorder program (covered later in this chapter).

6. Click the play button to hear the sound — a preview of sorts.

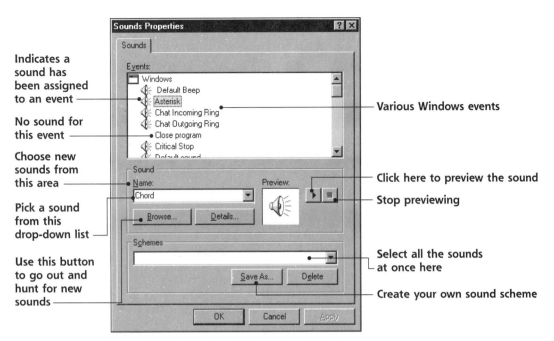

Indicates a sound has been assigned to an event —

No sound for this event —

Choose new sounds from this area —

Pick a sound from this drop-down list —

Use this button to go out and hunt for new sounds —

Various Windows events

Click here to preview the sound

Stop previewing

Select all the sounds at once here

Create your own sound scheme

Figure 23-4 The Sounds Properties dialog box

7. Continue assigning sounds to various Windows tasks. You can repeat Steps 3 and 4 for nearly everything Windows does.

8. Click OK when you're done. Before clicking OK, you can optionally click the Save As button to save all your sounds as a sound scheme on disk.

Scheming Sound Schemes

A collection of sounds is called a *scheme*. Windows has a few of them available for you to choose from, each has its own collection of specific sounds that work together in a certain way — call it a *sound motif*, though you'll have to look up what *motif* means in your dictionary.

You may not have any sound schemes installed on your computer. If not, you'll have to set them up manually. Refer to "Adding the Rest of Windows" in Chapter 11 for more information.

To use a preset sound scheme, choose one from the Schemes drop-down list in the Sounds Properties dialog box (see the previous section).

My personal favorite sound scheme is *Musica*, though I prefer a lot of the *Utopia* sounds.

Making Music mit MIDI

Your PC's sound capabilities aren't limited just to playing back recorded sounds. Most PC sound systems have their own built-in synthesizer. Special programs on disk can tickle the keys on this synthesizer and play little ditties.

The little ditties your PC can play are stored in Musical Instrument Digital Interface (MIDI) files on disk. (Pronounce it "middy.") You double-click on one to play the MIDI music, which then launches a multipurpose program called the Media Player (see Figure 23-5). In the case of the MIDI file, the Media Player plays the musical instruments in your PC's synthesizer. In Figure 23-5, Mozart's Turkish march, *Rondo alla turca*, is being played (you can't hear it; this is a book).

Turkish

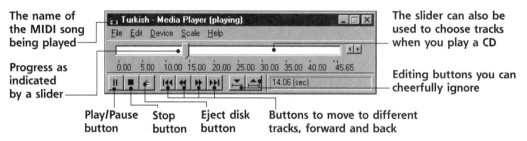

The name of the MIDI song being played — Progress as indicated by a slider — Play/Pause button · Stop button · Eject disk button · Buttons to move to different tracks, forward and back · The slider can also be used to choose tracks when you play a CD · Editing buttons you can cheerfully ignore

Figure 23-5   The Media Player pounds out Mozart at the computer keyboard.

There's nothing more you can do with MIDI files other than play them. Special hardware and software is required to create these files. They do, however, make a refreshing musical break if you collect a bunch of them and want to entertain yourself; the MIDI songs will play "in the background" while you do something else.

To play the music continuously, choose **Edit** → **Options** from the Media Player's menu. Then click the *Auto Repeat* option to put a ✔ check mark there. The music will play over and over, driving you nuts.

 X-REF   Another way your computer can play music is by sticking a musical CD into its CD-ROM player. Check out Chapter 12, "Playing a Musical CD" for more information.

The Media Player can also play videos and CDs, depending on which file types you choose when you select its **File** → **Open** command. See "Behold Computer Video!" later in this chapter for another run at the Media Player.

TIP Chances are good you don't have any MIDI files. Because I can't second guess what was installed in your computer, use the finding files skill you've learned and hunt for some MIDI files in Windows. Try searching for Mozart or *.MID.

Follow these steps to search for MIDI files:

1. Click on the Start button.

2. Point your mouse on Find.

3. Click on Files or Folders.

4. Click on the Advanced tab.

5. Use the scroll-down list on the *Of type:* box and click on *Midi Sequence.*

6. Click on Find Now.

If you have any MIDI files, they will be listed there. Double-click on the icon (not the name) and music will play.

Recording Your Own Sounds for Fun and Profit

If your computer has sound capabilities plus a little hole for plugging in a microphone, then you can record your own sounds in Windows. You do it with a little program called the Sound Recorder. (Clever names just ooze from the corporate offices of Microsoft.)

Follow these steps to create your own sounds:

1. Hook up the microphone to your computer. Make sure you plug it into the microphone connector, not a "line in" connector. (One is amplified, the other is not.) Likewise, you can plug in your stereo, VCR, or a tape recorder and copy sounds from them. Just go to Radio Shack and get a cable to connect your stereo's line out with your computer's line in.

2. Run the Sound Recorder program (Figure 23-6). You'll find it lurking off the Start Thing menu; Programs → Accessories → Multimedia → Sound Recorder is the way to get there.

3. Choose File → New. The New Sound dialog box appears. You can make various settings here to change the quality of the sound you record. The higher the quality, though, the larger the sound file on disk. If you've been messing around and haven't yet saved your sound to disk, you'll see a warning dialog box here giving you a chance to save.

23

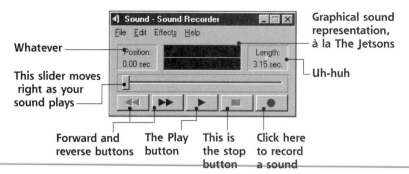

Whatever — Position: 0.00 sec.

Graphical sound representation, à la The Jetsons

This slider moves right as your sound plays

Length: 3.15 sec.

Uh-huh

Forward and reverse buttons

The Play button

This is the stop button

Click here to record a sound

Figure 23-6   The Sound Recorder is poised to record something.

4. Click OK to close the New Sound dialog box.

5. Clear your throat. Ah-hem. Test. One-two-three. Test . . . Test!

6. Click the Record button and start speaking into the mic. Blah-blah-blah. "Here's what I had for lunch today." Blah-blah-blah.

7. Click on the Stop button when you're done recording. If you don't click Stop, then you'll have a really big sound file with carefully recorded sounds of you muttering and shifting position in your chair.

8. Or click on the Play button to hear your recording. This can be fun. It's almost like the time you got your first tape recorder. If you don't like what you hear (which probably happened with your first tape recorder as well), repeat Steps 3 through 7. Again. And again. It takes a while to get things right.

9. Save your sound file to disk. Choose File → Save ; find a proper place and give a proper name to your sound file.

You can make your sound file a part of Windows by assigning it to a specific Windows event. For example, have your kids scream "Bye-bye" when Windows quits. See the section "Making Windows Noisy" earlier in this chapter for more information.

BONUS

Behold Computer Video!

Playing a video in Windows turns your $2,000 personal computer into a cheapy TV set, one that looks like it's picking up transmissions from Brezhnevian, Russia. Okay, maybe it's not that bad. Watching a video in Windows can be really fun.

Sunset
Blvd

The first thing you must do is find a video file. They're marked with a special icon and you might have such a file lurking in the Media folder off Windows' main folder. Just double-click on that file to start playing it. A window appears, such as the one shown in Figure 23-7, where your video plays.

She should have
won the Oscar

Stop button

Play/pause
button

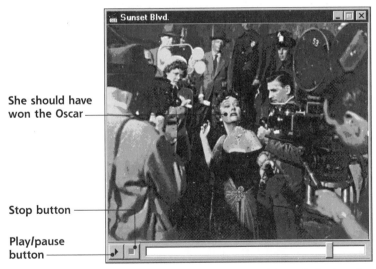

Figure 23-7   Norma Desmond is ready for her close-up.

The only drawback to videos on the screen, aside from the fuzzy, jerky quality, is they occupy a humongous amount of disk space. One little clip of Hannibal Lector describing the ideal wine to have with liver will chew up some 4MB of disk space. Other files take up even more space; a music video included with the Windows 95 beta test kit sucked up some 30MB of space.

Obviously, you didn't buy a computer to watch TV. In most cases, you'll find videos used as accompaniment in multimedia products. For example, clips from *Star Wars* and *Sunset Blvd.* are in Microsoft's Cinemania product. It's not the whole picture, but it's pretty fun to watch — yet another crazy thing Windows can do.

Summary

Windows could never be boring with all the fun gadgets that are added. Things such as animated mouse pointers, screen savers, sounds, videos, and a host of other interesting and sweetly charming goodies are all what makes Windows a hoot and hollerin' good time.

To make sure you can hoot and holler your best, don't leave this chapter without learning the following:

- ☐ How to start a screen saver for your monitor.
- ☐ How to use the password option for your computer.
- ☐ How to change the mouse pointer.
- ☐ How to program your computer to make noise.
- ☐ How to search for a MIDI file.
- ☐ How to create your own sounds.

CHAPTER TWENTY-FOUR

FUN, GAMES, AND FRIVOLITY

IN THIS CHAPTER YOU LEARN THESE KEY SKILLS

PLAYING SOLITAIRE   PAGE 308

PLAYING MINESWEEPER   PAGE 309

PLAYING FREECELL   PAGE 311

PLAYING HEARTS   PAGE 312

SETTING UP YOUR COMPUTER FOR DOS
     GAMES   PAGE 314

One thing about Windows being graphical and all that is it opens the doors to some fun games. Just about everything you've ever played — in real life, in an arcade, or on any computer — has a Windows equivalent. Not only that, Windows itself comes with a handful of interesting games, wonderful toys to obsess over. So here's a chapter devoted to Windows' games because, after all, you play them more than you should.

Look at me!
Look at me!
Look at me now!
It is fun to have fun
But you have to know how.
— *The Cat in the Hat*, by Theodor Geisel (Dr. Seuss)

Finding the Games

There are a ton of Windows games out there, games for all types. There are strategy games, blow-'em-up games, adventure games, card games, board games, you name it. Unfortunately, not all games come with Windows.

But look on the bright side: Those games that do come with Windows can be fun and addicting, two of the highest qualifications of any computer game.

Windows keeps all its games in the same menu off the Start Thing.

Follow these steps to find the games:

1. Pop up the Start Thing menu. Press CTRL+ESC or click the Start button on the taskbar.

2. Choose Programs . The Programs submenu appears.

3. Click on Accessories . The Accessories submenu appears.

4. Click on Games . The Games submenu appears, which may look like Figure 24-1. You'll see a list of the games installed with Windows, plus maybe some additional games you've added.

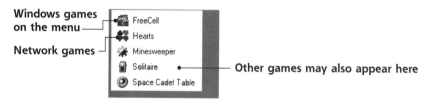

Figure 24-1   Your typical Games submenu

5. Click on the game you want to start. Pluck out a game. Try Solitaire first. Minesweeper involves a lot of mental energy most people don't want to expend. FreeCell is another frustrating card game.

If you find one game severely addictive, consider adding it to the Start Thing main menu. See Chapter 5.

Solitaire: The Art of Playing by Yourself

Perhaps the most addictive computer game is Solitaire, the card game of old. But don't use that as an excuse to play it. Solitaire is a great way to learn how to use the mouse. You get to point, click, drag, double-click. It's not fun it's . . . *exercise.* Yeah. That's it. Take a look at Solitaire in Figure 24-2.

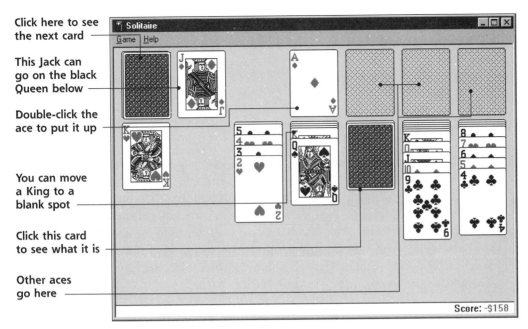

Click here to see the next card

This Jack can go on the black Queen below

Double-click the ace to put it up

You can move a King to a blank spot

Click this card to see what it is

Other aces go here

Figure 24-2   Old Sol can really get you going.

Start Solitaire according to the instructions offered in the section "Finding the Games" earlier in this chapter.

You click face-down cards to turn them over.

Drag cards from one column to another, putting red cards on black in descending order.

Double-click cards to put them up.

You can drag whole columns or just parts of columns.

Choose ▏**Game**▕ → ▏**Options**▕ to play some variations.

Yes, there is a way to cheat, but you'd be so pitiful if you tried it, I think there's no point in bothering.

TIP   Remember, you can minimize a game when you're done playing without quitting. That way you can quickly resume later, such as after the boss comes in. See "Done for the Day? To Quit or Put Away?" in Chapter 4.

Minesweeper, or How Not to Blow Up Bob

Minesweeper is one of those old computer logic puzzles. It goes like this: Suppose you have a grid under which are several mines. You can look under any tile in the grid for a mine. If you find a mine — Boom! — you blow up (actually, Bob blows up). If you don't find a mine, then you see a number that tells you how many tiles in the grid around you have mines under them. See? It's annoying.

For example, the grid nearby shows several uncovered tiles, but two of them have been flagged as mines. (That's because the 1 by each tile is only touching that one tile, meaning a mine is there.) The 2 right between the two flagged mines is already touching two mines, so the other blank tiles it's sitting next to are probably not mines. You can click the mouse on them to uncover their secret numbers, which will tell you more about the rest of the tiles, and so on, until you've solved the puzzle. (Supposedly.) Figure 24-3 shows you how a more advanced Minesweeper game looks.

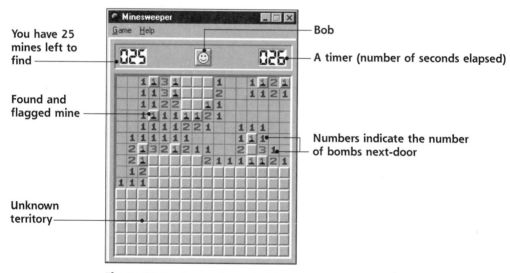

Figure 24-3 Sweep dem mines!

To start a new game, click Bob. Then start clicking blank tiles. Use your brain to determine where a mine lies based on the numbers you see. Use cunning, guile, and your computer mouse.

When you think you've found a mine, right-click that tile. This marks the tile with a little flag, meaning *Mine here!*

As you click on each tile to see what's underneath, Bob gets nervous.

If you find a mine, all the hidden mines are shown and, regrettably, Bob dies.

You can set the size of the mine field by choosing various options in the Game menu: Beginner, Intermediate, Expert, and Custom. Each size is larger with more mines to uncover.

If you win, Bob gets cool and you get to enter your name into the high score sheet.

By the way, not to brag or anything, but my best times are: Beginner, 9 seconds; Intermediate, 51 seconds; Expert, 138 seconds. Use these scores only for comparisons; your mileage may vary.

FreeCell (Another Annoying Solitaire-like Game)

A combination logic puzzle and Solitaire, FreeCell will keep you busy for hours — once you unlock its secrets. Perhaps the most annoying part of FreeCell is every puzzle has a solution. Unlike Solitaire, where you can be zoinked out of success by a bad shuffle, every single FreeCell game has a solution, sometimes several solutions. Now that smells of a challenge!

Start yourself a FreeCell game by following the instructions in "Finding the Games" earlier in this chapter. Then just play. See what you can do. The game is smart and will offer you suggestions about where cards can and cannot go. Take a look at FreeCell in Figure 24-4.

Unlike Solitaire, you do not drag cards with the mouse. Instead, you click on a card to select it, and then click where you want the card to move. The game will tell you if it's a valid move. If you can move a stack of cards, the game will ask if you want to move the whole stack or just the top card. Here are some of my own hints:

Free those aces up first!

Look for trouble spots, such as three of a kind in a row. That spells certain doom unless you can play all three cards.

FUN, GAMES, AND FRIVOLITY   **311**

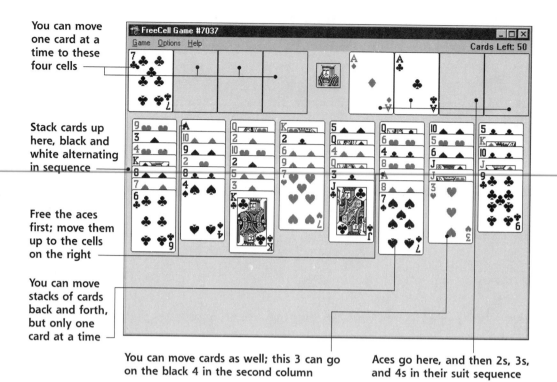

You can move one card at a time to these four cells

Stack cards up here, black and white alternating in sequence

Free the aces first; move them up to the cells on the right

You can move stacks of cards back and forth, but only one card at a time

You can move cards as well; this 3 can go on the black 4 in the second column

Aces go here, and then 2s, 3s, and 4s in their suit sequence

Figure 24-4   A typical, maddening FreeCell game

Try not to fill up the free cells, especially with high-suited cards, such as face cards.

If you can clear one whole column, you're halfway to winning the game.

Try to look several moves in advance.

Every puzzle has a solution. If you don't win the first time, try playing the same card layout again (it will ask if you want to when it announces that you've lost). I've done this hundreds of times and have yet to find a puzzle I can't defeat. Some of them are real boogers, though.

Hearts Attack

A great network game to play, and one you can play on a nonnetworked computer as well, is Hearts. It's the traditional game of Hearts, with the traditional rules (no cheating!). On a network, you can play with three of your nonworking coworkers, or you can start your own game by choosing to be the dealer and then by trying to beat the pants off the computer.

Refer to the instructions in "Finding the Games" earlier in this chapter for information on starting Hearts. I won't bother going into any details on how to play or strategy here, though you can rest assured, if one of the computer players has The Queen, he or she will pass it to you. Here are some other hints:

If you can't seem to play, then you probably have the 2 of Clubs — that card always leads.

Click a card to pass or play.

The computer will always know when you try to *run them*, so don't unless you really can and there's no way to stop you.

Pass your clubs when you start.

By the way, in Figure 24-5, Shirley passed me the Queen on the first hand. Predictable.

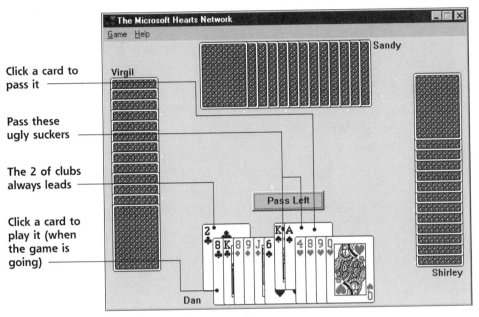

Figure 24-5   Hearts in action

Other Games Abounding

If you have a modem and access to an online service or the Internet, you have an open door to thousands of Windows games. Microsoft even makes Entertainment Packs, which contain all sorts of games (plus interesting wallpaper and fonts). There's even an Arcade Entertainment Pack that contains some classic old, early '80s arcade games you can play right in Windows. (Games include Tempest, Asteroids, Missile Command, BattleZone, Centipede, and so on.)

Unfortunately, about the only type of game unavailable for Windows is the flight simulator type. Although I wouldn't be surprised if such a game was available by the time you read this.

Wrestling with DOS Games

This is serious business. DOS games are perhaps some of the best, most sophisticated computer games ever devised. The reason is simple: DOS enables just about any program to take complete control over the computer. DOS is easy to push around. So DOS games just shove it out of the way and, lo, soon the game has control over more computing power than existed on the planet earth in the '50s. That's pretty impressive.

To run a DOS game under Windows, you must properly configure Windows to sacrifice as much control as it can over to the DOS game. This is a tall order. In fact, most true Game Zanies will start their computers in DOS mode only, bypassing Windows altogether. But Microsoft has made great strides in enabling greedy DOS games to run under Windows.

DOS Games? Forget Windows!

Those purists exist who will insist DOS games are best played in DOS, forget Windows. This is quite easy to do. You have three options:

First, you can start your computer under DOS instead of Windows. This is done right when the computer first starts, just after you see the *Starting Windows* message appear on the screen. You press the F8 key, and then press 6 to choose *Command prompt only* from the menu. This starts your computer in MS-DOS 7 mode, from which you can run your game without interference from Windows.

SIDE TRIP

EXCELLENT, IF NOT SELF-PROMOTING, BOOKS FOR USING DOS

If you're serious about games, you'll need to understand DOS a little better than most and be prepared for some tweaking beyond that offered in any Windows book. Two books I recommend are *MORE DOS For Dummies* and *The Microsoft Guide to Managing Memory with MS-DOS*. (Yeah, I wrote them both).

Although it's a *For Dummies* book, *MORE DOS For Dummies* contains ample information on using DOS and configuring your system. The *Managing Memory* book will tell you how to optimize a DOS session for the most memory possible, a sore subject among game players.

Much of the configuring these books suggest can be entered directly into the Advanced Program Settings dialog box, shown in Figure 24-6. Click on the *Specify a new MS-DOS configuration* option, and then click on the *Configuration* button to make the suggested settings for your game's *MS-DOS mode*. Good luck!

Second, you can just bolt from Windows and restart your computer in MS-DOS mode. Do this by choosing that option from the Shut down dialog box when you shut down Windows; click *Restart the computer in MS-DOS mode* and you'll soon see a cheery DOS prompt awaiting your DOS game commands.

Third, you can configure your DOS game program to fly solo in Windows. This is a special advanced option discussed in the next section. Basically it tells Windows to go away while your DOS program (such as a game) takes complete control over the computer.

All three of these methods achieve the same madness: Windows is shoved aside and your game or DOS takes over the computer. That's always the safest and best way to play your DOS game in Windows.

X-REF **For more information on startup options for Windows, including starting your computer in DOS mode, see the section titled "Windows' Special Startup Key Commands" in Chapter 29.**

See Chapter 1, "Quitting Windows and Turning Off Your PC" for more information on the Shut down command.

Properly Configuring a DOS Game Session in Windows

Suppose you want to run that DOS game in Windows. If so, you will have to be picky about how it runs. To be picky, you need to hunt down your DOS game using My Computer or the Explorer, and then bring up its Properties dialog box for some adjustments.

Follow these steps to configure a DOS game in Windows:

1. Locate your DOS game using My Computer or the Explorer.

2. Click on your game once using the mouse. This highlights or selects the game for action. Don't double-click here; you want to make some adjustments before starting your game.

3. Right-click the program's icon and choose Properties from the menu; press ALT+ENTER, or choose File → Properties . The program's Properties dialog box appears.

4. Click on the Program tab to bring that panel forward.

5. Click on the Advanced button.

   This brings up the Advanced dialog box (Figure 24-6) where it all boils down to two choices: Do you want to attempt to run this program inside Windows or do you want the program to shut down Windows and run by itself?

X-REF See Chapter 10 for more information about dealing with a DOS program's properties; however, most of the special stuff surrounding games is covered here.

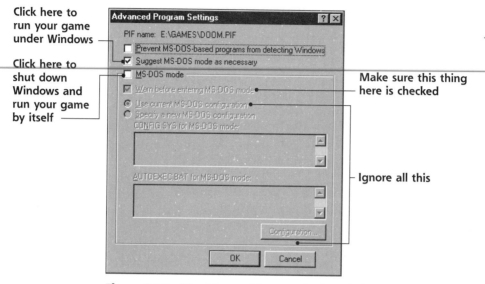

Click here to run your game under Windows

Click here to shut down Windows and run your game by itself

Make sure this thing here is checked

Ignore all this

Figure 24-6 The Advanced Program Settings dialog box

If you're daring, try running the game under Windows; leave the box by *MS-DOS mode* blank. This means Windows will start your game and try to run it in a window on the screen. Most of the time this meets with success, though the game may run slowly and may have to be run full-screen (as opposed to in its own window).

To run the game full-screen, press ALT+ENTER.

X-REF For more program secrets, check out Chapter 10.

If you find your game runs too slowly in Windows, put a ✔ check mark in the box by MS-DOS mode. This tells Windows to shut itself down and run your game in DOS. Make sure there's a ✔ check mark in the box by *Warn before entering MS-DOS mode.* This directs Windows to display a proper warning dialog box (Figure 24-7) before it dives into your game-only mode.

The warning in Figure 24-7 is kinda inaccurate. It makes it sound like Windows will merely close your programs but, in fact, it really shuts down entirely. When you quit your game, Windows will restart.

My advice is to run all your DOS games in the MS-DOS mode, or just consider restarting your computer in the MS-DOS mode (as described in the previous section). This way you'll be certain your game won't interfere with Windows and vice-versa.

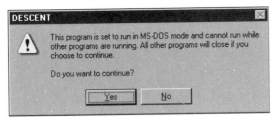

Figure 24-7 The warning dialog box you see when your game is about to take over

BONUS

How to Cheat the Games

You know, there is a way to cheat at these games, but I decided you shouldn't know this. Then you would be tempted to cheat, and that wouldn't be very good, now would it?

3D Space Cadet Pinball

You'll notice the last game listed is a pinball table. The sound and graphics are pretty cool. There are no secrets here. It's simply a pinball game. These are the keys you need to know:

?	Moves the right paddle.
>	Tilts the table to the right.
z	Moves the left paddle.
x	Tilts the table to the left.
	To get the game going, press the spacebar. The longer you hold down the spacebar, the more oomph the puller has.
F2	Restarts the game when you're doing a really bad job.
F3	Pauses the game, so your boss doesn't wreck your score when he or she walks in your office and wants to talk.
F8	Player Controls; you can change the keys for the paddles and tilting.

The dialog box on the right lets you know what's going on with the game. You'll see notices such as *Wormhole opened* and *Spaceship Refueled.* Good to know.

My top score is 2,980,500. My nine-year old's top score is 3,470,500. I have some work to do here.

Summary

Hearts, Solitaire, FreeCell, and Space Cadet Pinball. Wow! More fun than humanly possible. Now, enough play. It's time to work.

In the chapter, you should have picked up the following. Learning this, per se, isn't really necessary because, well, these are games.

☐ Where to find the games.

☐ How to play Solitaire.

☐ How to play Minesweeper.

☐ How to play FreeCell.

☐ How to play Hearts.

☐ How to configure a DOS game.

WINDOWS IS AS WINDOWS DOES

THIS PART CONTAINS THE FOLLOWING CHAPTERS

CHAPTER **25** YOUR BASIC WINDOWS' WINDOWS CONCEPTS

CHAPTER **26** TRAPPED IN A DIALOG BOX

CHAPTER **27** MOUSY CONCEPTS

CHAPTER **28** WORKING WITH TEXT AND GRAPHICS

CHAPTER **29** PROBLEMS AND SOLUTIONS

Eurystheus sat in front of the locked door to his computer room, sour and depressed. He questioned the gods. Was it Heracles or he himself they were driving mad?

Eventually the door opened and Heracles emerged. But this wasn't the same man who two weeks earlier had performed the twelve labours. This man could barely stand before the Hydra or Cerberus.

"Heracles," Eurystheus said, amazed at the tiny, pale man, "is that you?"

Heracles snorted. His arms were reed thin, his chest hollow, his ribs protruding. The tiny, drawn face spoke to Eurystheus. "I am immortal."

A glowing figure appeared: tall, brave-looking, white haired, bearded. Eurystheus recognized him as Zeus, father of the gods.

"Behold Heracles," Zeus boomed. "He has completed his tasks and is granted his reward. I have returned to him his sanity. And as part of the bargain, he now becomes immortal, one of the gods."

Eurystheus nodded. Another glowing figure appeared.

"Zeus, you are a fool," said Hera. "Heracles has not completed his final task. He is not the master of that device!"

Heracles looked away from the beautiful goddess as he spoke. "I think I've mastered the PC. I need to move now to that decaying IBM system you have installed on Olympus. It needs new software, and then I'll sell it to you."

Hera stood stunned. Zeus beamed like a proud father.

"No. I won't sell it to you. I'll *license* it to you," Heracles said. "You'll pay me a little bit every month, for eternity. And there will be upgrades . . ."

"Okay, okay," laughed Zeus. "We'll get into that soon enough." He turned to his wife. "Hera, only twelve labours were in this bargain. Why did you give him a thirteenth?"

"I didn't. Dave did it on his own." Hera pointed at Eurystheus, cowering in a corner.

"Is this true?" asked Zeus. Eurystheus wet himself.

"It is true," Zeus said. He turned to the computer to determine Eurystheus' punishment. He winked at Heracles, who smiled.

"Are you taking away my computer?" Eurystheus asked.

"No. I wouldn't do that," Zeus said. "Your punishment is far worse." Zeus laughed. Then he vanished with Heracles.

Eurystheus turned to Hera, who also vanished.

Gingerly, Eurystheus walked into his computer room, expecting the worst.

Nothing had changed. The computer was still there. The monitor. The printer. All was as he'd left it.

But then, up on the screen, instead of bright colors and graphical fun, Eurystheus saw something that shook him with cold terror. It was a simple thing, but it made his spine tingle.

The computer said: C:\>

CHAPTER TWENTY-FIVE

YOUR BASIC WINDOWS' WINDOWS CONCEPTS

IN THIS CHAPTER YOU LEARN THESE KEY SKILLS

IDENTIFYING VARIOUS WINDOW PARTS   PAGE 319

CHANGING A WINDOW'S SIZE AND
    POSITION   PAGE 322

WORKING SCROLLBARS   PAGE 325

UNDERSTANDING AND WORKING THE
    MENUS   PAGE 327

WORKING WITH MULTIPLE DOCUMENT WINDOWS
    (THE MULTIDOCUMENT INTERFACE)   PAGE 329

In Windows, information appears on the screen in a window. If the information appeared in an envelope, Microsoft would probably have called their operating system Envelopes, but it doesn't and they didn't. The philosophy is it's easier to manage information when it appears in a contained space, especially if you're doing several things at once. This way, each application runs in its own window, without elbowing others out of the way. The ability to control these windows is central to Windows' operation, which is why this chapter was written.

Windows' Windows (or "Pains of Glass")

All windows have two basic parts: the frame and the insides. Subtle variations exist, but certain gizmos are common to all windows and these gizmos work the same. Knowing what the gizmos are and how to work them brings you one step closer to feeling in charge of your computer.

321

I've Been Framed!

There are six basic elements to a typical window on the screen, as outlined in Table 25-1.

TABLE 25-1 Basic Window Screen Elements

Element	Description
CONTROL MENU	This menu contains several commands for adjusting the window. Each of these commands is more easily done using the mouse and other window gadgets. And, in case your mouse is ever broken, the keyboard equivalent for this menu is ALT+SPACEBAR.
TITLE BAR	Everything must have a name.
MINIMIZE BUTTON	Click on the Minimize button to shrink the window down to a button on the taskbar. *Thwoop!* The button even looks like a shrunken-down window. Kinda.
RESTORE/MAXIMIZE BUTTON	The Restore button looks like two overlapping windows. Click it to restore the window to its size and position after maximizing. The Maximize button lets you zoom out the window full-screen size, which is the preferred mode of operation for most windows.
CLOSE BUTTON	Click here to make the window go bye-bye. Other ways to do this include choosing Close from the window's control menu; choosing Exit, Quit, or Close from the application's File menu; pressing ALT+F4 or ALT+SPACEBAR+C on the keyboard; and double-clicking on the control menu icon. They really want to give you ample opportunities to stomp a window into the dirt.
EDGES	You can "grab" any edge of the window using the mouse and drag it to a new size. If you drag a window's corner, you can resize a window in two directions at once.

 X-REF Another button that may appear on dialog box windows is the question-mark button. See the box, "The Weird "?" Button on Some Windows," in Chapter 4 for more information.

Figure 25-1 shows a typical window on the screen.

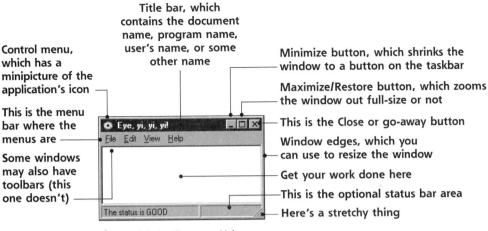

Title bar, which contains the document name, program name, user's name, or some other name

Control menu, which has a minipicture of the application's icon

This is the menu bar where the menus are

Some windows may also have toolbars (this one doesn't)

Minimize button, which shrinks the window to a button on the taskbar

Maximize/Restore button, which zooms the window out full-size or not

This is the Close or go-away button

Window edges, which you can use to resize the window

Get your work done here

This is the optional status bar area

Here's a stretchy thing

Figure 25-1 Fenestra Usitata

Inside Information

A window's contents depend on what the window does. Table 25-2 lists four common things you may find inside any window.

TABLE 25-2 Common Window Contents

Element	Description
MENU BAR	A list of commands going from left to right just under the window's title bar
TOOLBARS	A row of buttons, command shortcuts, and other gizmos that may appear below the menu bar
WORK AREA	Where it happens
STATUS BAR	A strip of helpful information about a program, typically low toward the bottom of the window

Review Figure 25-1 to find out where these things are, but remember, not every window will sport them.

Adjusting a Window's Position and Size

Any time you start an application, its window appears on the screen at some random position and size. Sometimes this is great. Other times you'd like to rearrange the window's position and size, which is cinchy to do, providing you know how to stretch a window to another size.

The Joy of Stretch

Windows on the desktop can change their size because their edges are made of rubber. To move a window's edge, you grab it with the mouse and stretch it to a new position. Look at Figure 25-2 to see this rubber edge.

Follow these steps to change the edges of a window:

1. Point the mouse at one of the window's edges you want to move. When the mouse is positioned right, it changes into an up-down or left-right pointy arrow. This shows you which direction you can move the window's edge.

2. Press and hold the mouse button down, and then move the mouse in or out to make the window larger or smaller along that one edge. As you drag around the mouse, you'll see a fuzzy bar showing you approximately where the window's edge will be.

3. Release the mouse button when you're pleased. The window snaps to the new edge, changing its size larger or smaller.

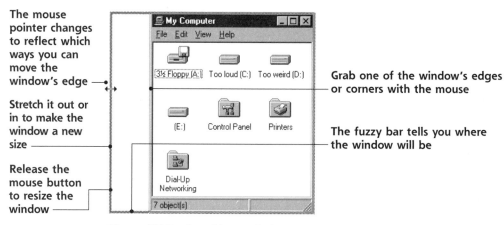

The mouse pointer changes to reflect which ways you can move the window's edge

Stretch it out or in to make the window a new size

Release the mouse button to resize the window

Grab one of the window's edges or corners with the mouse

The fuzzy bar tells you where the window will be

Figure 25-2 Stretching a window

You can also move two of the window's edges at once. You do this by grabbing one of the window's corners and not an edge.

Follow these steps to move two edges at once:

1. Point the mouse at one of the window's corners. Any of the four corners will do, though the most popular corner to grab is the lower right (don't ask me why; just try it). The mouse pointer changes to a diagonally pointing arrow when it's positioned right. Like dragging a window's edge, this shows you which direction you can move.

2. Drag the corner to a new position. You can drag the corner in two directions at once, making the window taller and wider, or shorter and narrower. If you drag the window too small, the menu bar will "wrap" itself down to a second or third line. Also, toolbars will disappear when a window is too narrow. The moral? Don't make your window too narrow if you have a toolbar displayed.

3. Release the mouse button. The window snaps to its new size.

SIDE TRIP

LOOK OUT FOR THE STRETCHY THING IN THE LOWER-RIGHT CORNER

Some windows may not stretch in the traditional way. You'll notice these because they sport what I call the *stretchy thing* in their lower-right corner — like a ribbed triangle. With those types of windows, often the only way to change their size is to drag them by their stretchy thing. These windows can usually only be dragged in one direction or another, or they must maintain some minimum size so you can see their contents.

Note, most status bars have a stretchy thing in their lower-right corner. This may or may not mean this is the only way to stretch the window.

The Wonder of Maximize and Restore

If you want to resize the window to fill the entire screen, click on the Maximize button. This makes the window full-size, no matter what size or shape your screen.

After clicking on the Maximize button, it changes to another button — the Restore button. This button returns your window to the size and position it was before maximizing.

 TIP You can also maximize and restore any window by double-clicking on its title bar. This is actually an old Macintosh trick, one Microsoft probably borrowed from Apple a long time ago and never got sued.

You cannot stretch a window when it's maximized. In fact, you can't even see the window's edges.

Moving Windows

Just as cartoons used to show cavemen dragging women around by their hair, you drag a window around. But because most windows are bald, you must instead use their title bar.

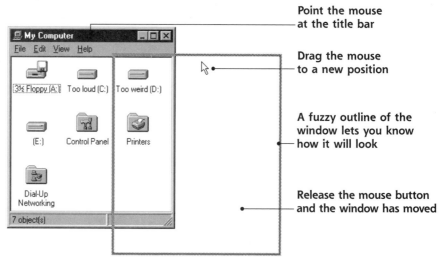

Figure 25-3 Dragging a window around by its head

Follow these steps to drag a window around (also illustrated in Figure 25-3):

1. Point the mouse at the window's title bar.

2. Press and hold the mouse button down.

3. Move the mouse — and the window — to a new position. As you drag the mouse on your desktop, an outline of the window on the screen will mimic those movements. This gives you a rough idea of where your window will fit.

4. Release the mouse button. Plop! The window falls into place.

Cleaning Stray Windows

Sometimes a window will wander to the side of the screen, slipping out of mouse reach. When this happens, it can be darn hard to reach the window, and nearly impossible to read anything the window may say.

Who knows why windows wander? But a straying window is no reason to turn off the computer or painfully reinstall Windows. Instead, try the following trick.

Follow these steps to get your wandering window back:

1. Close or minimize any windows on the screen, except for the one you can't get to (of course). You want your stray window to be the only one "open."

2. Bring up the taskbar's shortcut menu.

3. If you can't find a blank spot on the taskbar, right-click the current time, shown on the far-right side of the taskbar. That shortcut menu looks a little different, but it still contains the vital command you need.

4. Choose Cascade from the menu.

The window is instantly resized and placed in the upper-left corner of the screen.

Now you can get at it, change its size, read its contents, whatever. Whew! Aren't you lucky?

To Deal with Scrollbars

What you see in a window is merely a small representation of something that can be much bigger. For example, a chapter in your great American novel can be several pages long, but you can only see 23 lines or so on the screen at a time. To see the rest of the document, you need to scroll.

You can make a window's scrollbars disappear, providing you can stretch the window out to a larger size. See "The Joy of Stretch" earlier in this chapter. (By the way, I once saw a PC hooked up to a special "virtual" monitor where some computer geeks had stretched out a window to 32 feet X 32 feet in size. Talk about a slow day. . . .)

Scrolling for Dollars

Scrolling is done in two directions: up and down and left and right. To control how you scroll, and which parts of your document you can see, you use a vertical or horizontal scrollbar.

Left and right is horizontal. Think about the horizon. It goes left and right, a straight line (minus the mountains) going left and right is horizontal.

Up and down is vertical. There is no cute way to remember vertical.

Working a Scrollbar (Scrollin', Scrollin', Scrollin')

You use the scrollbar to see a different part of the image inside the window. But the scrollbar doesn't really move the image; instead it moves the window. For example, to see the *left* side of your document, you click the *left* arrow on the horizontal scrollbar. But that moves your document to the *right*. This confuses some beginners, but you can get used to it snappy-quick.

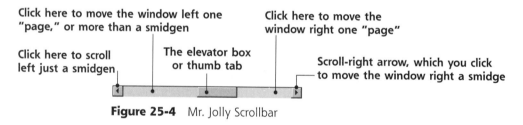

Figure 25-4 Mr. Jolly Scrollbar

Figure 25-4 shows a typical scrollbar, which could be either a vertical or horizontal scrollbar, but it's horizontal here because that fits best on the page. Note, several ways exist to use the scrollbar, not just the arrows at the end.

The most curious part of the scrollbar is the elevator box or thumb tab. First, its position gives you a vague idea of where the window is looking in relation to the entire document. For example, if the elevator box is at the top of the vertical scrollbar, you know you're looking at the beginning of your document.

Second, the elevator box's size lets you know how much of the document you can see at once. If it's really long, your document is relatively short and you can see most of it in the window at one time. If it's squat, then you have a hefty document.

Third, you can drag the elevator box with the mouse to scroll anywhere in your document at once.

Chasing Menus

A key part of most application windows is their menu bar. This is where the commands live that control that application. What the commands do and how they work depends on the application. The following sections tell you how the menus operate.

 Many menu commands are common to all Windows applications. Refer to Chapter 4, "Use One Program, You've Used Them All" for more information on those common menu commands.

Working the Menus

The best way to work Windows' menus is with your mouse. This involves a lot of pointing, clicking, and, occasionally, some dragging. Before doing so, gawk at Figure 25-5 to glean some menu terminology knowledge.

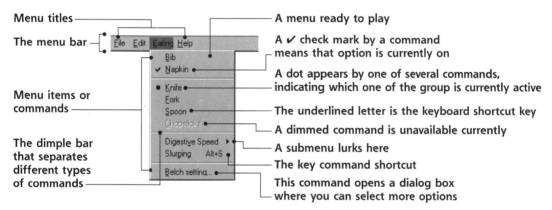

Figure 25-5   Menu pieces' parts

Menus consist of titles and the menu itself. You click the menu name on the menu bar to see the menu.

Located on each menu are various commands. The commands are often divided into groups on longer menus, separated by dimple bars.

A ✔ check mark next to a menu command means the option is on. Choosing the command again removes the ✔ check mark, turning it off. Choose the command a third time to switch it on again.

Sometimes only one of several menu items can be selected at once. For example, in Figure 25-5, you can choose either *Knife*, *Fork*, or *Spoon* (the *Chopsticks* item is unavailable). Whichever item you pick from the group has a dot (●) by it.

When a menu item isn't available, it appears "dimmed" in the menu. You can't choose that item no matter what; typically you'll need to rework some part of the program to make it available as an option (such as choosing Chinese food).

A triangle next to a command indicates a submenu. Choosing that command displays the submenu, which pops up on the screen. Sometimes there are sub-submenus, such as the disaster that naturally befalls the Start Thing menu.

Finally, some commands have ellipses, or three dots, after their names. That means the command opens a dialog box where you can set more options. This isn't a hard and fast rule, though. Lots of the commands that should have dots after them don't, and some that don't should have.

Beware the Instant Menu!

Watch out for some "instant" menu titles. These really aren't titles but are, in fact, commands on the menu bar. Some programmers are nice and let you know they really are commands by putting an exclamation point after them. So your menu bar may look like this:

File Edit Schedule!

The *Schedule!* menu is really a command. This isn't a hard and fast rule, so be on the lookout for certain menu titles that are commands and offer you no clue about it either way.

Working Menus with Your Keyboard

Every menu item and command has a key equivalent. This means you can get at any menu using the keyboard, often faster than you can using the mouse. The key is to look for the underlined letter in the menu. Press that letter, plus the ALT key, to activate that menu or command.

For example, the Edit menu has an underlined E. If you press ALT+E you'll drop down the Edit menu. You can then choose any item in that menu by pressing the underlined letter: T for Cut; C for Copy, P for Paste, and so on. You don't need to press the ALT key once you have the menu open.

You can also press each key separately. For example, just press and release the ALT key. This activates all the menus. From this point on, you need only press the underlined letter to make something happen: ALT, E, T for **Edit** → **Cut** , for example.

X-REF Some people find these keyboard shortcuts much faster than working the mouse, especially when using a word processor or any application where your fingers are already on the keyboard. Also check out the box "Quick Key Shortcuts" in Chapter 4 for some command equivalents to certain common menu items.

BONUS

The Old Multidocument Interface Gag

Some sophisticated applications enable you to work on multiple documents at once. To handle this, each document appears in its own window inside the application's main window. This is windows within windows within Windows! It's called the *multidocument interface*.

The key to knowing whether your application supports the multidocument interface is to find a *Window* menu. This menu usually indicates the application can support multiple document windows open at a time.

Like the application's window, the document windows will have basic parts (go back to Figure 25-1); each document window has a Minimize, Maximize/Restore, and Close button, for example.

When the document window is maximized (as shown in Figure 25-6), its buttons appear following the application's buttons on the menu bar.

Here is the document's control menu

The "red" underlined words are flagged by Word as misspelled

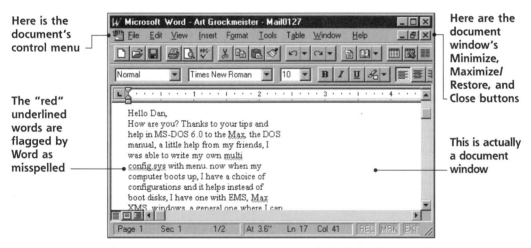

Here are the document window's Minimize, Maximize/Restore, and Close buttons

This is actually a document window

Figure 25-6 A document window "maximized" inside an application

When the document window is minimized, it appears like a button on the taskbar, but the button floats in the bottom of the application's work space (see Figure 25-7).

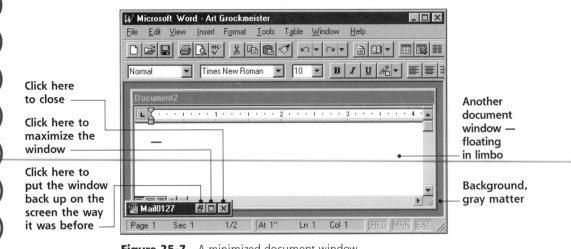

Click here to close

Click here to maximize the window

Click here to put the window back up on the screen the way it was before

Another document window — floating in limbo

Background, gray matter

Figure 25-7 A minimized document window

When the document window floats in the application's work space, you can change its size or position just like a window on the desktop. See "Adjusting a Window's Position and Size" earlier in this chapter. The instructions there also apply to document windows.

Summary

The whole philosophy behind windows is: Information is easier to manage when it appears in a contained space, especially if you're doing several things at once. The ability to control these windows is why this chapter was written.

In this chapter, you should have picked up the following:

☐ What the six basic elements to a typical window are.

☐ How to change the edges of a window.

☐ How to move two edges of a window at once.

☐ How to click and drag a window.

☐ How to get a wandering window back.

☐ How to work with scrollbars.

☐ The pieces and parts of a menu.

☐ How to work the menus with your keyboard.

TRAPPED IN A DIALOG BOX

26

IN THIS CHAPTER YOU LEARN THESE KEY SKILLS

UNDERSTANDING DIALOG BOXES   PAGE 332

WORKING THROUGH A DIALOG BOX   PAGE 334

USING THE KEYBOARD IN A DIALOG BOX   PAGE 334

PLAYING WITH ALL THE DIALOG BOX GIZMOS
   (LOTS OF THEM)   PAGE 335

W hen Windows wants your opinion, it asks. Then it ignores you. But when it needs information, it presents you with a dialog box. A dialog box is a special window on the screen, like an information sheet. You fill in various options, set various settings, and generally goof around until you think you have everything set just right. Then you tell Windows it's all OK, or you chicken out and Cancel.

Dialog boxes are useful because they enable you to set numerous options without fussing with a lot of menus. On the downside, Windows tosses up dialog boxes on the screen like dough in a pizza parlor on a Saturday night. Some dialog boxes are so complex, they make you think you've just sat down in a space shuttle cockpit; things can get confusing. The purpose of this chapter is to tell you how a dialog box works, so the gizmos and gadgets you encounter will actually help you get done what you want done.

Anatomy of a Dialog Box

Dialog boxes range from the utterly simple to a variation of a Boeing 747 cockpit. Even so, all of them tend to look and work the same.

The most basic of all dialog boxes is the "info" dialog box, such as the About Windows dialog box shown in Figure 26-1. It contains basic information, some blah-blah text, and an OK button.

Choose Help → About Windows 95 from My Computer window to see this dialog box

Information about Windows. La-di-da

Good to know stuff, but nothing you can do about it

Click here when you've been impressed enough

Figure 26-1   Windows! Read all about it!

Another simple dialog box is the warning dialog (see Figure 26-2), which lets you know something is amiss and may even give you a chance to remedy the situation.

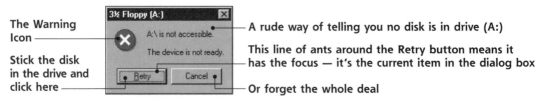

The Warning Icon

A rude way of telling you no disk is in drive (A:)

Stick the disk in the drive and click here

This line of ants around the Retry button means it has the focus — it's the current item in the dialog box

Or forget the whole deal

Figure 26-2   Oops. Musta taken a wrong turn.

NOTE   Other icons include a question mark (?) for a question, an exclamation point (!) for *what the huh?*, and maybe more I haven't seen yet.

Basic Pieces' Parts

Every dialog box has three main elements: The title bar, the contents, and a button. The title bar gives the dialog box a name, the contents are the "dialog" part for the computer, and the button is your dialog part.

Often times the button says "OK" when, in fact, it should say "Oh well."

Don't confuse the buttons in the dialog box with the main dialog box control buttons. Typically, there will be one to three main control buttons, all of which you'll find at the bottom of the dialog box.

The more complex dialog boxes will sport a question-mark button, next to the Close button in the dialog box's upper-right corner (see Figure 26-3). Click this button and the mouse pointer changes to a mouse pointer/question-mark thing. Then you can click any other gadget in the dialog box to get pop-up help.

Another way to get pop-up help is to right-click something in a dialog box. This usually displays the *What's This?* shortcut menu. Click *What's This?* to get some bubble help.

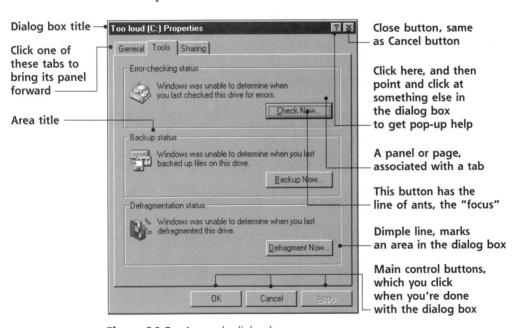

Dialog box title
Click one of these tabs to bring its panel forward
Area title

Close button, same as Cancel button
Click here, and then point and click at something else in the dialog box to get pop-up help
A panel or page, associated with a tab
This button has the line of ants, the "focus"
Dimple line, marks an area in the dialog box
Main control buttons, which you click when you're done with the dialog box

Figure 26-3 A sample dialog box

TIP Use the TAB key to move the focus to another part of the dialog box. Also, pressing the ENTER key is the same as choosing the focused item.

Panels, Pages, and Tabs

Some dialog boxes have more than one face. The *faces,* also called *panels* or *pages*, are each connected to a tab, such as the tab on a file folder. Click on the tab and that panel moves forward in the dialog box.

Areas, Regions, and Asylums

Within each dialog box you may find various areas or regions. These are groupings of gadgets within the dialog box, usually controlling some related item.

Areas are each given a title and then surrounded by a dimple line. While this serves to look cool, it also keeps those related items together. And if you're hunting for something inside one of those 747-cockpit dialog boxes, it can make finding that something easier.

Working the Dialog Box

Some dialog boxes just give up and tell you something (see Figure 26-4). Most others are there to get information from you. That's done primarily through the gizmos, covered later in this chapter. But certain rules apply to using all dialog boxes, which are covered in the next few, brief sections.

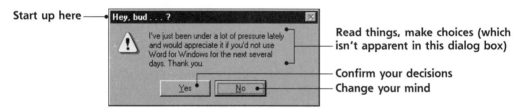

Figure 26-4 The briefest of dialog boxes

The Mousy Way of Using a Dialog Box

The best way to control the stuff in a dialog box is to use the mouse; dialog boxes are mouse-friendly. You'll need a keyboard to type in various text items in a dialog box, which the mouse is lousy at doing. Otherwise, it's point-and-click, drag, click-click, and so on.

The Keyboardy Way of Using a Dialog Box

Keyboards and dialog boxes can go together, but normally it's rather awkward. To use a keyboard to control a dialog box, you need to know about the line of ants and understand how the TAB key works.

The focal point of every dialog box is in the line of ants, a dotted rectangle that surrounds the current item in a dialog box. For example, in Figure 26-1, it's the OK button that has the focus; in Figure 26-2, it's the Retry button; in Figure 26-3, it's the Check Now button. In Figure 26-4, the No button has the focus.

You can move the focus either by clicking the mouse on another gadget in the dialog box or by pressing the TAB key. The line of ants jumps from item to item each time you press the TAB key.

Pressing the ENTER key selects the gizmo with the line of ants around it. This is the same as clicking the mouse on that item.

To switch from one panel to another, press the TAB key until the current panel's tab is highlighted. Then use the left and right arrow keys to switch to another tab.

You can instantly choose any gizmo in a dialog box by using a keyboard shortcut. You'll notice various items in the dialog box have one letter underlined. If you press the ALT key plus that letter, you'll choose that item — similar to clicking on it. For example, in Figure 26-3, you can choose the Backup Now button by pressing ALT+B in that dialog box.

Backup Now...

The universal cancel key in any dialog box is ESC. Pressing that key is the same as clicking the mouse on the Cancel button.

Time to Commit to Something

Nothing you do in a dialog box happens until you tell Windows it's OK. So after making your selections and settings, you need to click OK to make it happen. Or, if you change your mind, you can click the Cancel button.

A third button, Apply, may appear in some dialog boxes. This button allows you to preview your settings without leaving the dialog box. It's the same as clicking OK, but the dialog box's window doesn't close. This way you can take a peek at how your decisions affect the rest of Windows, then make minor tunes and tweaks — or toss the whole thing out — and then click OK to confirm.

Apply

All Them Gizmos

What makes a dialog box work are all the doodads and gizmos you'll find lurking inside it. The following sections discuss how to use the various gadgets you may find lurking in a dialog box near you.

This list may not be complete; programmers can create new gadgets every day, including some truly intuitive and creative stuff. Don't be afraid of them! Nothing you do in a dialog box has serious consequences unless you click the OK button. So feel free to goof around if some gadget seems like a fun toy.

For example, the Time Zone gadget in the Date/Time Properties dialog box is a fun one. Goof around there, but click Cancel when you leave — unless you're in the process of moving, of course.

 X-REF For more information on the Date/Time Properties dialog box see Chapter 6, the section "Fooling with the Time (Setting the Time on Your PC)."

Buttons

Buttons aren't a typical dialog box gizmo. *Buttons* usually perform their actions immediately, such as a Save As button opening another dialog box.

Buttons work by clicking the mouse on them. This instantly selects whichever option is attached to the button. The name on the button should give you some hint as to what happens next.

You can activate a button using the keyboard in two ways: First, you can find an underlined letter in the button's name, and then press the ALT key plus that letter. Second, you can press the TAB key until the line of ants surrounds that button's name, and then press the ENTER key. (Obviously it's better to use the mouse.)

Also see the section "On/Off buttons" for information on another type of button.

Check Boxes

Check boxes are used when an option can be either on or off. A check mark ✔ in the box means the option is on; an empty box means the option is off.

You put a ✔ check mark in the box and remove it by clicking the mouse on that option, either in the box or on the option's name. Click once to put a ✔ check mark there; click again to remove it.

Using the keyboard, you press the ALT key plus the underlined letter in the command name, such as ALT+K to activate *Slovakia*.

Computer geeks call this type of gizmo a *toggle*; choose it once to turn it on, choose it again to turn it off. See? It toggles back and forth like the togs of old.

The Collapsible Tree Structure Thing

The *collapsible tree structure* thing appears a lot in Windows. It's used to display something with a *hierarchical structure*, for example, an outline or the way folders are organized on a hard drive.

The idea is: Some items in the tree structure contain other items, just like one folder on the hard drive can contain other folders. The collapsible tree structure thing comes in handy because it enables you to hide the contents of folders so you don't see everything at once. In the outline example, it's possible to view only the major headings in your outline. Then you can open each heading to see the details as you want. This is truly less mind-boggling than seeing everything at once.

An icon in a tree structure with a plus (+) by it contains more branches in the tree. Click once on the + to open the branches and look. But stand back! Sometimes this opens a whole can of worms, often a lot more stuff than can be displayed in the window at once.

After being opened, the plus thing changes into a minus thing (-).

An icon with a minus by its name is already open. To close this part of the tree, click the minus once with the mouse.

When you close a branch of the tree, the minus thing changes to a plus thing.

A missing plus or minus thing means no more branches are inside it, nothing more to be opened.

X-REF Icons appear by the plus or minus signs in a collapsible tree structure. In the Explorer, the icons are of little folders: Pluses have closed folders by them, minuses have open folders. See Chapter 13, the section "Climbing the Folder Tree," for more information.

TIP The collapsible tree structure thing appears in several other places in Windows, most often in the Control Panel. I can tell you quite assuredly, if you ever see one of these beasts and it's not in the Explorer, *don't mess with it!* Usually that tree structure controls advanced aspects of Windows that are best left untouched. See Chapter 18 for more information on the Control Panel.

Drop-Down Lists

A *drop-down list* displays a bunch of fill-in-the-blanks options. These you either typed in earlier or they're preset options you can't change. Either way, the drop-down list works the same.

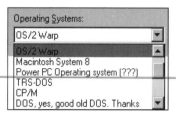

You activate a drop-down list by clicking the arrow button to the right of the list. This displays the list like a menu.

If the list is long, you can use its scrollbar to browse through the options.

When you see the option you want, click it once using the mouse. The drop-down list disappears and your choice appears in the list's text box.

These things are a bear to work using the keyboard alone. Basically, you set the focus on the list box using the TAB key or by pressing the ALT key plus the underlined letter in the list box's title. Then press ALT+↓ (the down-arrow key) to drop down the list. Use the up- or down-arrow keys to find an item in the list, then press the ENTER key. (Or just use the mouse.)

By the way, sometimes when the dialog box hovers at a low altitude on the screen, the list box drops "up." This is so you can see all the options; nothing's wrong with your computer.

Some list boxes don't drop down. See "List Boxes" later in this section.

Drop-Down Palettes

A *drop-down palette* works like a drop-down list box; the difference is a small table of selections appears instead of a scrolling list. Most often, you'll see this used in the Color palette, from which you choose a color for some such operation.

To pick an item, click on it with the mouse.

Unfortunately, you can't manipulate this one using the keyboard.

In the Color drop-down palette, there's a button for Other, which lets you custom create your own color. Clicking it brings up the interesting and fun Color dialog box where you can custom create your own color. It's an enormous time waster, so I won't bother describing how it works in this book.

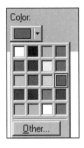

Input Boxes

An *input box* is merely an area in a dialog box where you can type in something. It contains editable text and can even be edited using common word processor commands.

To activate an input box, click on it with the mouse. Then just start typing.

If you want to replace the text in an input box, double-click on it with the mouse. This selects all the text and whatever you type will replace it.

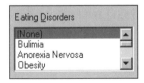

TIP **Always remember to press the** TAB **key when you're done typing in text. In most dialog boxes, pressing** ENTER **is the same as selecting some other option, such as the OK button, which probably isn't what you want.**

You can also cut, copy, and paste text in an input box. I amazed a coworker once when I selected a phone number from one application, and then pasted it into an input box in another application's dialog box. You save a lot of typing that way, and you're assured the number is entered exactly.

List Boxes

A *list box* is a scrolling list of options, though sometimes there aren't enough to them to warrant a scrollbar. Unlike a drop-down list box, most of these items are visible at once.

You pick an item by clicking it with the mouse. You can use the scrollbar to scroll the list up or down to see more options.

With the keyboard, you can use the up- or down-arrow keys to choose an item. First select the list box by pressing the ALT key plus the underlined letter in the list box's name, such as ALT+D for *Eating Disorder*.

On/Off Buttons

You'll mostly see on/off types of buttons on toolbars. On/off buttons work like check boxes; when the button looks pushed in, that option is on. When the button is left sticking out (an outtie), then the option is off.

To turn on an on/off button, click it once with the mouse. Click it again to turn that option off.

Keyboard equivalents for these types of buttons are rare because they appear mostly on toolbars and toolbars are nonkeyboard things.

Option Buttons

Option buttons are on/off buttons, similar to check mark boxes. The difference is option buttons are grouped in "families" of two or more. Only one option button in the family may be chosen at any one time. This works like the buttons on old car radios; you could only punch up one station at a time, unless you were four years old. (Incidentally, Macintosh users refer to option buttons as *radio* buttons.)

To choose one option button in a family, click it with the mouse. The circle will grow a dot in it, indicating that's the item you've chosen. To deselect this item, you must click a different option button in that family.

With the keyboard, simply choose the key shortcut for the option button by pressing the ALT key plus the underlined key in the command, such as ALT+A for *Wrap for Christmas*.

More than any other group of commands, you'll see option buttons in various areas roped off by a dimple line. This keeps one family of option buttons separate from any other option buttons that may live in the same dialog box. Without that dimple line, heck, it'd be the Hatfields and the McCoys all over again.

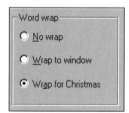

Sliders

A *slider* could be one of a number of controls, each of which is manipulated by grabbing the control with the mouse and moving it to a new position. Numbers nearby the slider usually tell you what the new position does.

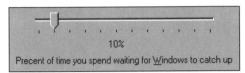

With a mouse, you need to point at the slider control, then drag the slider to a new position: Hold down the mouse button, move the mouse to move the slider, then release the mouse button when you're done. This works similarly to a scrollbar.

With the keyboard, you press the ALT key equivalent, such as ALT+W, and then use the left- and right-arrow keys to adjust the slider. Some sliders may have a text input box, in which case you can use it to input a precise value.

BONUS

Spinners

Spinners are delightful little gadgets that adjust a value up or down, such as setting the time of day, the year, or your weight in kilograms after a hearty meal.

To adjust the value, you click the tiny arrows — the spinner — using the mouse. Click the up arrow to make the value larger; click the down arrow to make the value smaller.

When you have multiple values, as with the time of day, you should double-click the mouse on the hour, minute, or seconds value to select it first. Then use the spinner to adjust the time.

The keyboard alternative to using a spinner is just to type in the proper value. Most spinner's text boxes can be edited. If not, try the up or down arrows to adjust the value.

Summary

A dialog box is when Windows needs your opinion about something. Your job is to slide sliders, click on and off buttons, and pull down drop lists until the right answer is found. Then you click, and Windows is happy with your answer and can continue with what it needs to do.

Before you continue, make sure you learned this stuff:

☐ What the three main elements of a dialog box are.

☐ What drop-down lists and drop-down palettes are.

☐ What on/off buttons, option buttons, sliders, and spinners do.

CHAPTER TWENTY-SEVEN

MOUSY CONCEPTS

IN THIS CHAPTER YOU LEARN THESE SKILLS

USING THE MOUSE   PAGE 345

LEARNING NEW MOUSE TERMS   PAGE 347

RECOGNIZING BEHAVIOR PATTERNS COMMON TO THE
   MOUSE   PAGE 347

UNDERSTANDING THE MOUSE POINTER   PAGE 351

27

You're fooling yourself if you think you can use Windows without a mouse. You need a mouse to use Windows. You must have one. Not only that, you need to understand how the mouse works and how to perform some common mouse tricks. This is all simple stuff, but something to practice until you're used to doing it. Think of the mouse as your nonfuzzy little friend. The happy rodent. Heck — Mickey! After all, it's not called the computer *rat*, you know.

"Here I Come to Save the Day!" (Using Mr. Mouse)

You don't need your hand on the mouse all the time you use your computer. You only need to grab it when something mousy is required, which isn't that often.

The mouse points away from you, with its tail trailing off toward the rear of your desk and back into the bowels of your computer. So, if the other end of the mouse were its head, you'd grab the mouse with its head under the palm of your hand. Remember: The tail points *away* from you, right beneath the tips of your fingers.

When it's time to grab the mouse, gently rest your hand upon it. Instead of resting the palm of your hand on the mouse, open your hand and place it on the mouse with your index finger on the left button and your middle finger on the right button. Your thumb and other fingers will rest off to the side and your wrist will be limp on your table top.

Some mice have three buttons; ignore the middle button for now.

If you're left-handed, you'll put your index finger on the right button and your middle finger on the left. See the sidebar "The Left-handed Mouse" later in this chapter.

The mouse gets going thanks to elbow movement on your behalf. Do not roll the mouse with your wrist; use your elbow to help glide Mr. Mouse around on your table top. The mouse controls a pointer or mouse cursor on the screen that mimics the movements of the mouse on your table top. Move the mouse wildly in a circle and the pointer on the screen follows suit.

It's best to roll your computer mouse on a soft, fuzzy mouse pad. This enables the mouse's rubber ball underneath to get some traction, and it makes for smoother mouse operations.

Another item you can buy is a wrist pad, which helps elevate your wrist when you use the mouse. This supposedly lessens the chance of wrist injury while using a mouse. (Mouse Wrist is the Tennis Elbow of the '90s.)

SIDE TRIP

THE BEST WAY TO LEARN THE MOUSE

Alas, Windows doesn't come with a mouse tutorial. Maybe it will someday, but for some reason Microsoft is afraid you'll master the mouse without any extra help offered by any software. Fortunately, a program exists you can use to help you understand how the mouse works: It's the Solitaire game!

When you play Solitaire, you use the mouse to click on menus, double-click on cards, and drag cards to certain positions. All the mouse techniques are used to play the game, which makes it an ideal mouse tutorial — if you like playing Solitaire.

See Chapter 24 for more information on wasting time with the Solitaire game.

Know These Mouse Terms

Y ou can do five things with the mouse, and five terms are used to describe them: point, click, double-click, drag, and selecting or highlighting. Each of these terms is elaborated upon in the following sections, and a brief description is given in Table 27-1.

TABLE 27-1 Things You Can Do with a Computer Mouse

Mouse Action	Description
POINT	To move the mouse pointer on the screen so it's hovering over some object, a button, or what have you.
CLICK	To press and release the mouse's main button, the one on the left.
DOUBLE-CLICK	Two quick clicks in a row, both pointing at the same spot.
DRAG	To press and hold the mouse button down, and then move the mouse around. In Windows, this technique is used to move objects around on the screen. The drag ends when you release the mouse button.
SELECTING	To click on something, highlighting it.

Behavior Patterns Common to the Computer Mouse

T he following sections contain descriptions of various things you can do with a computer mouse. This is not required reading. Only look here if you have trouble with the mouse concept or if you need a little extra help.

Getting to the Point

When you're told to point the mouse at something, you move the mouse pointer or cursor over to that something. For example, in Figure 27-1, the mouse is pointing at the drive (C:) icon in My Computer.

Remember, you move the mouse pointer on the screen by rolling the mouse around on your table top. The movements of the mouse pointer on the screen mimic those of the mouse on your table.

When you're told to point at something, point right at it. Do not point below it or off to the right. Hover the mouse right over that sucker to point at it.

A point is usually followed by a click.

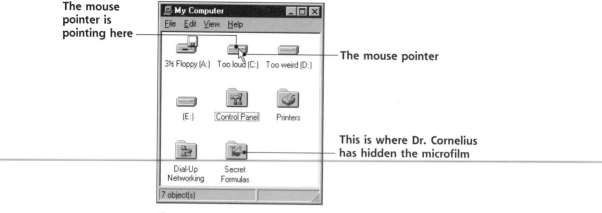

The mouse pointer is pointing here

The mouse pointer

This is where Dr. Cornelius has hidden the microfilm

Figure 27-1 Getting to the point

Some Things Just Click

Clicking the mouse requires you to press and release its button. But which button? Button, button, who's got the mouse button?

The main mouse button is the one you click — that's the index finger button, the left button. When you see instructions to click the mouse, that's the button you click.

A *double-click* is two quick clicks of the mouse in a row *and* in the same spot. Both clicks must be at the same spot on the screen or it doesn't work (and that describes most of your problems with a double-click).

You double-click most often to "open" something, such as a new program or document. Double-click, said the manual. Click, click, went the mouse. Run, run, went the program.

Of course, if you're left-handed, you click the right button, which is the button your index finger is on. See "The Left-handed Mouse" box.

If your hearing hasn't succumbed to old age, you can hear the clicking sound the mouse makes when you click its button. This is where this mouse technique got its name.

Most often you click the mouse to activate some graphical goody-goody on the screen, such as a button, menu, or other interesting object.

THE LEFT-HANDED MOUSE

If you're one of the few lucky southpaws in this world, you can choose to use your mouse on the right side of your computer — like the rest of us — or you can use your mouse on the left side, where it's more intuitive for you. Heck, even some right-handers like a left-handed mouse. My friend Wally Wang, co-author of IDG Books *Illustrated Computer Dictionary For Dummies,* is one such righty who uses a lefty mouse.

To make your mouse left-hand friendly, follow these steps:

1. Pop up the Start Thing.

2. Choose Settings → Control Panel .

3. Double-click the Mouse icon to open it. You'll see the Mouse Properties dialog box (see Figure 27-2).

4. Click the *Left-handed* option button. You'll see the button highlight on the demo mouse shift from the left side to the right — where you want it.

5. Click OK. This closes the Mouse Properties dialog box. Then close the Control Panel's window as well.

You've just switched mouse buttons, so from here on, you'll use the *right* button to click, double-click, and open things. You'll be using the *left* mouse button to pop up shortcut menus. Remember this!

Doing the Right-Click

The *right-click* is used in Windows to bring up various shortcut menus. To do a right-click, you just click the mouse's right button. This works the same as the normal click, though it's called a right-click in this book and in Windows.

And if you're using a lefty mouse, you'll do a left-click. But, remember, this book uses the term "right-click" throughout. Don't get confused (as if can openers, door knobs, and bottle caps haven't driven you insane already).

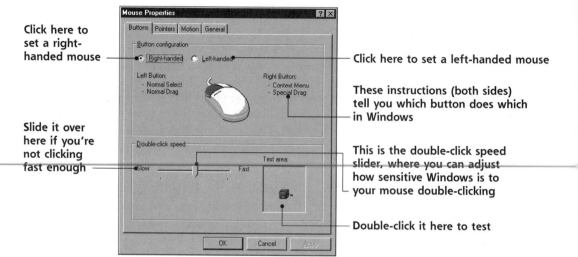

Click here to set a right-handed mouse

Click here to set a left-handed mouse

These instructions (both sides) tell you which button does which in Windows

Slide it over here if you're not clicking fast enough

This is the double-click speed slider, where you can adjust how sensitive Windows is to your mouse double-clicking

Double-click it here to test

Figure 27-2   The Mouse Properties dialog box

TIP   If you think you're Bill Gates, slide the slider all the way over toward *Fast*. You *really* have to double-click fast to get the jack-in-the-box icon up. If you're like me, you'll leave the slider in the middle, where most folks are happy with that double-click speed.

Moving Can Be Such a Drag

Dragging is the most complex mouse action to describe. Essentially, *dragging* is a combined click and move at the same time.

Follow these steps to practice dragging your mouse:

1. Point the mouse at something you want to drag. In Windows, this could be an icon, a graphical object, a window, the edge of a window, or any of a number of draggable things.

2. Press and hold the mouse button down. This is just like a click, except you're keeping the button held down.

3. Continue holding the button down (which isn't that hard) and move the mouse on the screen. This typically moves something on the screen so you get immediate visual feedback as to what you're doing. This is the drag part.

4. Release the mouse button.

When the mouse pointer is pointing at the new position, release the mouse button. You're done dragging.

TIP Normally you press and hold the main mouse button, the button on the left. There is a "right-drag" operation in Windows, though, in which case you press and hold the right mouse button instead. Southpaws, as usual, reverse the buttons in the previous paragraphs.

Selective Service

Selecting isn't really an official mouse operation. *Selecting* is just pointing and clicking at something. The difference is the thing you clicked becomes highlighted or selected. For example, you click an icon to select it and the icon becomes highlighted.

To select more than one object, you press and hold the CTRL (control) key while clicking. This is officially known as a CTRL+CLICK (control-click). Each item you CTRL+CLICK becomes selected. If you don't CTRL+CLICK, then only the last item you clicked is selected.

X-REF You can also select a group of items by dragging the mouse around them. This technique is covered at the end of Chapter 14, in the section "Calf Ropin' Files."

The Ever-Changing Mouse Pointer

The mouse pointer doesn't always look like an arrow. No, it changes. Depending on what you're doing in Windows at the time, the mouse pointer can take on a number of different personas. A few of the more popular ones are shown and described in Table 27-2.

The hourglass "Busy" pointer is your worst enemy. It means you have to sit and wait until Windows is done spinning its wheels before you can do something else. Sometimes this can be a long, long time. Other times, it's even longer.

The "Working in Background" pointer doesn't spell true death. You can actually click things while Windows is working, but everything will still move slowly.

X-REF The mouse pointer needn't look the way it does in Table 27-2. You can use other styles or schemes, each replete with its own stock of pointers. See Chapter 23 for the details.

TABLE 27-2 Different Mouse Pointers You May Find Loitering Around

Pointer	Name	Function
⬚	Normal Select	This is your typical mouse pointer.
⧖	Busy	This tells you Windows is off doing something. Wait.
⧖	Working in Background	You can still work, but Windows is busy doing something for which you just asked.
I	Text Select	This is used when editing text to position the cursor or select text.
?⬚	Help Select	This means you can click something to see help about it.
⊘	Unavailable, or "Uh-uh"	Whatever you're trying to do, don't bother.

BONUS

The Double-Quick Double-Click

A great place exists to practice your double-clicks in Windows. It's located in the Mouse Properties dialog box. You can double-click there on a tiny jack-in-the-box icon to test your double-clicking skills.

Follow these steps to practice your double-clicking skills:

1. Press CTRL+ESC to summon that fun-loving Start Thing.

2. Choose ⬚ Settings ⬚ → ⬚ Control Panel ⬚.

3. Double-click on the Mouse icon. This displays the Mouse Properties dialog box.

Mouse

4. Click on the Buttons panel to bring that panel forward if it isn't already. What you see will be similar to Figure 27-2. Look for the *Test area* in the lower-right corner of the Buttons panel.

5. Point the mouse right at the purple jack-in-the-box icon.

6. Click the button twice while you try to keep the mouse steady. It helps if you gently hold the mouse in your hand; if you have a death-grip on the sucker, a double-click will never work.

7. If you're successful, a clown pops up. Egads! Try double-clicking again to put him away.

8. Adjust the double-click speed by moving the slider to the *slow* end of the scale if you find double-clicking difficult. Then repeat Step 5.

9. Click OK to close the Mouse Properties dialog box.

Summary

You should be familiar with the single-click, double-click, left-click, right-click, and the drag. Kinda sounds like a new dance step you'd learn on a cruise ship!

You should have learned the following about Mr. Mouse:

☐ How to hold the mouse.

☐ What the five mouse terms are.

☐ Where the main mouse button is.

☐ What a double click is.

☐ How to configure your mouse for left-handers

☐ How to drag your mouse.

☐ What the different mouse pointers are.

WORKING WITH TEXT AND GRAPHICS

IN THIS CHAPTER YOU LEARN THESE SKILLS

WORKING WITH TEXT IN WINDOWS   PAGE 355

USING THE TOOTHPICK CURSOR   PAGE 356

CHANGING TEXT ATTRIBUTES   PAGE 358

STRETCHING GRAPHICS   PAGE 360

28

P art of Windows' common approach is it treats any text or graphics in any application the same way. A definite way exists to edit text, to change its size, style, and so forth. This is a constant, something done the same whether it's in a big program, such as Microsoft Word, or in a tiny text field in a dialog box. (Although Word has more features, there are basic text editing techniques.) The same holds true with graphics on the screen, though you can't do as much with them. This chapter covers the basic tenets of working with text and graphics nearly anywhere in Windows.

Basic Messing with Text Stuff

E ven though Windows is graphical, there is a lot of text. You still need a keyboard and a mouse to make things happen. In fact, I'd say a good chunk of your time spent working with Windows will be typing in text, either in an application or in a dialog box. No matter what, you can always rely on Windows' consistent rules for dealing with text.

All Hail the Flashing Toothpick Cursor

Windows uses two dealies when you play with text. The first is the Text Selection pointer, which is what the mouse pointer turns into when you hover it over text. This pointer says you can use the mouse to select text and position the flashing toothpick cursor on the screen.

The flashing toothpick cursor is used to help you edit your text. It marks the position on the screen where new characters appear as you type. New text appears behind the toothpick cursor, and the toothpick cursor moves to the right as you type.

You can move the toothpick cursor by clicking the mouse on a new spot in the text. This works whether you're working in a word processor or toiling away in some tiny text input box in some obscure dialog box. You can also move the toothpick cursor with your keyboard's arrow keys, as covered in the next section.

Basic Text Editing Stuff

To create new text, type away. If you make a mistake, you can use the BACK-SPACE key to back up and erase your text. Unlike with a typewriter, a computer's BACKSPACE key backs up and erases.

When you're done typing a line of text, press the ENTER key.

In a dialog box, when you're done filling in an Input box and want to continue to the next field, press the TAB key.

While you're working with text, use several special keys on the keyboard to edit as you go. These keys are listed in Table 28-1.

TABLE 28-1 Common Windows Editing Keys

Key	What It Does
BACKSPACE	Backs up the toothpick cursor and deletes the previous character
DELETE	Deletes the next character — the one after the toothpick cursor
CTRL+DELETE	Deletes all text from the toothpick cursor until the end of the word
HOME	Moves the toothpick cursor to the start of the line or the first character in an input box

Key	What It Does
END	Moves the toothpick cursor to the end of the line or to the last character in an input box
TAB	Moves the toothpick cursor to the next input box in a dialog box
ENTER	Ends a line or paragraph of text (use only in a word processor)
←	Moves the toothpick cursor back one character
→	Moves the toothpick cursor forward one character
↑	Moves the toothpick cursor up one line
↓	Moves the toothpick cursor down one line
CTRL+←	Moves the toothpick cursor back one word
CTRL+→	Moves the toothpick cursor forward one word

 X-REF Word processors will offer additional key combinations to enable the toothpick cursor to do other amazing things. See Chapter 7 for information on WordPad.

Making Text Feel Special by Selecting It

All text in Windows can be edited using the Cut, Copy, and Paste commands, even if an Edit menu isn't hanging around nearby. What you'll be using instead are the keyboard shortcuts for those commands: CTRL+X for Cut, CTRL+C for Copy, and CTRL+V for Paste. Also available is CTRL+Z for the Undo command.

Before you can cut or copy text, it needs to be selected. There are several ways to do this in Windows. The best way to select text is to drag over it with the mouse's Text Selection pointer. This is illustrated in Figure 28-1. Begin the drag at the start of your text, and then drag to select and highlight. Release the mouse button when you've selected the necessary text.

To select all the text in a dialog box's input box, double-click that box. This highlights all the text.

You can also select text by using the SHIFT key while moving the toothpick cursor. For example, SHIFT+← selects one character to the left of the toothpick cursor. Keep pressing SHIFT+← to select more characters.

After the text is selected, you can use the Cut or Copy commands to cut or copy the text: press CTRL+X to cut; press CTRL+C to copy.

You can also press the DELETE key to delete all the selected text.

Press CTRL+V to paste previously copied text.

Press CTRL+Z, the Undo command, to give up and undo whatever editing changes you've made.

"Are you sure you don't have any insurance?" the lawyer asked again.
Hawkins answered no for the nth time. The lawyer began flipping through some notes.

"Ah-ha!" he said, reaching for a lighter to blaze up another cigar. "I see that the tree you plowed into is owned by a rich farmer. Some jerk back east. The guy doesn't even live here. Must have pockets full of money." T

Hawkins was confused. "I don't get it. I plow into some poor guy's ancient oak tree, one of this town's historic landmarks, and we're going to sue the guy who owns the tree? I was drunk!"

The lawyer waved Hawkins off. "Doesn't matter. It's the law. He's negligent for having that tree there in the first place. Dumb sucker."

The logic escaped Hawkins who, for the moment, could only think of continuing the practice of running into trees around the country and collecting massive sums of money. All that while being drunk too. This certainly is a great country.

Start dragging the mouse here

This text is selected— ready for cutting or copying

This was edited so as not to offend lawyers

Release the mouse button here

The Text Selection mouse pointer design

Figure 28-1 Text is selected.

X-REF See Chapter 8 for more information on the Cut, Copy, Paste, and Undo commands. They apply to any selected text in Windows, even text in a dialog box.

Refer to Chapter 27 for more help with using the mouse to drag and select text.

Changing the Way Text Looks

The appearance of text in most applications can be changed. This doesn't apply to dialog boxes, where the text is pretty boring. But in a word processor or similar application, you can change the way the text looks.

You can change two major things about text: the font or typeface, which is the text style, and the text's size. You can also change various attributes of the text, making it **bold**, *italics*, underlined, or a number of other effects, depending on what your software offers and how well your creative juices are flowing.

A Font of Typefaces

The way text appears, its style, is called a *typeface.* This is the official typesetter's term. The unofficial computer term is a *font,* which isn't exactly a typeface, but no one's watching and no professionals are in the room.

Fonts are changed in one of two ways. The first is from a Font menu item. The second is using a Font drop-down list on a toolbar. In both cases, you fetch a new style for your text by scrolling through a list of fonts installed on your computer.

The new font you choose affects any selected text in your document or, if no text has been selected, it affects any new text you type.

Text Sizes from Petite to Full-Figured

The size of your text can also be changed, from teensy-tiny to relatively huge. The value used is *points*, which is another typesetter's term. A point is essentially a tiny piece of a letter, about as big as an ant could eat in one bite.

Text typically appears on the screen in 8-, 10-, or 12-point sizes. The larger the point value, the bigger the text. If you set the point size to about 72, then you get text about 1-inch high. Or, if you're in Canada, if you set the point size to about 28 you get text a hair over 1 centimeter in height.

As with the font, setting a new point size is typically done with a drop-down list box, either on a toolbar or hidden in a menu. You can usually type in a size value in addition to selecting it from a list.

The new point size affects any selected text in your document or, if no text is selected, it affects anything new you type. Figure 28-2 illustrates how this works.

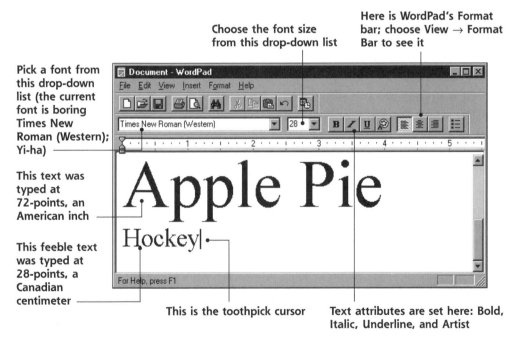

Figure 28-2 Text of different point sizes in WordPad

TIP I use color in my work to make comments and to emphasize text I think needs reworking. For example, I color text blue if I'm not sure about something; red if it needs reworking; green if it's a comment to me, not to be printed. If you try this approach, remember to remove the comments or to fix the text before you print.

Basic Messing with Graphics Stuff (Stretching)

Playing with graphics isn't as extensive as playing with text in Windows. Most high-end graphics programs will use their own techniques for drawing and creating images. Still, you can do one thing to most graphical images, especially those pasted into another program.

For example, suppose you plop a map of Mississippi into your report on Sam Clemens. After pasting it into your word processor, you realize it's a map of Missouri you really want, so you create a graphical bitmap of Missouri and paste it into your word processor instead. The graphic you see may look like Figure 28-3.

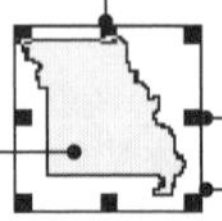

Click and drag here to
make the graphic taller

Click the graphic
object once to
select it

Click and drag here to make the graphic wider
Click any corner to change the graphic's size in two directions at once

Figure 28-3   Missouri awaits you.

Click the graphic once to select it. You'll see tiny handles appear on its sides and corners, just as in Figure 28-3. You can *grab* any of the graphic handles to stretch or shrink the graphic — just as you can resize a window on the screen (see Chapter 25).

If you hold the SHIFT key while you drag one of the handles, the image maintains its proportions. So if you want a larger Missouri all around, press the SHIFT key, and then grab one of the corners with the mouse. Drag the mouse outward and Missouri will still look like Missouri as it's resized.

X-REF   See "The Joy of Stretch" in Chapter 25 for instructions on resizing a window. The same techniques apply to resize a graphic image on the screen.

BONUS

Funky Things to Do with Text (Attributes)

Text attributes basically control four different things: Bold, Italic, Underline, and text color. The first three are set in a text dialog box or by using on/off buttons on a toolbar, as seen in Figure 28-2.

To change text attributes, select the text you want to change, and then choose the new attribute. Or you can choose an attribute and then type some new text, in which case the new text will be affected by that attribute.

Use **bold text** for strong emphasis or in titles. Use it sparingly; too much bold text can make your reader want to read something else.

In most cases, you should use *italics* for emphasis. Use italics whenever you were told to underline something in your typewriter class. For example, italicize book titles, films, foreign words, phrases, and stuff you *really* want to emphasize. Underline? Ha! No one uses it.

> **TIP** **If you want to create a blank line for input, perhaps for a form you're creating, use the underline key on your keyboard. Just press and hold the key down to make a nice, long underline for fill in the blanks type stuff.**

Text color is another attribute you can set. It looks nice on the screen and can make your documents rainbow beautiful. But if you don't have a color printer, you're wasting your time.

Summary

Windows has made this simple for you. If you want to edit text, whether it's in a big program like Microsoft Word or in a tiny text field in a dialog box, you do it the same way.

Stop! Don't go on to the next chapter until you understand the following:

- [ ] What the common Windows editing techniques are.
- [ ] How to select text.
- [ ] How to change the appearance of text.
- [ ] How to stretch graphics.

PROBLEMS AND SOLUTIONS

IN THIS CHAPTER YOU LEARN THESE SKILLS

USING THE WINDOWS TROUBLESHOOTER   PAGE

DEALING WITH ANNOYING HARDWARE
  CONFLICTS   PAGE

USING SPECIAL STARTUP OPTIONS   PAGE

USING THE EMERGENCY BOOT DISK   PAGE

FINDING LOST FILES   PAGE

29

P roviding you do the routine maintenance covered in Chapter 16, nothing
should ever go wrong with your computer. Oh, it will eventually wear out.
Time passes and new technology will make your PC seem slow. Your hard
disk will fill up, but you can always buy a second one. But the only time something strange will happen (aside from anything on the network) is when you
add new hardware or software. If anything odd goes on in your computer, it will
probably happen after one of those two events.

The biggest problem with computer catastrophe is not knowing what to do
next. Generally you can do two things. The first is to troubleshoot, which is easily accomplished using Windows' fancy Troubleshooter software. The second is
to start your computer with an Emergency Boot Disk and work repairs from
there. This chapter covers both of these solutions.

The All-Purpose Amazing Windows Troubleshooter

Any time your computer acts funny, you should set out to use the Troubleshooter. This is actually part of the Windows 95 help system. It's a series of dialog boxes that ask you simple questions. Eventually, the questions lead you to an answer or at least to the proper dialog box where amends can be made.

Follow these steps to work through the Troubleshooter:

1. Start Help by pressing CTRL+ESC to pop up the Start Thing menu, and then choose the Help command. Help may write in its little book for a while. Please wait. Eventually you'll see the Help dialog box (Figure 29-1).

Click this tab to bring this panel forward

Type the word trouble in here

Your options banquet

Scroll down through the list to see more options

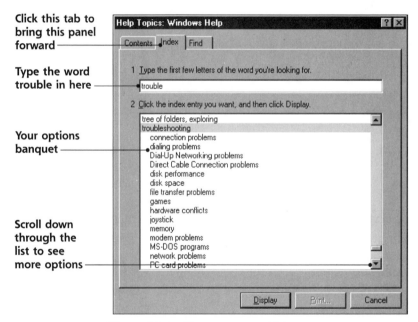

Figure 29-1 Here comes trouble!

2. Click the Index tab to bring that panel forward.

3. Type **trouble** into the first input box. This looks up the word Troubleshooting in the index and displays a banquet of options for getting your PC repaired.

4. There are 20 or so different items listed under *Troubleshooting* in the Help index. Pick the one that presently irks you. For example, if your hard disk seems sluggish, double-click *disk performance.* This brings up a dialog box (see Figure 29-2) that explains why your disk may be working so sluggishly. It also contains a link to the proper program to fix it.

Starts the Defragmenter program

Step-by-step instructions

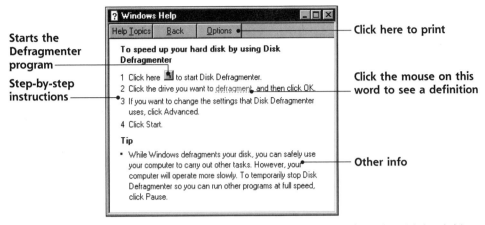

Click here to print

Click the mouse on this word to see a definition

Other info

Figure 29-2 The Troubleshooter's suggestions for a sluggish hard drive

 TIP When you see Help displayed, as in Figure 29-2, it's a good idea to click the Options button and choose the Print Topic command from the menu. This way you'll have a hard copy of the instructions the Troubleshooter is suggesting. That helps, especially if your PC crashes and you forget which step to take next.

5. Continue to work through the Troubleshooter.

Sometimes the Troubleshooter will ask you a series of questions. For example, suppose you choose Printing Problems from the list. The Troubleshooter will want you to narrow down the problem, as shown in Figure 29-3. Simply choose whichever item best reflects your situation. The Troubleshooter may even want to know more information, as shown in Figure 29-4.

Read this first

Then choose one of these options

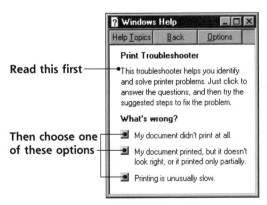

Figure 29-3 The Troubleshooter wants more information.

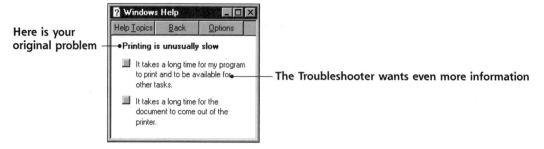

Here is your original problem — The Troubleshooter wants even more information

Figure 29-4 Even more questions are asked.

Eventually you'll encounter either a written explanation of what's wrong or one of those go-to buttons that takes you to a part of Windows where the problem can be solved. The Troubleshooter is sincere; it may want to be sure your problem is solved by asking you even more questions (see Figure 29-5).

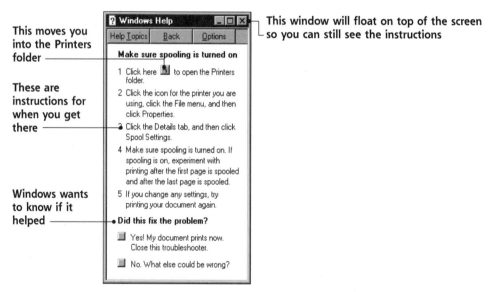

This moves you into the Printers folder

These are instructions for when you get there

Windows wants to know if it helped

This window will float on top of the screen so you can still see the instructions

Figure 29-5 The problem is, hopefully, resolved.

Dealing with Annoying Hardware Conflicts

Sometimes your problem may involve some new gadget you installed, one that refuses to work. Windows even asks you, after you run the Add New Hardware wizard, whether it works correctly. If not, you troubleshoot hardware.

Follow these steps to start the hardware conflict troubleshooter:

1. Waltz through the steps in the previous section and choose *hardware conflict* in Step 4 (from the Help system). A help dialog box is displayed with two button options.

2. Choose *Start the Hardware Conflict Troubleshooter.* Another dialog box is displayed.

3. Click the go-to button to display the Device manager. This displays the Device Manager tab in the System Properties dialog box (see Figure 29-6).

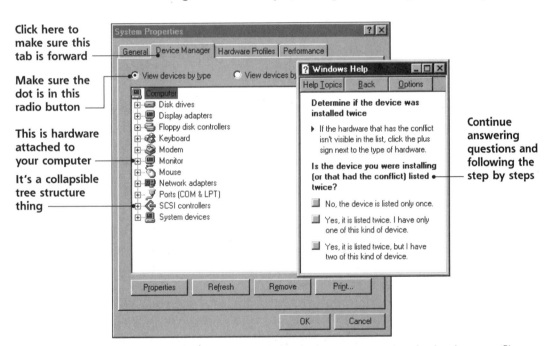

Click here to make sure this tab is forward

Make sure the dot is in this radio button

This is hardware attached to your computer

It's a collapsible tree structure thing

Continue answering questions and following the step by steps

Figure 29-6   Working through the Device Manager to resolve hardware conflicts

4. Click the button by *Click here to continue.*

5. Work through the questions.

The Troubleshooter continues to ask you questions and walk you through any modifications that should be made in the Device Manager. Beware: The Device Manager is scary stuff, so pay special attention to everything you read. Assume nothing!

> **TIP** If you're asked to double-click the hardware with a conflict, expand the part of the tree that deals with this piece of hardware. For example, if a sound card is not doing well, expand the *Sound video and game controllers* part of the tree to see your sound card. Then double-click your sound card. You'll see its special Properties dialog box, containing the *Device usage* section (toward the bottom) to which the Troubleshooting text refers.

There is a chance that you may have to reinstall your hardware. This may be required to reset a *jumper* to a new *IRQ* setting. (This only happens with older PC cards, not the newer Plug and Play-happy cards.) If so, turn off your computer and reinstall the device, configured as the Troubleshooter suggests.

Eventually, and hopefully, your hardware conflict will be solved — or at least you'll have the problem narrowed down and know what to tell tech support if the problem persists.

Special Ways to Start Your Computer

You may sometimes need to start Windows in a special way, for example in the *safe* mode. Or maybe you want to skip over Windows and start your PC using DOS or with a special Emergency Boot Disk. This all may be part of your troubleshooting strategy. Or maybe you just want to forgo Windows for now and play a DOS game. Whatever, the following sections tell you how.

Windows' Special Startup Key Commands

When your computer first starts, or after you reset, you'll see the following message on the screen:

Starting Windows 95...

If you sit there and drool while this message appears, Windows will start, hopefully, as it always does. But if you're quick, you can stab the F8 key on your keyboard. That displays a special startup menu with several options for starting Windows, all described in Figure 29-7.

Choose an option as described in the menu. For example, if you want to start your computer in DOS mode for playing DOS games, type **5** and press the ENTER key. If you're having trouble starting Windows, type **3** and press ENTER. ThIs will at least get Windows started; from there you can run the Troubleshooter as described earlier in this chapter. If you choose 1, Windows will start as it always does.

You may see strange messages on the screen when you accidentally press the ESC key when Windows starts. What this does is switch you over to the *text mode*, where you see various startup files run and display their confusing text messages. You'll have to remember not to press the ESC key next time to return to the happy *use the darn Start button, Windows in the blue sky* startup screen.

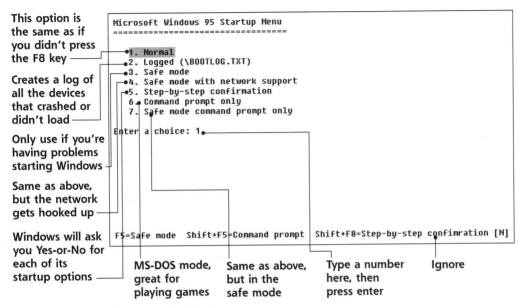

This option is the same as if you didn't press the F8 key

Creates a log of all the devices that crashed or didn't load

Only use if you're having problems starting Windows

Same as above, but the network gets hooked up

Windows will ask you Yes-or-No for each of its startup options

```
Microsoft Windows 95 Startup Menu
=================================
1. Normal
2. Logged (\BOOTLOG.TXT)
3. Safe mode
4. Safe mode with network support
5. Step-by-step confirmation
6. Command prompt only
7. Safe mode command prompt only

Enter a choice: 1

F5=Safe mode   Shift+F5=Command prompt   Shift+F8=Step-by-step confimration [N]
```

MS-DOS mode, great for playing games

Same as above, but in the safe mode

Type a number here, then press enter

Ignore

Figure 29-7 Windows' special startup menu

Mayday! Mayday! Stick in That Emergency Boot Disk!

If all hell does break loose, and you can't start Windows at all, you can always use the handy Emergency Boot disk (created in Chapter 12, "Creating a Disk to Start Your Computer, the Fun Yet Useful Emergency Boot Disk"). This disk will definitely start your computer when Windows stubbornly refuses to boot.

Follow these steps to use the Emergency Boot disk:

1. Place the Emergency Boot disk into your (A:) drive. It must be drive (A:).

2. Reset or turn on your computer. Remember, this is a desperate situation; I'm assuming you can't get your PC to start any other way. *Never* reset with Windows on the screen unless it tells you it's okay to do so.

3. The Emergency Boot disk starts.

Because the Emergency Boot Disk is in drive (A:), it will start your computer instead of Windows on your hard drive. You'll see something like the following displayed in — Yech! — ugly text mode:

```
Starting Windows 95...
Microsoft ® Windows 95
    (C)Copyright Microsoft Corp 1981-1995.
A:\>
```

That last entry is a DOS prompt. Welcome to 1981! Before you break out your copy of *DOS For Dummies,* there are only a few things you can do here.

When Windows built your Emergency Boot Disk, it copied over a few handy files, each of which plays a special role in getting your computer back into shape. All the files are listed in Table 29-1, along with their function and a reference to where you can read more about them elsewhere in this book.

Table 29-1 Commands and Programs Available on the Emergency Boot Disk

Command	What It Does
ATTRIB	Grants access to read-only files; use only if directed by technical support.
CHKDSK	Quickly scans a disk for errors; use ScanDisk instead.
DEBUG	A programmer's tool used to inspect memory, disks, and your PC's guts. Not for the fainthearted.
EDIT	Starts a text editor, which you can use to mess with the config.sys and autoexec.bat files on your hard drive (but only if tech support tells you so).
FDISK	Initializes a hard drive, which also erases the drive. Don't use this turkey.
FORMAT	Formats disks, typically used after fdisk when setting up a hard drive for the first time. Don't bother.
REGEDIT	Grants access to Windows' registry files, which may aid in disk recovery. Use only under the direction of Microsoft tech support personnel.
SCANDISK	At last! One you can use yourself. Run this program to examine and optionally fix disk boo-boos. Instructions are offered in Chapter 16.
SYS	A program to copy Windows boot files from the floppy disk to the hard drive. This may be required, but do so only under the direction of Microsoft tech support personnel.

To run one of these commands, carefully type in its name at the A:\>

prompt. Use the BACKSPACE key to backup and erase. Then press the ENTER key. For example:

```
A:\>scandisk
```

The ScanDisk program's name was typed. Press the ENTER key and ScanDisk runs.

Be aware that the programs will be run in the text-only mode. They will look and work similarly to their Windows graphical counterparts, but they may not be operated in the same manner. Also, the suggestions given in this book are best suited only to those daring enough to try these solutions on their own. If you're one of those people, great. Otherwise, my best advice is to dial up Microsoft technical support and beg them for assistance. (The phone numbers are listed in your Windows manual and, yes, it will probably cost you money — at least for the phone call.)

X-REF Only one cure exists for total hard disk disaster: Have a good backup handy. I cannot urge you strongly enough to keep good backup. Refer to Chapter 16 where I beat the concept into the dirt.

File? File? Here File! C'mon, Boy! Where'd You Go?

29

Things come and go. Sometimes a file is here, and then it's gone. It happens to everyone, but most likely the reason you lose files is you didn't store them in the proper folder. That's a sin. Fortunately Windows makes it easy to find your lost file, providing you know a few details about it — like its name, for one.

Follow these steps to find your file now, Mr. Inarush:

1. Open up My Computer or the Explorer.

2. Press the F3 key (or press CTRL+F). This brings up the Find: All Files dialog box (see Figure 29-8 when you have time).

3. Type the name of the file you want. Be as precise as possible. If you only know part of the filename, just type in that part. If you aren't sure of some letters, replace them with the question-mark character: POR???B.

4. Choose *My Computer* from the *Look in* drop-down list.

5. Make sure the *Include subfolders* item is checked.

6. Click on Find Now. Windows looks for your file.

7. The results are displayed in the bottom of the dialog box. Double-click

on the file to open it, or you can do whatever you want with it. The file has been found.

BONUS

Finding Files — The Relaxed Explanation

Follow these steps to look for a long lost file anywhere on your computer:

1. Open My Computer or the Explorer. My Computer is my favorite here. If you open the main My Computer window, you save yourself the trouble of going through Step 4 below.

2. Press the F3 key. This brings up the Find: All Files dialog box (see Figure 29-8). You can also summon the Find: All Files dialog box from My Computer's shortcut menu, as well as from the Start Thing menu: Press CTRL+ESC, F, F (think: *find files*).

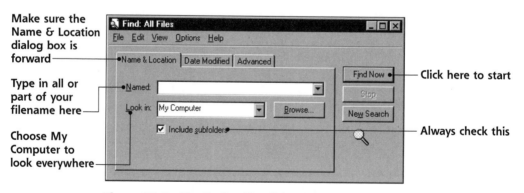

Make sure the Name & Location dialog box is forward

Type in all or part of your filename here

Choose My Computer to look everywhere

Click here to start

Always check this

Figure 29-8 The Finding files dialog box

3. Type the name of the file you want. You can type in all or only part of the filename. For example, if you're looking for the file *Sounds like an elephant who ate too many beans,* you need only type in *Sounds* or *elephant* and Windows will find the rest. (Actually, it finds all files matching the words you type.) If you aren't sure of some of the letters, you can replace

them with question marks, thusly:

SOU??S

Windows still searches for the proper matches.

4. Choose *My Computer* from the *Look in* drop-down list. This ensures Windows will look on every hard drive in your computer. If you're certain the file is on one hard drive or another, you can limit the search by choosing that drive from the drop-down list. Any network drives attached to your computer can also be selected for searching.

TIP **If you press the F3 key while in a folder deep down in My Computer, that folder also appears on the list. Although this is a great way to narrow the search to one folder (or one branch of your hard disk tree), I still recommend selecting My Computer. After all, the file is *lost*, you know.**

5. Make sure the *Include subfolders* item is checked. Put a ✔ check mark in the box. That way Windows looks everywhere.

6. Click the Find Now button. Windows looks for your file everywhere you suggested. This takes some time; as each potential match is located, it's displayed in a list at the bottom of the dialog box (see Figure 29-9). By the way, Windows will not look for any lost files in the Recycle Bin. If you suspect your lost file was deleted, you'll need to browse the Recycle Bin by yourself.

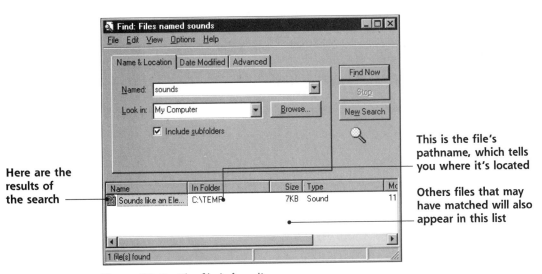

Here are the results of the search ⎯

This is the file's pathname, which tells you where it's located

Others files that may have matched will also appear in this list

Figure 29-9 The file is found!

7. The results are displayed in the bottom of the dialog box. You can

double-click the file to open it, or you can drag it out to the desktop or into a folder where you won't lose it again. (This moves the file from wherever it was hiding, by the way.)

Other Options You May Want to Try in the Find Dialog Box

If you click the Advanced tab in the Find files dialog box, you can look for files of a specific type or files that contain certain text. For example, if you're only looking for sound files, you can choose the Sound type from the list and then leave the filename blank. Windows will find all your sound files for you.

If you want to find a file that contains a specific snippet of text, type this text into the *Containing text* box in the Advanced panel. If you leave the filename blank, Windows will only hunt for files containing that bit of text.

If you do look for a file containing text, try to select the type of text file for which you're looking: Word, Rich Text, Text Document, and so on. Again, this helps speed the search by directing Windows to skip over nontext files.

Summary

Windows has supplied you with Troubleshooter software and, if you followed the directions in this book, you made yourself an Emergency Boot Disk. Both should help you with any catastrophes that may happen with Windows. Just hope nothing ever does happen. Hallelujah! The last chapter. No time to be skipping information.

Make sure you understand the following:

- ☐ How to work through the Troubleshooter.
- ☐ How to work the hardware conflict troubleshooter.
- ☐ How to start Windows (the *special* way).
- ☐ How to use the Emergency Boot disk.
- ☐ How to find a file

ERROR MESSAGES (AND HOW TO DEAL WITH THEM)

Error messages are a pain in the rump. Not because they pop up there and spoil your rhythm, but because it's really hard to understand them. Even with all they tried to do to make Windows easier to use, the scriveners at Microsoft can't remove the terms *invalid*, *default*, *specified*, and *illegal operation*. Yikes! It makes particle physics sound elementary.

The following sections divvy up some error messages, explaining why they happened and what, if anything, you can do to fix the problem.

Cannot Find the File

What happened: You typed in the name of a program to run and Windows couldn't find it. This usually happens when you type in the name of a program using the Start Thing's Run command.

How to fix it: Use the Browse button on the Run command's dialog box to hunt for the file. Or you can refer to the section "File? File? Here File! C'mon, Boy! Where'd You Go?" in Chapter 29 to try to hunt down the file elsewhere on your system.

The name of the program you tried to run

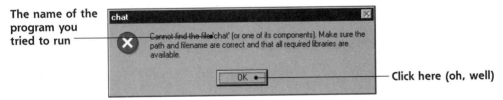

Click here (oh, well)

Figure A-1 This program refuses to run.

Cannot Find This File

What happened: You tried to open a file in WordPad or some other application by typing in that file's name. Tsk, tsk, tsk.

How to fix it: Use your mouse to pluck out the file from the scrolling list. Browse! Or you can edit the filename and try typing it in again.

Bizarre way to say you mistyped a filename

Figure A-2 Check your typing and try again error

Cannot Rename

What happened: You tried to give a file a new name and a file with that name already exists in the same directory.

How to fix it: Give the file another name.

This is the file you tried to rename

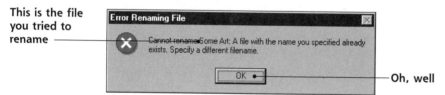

Figure A-3 The try-to-rename-the-file-again warning dialog box

The Device Is Not Ready

What happened: You tried to access a disk drive and, for some reason, Windows wasn't able to do so. Pray that it's a floppy disk; if it's a hard drive, there may be something horribly wrong with the drive.

How to fix it: For a floppy disk, stick a formatted disk into the drive. You either don't have a disk in the drive, the drive's door latch isn't closed, or the disk isn't formatted. If it's a hard drive, then you'll need to do some troubleshooting. Refer to "The All-Purpose Amazing Windows Troubleshooter" in Chapter 29 for more information.

You can click here after putting a proper disk in the drive

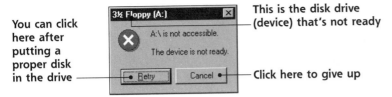

This is the disk drive (device) that's not ready

Click here to give up

Figure A-4   "I'm not ready yet!"

The Disk in the Destination Drive Is Full

What happened: You tried to move or copy something to a disk and, lo, there isn't enough room.

How to fix it: For a floppy disk, you can replace the disk and try again. For a hard drive, you'll have to delete some files to free some space. A great way to free space on a hard drive is to adjust the amount of disk space eaten by the Recycle Bin.

Follow these instructions

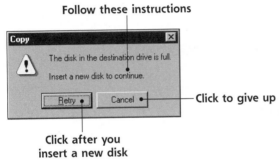

Click to give up

Click after you insert a new disk

Figure A-5   There's no room at the inn.

The Disk Is Write-Protected

What happened: You tried to alter a file on a write-protected disk. A write-protected disk cannot be written to and the information saved on that disk cannot be changed or deleted.

How to fix it: You can either use another disk or remove the write-protection from that disk. To change the write-protect status on a floppy disk, slide the tile so it covers the hole. (On the older 5¼-inch disks, you have to remove the sticker over the disk notch.)

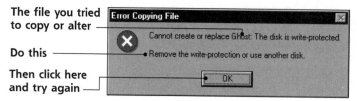

The file you tried to copy or alter

Do this

Then click here and try again

Figure A-6   Write-protection has stopped you cold.

Read-Only File Cannot Be Changed and Saved

What happened: You tried to save a file that's been marked *read-only* by Windows. Such a file cannot be altered or even deleted.

How to fix it: My best advice is not to fix it; read-only files are made that way for a reason. Obviously someone doesn't want you altering the file. If you're persistent, you can open up the file's Properties dialog box and in the Attributes section click on *Read-only* to remove the ✔ check mark from the box.

Here is the name of the read-only file

Oh, well

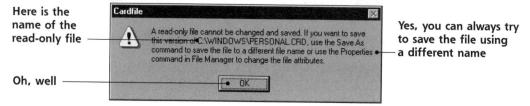

Yes, you can always try to save the file using a different name

Figure A-7   Don't mess with me!

Replace Existing File?

What happened: You've tried to save a file to disk, but a file with that same name already exists.

How to fix it: Click No unless you're absolutely sure you want to replace the already existing file. Remember, if you save, you cannot recover the original file — no matter what. Just type in a different name when you try to save the file again.

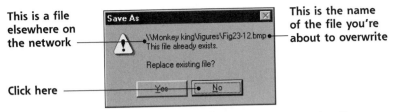

This is a file elsewhere on the network —

This is the name of the file you're about to overwrite

Click here —

Figure A-8 You shouldn't overwrite existing files.

Save Changes?

What happened: You were working on a document and decided to close it or start a new one, but the document has not been saved to disk. Omigosh!

How to fix it: Nothing to fix, really. Just click Yes to save the file.

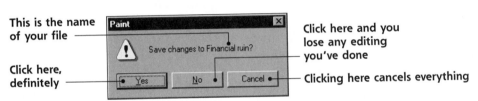

This is the name of your file —

Click here, definitely —

Click here and you lose any editing you've done

Clicking here cancels everything

Figure A-9 Save your files before it's too late!

The Item This Shortcut Refers to Has Been Changed or Moved

What happened: Shortcuts can get you there quickly and they can get you lost. Sometimes the file a shortcut points to may be moved or deleted. Windows catches most of that, but sometimes it misses a file or two. You'll be warned when that happens, but Windows will also try to make amends by finding the file.

How to fix it: See if the match suggested in the dialog box (see Figure A-10) is okay. If so, click Yes. Otherwise, you may want to scour the Recycle Bin for the original file. And if the file can't be found at all, just delete the shortcut; it doesn't point to anything anyway.

Here is the long, boring pathname to the file

C:\OFFICE95\EXCEL\EXCEL.EXE

Here is the filename part (this is Excel)

The specified path is invalid.

Oh well

OK

Figure A-10 Missing shortcuts can get Windows lost.

The Specified Path Is Invalid

What happened: You tried to run a program from the Start Thing menu and Windows couldn't find it.

How to fix it: You can follow the steps in the section "File? File? Here File! C'mon, Boy! Where'd You Go?" in Chapter 29 to try to find the file on your disk.

This error message may follow another error message warning you that some of the program's pieces' parts are missing. In that case, you probably have an installation problem. Consider reinstalling the software. See Chapter 11 for more information on installing software.

If the program lives on the Start Thing menu, you may consider removing it.

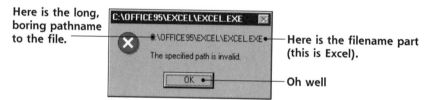

Here is the long, boring pathname to the file.

C:\OFFICE95\EXCEL\EXCEL.EXE

Here is the filename part (this is Excel).

The specified path is invalid.

Oh well

OK

Figure A-11 Windows can't find this program.

This Filename Is Not Valid

What happened: You tried to save a file to disk and typed in a forbidden file-name character.

How to fix it: Retype the filename, but don't use any of the following characters:

" * / : < > ? \ | .

Also see Chapter 14, the side trip "Basic File-Naming Rules and Regulations."

Contains the slash character—Heavens!

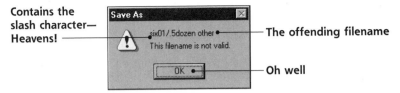

The offending filename

Oh well

Figure A-12 You can't name a file that!

This Program Has Performed an Illegal Operation

What happened: This is a scary one. For some reason, the program you were using *crashed*. It died. It's gone. Who knows why this happened? The dialog box suggests contacting whoever developed the software to let them know about it. Sounds like a good idea.

How to fix it: You can't. Click on the Close button to close the offending application. Further, I would advise saving everything you're working on and restarting the computer. In some rare cases you may not be able to do that, but try anyway. Stubborn programs that refuse to be shut down can be killed off in Windows using the CTRL+ALT+DELETE key combination. See Chapter 3 "The Drastic Way to Quit."

This is the program that died

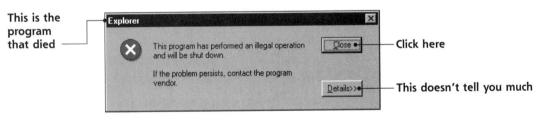

Click here

This doesn't tell you much

Figure A-13 The big *OOPS* has happened!

You Must Type a Filename

What happened: You tried to rename a file but you didn't type in a name. Foolishly, you just pressed the F2 key, and then ENTER. All files must have a name, silly.

How to fix it: Try again. This time, type in a name for the file.

The Rename program caused this error ——

Like, duh

Oh well

Figure A-14 Gotta name that file.

FREEBIES

When you see an advertisement that something is *free*, chances are good it really isn't. Something is always attached. Even when you get an annoying phone call saying, "Hey, Mr. and Mrs. Hardin, you've just won a new TV! To receive your prize, you must come down to our office and claim it!" OK. You know what happens next. The Hardins go down for their prize and, lo and behold, there's a group of top-notch (pushy) sales people who are going to pressure — er . . . encourage — the Hardins to buy something they don't need that costs too much. In return, the Hardins get a set of tea cups (because the company offering the prize always runs out of whatever the winner supposedly won).

Microsoft has thrown in a few freebies for you. But they've saved you from the pushy sales people and, in this case, no strings are attached.

TABLE B-1 The Freebies of Windows 95

Icon	Name	Path
Sounds	Sound Recorder	Start → Programs → Accessories → Multimedia → Sound Recorder
	CD Player	Start → Programs → Accessories → Multimedia → CD Player
	Phone Dialer	Start → Programs → Accessories → Phone Dialer
	Clipboard Viewer	Start → Programs → Accessories → Clipboard Viewer
	Paint	Start → Programs → Accessories → Paint

(continued)

TABLE B-1 The Freebies of Windows 95 (*continued*)

Icon	Name	Path
	WordPad	Start → Programs → Accessories → WordPad
	Calculator	Start → Programs → Accessories → Calculator
	Notepad	Start → Programs → Accessories → Notepad
	Hyper Terminal	Start → Programs → Accessories → HyperTerminal
	Character Map	Start → Programs → Accessories → Character Map
	Solitaire — Game	Start → Programs → Accessories → Games → Solitaire
	FreeCell — Game	Start → Programs → Accessories → Games → Free Cell
	Minesweeper — Game	Start → Programs → Accessories → Games → Minesweeper
	Hearts — Game	Start → Programs → Accessories → Games → Hearts
	Space Cadet Table — Game	Start → Programs → Accessories → Games → Space Cadet Table

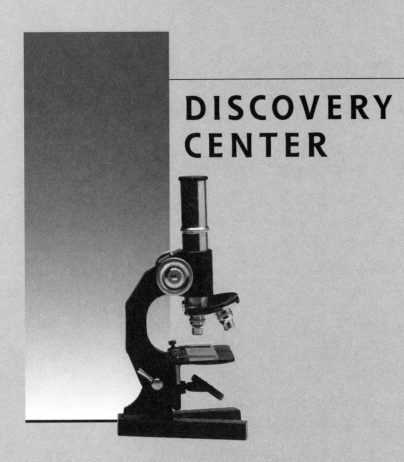

DISCOVERY CENTER

What you'll discover is most of the important steps on how to do things in Windows are found in this part of the book. The Discovery Center serves as a handy reference to the most important tasks in the chapters. The steps in the Discovery Center have few explanations (you'll have to read the book!); they only sport minimal steps. Just the facts, ma'am.

CHAPTER 1

How to start Windows (page 3)

Flip on the switch on the computer box, and then turn on the switch on the computer's monitor.

How to log in to Windows (page 5)

1. Type your first and last name or login ID in the *User name* box of the log-in dialog box.

2. Type your secret password in the *Password* box.

3. Click OK.

If you've never typed in your name and password, Windows asks you to confirm your password:

1. Type that same password again in the *Confirm new password* box of the New Password dialog box.

2. Click OK and Windows will remember you.

How to bypass typing in a name and password (page 7)

If you don't want to log in to Windows, just click on the Cancel button in the "who are you?" dialog box.

How to activate the Start Thing (page 10)

Do any of the following:

* Click your mouse on the Start button.
* Press CTRL+ESC.
* Press the Window button (between the CTRL and ALT buttons on the lower-left side of the keyboard), if you have one.

How to shut down your computer (page 13)

1. Activate the Start Thing's pop-up menu.

2. Select the bottom item Shut Down .

3. Make sure the option *Shut down the computer?* is selected.

4. Click on the Yes button.

5. The final screen displays the Windows 95 logo and tells you it's safe to turn off your computer.

6. Turn off the computer.

How to turn off the "Welcome to Windows" Dialog box (page 9)

1. Click in the *Show this Welcome Screen next time you start Windows* box.

2. The ✔ check mark in the box disappears. You're done.

CHAPTER 2

How to look at the files on My Computer (page 18)

Open the My Computer icon to see the disk drives, folders, and files living on your computer.

How to open and close a folder (page 19)

1. Double-click on a disk drive icon.

2. Double-click on a folder.

3. Close the folder when you're done by clicking on the Close button.

How to organize your windows (page 22)

1. Find the taskbar; it should be the line on the bottom of the desktop.

2. Point the mouse at a blank part of the taskbar.

3. Click on the right mouse button once and the taskbar shortcut menu pops up.

4a. Choose Cascade from the menu. This arranges all the windows in a nice, overlapping fashion.

4b. Click on Tile Horizontally or Tile Vertically to arrange the windows in a tiled (not overlapping) fashion.

How to close windows (page 22)

Click on the X close button.

How to change the way My Computer displays information (page 25)

* Big Icon View (recommended): Choose [View] → [Large Icons], or click on the Large Icon button from the toolbar.
* Small Icon View: Choose [View] → [Small Icons], or select the Small Icons button from the toolbar.
* Details View (for nerds): Choose [View] → [Details], or click the Details button on the toolbar.

How to see the toolbar if it's hidden (page 24)

Choose [View] → [Toolbar] from the menu.

How to make the status bar visible (page 25)

Choose [View] → [Status Bar]. Choose that command again to remove the status bar, enabling you to see more of your stuff in the window.

How to use the single-window approach in My Computer (page 27)

1. Choose [View] → [Options] from My Computer.
2. Click the Folder tab if it's not in front.
3. Click the text *Browse folders by using a single window that changes as you open each folder.*
4. Click OK.

CHAPTER 3

How to start a new program (page 31)

1. Click on the Start Thing button.
2. Select [Programs].
3. If one of your programs appears at the top of the Start Thing menu, you're ready to start it now. Move on to Step 5.
4. If you don't see the program you want, click on a submenu folder to look for more programs.
5. When you find your program, click on it.

How to start a new program in My Computer (page 34)

1. Double-click on the My Computer icon.

2. Double-click on the drive (C:) icon.

3. Double-click on the folder where your file is located.

4. Double-click on the file.

How to use the Run command (page 34)

1. Click on the Start Thing button if a mouse is handy.

2. Click on `Run`.

3. Type the name of the program you want to run in the *Open* box of the Run Dialog box.

4. Click on the OK button.

How to start working on a document in the Documents menu (page 35)

1. Click on the Start Thing.

2. Choose `Documents`.

3. Click on a recent document.

4. The document is opened.

How to quit a program (page 37)

Quit any program by selecting the `Exit` command at the bottom of the File menu. The command may be called `Close`; in some rare instances, you may even see the word `Quit` used.

How to clear the Documents menu (page 39)

1. Choose `Settings` → `Taskbar` from the Start Thing menu.

2. Click on the Start Menu Programs panel.

3. Click the Clear button in the bottom, Documents Menu area.

4. Close the Taskbar Properties dialog box by clicking its Close button.

CHAPTER 4

How to start WordPad (page 42)

1. Click on `Start`.
2. Choose `Programs` → `Accessories`.
3. Click on `WordPad`.

How to print a document (page 45)

1. Choose `File` → `Print` from the menu.
2. Click on OK.

How to save a document (page 46)

1. Choose `File` → `Save` from the menu.
2. Choose a disk drive for your document.
3. Choose a folder for your document.
4. Click on the *File name* box and type in a document name.
5. Choose a document type.
6. Click the Save button or press ENTER.

How to open a document (page 48)

1. Choose `File` → `Open` from the menu.
2. Locate the folder or disk drive where the file is located.
3. Double-click on the file. Voila.

How to find Help (page 50)

The F1 key is the Help key.

How to use Help for a specific topic (page 51)

1. In your application, press the F1 key to activate the Help system.
2. Click on the Index tab.

3. Search for your topic by typing the first few letters of the word in the box at the top of the panel.

4. Double-click on the index entry for which you're looking and read up on the topic you've chosen.

How to save time with quick key shortcuts (page 57)

Key Combo	Command
CTRL+A	Select All
CTRL+C	Copy
CTRL+F	Find
CTRL+N	New
CTRL+O	Open
CTRL+P	Print
CTRL+S	Save
CTRL+V	Paste
CTRL+X	Cut
CTRL+Z	Undo
F1	Help
ALT+F4	Quit/Exit

CHAPTER 5

How to place a program on the Start menu (page 63)

1. Open My Computer, and then open drive (C:), the Program Files folder, and look inside the Accessories folder. WordPad's program icon should be there.

2. Drag the program icon to the Start button on the taskbar.

3. To verify that a shortcut copy of the program is now on the menu, activate the Start Thing. You'll see your program's icon there.

How to use the Start Thing menu (page 61)

Icon	Text	What It Does
	Programs	Lists a sublist of submenu of programs (see Chapter 3)
	Documents	Lists a submenu of recent documents
	Settings	Lists a submenu for quick access to Windows' dinking tools
	Find	A special command that helps you find files, folders, and programs on disk
	Help	Activates Windows' main Help system
	Run	Brings up a dialog box where you can type the name of a command to run
	Shutdown	Forces Windows into bankruptcy— seriously, offers several options for quitting Windows or shutting down for the day
	Suspend	Saves energy by forcing energy-efficient and laptop computers into a *sleep* mode

How to add a program to the Start Thing submenu (page 64)

1. Pop up the Start Thing menu.
2. Choose `Settings` → `Taskbar`. This brings up the Taskbar Properties dialog box.
3. Click on the Start Menu Programs panel.
4. Click on the Add button which brings up another dialog box, Create Shortcut.
5. Click on the Browse button.

6. Find your program.

7. Choose the drive where your program lives from the *Look in* list box.

8. Double-click on the folder.

9. Use the scrollbar at the bottom of the window to find your program.

10. Click once on the program's icon.

11. Click on Open. This closes the Browse dialog box and puts the program's geeky pathname into the Create Shortcut dialog box.

12. Click on Next. Now you select a Start Thing submenu for your program. Just click on the folder in which you want your program shoved.

13. Click on the Next button again.

14. Click on Finish.

15. Click on OK and you're finished.

How to remove a program from the Start Thing (page 66)

1. Open the Taskbar Properties dialog box.

2. Click on the Start Menu Programs panel.

3. Click on Remove.

4. Double-click on a folder to open it and see its menu items.

5. Click once on the program you want to remove.

6. Click on the Remove button.

7. Click on the Close button.

8. Click on the OK button.

CHAPTER 6

How to stretch the taskbar (page 77)

1. Hover the mouse over the top edge of the taskbar.

2. Press and hold the mouse's left (main) button.

3. Drag up the mouse, making the taskbar fatter.

4. Release the mouse button when the taskbar is two or even three times as large.

How to restore a vanished taskbar (page 78)

1. Open the Start Thing menu.

2. Press ALT+spacebar. This displays the taskbar's control menu, which replaces the Start Thing menu.

3. Press s for size.

4. Press the ↑ key on the keyboard. Every time you press the ↑ key, the taskbar grows in size.

5. Press ENTER. This restores the taskbar to the size you see it on the screen.

How to see the clock if it is hidden (page 81)

1. Click on the Start button.

2. Choose Settings → Taskbar. The Taskbar Properties dialog box appears.

3. Click in the *Show Clock* box. If a ✔ check mark appears in the box, the current time appears on the taskbar.

4. Click on OK. You now have a clock (or not) on the taskbar.

How to see the volume control (page 80)

1. Open My Computer.

2. Open the Control Panel.

3. Locate the Multimedia icon.

4. Double-click on the Multimedia icon.

5. Click on the Audio panel to bring it in front.

6. Click in the *Show volume control on the taskbar* box. This puts a ✔ check mark in the box, causing Windows to display the volume button.

7. Click on OK in the Multimedia Properties dialog box to close it.

8. Close the Control Panel window and My Computer's window.

CHAPTER 7

How to find Windows' applets (miniapplications) (page 87)

Choose Programs → Accessories.

1. Activate the Start Thing menu.
2. Choose [Programs] → [Accessories] → [Paint].

How to use Paint (page 92)

Art	Tool	Do This . . .
	Selection	Use the selection tools to select graphics on the screen for dragging, copying, or cutting. Use the star-shaped selection tool to drag unusual shapes and select them; the rectangle selection tool selects only rectangular shapes (duh).
	Color Eraser	Click on the right mouse button while using the Eraser tool to use the *color eraser*. In that mode, only the selected foreground color will be erased.
	Paint bucket	Click with the left mouse button to fill an area on the screen with the foreground color; click with the right mouse button to fill it with the background color.
	Eyedropper	The Eyedropper tool is used to choose a color from the canvas's image.
	Pencil	The pencil is used to draw a thin line. It's best used when you zoom in on a graphic for tight or tiny work. Press CTRL+PAGE DOWN to zoom in; press CTRL+PAGE UP to zoom out.
	Brush	The brush draws a thicker line than does the pencil.

(continued)

(*continued*)

Art	Tool	Do This . . .
A	Text	Text enables you to type in graphical text. Choose	View |→| Text Toolbar	so you can choose the font, size, and style for the text. Note, the text is drawn in the current foreground color; if you don't see the text, it's probably because you've selected white as the foreground color.
╲	Line Draw	This tool enables you to draw a straight line from one point to another. You do this by dragging the mouse. Choose a line width from the tool options palette.
▢ ⬭ ⬭	Shape tools	These tools draw their respective shapes. Click on the Line Draw tool to set the width of the line, and then you can choose how the shape will be filled by clicking in the tool option palette.

How to start Notepad (page 94)

1. Press CTRL+ESC to fire up the Start Thing menu.
2. Choose | Programs |→| Accessories |→| Notepad |.

How to start the Calculator (page 99)

1. Pop up the Start Thing menu.
2. Choose | Programs |→| Accessories |→| Calculator |.

Or, for a nerdier version of the Calculator . . .
3. Choose | View |→| Scientific | from the menu.

How to use the phone dialer (page 100)

1. Pop up the Start Thing menu.
2. Choose | Programs |→| Accessories |→| Phone Dialer |.

3. Type a number in the *Number to dial* box, or click on it using the mouse on the phone keypad.

4. Click on the Dial button.

5. When the other party answers, click on the Talk button in the Call Status dialog box.

6. Click the Hang Up button in the Active Call dialog box when the call is over.

CHAPTER 8

How to multitask using the taskbar (page 104)

1. Minimize all your programs by clicking on the minimize button.

2. The program icon becomes a button on the taskbar.

3. Click on the program icon when you want to open that window.

How to use ALT + TAB for multitasking (page 106)

* Press the ALT+TAB keys. This will take you from one program to another.

* If you have more than one program to which you are switching back-and-forth, continue holding down the ALT key and tap the TAB key.

How to find the Cut, Copy, and Paste commands (page 107)

Toolbar Button	Command	Menu	Keyboard Shortcut
	CUT	Edit → Cut	CTRL+X
	COPY	Edit → Copy	CTRL+C
	PASTE	Edit → Paste	CTRL+V

How to run the Clipboard Viewer (page 112)

1. Pop up the Start Thing menu.

2. Choose Programs → Accessories → Clipboard Viewer .

CHAPTER 9

How to get on the Internet (page 114)

To use the Internet, you need the following:

* A modem (connected to a COM or serial port)
* A phone line
* *Software* to control your modem
* An Internet Service Provider (ISP)
* Money, money, money, money.

How to connect to the Internet (page 119)

1. Double-click on My Computer.
2. Double-click on the Dial-Up Networking folder.
3. Open the icon representing your Internet provider (which was placed in the folder when you installed your Internet software).
4. Type your password (if needed) in the Connect To dialog box.
5. Click on the Connect button.
6. If a connection is made, you'll see the Connected dialog box. You can now start using your Internet software.

How to start HyperTerminal (page 124)

1. Click on the Start button.
2. Choose [Programs] → [Accessories] → [HyperTerminal].

How to create a session for the Microsoft Download computer (page 125)

1. Open the HyperTerminal program by double-clicking on its icon in the HyperTerminal folder.
2. Type in a name for the system you're calling.
3. Pluck out a handy icon for the session.
4. Click on the OK button.
5. Enter the country code of the computer you're dialing.
6. Don't mess with the Connect using box.

7. Click on the OK button.

8. The Connect dialog box is displayed. Now you're ready to call the other computer.

CHAPTER 10

How to work with DOS programs (page 134)

1. Pop up the Start Thing menu.

2. Choose [Programs], and then choose any submenus where your DOS program is located.

3. Click on your DOS program to start it.

4. If you don't see your DOS program on the menu, start the MS-DOS Prompt program, which lives on the main Programs menu.

How to use the MS-DOS Troubleshooter (page 141)

1. Choose Help from the Start Thing menu.

2. Click on the Index tab if that panel isn't already forward.

3. Type the word **Installing** into the number-one box on the Index panel.

4. Click on MS-DOS programs once to highlight that item.

5. Click on the Display button. You'll see the MS-DOS Program Troubleshooter on the screen.

6. Choose the item that bugs you.

How to learn more about DOS (page 142)

Buy *DOS For Dummies*, by Dan Gookin.

CHAPTER 11

How to practice installing software (page 144)

1. Double-click on My Computer.

2. Double-click on the friendly Control Panel.

3. Double-click on the Add/Remove Programs icon.

4. Click on the Install/Uninstall tab if that panel isn't up front already.

5. Click on the Install button.

6. Stick the installation disks into the appropriate drive.

7. Click on Next.

8. Click on Finish (or Install).

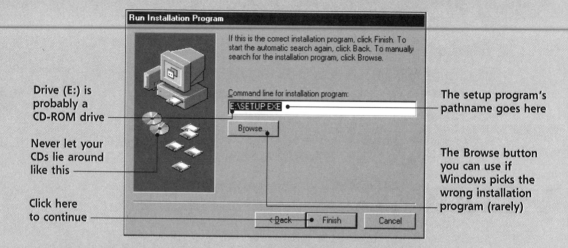

Drive (E:) is probably a CD-ROM drive

Never let your CDs lie around like this

Click here to continue

Run Installation Program

If this is the correct installation program, click Finish. To start the automatic search again, click Back. To manually search for the installation program, click Browse.

Command line for installation program:

E:\SETUP.EXE

Browse...

The setup program's pathname goes here

The Browse button you can use if Windows picks the wrong installation program (rarely)

< Back   Finish   Cancel

How to install the rest of Windows (page 146)

1. Pop up the Add/Remove Programs Properties dialog box.

2. Click on the Windows Setup tab.

3. Put a ✔ check mark in the box by those items you want to add to Windows.

4. Click on the Details button if the item has more than one option.

5. Click on the OK button when you're ready to add your stuff.

6. Stick the Windows setup disk into your disk drive.

7. You're done.

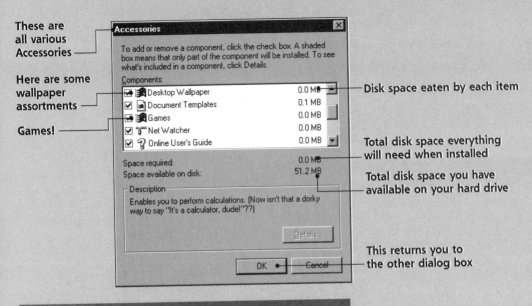

These are all various Accessories

Here are some wallpaper assortments

Games!

Disk space eaten by each item

Total disk space everything will need when installed

Total disk space you have available on your hard drive

This returns you to the other dialog box

How to uninstall programs (page 149)

1. Summon the Add/Remove Programs Properties dialog box.

2. Click on the application you want to remove in the Install/Uninstall list.

3. Click the Remove button. You'll see a Confirm File Deletion dialog box.

4. Click Yes.

5. Resume your deinstallation.

CHAPTER 12

How to create or change the name of your disk drives (page 158)

1. Double-click on My Computer.

2. Locate the hard drive you want to rename.

3. Right-click on the disk drive icon to bring up its shortcut menu.

4. Click on Properties .

5. Click on the General tab to bring that panel forward.

6. Look for the Label input box.

7a. If you don't want any name for your disk drive, press the DELETE key to erase the current name, and then skip to Step 8.

7b. If you want to type in a new name, do so.

8. Click on OK. This closes the disk drive's Properties dialog box.

How to format a disk (page 160)

1. Place a floppy disk into drive (A:), your computer's first floppy drive. If you want to format a disk for drive (B:), put a disk in there instead.

2. Double-click on My Computer.

3. Right-click the mouse on drive (A:) to display its shortcut menu. Or, right-click on drive (B:) if you're formatting a disk in that drive.

4. Click on Format . The Format dialog box appears.

5. Click Start. The formatting operation starts a-hummin'.

6. Click Close in the Formatting dialog box. You're done.

7. Remove the formatted disk from the drive and label the disk right now!

8. If you want to format another disk, start again with Step 1.

How to avoid ultimate trouble (page 161)

Never format a hard drive!

How to start a musical CD disk (page 163)

✳ Insert a musical CD, and you'll see the music-is-playing CD icon in My Computer indicating that the CD Player program is running.

✳ If that doesn't happen, you can manually start the CD Player program; press CTRL+ESC to bring up the Start Thing menu, and then choose Programs → Accessories → Multimedia → CD Player .

How to see if you have a RAM drive (page 164)

Look for a RAM drive icon in My Computer. If you find one there, you have a RAM drive.

How to remove your RAM drive (if you have one) (page 164)

Refer to the chapter. This is a long process and you need to read the complete steps to understand this.

CHAPTER 13

How to create a new folder (page 169)

1. Start in the root folder (go to My Computer and open drive (C:). The window you'll see is the root folder, the parent of your new folder baby.)
2. Choose `File` → `New` → `Folder` from the menu. The new folder appears in the window.
3. Type a new name for the new folder.
4. Press the ENTER key when you're done.

How to explore the bowels of the folder tree on your (C:) drive (page 172)

1. Open My Computer.
2. Right-click the mouse on your (C:) drive icon. This displays drive (C:)'s shortcut menu.
3. Choose *Explore* from the shortcut menu.

How to use the Explorer (page 172)

1. Use the All Folders side of the window to locate the disk drive you want to examine.
2. Open the folders on that disk drive until you get to the one you want.
3. Look in the Contents window for the icons or files you want.

How to keep your folders organized (page 174)

Adopt this work folder strategy, courtesy of Dan and Sandra Gookin.

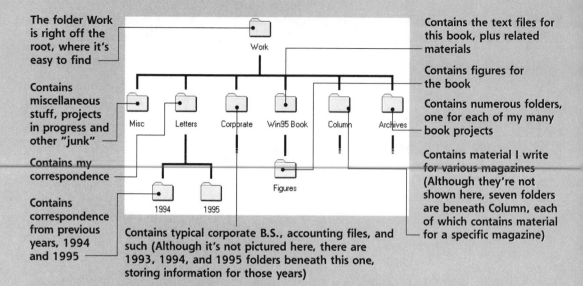

The folder Work is right off the root, where it's easy to find

Contains miscellaneous stuff, projects in progress and other "junk"

Contains my correspondence

Contains correspondence from previous years, 1994 and 1995

Work

Misc   Letters   Corporate   Win95 Book   Column   Archives

1994   1995

Figures

Contains the text files for this book, plus related materials

Contains figures for the book

Contains numerous folders, one for each of my many book projects

Contains material I write for various magazines (Although they're not shown here, seven folders are beneath Column, each of which contains material for a specific magazine)

Contains typical corporate B.S., accounting files, and such (Although it's not pictured here, there are 1993, 1994, and 1995 folders beneath this one, storing information for those years)

CHAPTER 14

How to change a file's name (page 177)

1. Click on the icon once.

2. Press the F2 key.

3. Type in a new name for the icon.

4. Press ENTER when you're done. The new name is in place.

How to see the filename extension (page 179)

1. Choose **View** → **Options**. This displays the Options dialog box.

2. Click on the View panel to bring that forward.

3. Click on the box by *Hide MS-DOS file extensions for file types that are registered*. If a ✔ check mark appears in the box, the extensions are hidden. If the box is empty, you can see the extensions.

4. Click on OK to close the Options dialog box.

How to copy or duplicate a file (page 180)

1. Click on the file once to select it. The file becomes highlighted on the screen.

2. Choose `Edit` → `Copy`.

3. Go to the destination. Open the folder to which you want to copy the file.

4. Choose `Edit` → `Paste`.

How to move a file (page 182)

1. Click on the file's icon once to select it.

2. Choose `Edit` → `Cut`.

3. Open the folder to which you want to move the file.

4. Choose `Edit` → `Paste`.

5. The file now lives in the new folder.

How to delete a file (page 182)

1. Click on the file's icon to select it.

2. Choose `File` → `Delete`.

3. The Confirm File Delete dialog box appears. Click Yes.

How to undo what you just did (page 183)

Choose `Edit` → `Undo` from the menu.

How to select more than one object on the screen (page 184)

1. Point the mouse at the icon you want to select.

2. Press and hold the CTRL key on your keyboard.

3. Click on each file you want to select.

4. Repeat Step 3 for every file you want to select in the group. Just keep CTRL+clicking.

How to select a group of files (page 184)

1. Select the first file in the group.

2. Select the last file in the list and SHIFT+click on it. This selects that file and all the files between it and the first file you selected.

How to select all the files in a folder or window (page 187)

1. Go to the window containing the hoard of files you want to select.

2. Choose [Edit] → [Select All].

CHAPTER 15

How to use the Recycle Bin (page 191)

1. Open the file you want to delete.

2. Click on the file.

3. Drag the file over to the Recycle Bin.

4. Are you sure? Click Yes.

How to restore a document from the Recycle Bin (page 192)

1. Double-click on the Recycle Bin on the desktop.

2. Click once on the file you want to recover and restore using the mouse.

3. Choose [File] → [Restore] from the menu. The file is removed from the Recycle Bin and put back on disk, in the exact folder from which it was deleted.

4. Select [File] → [Close] to close the Recycle Bin or click on its Close button in the window's upper-right corner.

How to selectively delete files from the Recycle Bin (page 194)

1. Click on the file(s) you want to delete. You can hold the CTRL key down while clicking to select more than one file, or you can "drag-lasso" a group of files.

2. Click [File] → [Delete]. The Delete command in the Recycle Bin zaps files for good. The Confirm File Delete dialog box appears.

3. Click the Yes button. The files are gone.

CHAPTER 16

How to locate your hard drive's Properties dialog box (page 202)

1. Open the My Computer icon on the desktop. This displays a window in which you see all your PC's disk drives.

2. Right-click on a disk drive. The drive's shortcut menu is displayed.

3. Choose **Properties**. The Properties dialog box appears.

4. Click on the Tools tab to bring that panel forward.

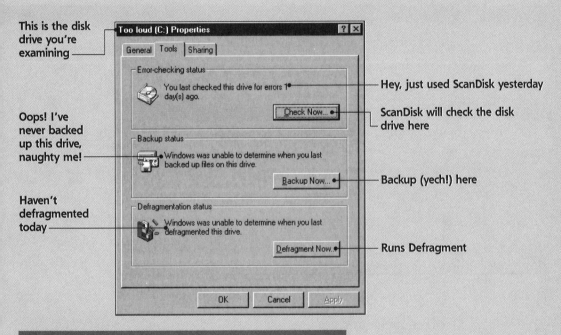

This is the disk drive you're examining

Hey, just used ScanDisk yesterday

ScanDisk will check the disk drive here

Oops! I've never backed up this drive, naughty me!

Backup (yech!) here

Haven't defragmented today

Runs Defragment

When you should back up (page 204)

* Every day, back up the work you did that day.
* Every week, back up your entire hard drive.

How to back up your computer (page 204)

1. Start the Backup program. Click on the Backup Now button.

2. Read the Welcome screen which outlines the process.

3. You might see a dialog box saying *Backup has created the following full backup set for you.* If so, click on the OK button.

4. The main Backup screen appears.

5. Select disk drives, folders, or files to back up.

6. In the next screen tell Windows where to back up your files.

7. Click on the Start Backup button.

8. Type in a Backup Set Label. Click on the OK button when you're done.

9. Make sure the disk or tape to which you are backing up is ready, in the drive, formatted, and willing.

10. Click OK. The backup begins.

11. If the disk already contains files, you'll see a warning dialog box.

12. You might be asked to switch disks. If you're backing up to floppy disks and, face it, one floppy disk doesn't hold a whole hard drive's worth of information, you'll need to switch disks.

13. Remove the current disk. Yank it from your disk drive and set it aside. Insert the next disk. Close the drive door latch if it's a $5\frac{1}{4}$-inch drive.

14. The backup is complete. Close stuff.

15. Remove and number the final disk. If you did a tape backup, remove it and label it, as well.

16. Click OK to close the backup complete dialog box.

17. Click OK to close the other dialog box.

18. Close the Microsoft Backup application window.

How to restore something you backed up (page 208)

1. Start the Backup program.

2. Click on the Restore tab to bring that panel forward.

3. Put your first backup disk or tape into the proper PC orifice. *Kee-lunk!*

4. Click on that backup device in the Restore panel.

5. Choose the files you want to restore.

6. Click the Start Restore button.

7. Swap disks (if necessary).

8. And suddenly . . . you're done.

How to run ScanDisk (page 209)

1. Start the ScanDisk program.

2. When ScanDisk starts, you'll see its window displayed.

3. Pick a drive to scan from the scrolling list.

4. Make sure the *Standard* option is chosen.

5. Make sure the *Automatically fix errors* item is checked.

6. Click the Advanced button.

7. Click OK to close the Advanced Options dialog box.

8. Click the Start button.

9. If you encounter any errors, ScanDisk should fix them automatically. If not, a dialog box may be displayed explaining the problem. Just click the OK button and everything will be fixed all happily-bappily.

10. ScanDisk is done.

How to defragment (page 211)

1. Start the Defragment program. Click the Defragment Now button if you're running the defragment program from a disk's Properties dialog box.

2. Decide whether you really need to do this. The cool thing about the Disk Defragmenter is it immediately lets you know whether you're wasting your time.

3. If Windows suggests you defragment your drive, or if you'd just like to do it for the heck of it, click the Start button.

4. Wait. If your screen saver kicks in, press the CTRL key or wiggle the mouse to get rid of it.

5. You're done!

CHAPTER 17

How to pick a main printer (page 217)

1. Go to the Printers folder (located in My Computer).

2. Point the mouse at the printer you want to choose as your main printer.

3. Bring up the printer's shortcut menu. Right-click the mouse. The shortcut menu appears.

4. Choose *Set As Default*. If a ✔ check mark is already by this item, this printer is your main printer. If not, choosing *Set As Default* makes it your main printer. That will now be the printer Windows uses whenever you print anything.

How to pause your printer (page 220)

Choose `Printer` → `Pause Printing` from the menu in your printer's dialog box (the queue box).

How to pause individual documents (page 220)

Click on your document in the queue and choose `Document` → `Pause Printing` from the menu.

How to kill your document in the queue (page 221)

Locate the offending document and click on it once with the mouse to highlight it. Then choose `Document` → `Cancel Printing`.

CHAPTER 18

How to find the Control Panel (page 227)

* Double-click on My Computer, or;
* Click on the Start Thing, and then choose `Settings` → `Control Panel`.

How to change the language on your keyboard (page 232)

1. Locate the Control Panel; double-click on the Keyboard icon to open it.
2. Click on the Language tab to bring that panel forward.
3. Click on the Add button. The Add Language dialog box appears.
4. Choose the new language from the drop-down list.
5. Click on OK.
6. Click on OK to exit the Keyboard Properties dialog box.

CHAPTER 19

How to find the Fonts folder (page 242)

1. Open the Control Panel in My Computer's main window.
2. Double-click on the Fonts folder to open it.

How to view a font (page 244)

Double-click on the font icon in the Fonts folder, located in the Control Panel.

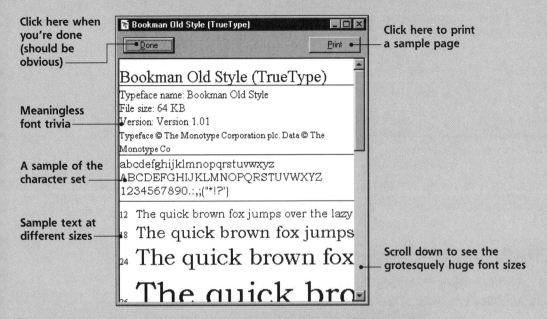

Click here when you're done (should be obvious)

Click here to print a sample page

Meaningless font trivia

A sample of the character set

Sample text at different sizes

Scroll down to see the grotesquely huge font sizes

How to add new fonts to your system (page 245)

1. Open the Fonts window.

2. Choose File → Install New Font . The Add Fonts dialog box appears.

3. Use the Drives and Folders windows to locate your font files.

4. Choose the fonts you want to install from the *List of Fonts* list.

5. Click OK. *Chugga-chugga.* Soon the fonts are copied to the Fonts folder window on your hard drive. There's no need to reset; the fonts are ready to use.

How to kill off old unused fonts (page 246)

1. Open the Fonts window.

2. Select the font(s) you want to kill off by clicking on that font.

3. Choose File → Delete . A warning box appears, asking if you're sure you want to delete the font.

4. Click Yes. The font is deleted.

From the Start Thing menu, choose Programs → Accessories → Character Map .

Choose a font here ——

Click a character to see it magnified ——

Double-click to paste the character ——

Characters are pasted here for copying

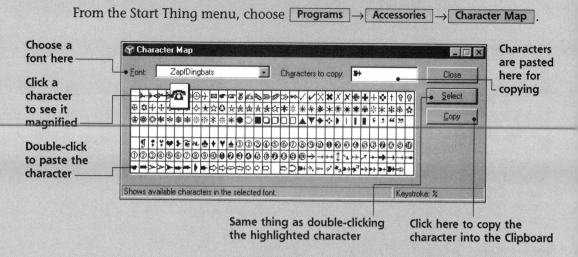

Same thing as double-clicking the highlighted character

Click here to copy the character into the Clipboard

CHAPTER 20

1. Open a file you would like to save elsewhere.

2. Choose File → Save As from the menu. The standard Save As dialog box appears.

3. Use the *Save in* drop-down list and choose Network Neighborhood from the list.

4. Open the computer on which you want to save by double-clicking on the computer's icon.

5. Double-click on the folder you want to open.

6. You may be asked to enter a password here.

7. Continue double-clicking on folders until you find the one where you want to save your file.

8. At this point, using the Save As dialog box works exactly as it would for your own computer. In fact, it's often hard to tell the difference.

9. After finding the proper folder, type in a file name next to the *File name* box. Do this just as you would on your computer.

10. Choose a file type.

11. Click the Save button. The file is saved on another computer.

How to open a file from another computer (page 255)

1. Choose `File` → `Open` from the menu.

2. Choose Network Neighborhood from the *Look in* drop-down list.

3. Find the computer on which you want to open a file and double-click on its icon.

4. Double-click on a folder to open it. The folder's contents are then displayed in the window. Type in a password if you're asked.

5. Continue opening folders until you find the file for which you're looking.

6. Eventually you'll find what you're looking for — a document, file, program, whatever. Double-click on it and it opens.

How to share any hard drive or folder on the network (page 259)

1. Locate the disk drive or folder you want to share by using My Computer or the Explorer.

2. Click on the folder or disk drive once to select it.

3. Choose `File` → `Sharing`.

4. Click on *Shared As*. This surrenders the disk drive or folder for sharing.

5. Click on OK. *Humma-humma-humma!*

How to share your printer (page 260)

1. Open the Control Panel.

2. Double-click on the Printers folder to open it.

3. Select the printer you want to share by clicking once on your printer's icon.

4. Choose `File` → `Sharing`.

5. Click on the *Shared As* option button.

6. Click on OK. You're done.

How to find Microsoft Exchange (page 262)

✳ Click on the Start Thing menu; choose `Programs` → `Microsoft Exchange`.

✳ You may also see the Inbox icon on your desktop, in which case you can click on it to start Exchange.

How to get your mail (page 263)

* When new mail arrives, your computer will beep and you'll see the friendly mail guy appear near the loud time on the taskbar. Double-click on him to pop up the Exchange and read your new mail.

How to send a new mail message (page 264)

1. Choose `Compose` → `New Message` from the Exchange's menu.
2. Fill in the *To* and *Subject* input boxes and, optionally, the *CC* (carbon copy) box.
3. Fill in the message text.
4. When you're done, choose `File` → `Send` to send your message, or click on the wee little send button on the toolbar.

How to use your WinPopup (page 266)

1. Start WinPopup by choosing it from the Start Thing menu. It should be in the `Programs` → `Accessories` submenu.
2. To send a message, click on the little envelope button.
3. Type in the user's name (how they're logging into their computer) or type in the computer name.
4. Press the TAB key and then type the message.
5. Click on OK to send it.
6. A dialog box pops up saying your message was successfully sent.
7. Click on OK.
8. You are now ready to send another message.

CHAPTER 21

How to install hardware (page 269)

1. Close all open programs.
2. Double-click on My Computer.
3. Double-click on the Control Panel.
4. Double-click on the Add New Hardware icon.

5. Click Next in the Add New Hardware Wizard box.

6. Follow the directions of the Wizard.

How to install your printer (page 273)

1. Double-click on My Computer.

2. Double-click on the Control Panel.

3. Double-click on the Printers folder.

4. Double-click on the Add Printer icon.

5. Click the Next button. The *How is this printer attached to your computer?* panel appears.

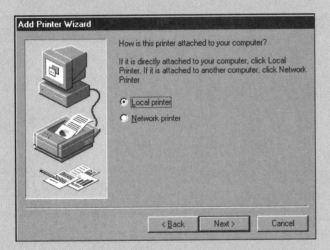

6a. If your PC has its own printer, choose *Local printer*.

6b. If your PC doesn't have its own printer but must share a printer elsewhere on the network, choose *Network printer*.

7. Click on the Next Button.

8a. If you're installing a network printer, click on the Browse button to find the printer to which you want to connect and click on the printer's name. Then click on OK.

8b. If you chose *Local printer,* click on the Next button.

9. Now you get to tell Windows which brand and model of printer you have.

10a. Pick the *Manufacturers* first.

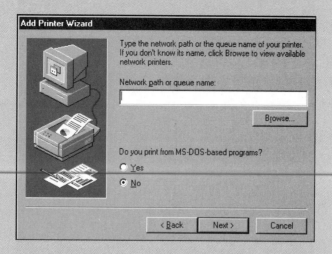

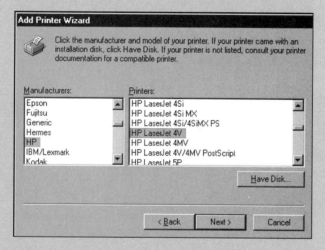

10b. If your printer isn't on the list, but it came with an installation disk, stick the disk in drive (A:), and click the Have Disk button.

11. Pick the model number second.

12. Click on the Next button.

13. Choose how the printer is connected to your computer.

14. Click on the Next button.

15. Now you get to give your printer a name.

16. Click on the Next button.

17. Print a test page.

18. Click on the Finish button.

CHAPTER 22

How to change the way Windows looks (page 283)

1. Right-click on a blank part of the desktop.

2. Choose Properties from the shortcut menu.

3. Click on the proper tab to bring whichever panel forward. There are four panels, each of which adjusts something clever with the screen or desktop background.

How to select a pattern for your window (page 284)

1. Bring up the Display Properties dialog box.

2. Click on the Background tab to bring that panel forward.

3. In the Wallpaper area, make sure the *(None)* option is selected.

4. Choose a pattern.

5. Click on the pattern once with the mouse to preview it in the monitor preview window.

6. Click on OK.

How to pick out wallpaper for the desktop (page 285)

1. Summon the Display Properties dialog box.

2. Click on the Background tab to bring that panel forward.

3. In the Pattern area, make sure the (None) option is selected.

4. Choose a Wallpaper image. Scroll through the list and click on each image name using the mouse.

5. Experiment with the Tile and Center buttons to see which method best displays your image. If you don't see your graphic file here, click on the Browse button to find it elsewhere on your computer.

6. Click on OK.

How to change the color of your Windows screen (page 288)

1. Muster the Display Properties dialog box.

2. Click on the Appearance panel to move it center stage. It shows several onscreen elements, colors, fonts, and whatnot, all of which can be changed.

3a. Preview a bunch of color schemes using the drop-down list box below *Scheme.*

3b. Make up your own color scheme.

4. Click on the Apply button.

5. If everything looks fine, click OK to lock in your choices. If it looks horrid, go back a step and reset your choices. Then click Cancel and be done with it.

How to stretch the taskbar (page 291)

Just click the mouse on the taskbar's inside edge to *s-t-r-e-t-c-h* it.

How to change the way the taskbar works (page 291)

1. Call up the taskbar Properties dialog box.

2. Click on the taskbar Options tab to bring that panel forward.

3. Click on *Always on top* to change that option.

4. Click on *Auto hide* to change that option.

5. Click on the OK button in the taskbar Properties dialog box to lock in your changes.

CHAPTER 23

How to activate a screen saver for your monitor (page 296)

1. Summon the Display Properties dialog box (right-click on the desktop).

2. Click on the Screen Saver tab.

3. Pick a screen saver.

4. Set the *Wait* time.

5. Click OK.

How to set a password for your screen saver (page 297)

1. Click the Change button. The Change Password dialog box appears.

2. Type your new password into the *New password* box.

3. Type the same password again into the *Confirm new password* box.

4. Click on OK.

How to change your mouse pointer (page 298)

1. Open a handy control panel near you.

2. Double-click on the little mouse guy.

3. Click on the Pointers tab to bring it forward.

4. Click on a pointer to change it.

5. Click on Browse.

6. Double-click on a new pointer in the Browse dialog box to select it and return to the Mouse Properties dialog box.

7. Repeat Steps 4 and 5 for each pointer you want to change.

8. When you're done making changes, click on OK.

How to make noises on your computer (page 299)

1. Open the Control Panel.

2. Double-click on the Sounds icon.

3. Pick a Windows event from the *Events* list.

4. Choose a sound to associate with that event from the drop-down list by picking a sound from the *Sound* list.

5. Use the Browse button to look for a specific sound on your hard drive.

6. Click on the play button to hear the sound — a preview of sorts.

7. Click on OK when you're done. Before clicking on OK you can optionally click on the Save As button to save all your sounds as a sound scheme on disk.

How to search for MIDI files (page 303)

1. Click on the Start button.

2. Point your mouse on `Find`.

3. Click on `Files or Folders`.

4. Click on the Advanced tab.

5. Use the scroll-down list on the *Of type* box and click on *Midi Sequence*.

6. Click on Find Now.

How to create your own sounds (page 303)

1. Hook up the microphone to your computer.

2. Run the Sound Recorder program. You'll find it lurking off the Start Thing menu; `Programs` → `Accessories` → `Multimedia` → `Sound Recorder`.

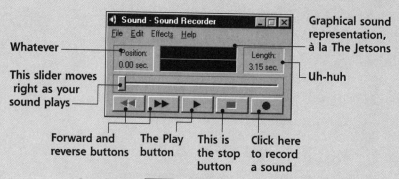

Whatever

This slider moves right as your sound plays

Graphical sound representation, à la The Jetsons

Uh-huh

Forward and reverse buttons

The Play button

This is the stop button

Click here to record a sound

3. Choose `File` → `New`.

4. Click on OK to close the New Sound dialog box.

5. Clear your throat. *Ah-hem. Test. One, two, three. Test. Test!*

6. Click on the Record button and start speaking into the mic. Blah-blah-blah.

7. Click on the Stop button when you're done recording.

8. Optionally click on the Play button to hear your recording.

9. Save your sound file to disk. Choose `File` → `Save` and find a proper place and give a proper name to your sound file.

CHAPTER 24

How to find the games (page 307)

1. Pop up the Start Thing menu.

2. Choose `Programs`.

3. Click on `Accessories`.

4. Click on `Games`.

5. Click on the game you want to play.

1. Locate your DOS game using My Computer or the Explorer.

2. Click on your game once.

3. Right-click on the program's icon and choose Properties from the menu.

4. Click on the Program tab to bring that panel forward.

5. Click on the Advanced button.

6. This brings up the Advanced dialog box. You have two choices: You can attempt to run this program inside Windows or you can let the program shut down Windows and run by itself.

Click here to run your game under Windows

Click here to shut down Windows and run your game by itself

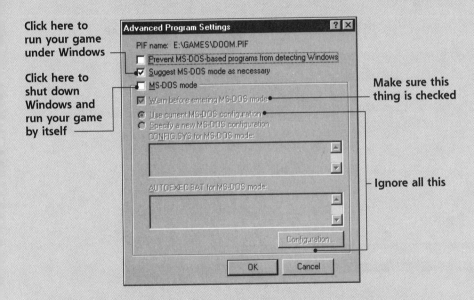

Make sure this thing is checked

Ignore all this

CHAPTER 25

How to change the edges of a window (page 324)

1. Point the mouse at one of the window's edges you want to move. When the mouse is positioned correctly, it changes into an up-down or left-right pointy arrow. This shows you which direction you can move the window's edge.

2. Press and hold the mouse button down, and then move the mouse in or out to make the window larger or smaller along that one edge.

3. Release the mouse button when you're pleased. The window snaps to the new edge, changing its size larger or smaller.

How to move two edges at once (page 325)

1. Point the mouse at one of the window's corners.

2. Drag the corner to a new position.

3. Release the mouse button. The window snaps to its new size.

How to drag a window around (page 326)

1. Point the mouse at the window's title bar.

2. Press and hold down the mouse's button.

3. Move the mouse — and the window — to a new position.

4. Release the mouse button. *Plop!* The window falls into place.

How to line up your windows (page 327)

1. Close or minimize any windows on the screen, except for the one you can't access (of course).

2. Bring up the taskbar's shortcut menu.

3. Choose Cascade from the menu.

CHAPTER 26

How to navigate dialog boxes (page 335)

Element	To Use . . .	Do This . . .
Belly	BUTTON	Click on it with the mouse pointer
☐ Slovakia	CHECK BOX	Click on it to check (turn on) or uncheck (turn off) the option
10: 07: 61 PM	SPIN BOX	Click the spin arrows to scroll through preassigned values or to type an entry into the box

Element	To Use . . .	Do This . . .
Word wrap ○ No wrap ○ Wrap to window ⊙ Wrap for Christmas	OPTION BUTTON	Click on it to turn on (a dot appears) or off (blank) the option
File name: Blech-o-matic	TEXT BOX	Click on it and start typing
Eating Disorders (None) Bulimia Anorexia Nervosa Obesity	LIST BOX	Click on the item you want
Operating Systems: OS/2 Warp OS/2 Warp Macintosh System 8 Power PC Operating system (???) TRS-DOS CP/M DOS, yes, good old DOS. Thanks	DROP-DOWN LIST	Click on the arrow next to the item to display other choices
10% Precent of time you spend waiting for Windows to catch up	SLIDER	Point at the slider control with your mouse—click the mouse button down and keep it held down while you drag the slider to a new position

How to open and close a collapsible tree structure (page 339)

* An icon in a tree structure with a plus (+) by it contains more branches in the tree. Click once on the (+) to open the branches and look.

* After being opened, the plus thing changes into a minus thing (-). To close the tree, click on the (-).

CHAPTER 27

How to control your mouse (page 347)

Mouse Action	Description
POINT	Move the mouse pointer on the screen so it's hovering over some object
CLICK	To press and release the mouse's main (left) button
DOUBLE-CLICK	Two quick clicks in a row, both pointing at the same spot
SELECT	To click on something, highlighting it
DRAG	To select something, and then press and hold the mouse button down while moving the mouse around—the drag ends when you release the mouse button

How to make your mouse left-hand friendly (page 349)

1. Pop up the Start Thing.
2. Choose Settings → Control Panel .
3. Double-click on the Mouse icon to open it.
4. Click on the *Left-handed* option button.
5. Click on OK.

CHAPTER 28

How to edit text with common editing keys (page 356)

Key	What It Does
BACKSPACE	Backs up the toothpick cursor and deletes the previous character
DELETE	Deletes the next character—the one after the toothpick cursor
CTRL+DELETE	Deletes all text from the toothpick cursor until the end of the word

Key	What It Does
HOME	Moves the toothpick cursor to the start of the line or the first character in an input box
END	Moves the toothpick cursor to the end of the line or the last character in an input box
TAB	Moves the toothpick cursor to the next input box in a dialog box
ENTER	Ends a line or paragraph of text (use only in a word processor)
←	Moves the toothpick cursor back one character
→	Moves the toothpick cursor forward one character
↑	Moves the toothpick cursor up one line
↓	Moves the toothpick cursor down one line
CTRL+←	Moves the toothpick cursor back one word
CTRL+→	Moves the toothpick cursor forward one word

CHAPTER 29

How to use the Windows Troubleshooter (page 364)

1. Choose Help from the Start Thing menu.
2. Click on the Index tab to bring that panel forward.
3. Type **trouble** into the first input box. This looks up the word Troubleshooting in the index and displays a banquet of options for getting your PC repaired.
4. There are 20-or-so different items listed under *Troubleshooting* in the Help index. Pick the one that irks you presently.
5. Continue to work through the Troubleshooter until you find the answer to your problem.

How to use the hardware conflicts troubleshooter (page 367)

1. Choose Help from the Start Thing menu.
2. Click on the Index tab to bring that panel forward.

3. Type **trouble** into the first input box. This looks up the word Troubleshooting in the index and displays a banquet of options for getting your PC repaired.

4. Choose *hardware conflict*. A help dialog box is displayed with two button options.

5. Choose *Start the Hardware Conflict Troubleshooter*. Another dialog box is displayed.

6. Click on the go-to button to display the Device manager. This displays the Device Manager tab in the System Properties dialog box.

7. Click on the button by *Click here to continue*.

8. Work through the questions.

How to find a file when you're in a rush (page 371)

1. Open My Computer or the Explorer.

2. Press the F3 key (or press CTRL+F). This brings up the Find: All Files dialog box.

3. Type the name of the file you want. Be as precise as you can. If you only know part of the filename, just type in that part. If you aren't sure of some letters, replace them with the question-mark character: **POR???B**

4. Choose *My Computer* from the *Look in* drop-down list.

5. Make sure the *Include subfolders* item is checked.

6. Click *Find Now*. Windows looks for your file.

7. The results are displayed in the bottom of the dialog box. Double-click on the file to open it or do whatever you want with it. The file has been found.

VISUAL INDEX

The Windows Desktop

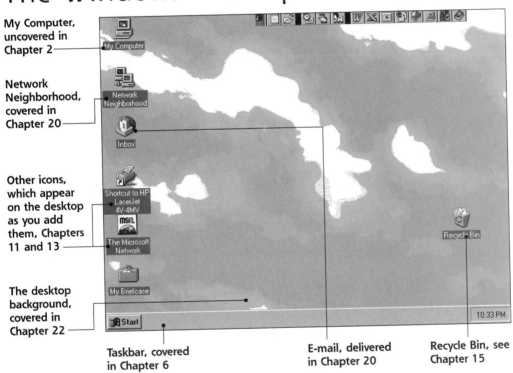

My Computer, uncovered in Chapter 2

Network Neighborhood, covered in Chapter 20

Other icons, which appear on the desktop as you add them, Chapters 11 and 13

The desktop background, covered in Chapter 22

Taskbar, covered in Chapter 6

E-mail, delivered in Chapter 20

Recycle Bin, see Chapter 15

The Start Thing Menu

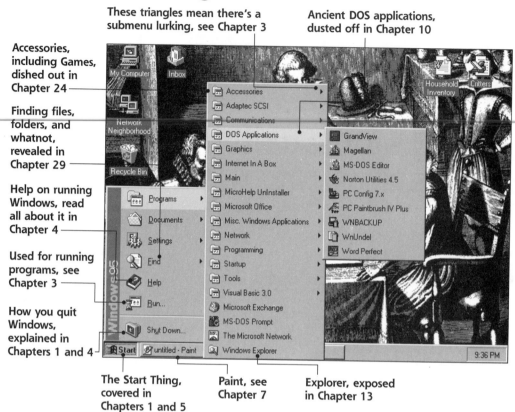

These triangles mean there's a submenu lurking, see Chapter 3

Ancient DOS applications, dusted off in Chapter 10

Accessories, including Games, dished out in Chapter 24

Finding files, folders, and whatnot, revealed in Chapter 29

Help on running Windows, read all about it in Chapter 4

Used for running programs, see Chapter 3

How you quit Windows, explained in Chapters 1 and 4

The Start Thing, covered in Chapters 1 and 5

Paint, see Chapter 7

Explorer, exposed in Chapter 13

My Computer's First Window

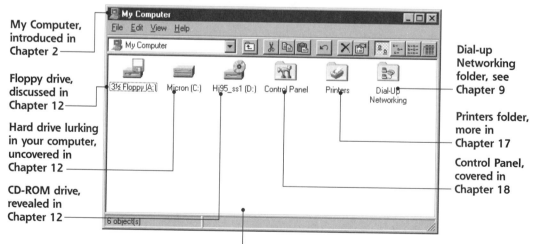

My Computer, introduced in Chapter 2

Floppy drive, discussed in Chapter 12

Hard drive lurking in your computer, uncovered in Chapter 12

CD-ROM drive, revealed in Chapter 12

Dial-up Networking folder, see Chapter 9

Printers folder, more in Chapter 17

Control Panel, covered in Chapter 18

You can change the way My Computer displays information; details revealed in Chapter 2.

The WordPad Program

The menu bar, also in Chapter 4

Formatting bar (specific to WordPad), introduced in Chapter 4

The window's control buttons, covered in Chapter 4

The WordPad program, discussed in Chapter 4

Saving a document, covered in Chapter 4

Printing stuff, see Chapter 4

Creating stuff, explained in Chapter 4

Formatted text, discussed in Chapter 28

The Windows way of offering help, extended in Chapter 4

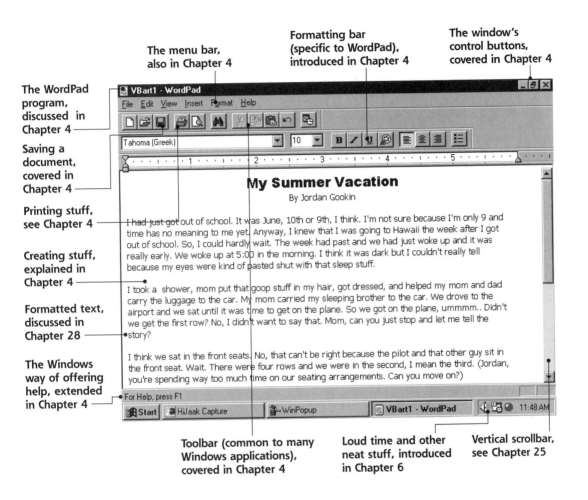

Toolbar (common to many Windows applications), covered in Chapter 4

Loud time and other neat stuff, introduced in Chapter 6

Vertical scrollbar, see Chapter 25

The Explorer

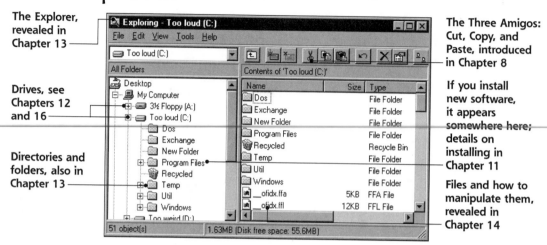

The Explorer, revealed in Chapter 13

Drives, see Chapters 12 and 16

Directories and folders, also in Chapter 13

The Three Amigos: Cut, Copy, and Paste, introduced in Chapter 8

If you install new software, it appears somewhere here; details on installing in Chapter 11

Files and how to manipulate them, revealed in Chapter 14

The Control Panel Window

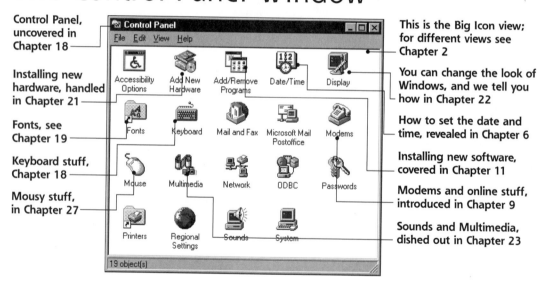

Control Panel, uncovered in Chapter 18

Installing new hardware, handled in Chapter 21

Fonts, see Chapter 19

Keyboard stuff, Chapter 18

Mousy stuff, in Chapter 27

This is the Big Icon view; for different views see Chapter 2

You can change the look of Windows, and we tell you how in Chapter 22

How to set the date and time, revealed in Chapter 6

Installing new software, covered in Chapter 11

Modems and online stuff, introduced in Chapter 9

Sounds and Multimedia, dished out in Chapter 23

INDEX

NUMBERS
3D Space Cadet Pinball, 317–318

A
About Windows 95 dialog box, 334
Accessibility Options, physically challenged users, 229–230
actions, undoing last, 183
active command, menu dot indicator, 329
Add Fonts dialog box, 245
Add New Hardware Wizard, 235, 270–273
Add Printer Wizard, network printer addition, 257–258
Add/Remove Programs Properties dialog box, 144, 147
Alt key, keyboard command equivalents, 330
America Online, 130
applets
  See also applications
  Calculator, 99–100
  described, 87
  Notepad, 99
  Paint, 88–94
  Phone Dialer, 100–101
  Scientific Calculator, 100
  WordPad, 94–98
applications
  See also applets and programs
  Add/Remove Programs option, 235
  automatic startup, 68–72
  CD-Player, 163
  Character Map, 246–248
  Clipboard information sharing, 107–111
  closing documents without exiting, 50
  common dialog box elements, 334–343
  common editing keys, 356–357
  common menu elements, 329–330
  common window elements, 321–325
  common Windows 95 elements, 41–42

Cover Page Editor, 224
cutting/copying/pasting selected text, 357–358
Defragmentation, 211–212
disk tools, 202–213
document saving, 46–48
DOS, 133–142
Drive Space, 213
exiting before installing new software, 146
games, 12–13
installation types, 145–146
installation/removal, 143–152
Media Player, 302–303
menu command elements, 43–44
Microsoft Exchange, 238, 262–265
Microsoft Fax, 222–224
minimizing versus quitting, 56
new document creation, 49
opening previously saved documents, 48–49
recently opened document list, 49
ribbed triangle window sizing handle, 325
running maximized/minimized on startup, 70–72
ScanDisk, 209–211
Sound Recorder, 303–304
starting from StartUp submenu, 68–72
status bars, 44
switching between, 104–106
switching between Help system, 55
System Agent, 213
toolbar elements, 43–44
uninstalling, 149–150
Winpopup, 266–267
work uses, 44–45
Apply button, dialog box change acceptance, 337
Attributes dialog box, Paint, 89–90
attributes, font emphasis, 358–359, 361

B
backgrounds, desktop, 282–286. 293
backslash (\) character, file/folder pathnames, 176
Backspace key, text corrections, 356
Backup program, 203–209
  file/folder backup selections, 205–206
  media type selections, 206
  restoring from backups, 208–209
  scheduling, 204
  starting, 204
backup tapes
  numbering conventions, 207
  storage considerations, 204
backups, 203–209, 371
BBS (Bulletin Board Service), 113
bitmaps, described, 89
block copy, described, 108
block move, described, 108
boot, described, 4
boot disk, using, 369–371
buttons, dialog box element, 335, 338

C
Calculator program, 34, 99–100
canvas size, resolution settings, 88–90
Cardfile program, adding to StartUp submenu, 73
Cascade command, 22
CD Player program, musical CD playback, 163
CD-ROM, described, 156
CD-ROM drive
Character Map program, 246–248
characters
  See also symbols
  backslash (\), 176
  Character Map program, 246–248
  exclamation point (!), 330
check boxes, dialog box element, 338
check mark, command toggle indicator, 329–330
children (subfolders), 169

clicking
   menu activation, 43
   mouse, 348–349
Clipboard
   DOS program information,
      copying/pasting, 137–138
   files, copying/pasting, 180
   information sharing, 107–111
   items,
      cutting/copying/pasting,
      107–111
   OLE objects,
      cutting/copying/pasting,
      111
   selected text,
      cutting/copying/pasting,
      357–358
   special characters,
      copying/pasting, 247
   viewing contents, 112
Clipboard Viewer, 112
clock
   displaying/hiding, 81
   time/date settings, 83–84
Close (X) button
   closing windows, 19–20
   dialog box element, 335
   quitting program when
      closing window, 38
   windows element, 322
Close Program window,
   Ctrl+Alt+Delete key
   combination, 38
cold boot, described, 5
colors
   desktop schemes, 288–289,
      293
   text comments, 359
COM (serial port) connections,
   modems, 115–116
Command prompt only item,
   314
commands
   available on Emergency Boot
      disk, 370
   Cascade, 22
   check mark on/off toggle, 329
   Compose⇨New Message, 264
   dimmed (unavailable),
      329–330
   Document⇨Cancel Printing,
      221
   Document⇨Pause Printing,
      220
   Edit⇨Copy (Ctrl+C), 40, 107,
      180, 357–358
   Edit⇨Cut (Ctrl+X), 107,
      355–358
   Edit⇨Invert Selection, 187
   Edit⇨Options, 302
   Edit⇨Paste (Ctrl+V), 107, 180,
      357–358
   Edit⇨Paste Shortcut, 181
   Edit⇨Paste Special, 111

Edit⇨Select All (Ctrl+A), 187
Edit⇨Speed Dial, Phone
   Dialer, 101
Edit⇨Undo, 108, 183
ellipses (...) dialog box
   indicator, 330
File⇨Close, 50, 173, 193
File⇨Delete, 183, 191, 246
File⇨Exit, 37, 129
File⇨Install New Font, 245
File⇨New, 49
File⇨New⇨Bitmap Image, 88
File⇨New⇨Folder, 170
File⇨Open, 48, 255
File⇨Print, 46
File⇨Save, 47
File⇨Save As, 254
File⇨Send To, 180
File⇨Sharing, 259
File–Restore, 193
Help⇨About Windows 95, 334
hot key activation, 56–57
Image⇨Attributes, Paint, 89
Insert⇨Object, 111
Insert⇨Symbol, Microsoft
   Word, 247
instant menu title
   exclamation point (!)
   indicator, 330
keyboard equivalents, 330
keyboard shortcuts, 57–58
menu elements, 329
New⇨Shortcut, 181
Print Topic, 365
Printer⇨Pause Printing, 220
Printer⇨Purge Print Jobs, 221
Programs⇨Accessories⇨Hyper
   Terminal, 124
Run, 34–35
Settings⇨Control Panel, 216,
   227
Settings⇨Printers, 216
Settings⇨Taskbar, 39, 64, 292
Shut Down, 13
Switch (Alt+Tab), 55
Tile Horizontally, 22
Tile Vertically, 22
Tools⇨Show Log, Phone
   Dialer, 101
Transfer⇨Send File, 132
underlined letter shortcut key,
   329–330
Undo (Ctrl+Z), 357–358
View⇨Arrange Icons, 26
View⇨Arrange Icons⇨Auto
   Arrange, 26
View⇨Arrange Icons⇨by
   Date, 193
View⇨Details, 26, 228
View⇨Large Icons, 25, 228
View⇨Line Up Icons, 26
View⇨Options, 27, 179
View⇨Scientific, 100

View⇨Small Icons, 25
View⇨Status bar, 25
View⇨Toolbar, 24, 251, 256
communications, Phone Dialer
   connections,100–101
Compose New Fax dialog box,
   223
Compose⇨New Message
   command, 264
CompuServe, 130
computers
   browsing networked, 251–252
   Emergency Boot disk, 162–163
   exiting Windows 95, shutting
      down, 13–14
   laptop, 11, 15
   MS-DOS mode startup, 135
   new hardware installation,
      269–277
   overview, 17–29
   resetting after DOS
      applications installation,
      139
   resetting with Ctrl+Alt+Delete,
      38
   shared activities, 253–258
   starting, 3–5
   starting in DOS, 314
   surge protection, 4
   ways to start, 368–371
CONFIG.SYS file, RAM drive
   removal, 164–165
Confirm File Delete dialog box,
   183, 190, 194
Connect To Dialog box, 120
Connected To dialog box, 121
Connection Description dialog
   box, 125–126
control buttons, dialog box, 335
Control menu, windows element,
   322
Control Panel
   Accessibility Options, 229–230
   accessing, 227, 242
   Add New Hardware option,
      235
   Add/Remove Programs
      option, 235
   content viewing options, 228
   Date/Time option, 235
   Display option, 236
   Fonts folder, 241–248
   Fonts option, 236
   Joystick settings, 230
   keyboard properties, 231–233
   Mail and Fax settings, 238
   Mail Wizard, 238
   Microsoft Mail Postoffice, 238
   modem properties, 233–234
   Mouse option, 236
   mouse pointer settings,
      298–299
   Multimedia settings, 238
   My Computer element, 18

Network option, 236
ODBC settings, 239
Password option, 236
Printers folder, 216–219
Printers option, 236
Regional settings, 239
software installation/removal,
144–152
sound settings, 299–301
Sounds option, 236
System Properties, 239
Telephony settings, 239
cool switch, switching between
applications, 106
Cover Page Editor program, 224
cover pages, fax, 223–224
Ctrl key, keyboard command
equivalents, 330
Ctrl+Alt+Delete, Close Program
window, 38
current folder, title bar display, 22
cursors
double-headed arrow edge
handles, 324–325
Help system, 52
I-beam, 356
Text Selection pointer, 356
toothpick (text position), 356
Cursors folder, 298–299

D

Date/Time Properties dialog box,
83–84, 235
dates, day/date format settings,
83–84
daylight savings time, date/time
settings, 84
default printer, selecting, 217
Defragmentation program,
211–212
Delete key, text selection deletion,
357
desktop
color schemes, 288–289, 293
copying/pasting documents, 40
described, 281
Display Properties dialog box,
283–284
elements, 9–10
Inbox icon, 263
Internet shortcut, 124
My Computer icon, 17–26
Network Neighborhood icon,
250
patterns, 282, 284–285, 293
screen resolutions, 286–287
Start button, 10–11
starting programs from, 33
wallpaper, 282, 285–286, 293
Details view, file selection
techniques, 185–186
dialer, described, 116
Dialing Properties dialog box, 234
dialog boxes

Apply button change
acceptance, 337
areas/regions, 336
buttons, 338
check boxes, 338
closing, 335
control buttons, 335
described, 333
dimple line area/region
separator, 336
drop-down lists, 340
drop-down palettes, 340
elements, 334–343
Enter key option/item selections,
337
Esc key exit, 337
input boxes, 341
list boxes, 341–342
marquee (marching ants),
active item indicator, 337
mouse navigation, 336
option buttons, 342
panels, 336
question mark (?) button, 335
slider controls, 343
spinner adjustments, 343
Tab key navigation, 335, 337
toggles, 338
warning boxes, 334
Dial-Up Networking
connection information display,
121
desktop shortcut, 124
disconnecting, 123
Internet connection procedure,
119–121
Internet connection program,
116
dimple bar, menu/dialog box
separator, 329, 336
dinking, described, 13
directory See folders
disk compression, described, 213
disk drives, 155–166
See also CD-ROM drives and
floppy drives and hard drives
disk usage information,
159–160
Emergency Boot disk, 162–163
file save selection, 47
file/folder storage, 20–21
letter name hierarchy, 156–157
mapping a networked drive, 256
My Computer icon element
types, 18–19
naming conventions, 21,
156–159
Properties dialog box, 159
Recycle Bin folder, 189–190
tape backup, 203–209
types, 155
viewing contents, 20–21

disk tools
Defragmentation, 211–212
described, 202
ScanDisk, 209–211
System Agent, 213
disks, scanning for errors, 209–211
Display Properties dialog box, 235,
283–289
desktop color schemes, 288–289,
293
pattern settings, 285
screen resolutions, 286–287
screen saver settings, 296–298
wallpaper settings, 285–286
display settings, Accessibility
Options, 230
Document⇨Cancel Printing
command, 221
Document⇨Pause Printing
command, 220
Document menu, clearing
contents, 39
documents
adding to Start menu submenu,
65
closing without exiting
program, 50
copying/pasting to desktop, 40
creating new, 49
desktop placement, 40
loading when starting
programs, 35–37
moving to Recycle Bin, 191–192
opening, 48–49
previously opened list, 36
print pausing, 220
printing, 45–46, 110
recently opened list, 49
recovering from Recycle Bin,
192–193
removing from print queue, 221
saving, 46–48
searches, 36
special characters, 246–248
WordPad program creation, 45,
95–98
Documents menu, previously
opened document list, 36
DOS applications, 133–142
common window elements,
135–136
copying/pasting information
between, 137–138
full window display, 136
games, 314–317
installation, 139
multitasking, 138
Properties dialog box, 136,
139–141
quitting, 138–139
resetting computer after
installation, 139
sizing windows, 135–136

starting, 134–139
Text Selection Mode, 137
text-only display, 136
troubleshooting, 141–142
DOS games, configuring in
Windows, 315–316
dot indicator, active menu
command, 329
double-click
mouse, 348
speed, adjusting, 350
techniques, opening desktop
items, 19
double-quick double-click, 352–353
drag-and-drop
moving files, 188
mouse techniques, 350–351
printing, 277
drawings, Paint program, 88–94
Drive Space, 213
drop-down lists, described, 340
drop-down palettes, described, 340

E

edges, window sizing, 322, 324–325
Edit⇨Copy (Ctrl+C) command, 40,
107, 180, 357–358
Edit⇨Cut (Ctrl+X) command, 107,
355–358
Edit⇨Invert Selection command,
187
Edit⇨Options command, 302
Edit⇨Paste (Ctrl+V) command, 107,
180
Edit⇨Paste Shortcut command, 181
Edit⇨Paste Special command, 111
Edit⇨Select All (Ctrl+A) command,
187
Edit⇨Speed Dial command, Phone
Dialer, 101
Edit⇨Undo command, 108, 183
elevator boxes, scrollbars, 328
e-mail, 116
icon, taskbar display, 85
Microsoft Exchange program,
262–265
Winpopup program
management, 266–267
Emergency Boot disk, 162–163,
369–371
commands and programs
available, 370
creating, 162–163
End Task button, closing
unresponsive programs, 38
Enter key
dialog box option selections, 337
paragraph breaks, 356
Enter Network Password dialog box,
5
error messages, 375–382
Cannot find file, 375
Cannot find this file, 376

Device is not ready, 376–377
Disk in the destination drive is
full, 377
Disk is write-protected, 377–378
Item this shortcut refers to has
been changed or moved, 379
Program has performed an
illegal operation, 381
Read-only file cannot be
changed and saved, 378
Replace existing file, 378–379
Save changes?, 379
Specified path is invalid, 380
This filename is not valid,
380–381
You must type a filename, 382
Esc key
Help system exit, 54–55
quitting/closing dialog box, 337
events, sound settings, 299–301
exclamation point (!) character,
instant menu title command,
330
Explorer
exiting, 173
folder creation, 169–170
folder organization, 171–176
Network Neighborhood access,
253
Options dialog box, 27–28
versus My Computer, 26
viewing all file details, 179
Exploring-Accessories window,
automatic application startup,
68–72

F

Fax Wizard, 222–224
faxes
composing, 222
cover pages, 223–224
described, 222
features, free, 383–384
File⇨Close command, 50, 173, 193
File⇨Delete command, 183, 191,
246
File⇨Exit command, 37, 129
File⇨Install New Font command,
245
File⇨New⇨Bitmap Image
command, 88
File⇨New command, 49
File⇨New⇨Folder command, 170
File⇨Open command, 48, 255
File⇨Print command, 46
File⇨Save command, 47
File⇨Save As command, 254
File⇨Send To command, 180
File⇨Sharing command, 259
File⇨Restore command, 193
filename extensions, dot-three
conventions, 179

files
avoiding Recycle Bin when
deleting, 184
copying, 180–182
copying to floppy disk with Send
To command, 180
deleting, 182–183
described, 23
detailed view, 26
downloading/uploading,
131–132
drag-and-drop move, 188
duplicating in the same folder,
188
format type selection, 47
group selection techniques,
184–187
lost/found, 371–374
marquee drag selection, 185
MIDI, 302–303
moving, 182
moving to Recycle Bin, 190–191
naming conventions, 47,
177–179
opening from shared computer,
255–256
pathname conventions, 73, 176
RAMDRIVE.SYS, 164–165
Recycle Bin deletion bypass, 197
renaming, 187–188
renaming existing, 177–179
saving to shared computer,
254–255
shared file naming conventions,
255
shortcut copy alternative,
180–182
truncated names, 268
undoing deletions, 183
video, 305–306
viewing all details, 179
Find File dialog box, 374
Find panel, Help system search,
53–54
fixed fonts, 243
floating palettes, described, 43–44
floppy disks
copying files with Send To
command, 180
Emergency Boot disk, 162–163
formatting, 160–161
scanning for errors, 209–211
floppy drives, letter name
hierarchy, 156–157
folders
adding to Start menu submenu,
65
child/parent relationship, 169
collapsible tree structure, 339
Control Panel, 18, 227–239
creating, 169–170

creating when saving to disk, 170–171
Cursors, 298–299
described, 21–22, 167–168
expanding/collapsing tree structure, 339
Explorer organization, 171–176
file detail view, 26
file save selection, 47
Fonts, 235, 241–248
hierarchical structure, 339
Junk, 175
Media, 305–306
moving to Recycle Bin, 190–191
opening (viewing contents), 21–22
organization, 167–176
pathname conventions, 73, 176
Printers, 18, 216–219, 237
Recycle Bin, 189–198
Recycle Bin deletion bypass, 197
renaming cautions, 178
root, 168–169
sharing, 259–260
subfolder types, 168
Temp, 175
title bar display, 22
tree hierarchy structure, 171
viewing all file details, 179
Windows, 169
Work, 174–175
fonts
    character maps, 246–248
    fixed, 243
    installation/removal, 245–246
    points, 359
    previewing, 244
    printer, 243
    printing sample page, 244
    Quick View window, 244
    recovering from Recycle Bin, 246
    sizing/editing, 358–359
    substitutions, 243
    TrueType, 242–244
    Wingdings, 246–247
    Zapf Dingbats, 247
Fonts folder, 235, 241–248
    font types, 242–244
    TrueType font display, 242–244
foreign languages, keyboard settings, 231–233
Format dialog box, 160–161
Format Results dialog box, 161
freebies, 383–384
FreeCell game, 311–312
full backup, described, 204

G

games, 307–318
    3D Space Cadet Pinball, 317–318
    accessing, 12–13
    adding to Start menu, 308

cheating, 317
DOS, 314–317
finding, 307–308
finding online, 313
FreeCell, 311–312
Hearts, 312–313
Minesweeper, 309–311
minimizing, 309
Solitaire, 308–309
Games submenu, 308
Gookin, Dan, 122, 314
graphics, sizing handles, 360

H

handles, graphics sizing, 360
hard copy, described, 45
hard drives
    compression schemes, 213
    defragmenting, 211–212
    disk usage information, 159
    formatting cautions, 161
    letter name hierarchy, 156–157
    naming conventions, 158–159
    Recycle Bin storage requirements, 196–197
    root folder, 168–169
    scanning for errors, 209–211
    sharing, 259–260
hardware
    conflict troubleshooting, 367–368
    installation, 269–277
    Plug and Play technology, 269
    surge protectors, 4
hearing impaired users, Accessibility Options, 230
Hearts game, 312–313
Help (F1) key, 50
Help⇨About Windows 95 command, 334
Help system, 50–55
    accessing, 50
    components, 51–52
    exiting, 54–55
    Find panel search, 53–54
    hand cursor, 52
    Index panel search, 53
    links, 52
    MS-DOS Troubleshooter, 141–142
    question mark (?) button, 6, 52, 335
    switching between applications, 55
    tooltips, 20, 43
    What's This? shortcut menu, 335
hierarchy, folder tree structure, 171, 339
horizontal scrollbars, 328
hot keys
    See also keyboard shortcuts
    menu command access, 56–57

HyperTerminal
    accessing, 124
    disconnecting, 129
    existing session dial-up, 127–128
    modem connections, 124–128
    quitting, 129
    session creation, 125–127
    Zmodem protocol, 131–132

I

I-beam cursor, 356
icons
    See also screen elements
    desktop elements, 10
    e-mail, 85
    file, 23
    folders, 21
    Help system hand cursor, 52
    horizontal spacing, 289
    locating with keystrokes, 23
    minimize button, 56
    printer types, 81, 216
    reordering display, 26
    serving hand, 19, 259
    sizing, 289
    submenu item types, 32–33
    tooltips, 20, 43
    vertical spacing, 289
    view types, 26
Image⇨Attributes, Paint command, 89
images, size attributes, 89
Inbox, described, 10
Include subfolders item, 372–373
incremental backup, described, 204
indexes, Help system search, 53
information sharing, multitasking, 107–111
input boxes, described, 341
Insert⇨Object command, 111
Insert⇨Symbol command, Microsoft Word, 247
installation
    Accessibility Options, 229
    Add New Hardware Wizard, 270–273
    Add Printer Wizard, 273–276
    Add/Remove Programs option, 235
    DOS programs, 139
    exiting open programs before installing, 146
    fonts, 245–246
    hardware, 269–277
    Internet software, 118–119
    network printers, 257–258
    Windows applications, 145–148
Internet
    cost considerations, 117–118
    desktop shortcut, 124
    described, 10
    dialer program, 116

Dial-Up Networking connection procedure, 119–121
Dial-Up Networking program, 116
disconnecting, 123
hardware/software requirements, 114–118
ISP (Internet Service Provider) sources, 117
overview, 114–115
services, 116
site menus, 128–129
software installation, 118–119
URL (Uniform Resource Locator) address, 123
Web browser, 116
Web site listing, 123
Internet Explorer, 116
connecting on startup, 121
Internet software installation, 118–119
starting, 122
IRQ settings, 368
ISP (Internet Service Provider)
automatic disconnect, 123
cost considerations, 117–118
services, 117
items, undoing last action, 108

J
Joystick settings, 230
jumpers, resetting, 368
Junk folder, creating, 175

K
key commands, startup, 368–369
Keyboard Properties dialog box, 231–233
keyboard shortcuts
See also hot keys
Close (Ctrl+W), 50
commands, 57–58
Control Panel (Ctrl+Esc, S, C), 242
cool switch (Alt+Tab), 106
Copy (Ctrl+C), 40, 107, 180
Cut (Ctrl+X), 107
Delete (Shift+Delete), 184
described, 330
Full DOS Window (Alt+Enter), 136
Group Select (Shift+click), 185–186
menus, 57
MS-DOS Troubleshooter (Ctrl+Esc, H), 141
New (Ctrl+N), 49
Open (Ctrl+O), 48
Paste (Ctrl+V), 40, 107, 180
Reset (Ctrl+Alt+Delete), 38
Save (Ctrl+S), 48
Save As (Alt+F, S), 47
Select (Ctrl+click), 184

Select All (Ctrl+A), 187
Start (Ctrl+Esc), 11, 32
Taskbar Properties, (Ctrl+Esc ,S, T), 69
Undo (Ctrl+Z), 108, 183
keyboards
dialog box navigation, 336–337
foreign language settings, 231–233
menu command equivalents, 330
property settings, 231–233
selecting/editing text, 356–357
Sticky Keys, 229
Windows key, 32, 62
keys
Alt, 330
Backspace, 356
Ctrl, 330
Delete, 357
Enter, 337, 356
Esc, 54–55, 337
F1 (Help), 50
Shift, 357–358
Tab, 335, 337, 356

L
LAN (local area network), 114–115
languages, keyboard settings, 231–233
laptop computers
Suspend button, 11, 15
suspending operations, 15
left-handed mouse, 348–349
links, Help system, 52
list boxes, described, 341–342
lists, drop-down, 340
login ID, naming conventions, 6
logs, Phone Dialer, 101
long filenames, truncated appearance in MS-DOS mode, 268

M
Mail Wizard, Control Panel, 238
maintenance releases, Windows 95, 152
marquees (marching ants), 185, 337
Maximize/Restore button, windows element, 322, 326
Media folder, video files, 305–306
Media Player, MIDI file playback, 302–303
memory, RAM drives, 164–165
menu bar, windows content element, 323
menus
accessing, 56–58
activating with mouse click, 43
active command, 329
command elements, 329

command toggle (check mark) symbol, 329
common Windows 95 elements, 42–43
dimmed (unavailable) commands, 329–330
dimple bar (separator), 329
elements, 329–330
ellipses (...) command dialog box indicator, 330
hot keys, 56–57
instant command exclamation point (!) character, 330
keyboard shortcuts, 57
submenu indicator (right-pointing triangle), 329–330
titles, 329
Microsoft Download computer, HyperTerminal session, 125–129
Microsoft Exchange
accessing, 263
checking for mail, 263–264
e-mail management, 262–265
mail and fax settings, 238
reading new mail, 263–264
sending mail, 264–265
system tray mail envelope, 263
Microsoft Fax program, 222–224
Microsoft Fax Status dialog box, 224
MIDI (Musical Instrument Digital Interface) files, 302–303
Minesweeper game, 309–311
minimize button
quitting versus minimizing applications, 56
windows element, 322
minus (-) character, collapsing folder tree structure, 339
mistakes
correcting with Backspace key, 356
undoing last action, 108, 183
modem icon, system tray display, 81–83
modems
COM (serial port) connections, 115–116
connection information display, 121
connection software types, 129–130
connection speeds, 121
dialing properties, 233–234
fax capable, 222–224
HyperTerminal connections, 124–128
Internet hardware/software requirements, 114–118
Phone Dialer connections, 100–101
Properties dialog box, 131

property settings, 233–234
protocols, 131–132
speed settings, 131
uploading/downloading files, 131–132
Modems Properties dialog box, 233–234
monitors
screen resolutions, 286–287
screen savers, 295–298
mouse, 345–353
behavior patterns, 347–351
clicking, 43, 348–349
Cursors folder, 298–299
dialog box navigation, 336
double-click, 19, 348
drag-and-drop file moves, 188
dragging, 350–351
dragging windows to new positions, 326–327
file group selection techniques, 184–187
how to hold, 345–346
left-handed, 348–349
marquee drag file selection, 185
pointer types, 298–299
pointing, 347–348
right-click, 349
selecting, 351
selecting/editing text, 356–357
sizing windows with double-headed arrow cursor, 324–325
Solitaire to train, 346
system tray element details, 80
terms, 347
Text Selection pointer, 356
tooltips, 20
mouse pointer, 351–352
Mouse Properties dialog box, 236, 298–299, 352
MS-DOS mode startup, 135
MS-DOS Troubleshooter, 141–142
MS-DOS, Emergency Boot disk, 162–163
multidocument interface, described, 331
multimedia
described, 114
musical CDs, 163
settings, 238
multitasking
application switching, 104–106
described, 56, 103, 115
DOS applications, 138
information sharing, 107–111
musical CDs, 163
My Computer
accessing from the desktop, 18
adding programs to Start menu, 63

closing open window elements, 19–20
Control Panel, 227–239
described, 10
disk drive content viewing, 20–21
disk drive letter name hierarchy, 156–157
disk tools, 202–213
Emergency Boot disk creation, 162–163
floppy disk formatting, 160–161
folder content viewing, 21–22
folder creation, 169–170
icon view types, 26
large/small icon views, 25–26
opening (double-clicking) elements, 19
opening program from document icon, 36
Printers folder access, 216
program startup, 34
RAM drive removal, 164–165
root folder, 168–169
screen elements, 18–19
serving hand icon, 19
single-window approach, 27–28
software installation/removal, 143–152
status bar, 25
toolbar elements, 24–26
versus Explorer, 26
viewing all file details, 179
viewing file/folder details, 26

N
Netscape Navigator, 116
connecting on startup, 121
Internet software installation, 118–119
starting, 122
network drives, mapping, 256
Network icon, network settings, 236
Network Neighborhood
accessing, 250–251
browsing other computers, 251–252
described, 10
Explorer access, 253
mapping a networked drive, 256
opening files from remote computer, 255–256
saving files to remote computer, 254–255
shared device settings, 259–262
view options, 251
workgroup browsing, 252
network printers, adding/removing, 257–258
networked computers, browsing, 251–252

networking
described, 114–115, 249–250
shared devices, 253–258
networks
logging in, 5–6
login ID naming conventions, 6
Microsoft Exchange e-mail management, 262–265
Microsoft Mail Postoffice, 238
password log in, 6–7
shared file/folder deletion warning, 191
truncated filenames, 268
New⇨Shortcut command, 181
New dialog box, WordPad program, 96
newsgroups, 116
Notepad program, text editor, 99

O
objects, cutting/copying/pasting, 111
ODBC, settings, 238–239
OLE (Object Linking and Embedding), described, 111
on/off buttons, toolbars, 342
online games, finding, 313
online services, 130
Open dialog box, 48–49
option buttons, dialog boxes, 342
Options dialog box, My Computer options, 27–28

P
pages, dialog box faces, 336
Paint program, 88–94
bitmap format support, 89
document naming conventions, 89
image size attributes, 89–90
starting with new document, 88
switching between WordPad program, 104–106
tools, 90–94
wallpaper creation, 293
WordPad information sharing, 108–110
palettes, drop-down, 340
panels, dialog box faces, 336
Parker, Roger, Looking Good in Print, 245
passwords
bypassing on startup, 7
changing/forgetting, 236
confirming/changing, 7
forgetting, 8
multiple users, 237
network log in, 6–7
networked computers, 252
read-only access, 252
screen savers, 237, 296–298

shared device settings, 260
shared printer guidelines, 262
Paste (Ctrl+V) command, 357–358
patches, Windows 95, 152
pathnames
    described, 73
    file/folder conventions, 176
    networked drives, 256
patterns
    creating custom, 293
    desktop background, 282,
        284–285
Phone Dialer program, 100–101
physically challenged users,
    Accessibility Options, 229–230
Plug and Play standard, 269
plus (+) character, expanding folder
    tree structure, 339
pointing, mouse, 347–348
points, described, 359
power-on, described, 4
power-up, described, 4
Print dialog box, 46
Print dialog box, printer properties,
    217–219
Print icon, 46
Print Topic command, 365
Printer➪Pause Printing command,
    220
Printer➪Purge Print Jobs command,
    221
printer fonts, 243
printer icon, system tray display, 81
printers
    accessing shared, 257–258
    Add Printer Wizard, 273–276
    clearing partially printed
        documents, 221
    detail settings, 217, 219
    locations, 215
    naming conventions, 221
    properties, 217–219
    share settings, 260–262
    uninstalling, 277
Printers folder, 216–219, 237
    default printer settings, 217
    My Computer element, 18
printing
    canceling print jobs, 221
    documents, 45–46, 110
    drag-and-drop, 277
    faxes, 222–224
    hard copy, 45
    pausing, 220
    queues, 219–221
    reordering print jobs, 221
    sample font page, 244
    problems/solutions, 363–374
Prodigy, 72, 130
Programs➪Accessories➪
    HyperTerminal command, 124

programs
    See also applets and applications
    available on Emergency Boot
        disk, 370
    closing unresponsive, 38
    common Windows 95 elements,
        41–42
    desktop icon startup, 33
    disk tools, 202–213
    exiting before installing new
        software, 146
    exiting from Close Program
        window, 38
    moving to Recycle Bin, 190–191
    quitting, 37–39
    rerunning previously opened, 35
    Run command startup, 34–35
    Start menu addition, 63
    Start menu submenu
        addition/removal, 64–68
    starting, 31–35
    starting from document icon,
        35–37
    submenu item types, 32–33
protocols, Zmodem, 131–132
publications
    Illustrated Computer Dictionary
        for Dummies, Wally Wang,
        349
    Looking Good in Print, Roger
        Parker, 245
    Microsoft Guide to Managing
        Memory with MS-DOS, Dan
        Gookin, 314
    Modems For Dummies, Tina
        Rathbone, 234
    More DOS for Dummies, Dan
        Gookin, 314
    Web Wambooli, Dan Gookin,
        122

Q

question mark (?) button, Help
    system, 6, 52, 322, 335
queues
    described, 219–220
    print, 219–221
    print spooling, 220
    reordering documents, 221
    viewing print jobs, 220
Quick View window, font
    previewing, 244

R

RAM drive, removing, 164–165
RAMDRIVE.SYS file, removing from
    CONFIG.SYS file, 164–165
Rathbone, Tina, Modems For
    Dummies, 234
read-only passwords, 252
reboot, described, 5
Recycle Bin
    bypassing when deleting files,
        197

deleted file storage, 183
described, 10
disabling/displaying warning
    message, 195
document deletion, 191–192
emptying, 194
exiting, 193
file arrangements, 193
file search, 193
moving programs to, 190–191
property settings, 195
recovering deleted fonts, 246
restoring files/folders from,
    192–193
storage capacity settings,
    196–197
Recycle Bin Properties dialog box,
    195
Regional settings, Control Panel,
    239
releases, Windows 95, 152
reset, described, 4
resolutions, screen settings,
    286–287
Restore/Maximize button, windows
    element, 322, 326
ribbed triangle, window sizing
    handle, 325
right-click mouse, 349–350
right-pointing triangle, submenu
    indicator, 329–330
root directory See root folder
root folder, 168–169
ruler, WordPad program, 95
Run command, 34–35
Run dialog box, 34–35

S

Save As dialog box, 47
    creating folder when saving,
        170–171
    file/folder paths, 173–174
    Network Neighborhood access,
        254
Scientific Calculator, 100
screen elements
    See also icons
    My Computer, 18–19
screen savers
    described, 295
    password-protected, 237,
        296–298
    wait time settings, 297
screens, canvas size settings, 88–90
scrollbars, 327–328
searches
    Help system Find panel, 53–54
    Help system index, 53
    Recycle Bin, 193
selecting, mouse, 351
serial port (COM) connections,
    modems, 115–116

serving hand icon, shared devices, 19, 259
sessions, HyperTerminal, 125–127
Set Windows Password dialog box, 7
Settings⇨Control Panel command, 216, 227
Settings⇨Printers command, 216
Settings⇨Taskbar command, 39, 64, 292
Setup dialog box, printer details, 219
shared devices
    password settings, 260
    serving hand icon, 259
shared drives
    opening files from, 255–256
    saving files to, 254–255
    serving hand icon, 19
shared files, naming conventions, 255
shared folders
    accessing, 251–252
    Recycle Bin warning, 191
shared printers
    accessing, 257–258
    password guidelines, 262
    share settings, 260–262
sharing, Clipboard information, 107–111
Shift key, text selection techniques, 357–358
shortcut keys, command underlined letter, 329–330
shortcuts
    creating, 181–182
    described, 180–181
    file copying, 180–181
    naming conventions, 181
    Start menu program, 63, 65–66
Shut Down command, turning computer off, 13, 39
shutting down, exiting Windows 95/turning off computer, 13–14
sizing handles, graphics, 360
sliders, dialog box control, 343
software
    Add/Remove Programs option, 235
    installation/removal, 143–152
    Internet, 116
    modem connection types, 129–130
Solitaire game, 308–309, 346
solutions to problems, 363–374
Sound Recorder, 303–304
Sound Sentry, Accessibility Options, 230
Sound Properties dialog box, 300–301, 327
sounds
    events, 299–301
    Media Player, 302–303

MIDI file, 302–303
musical CDs, 163
property settings, 299–301
recording, 303–304
schemes, 301
visual clue options, 230
speakers
    visual clue options, 230
    volume settings, 80–81
special characters, 246–248
spinners, value adjustments, 343
spooling, described, 220
Start button
    described, 10–11
    keyboard access, 62
    Start menu elements, 61–68
    starting programs from, 32–33
    StartUp submenu, 68–72
Start menu
    adding games to, 308
    adding programs to, 63
    elements, 11, 61–68
    Shut Down command, 13
    submenu program addition/removal, 64–68
Startup menu, 369
StartUp submenu
    automatic application startup, 68–72
    program additions, 72–73
status bar
    application information display, 44
    described, 25
    displaying/hiding, 25
    My Computer, 25
    ribbed triangle window sizing handle, 325
    windows content element, 323
Sticky Keys, Accessibility Options, 229
subfolders
    child/parent relationship, 169
    types, 168
submenus
    Games, 308
    item types, 32–33
    right-pointing triangle indicator, 329–330
surge protectors, computer power strips, 4
Suspend button, laptop computers, 11, 15
Switch (Alt+Tab) command, 55
symbols
    See also characters
    Character Map program, 246–248
    check mark, 329
    dimple bar (menu/dialog separator), 329, 336
    dot indicator (active menu command), 329

ellipses (...) dialog box indicator, 330
right-pointing triangle, submenu indicator, 329–330
System Agent, 213
system tray
    element details display, 80
    hiding/displaying clock, 81
    mail envelope, 263
    modem icon display, 81–83
    printer icon display, 81
    speaker volume settings, 80–81
    taskbar elements, 79–84
Systems Properties dialog box, 239

T
Tab key, dialog box navigation, 335, 337, 356
tabs, dialog box faces, 336
tape backup drives, 203–209
taskbar
    application access, 75
    button types, 76–78
    clearing Documents menu, 39
    closing windows, 22
    described, 10
    display options, 291–292
    displaying/hiding, 11, 291–292
    displaying/hiding clock, 81
    elements, 75–86
    e-mail icon, 85
    hiding/displaying, 78–79
    locating lost windows, 20
    moving on screen, 290–291
    recovering vanished, 78
    shortcut menu elements, 85
    stretching/collapsing, 77–78
    stretching/shrinking, 291
    switching between applications, 104–106
    system tray elements, 79–84
Taskbar properties dialog box
    clearing Documents menu, 39
    Start menu submenu program addition, 64–66
telephones, Phone Dialer connections, 100–101
Telephony settings, Control Panel, 239
Temp folder, creating, 175
terms, mouse, 347
text
    font attribute elements, 358–359, 361
    selection techniques, 357–358
text editing, font selections, 358–359
text editors
    Notepad program, 99
    WordPad program, 94–98
text position (toothpick) cursor, 356
Tile Horizontally command, 22
Tile Vertically command, 22
time zones, time/date settings, 84

title bar
    current folder display, 22
    dialog box, 335
    moving (dragging) windows,
        326–327
    windows element, 322
titles, menus, 329
toggles, described, 338
toolbars
    common Windows 95 elements,
        43–44
    floating palette, 43–44
    My Computer, 24–26
    on/off buttons, 342
    Web browser, 122
    windows content element, 323
    WordPad program, 95
Tools⇨Show Log command, Phone
    Dialer, 101
tools, Paint program, 90–94
tooltips
    described, 20
    system tray elements, 80
    toolbar elements, 43
toothpick (text position) cursor, 356
topic windows, Help system, 51–52
Transfer⇨Send File command, 132
troubleshooting
    backups, 371
    DOS applications, 141–142
    Emergency Boot disk, 162–163,
        369–371
    error messages, 375–382
    Find Dialog box, 374
    finding files, 371–374
    forgotten password, 8
    hardware conflicts, 367–368
    lost files, 371–374
    MS-DOS Troubleshooter,
        141–142
    printing help topic, 365
    ScanDisk program, 209–211
    special ways to start computers,
        368–371
    Windows Troubleshooter,
        364–366
TrueType fonts, 242–244
truncated filenames, deciphering,
    268
typeface, described, 358

U
underlined letter, command
    shortcut key, 329–330
Undo (Ctrl+Z) command, 357–358
undoing last action, 108, 183
updates, Windows 95, 152
URL (Uniform Resource Locator),
    123
utilities, disk tools, 202–213

V
vertical scrollbars, 328
video files, 305–306
View⇨Arrange Icons⇨Auto
    Arrange command, 26
View⇨Arrange Icons⇨by Delete
    Date command, 193
View⇨Arrange Icons command, 26
View⇨Details command, 26, 228
View⇨Large Icons command, 25,
    228
View⇨Line Up Icons command, 26
View⇨Options command, 27, 179
View⇨Scientific command, 100
View⇨Small Icons command, 25
View⇨Status bar command, 25
View⇨Toolbar command, 24, 251,
    256
visually impaired users,
    Accessibility Options, 230
Volume Control panel, speaker
    volume settings, 80–81

W
wallpaper
    creating custom, 293
    described, 281–282
    sources, 285–286
Wang, Wally, 349
warm boot, described, 5
warning dialog boxes, 334
Web browsers, 116, 122
Web sites
    dummies.com, 234
    listing, 123
    Louvre museum, 285
Welcome to Windows dialog box, 6,
    8, 65
    adding to Start menu submenu,
        65
    disabling on startup, 9
    displaying/hiding, 9
What's This? shortcut menu, 335
Window menu, multidocument
    interface, 331
Windows 95
    component installation,
        145–148
    exiting/shutting down
        computer, 13–14
    network log in, 5–6
    System Agent, 213
    uninstalling applications,
        149–150
    updating, 152
    uses, 12–13
Windows button, keyboard Start
    menu access, 32
Windows folder, 169
Windows Troubleshooter, 364–366
windows
    cascading, 22
    cascading to recover missing,
        327

    closing, 19–20, 22
    configure a DOS game, 315–316
    DOS application elements,
        135–136
    edges, 322, 324–325
    elements, 321–325
    icon view types, 26
    locating with taskbar, 20
    maximizing/minimizing,
        331–332
    maximizing/restoring, 326
    menu elements, 329–330
    moving (dragging), 326–327
    quitting program when closing,
        38
    ribbed triangle sizing handle,
        325
    scrollbars, 327–328
    sizing with edge handles,
        324–325
    Special Startup Key commands,
        368–369
    tiling, 22
Wingdings fonts, 246–247
Winpopup, 73, 266–267
Wizards
    Add New Hardware, 235,
        270–273
    Add Printer, 257–258, 273–276
    Fax, 222–224
    Mail, 238
word processors, common text
    editing keys, 356–357
WordPad program, 94–98
    Close command non-support,
        50
    document creation, 45, 95–98
    Paint information sharing,
        108–110
    printing documents from, 45–46
    ruler, 95
    starting, 42
    switching between Paint
        program, 104–106
    text editor, 94–98
    toolbar, 95
work area, windows content
    element, 323
Work folder, creating, 174–175
WWW (World Wide Web), 113
    site menus, 128–129
    URL (Uniform Resource Locator)
        address, 123

Z
Zapf Dingbats fonts, 247
Zmodem protocol, file transfers,
    131–132
zones, time, 84